Private Collecting, Exh Shaping of Art History in London

The Burlington Fine Arts Club was founded in London in 1866 as a gentlemen's club with a singular remit – to exhibit members' art collections. Exhibitions were proposed, organized, and furnished by a group of prominent members of British society who included aristocrats, artists, bankers, politicians, and museum curators. Exhibitions at their grand house in Mayfair brought many private collections and collectors to light, using members' social connections to draw upon the finest and most diverse objects available. Through their unique mode of presentation, which brought museum-style display and interpretation to a grand domestic-style gallery space, they also brought two forms of curatorial and art historical practice together in one unusual setting, enabling an unrestricted form of connoisseurship, where new categories of art were defined and old ones expanded. The history of this remarkable group of people has yet to be presented and is explored here for the first time. Through a framework of exhibition themes ranging from Florentine painting to Ancient Egyptian art, a study of lenders, objects, and their interpretation paints a picture of private collecting activities, connoisseurship, and art world practice that is surprisingly diverse and interconnected.

Stacey J. Pierson is a Senior Lecturer in the Department of Art and Archaeology at the School of Oriental and African Studies, University of London. Her areas of specialization include ceramic history (China) and the history of collecting and display. Her most recent publication was *From Object to Concept: Global Consumption and the Transformation of Ming Porcelain* (Hong Kong University Press, 2013).

The Histories of Material Culture and Collecting, 1700–1950

Series Editor: Michael Yonan
University of Missouri-Columbia, USA

The Histories of Material Culture and Collecting, 1700–1950 provides a forum for the broad study of object acquisition and collecting practices in their global dimensions. The series seeks to illuminate the intersections between material culture studies, art history, and the history of collecting. It takes as its starting point the idea that objects both contributed to the formation of knowledge in the past and likewise contribute to our understanding of the past today. The human relationship to objects has proven a rich field of scholarly inquiry, with much recent scholarship either anthropological or sociological rather than art historical in perspective. Underpinning this series is the idea that the physical nature of objects contributes substantially to their social meanings, and therefore that the visual, tactile, and sensual dimensions of objects are critical to their interpretation. This series therefore seeks to bridge anthropology and art history, sociology and aesthetics.

For a full list of titles in this series, please visit *www.routledge.com/The-Histories-of-Material-Culture-and-Collecting-1700-1950/book-series/ASHSER2128*

7 **Manufacturing the Modern Patron in Victorian California**
Cultural philanthropy, industrial capital, and social authority
John Ott

8 **Craft, Community and the Material Culture of Place and Politics, 19th–20th Century**
Edited by Janice Helland, Beverly Lemire, and Alena Buis

9 **British Models of Art Collecting and the American Response**
Reflections across the pond
Edited by Inge Reist

10 **Textiles, Fashion, and Design Reform in Austria-Hungary before the First World War**
Principles of dress
Rebecca Houze

11 **William Hunter's World**
The art and science of eighteenth-century collecting
Edited by Geoffrey Hancock, Nick Pearce, and Mungo Campbell

12 **Materializing Gender in Eighteenth-Century Europe**
Edited by Jennifer G. Germann and Heidi A. Strobel

13 **Silver in Georgian Dublin**
Making, selling, consuming
Alison Fitzgerald

14 **Private Collecting, Exhibitions and the Shaping of Art History in London**
The Burlington Fine Arts Club
Stacey J. Pierson

Private Collecting, Exhibitions and the Shaping of Art History in London

The Burlington Fine Arts Club

Stacey J. Pierson

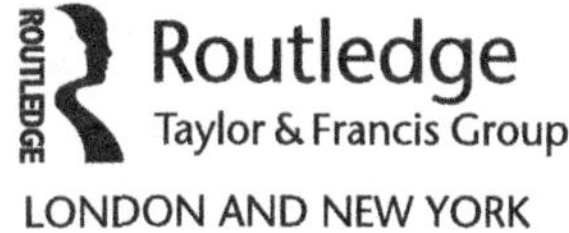

LONDON AND NEW YORK

First published 2017
by Routledge

2 Park Square, Milton Park, Abingdon, Oxfordshire OX14 4RN
52 Vanderbilt Avenue, New York, NY 10017

Routledge is an imprint of the Taylor & Francis Group, an informa business

First issued in paperback 2019

Library of Congress Cataloging in Publication Data
A catalog record for this book has been requested

ISBN: 978-1-138-23262-4 (hbk)
ISBN: 978-0-367-33142-9 (pbk)

Typeset in Sabon
by Book Now Ltd, London

Contents

Figures

Plates

Preface

In 1910, an exhibition opened in London which introduced visitors to a new category of Chinese ceramics: Early Chinese Pottery and Porcelain. The exhibition was presented by the Burlington Fine Arts Club and included over 480 club members' objects, ranging from Han pottery to Ming porcelain. The ceramics were lent by prominent collectors and specialists, such as George Eumorfopoulos (1863–1939), R. L. Hobson (1872–1941), and W. C. Alexander (1840–1916). A total of 3548 visitors (excluding Club members) saw the show and among these were local potters who noted that the exhibition introduced them to a new aesthetic.[1] Prior to this, exhibitions of Chinese ceramics had tended to focus on more recent works of the later Ming and Qing periods (sixteenth–nineteenth centuries). Here for the first time visitors could see something entirely different: Han pottery (second century BC–second century AD) and Song stoneware (eleventh–thirteenth centuries) (Figure P.1). 'Early Chinese Pottery and Porcelain' was not a museum exhibition, however, but rather a display that was organized by a group of private collectors who belonged to an unusual social club in London.

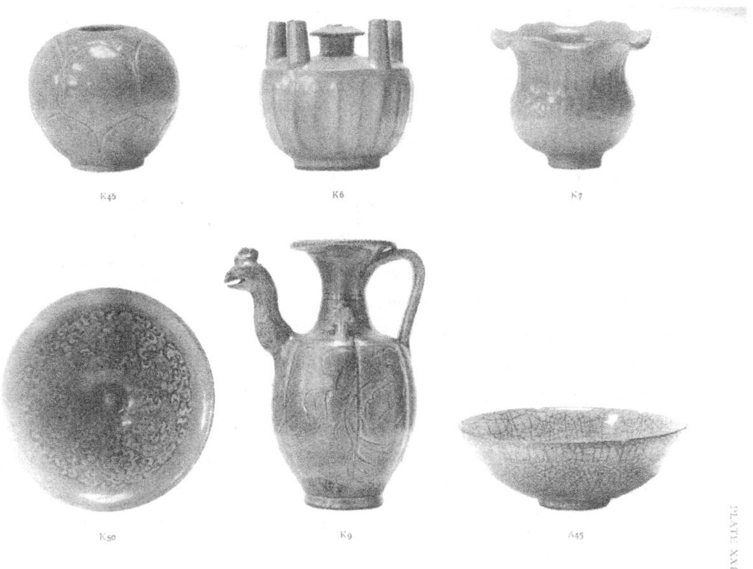

Figure P.1 Song stoneware, plate from Burlington Fine Arts Club, *Illustrated Catalogue of an Exhibition of Early Chinese Pottery and Porcelain*, London, 1911

The Burlington Fine Arts Club was founded in 1866 as a gentlemen's club with a singular remit – to exhibit members' objects in both ordinary and biannual 'special' exhibitions, the latter usually being accompanied by a catalogue. Both types of exhibitions were proposed, organized, and furnished by members of the Club, and special exhibitions were further open to the public by invitation. The Club was founded by a small group of private collectors, politicians, and museum curators and its exhibitionary activities made it unique both among gentlemen's clubs in London in the nineteenth century and exhibition spaces. Their exhibitions were entirely privately funded and organized within their own premises in Mayfair. This was, therefore, a significant venue for art displays in London that was not attached to a publicly-funded institution or an artists' society. In consequence, the exhibitions reflected the members' personal and collective interests in art and objects at that time. Their interpretation of these collected items also reflected the members' and associated specialists' views of connoisseurship, art history and thematic display.

The Club members were not restrained in their exhibition work by the politics or economics of an institution in the same way as one of the national museums or other exhibition spaces, such as the Royal Academy, for example. Exhibition themes and contributors were agreed by the Club's executive committee and members normally would volunteer to organize the show and write the catalogues, which began to be produced from 1868. Perhaps because of a lack of institutional constraints, much of their exhibition work can today be seen as innovative. Essentially, they could display what they wanted, when, and how. They also had an early interest in what is today called 'world art' and within this they chose to define a wide range of objects as 'art'. With its frequent, curated exhibitions, featuring an unusually broad range of members' objects, the Club therefore played a significant yet unacknowledged role in reflecting and shaping art history, collecting, and exhibition culture in London in its time. The legacy of these exhibitions is still felt today as some art historical themes and categories were first presented to (and defined for) the public by the Club – including Persian art, Chinese ceramics, and Egyptian art. The objects included in the exhibitions further gained recognition and a recognizable provenance.

In addition to the members' wide-ranging tastes and collections, the members themselves were equally diverse (apart from being all men). From its founding, the Club was joined by people across the social categories, ranging from Members of Parliament, wealthy landowners and aristocrats, to bankers, artists, art critics, diplomats, and museum professionals. A survey of the membership over its nearly 100-year history reveals an interesting congregation of often prominent members of British society who today are not known to have been associated with each other or in some cases to have been art collectors. It also reveals collaborative work between these various individuals, for whom, in many cases, exhibitions and curatorship were not part of their professional work or daily life. It is this remarkable mix of people and their collections that ultimately made the Club so creative in its exhibitionary work and so fortunate in having the best works of art readily available for study and display.

The Burlington Fine Arts Club's (BFAC) history has yet to be told from the perspective of either a gentleman's club or a venue for and originator of art exhibitions in the nineteenth and twentieth centuries. Fortunately a nearly complete archive of the Club's activities survives, along with its published catalogues. These enable us to formulate a picture of a significant yet unstudied source of art historical, exhibitionary, and collecting activity in London. BFAC exhibitions are consistently cited in histories of art historical themes and in the exhibition histories of specific art historical categories and objects, yet the activities of the Club are only noted in passing, with reference to other groups, exhibitions, or individuals. The collective power and impact of the Club, as a private collectors' exhibiting space, will be explored here for first time, therefore. This study will also introduce a members' club that had a different approach and broader scope than other clubs at the same time – one which focussed on art and concentrated on comparative exhibitions. This book therefore will enable the Club to be situated in the wider history of art collecting and exhibitions in nineteenth- to twentieth-century London and will demonstrate through a survey of what was exhibited that the so-called 'global turn' in art history began to take place well before the mid-twentieth century. This book will paint a picture of private collecting activities and art world practice that is somewhat different from what the studies of individuals and institutions have suggested. It is the association of the Club's members and their desire for display that makes it an ideal model for a comparative study of collecting and exhibitionary activities, as well as the impact of these activities on art historical practice.

In order to characterize and position the activities of the Club in the history of collecting, exhibitions, and art history in London, the structure of this book will be thematic and organized around exhibition subject areas. These have been selected from over 100 exhibitions to characterize major thematic categories and developments. In each chapter the discussion will cover a progressive chronological period in the Club's history to show how the exhibition category in focus developed and was presented over time. Representative objects and object categories presented in the exhibitions will be discussed to illuminate aspects of contemporary connoisseurship and critical responses. In conjunction with this the biographies of key individuals associated with the exhibitions will also be explored in order to contextualize their participation as well as their collecting activities. The approach is essentially art historiographical but within a socio-historical framework.

This book begins with an introductory chapter which presents a general history of the club as an institution, its activities, and some of the prominent and more active members of the group. The social and cultural background of the members is an important contributing factor in the Club's ability to access and present an unusually wide range of very high quality objects and art works. The Club's history foregrounds an analysis of its impact, raising some interesting questions about the supposed boundaries between the different aspects of art collecting practice and the London art world at that time. The main chapters which follow the introduction will examine the mechanics, significance, and legacy of key thematic categories of art and objects and the related exhibitions devised, mounted, and published by the Club. Within this, each exhibition selected for discussion will be presented and analysed in detail, including participants and objects, and will be situated in the context of the time and place in which it was mounted. For the most part, the exhibitions were defined by the Club in either material or cultural terms so this will be the broad categorization adopted here, for example 'ceramics', 'paintings', 'primitive art', etc. From 1878, geographical and national categories also come into play and will necessitate a discussion of this approach to object classification and its implications for the development of art history and the related field of art historiography. Certain materials, particularly ceramics, played a prominent part in the Club's collecting and exhibition activities, which seems unusual when considered against the usual narrative of art history in this time period, but not, as we will see, that of collecting in England. A number of hitherto unrecognized but influential and illuminating ceramics exhibitions therefore will be considered in a dedicated chapter (Chapter 2) that will provide a noteworthy contrast to the chapter on paintings and prints (Chapter 1), a category of art that is normally assumed to have been the benchmark for art collecting in the time period covered by this book. On the surface, interest in paintings and prints seem to be what united many of the Club's members but in fact this subject area was only treated in about half of the Club's special exhibitions, as we will see.

In spite of the Club's diverse membership and collections, there is as yet no publication which addresses both the history of the Club and its activities. Such a study has never been written, except by the Club itself at various times, for its members, and these internal histories are not critical studies of methodology or impact. There is a brief history of the Club's predecessor (the Fine Arts Club, FAC) in the *Journal of the Decorative Arts Society* (Eatwell 1994) but this does not cover the later history of the FAC or its new offshoot, the BFAC. It is also therefore not a study of the work of the Club, its activities, impact, or legacy, discussions of which appear only in passing references to the BFAC in related studies on other subjects (e.g. Griffiths 1996; Haskell 2000; Yallop 2011). With reference to what is identified as the main and most influential activity of the BFAC, display, there are survey histories of art exhibitions in general during this time period but these necessarily address the art exhibition as a particular type of exhibiting activity (e.g. Taylor 1999; Altschuler 2008). There are also selective, canonical histories of 'key' survey exhibitions in this period, such as the Manchester Art Treasures Exhibition of 1857 (Pergam 2011) or themed displays such as the 1931 International Exhibition of Persian Art (Wood 2000) but nothing in the current literature discusses exhibition work through the prism of a physical and conceptual exhibiting space, which the Club represents. Furthermore, studies of exhibitions organized by private groups (non-institutional, non-governmental) such as artists' societies or galleries in this time period (e.g. Denney 2000; Helmreich 2012) do not include the Club, even though, as this book will demonstrate, their work often intersected. In terms of critical frameworks, Haskell's influential art historical study of old master pictures considered the role of an art-collecting category in exhibition practices (Haskell 2000) and this has inspired similar studies on other categories such as Mexican art in Britain (Locke 2002). The social-historical context of the Club has been considered with reference to the histories of gentlemen's clubs and clubs in London (e.g. Lejeune 1979; Field 2009; Milne-Smith 2011) as the Club was modelled on these and their administration but does not feature in such histories. The Club is also considered as a locus for the intersection of various aspects of the London art world, drawing on socio-geographical studies such as Helmreich (2012). The fact that there was a gentlemen's club whose main activity was exhibiting, and by extension, classifying collected art, is essentially unacknowledged in any field however. In one exception, the BFAC was noted in the University of Glasgow research project on 'Exhibition Culture in London, 1878–1908' and included in its database[2] suggesting at the very least that it merits further investigation as a contributor to this regional display phenomenon. The BFAC was essentially a club for art collectors in London, and the role of collectors' clubs in general and of collectors within the wider London art world is not itself well studied. Nonetheless, with increasing attention being paid to the commercial aspects of collecting and the art market (e.g. Westgarth 2012; Helmreich and Fletcher 2013), the interrelationships between the various parts of the art world are becoming more apparent.

Thus, this book will bring the significant and influential activities of a unique gentlemen's club to light for the first time. It will also form the only published history of this Club, calling attention to the role of sometimes very prominent members of British society in art world practices, which in many cases is unknown at present. Through this, it will demonstrate the surprising way in which many of these people were known to each other, sharing a common interest in and shaping cultural life in London. We will also see how multiple facets of the London art world and art historical practice intersected in the later nineteenth and twentieth centuries through the lens of a single and indeed singular group of connoisseurs and experts who collected, presented, and interpreted a wide range of objects as 'art'.

Notes

1 See Stacey Pierson, 'The Sung Standard: Chinese Ceramics and British Studio Pottery in the 20th Century', in Stacey Pierson, ed., *Song Ceramics: Art History, Archaeology and Technology*, Colloquies on Art and Archaeology in Asia, no. 20. London, December 2004, p. 90.

2 University of Glasgow research project, 'Exhibition Culture in London, 1878–1908'. Available at: www.exhibitionculture.arts. gla.ac.uk/gall_exhlist.php?gid=226 (accessed 22 Dec. 2015).

Acknowledgements

This book began with a study of the work of a single collector whose activities did much to shape my professional life. In researching his area of interest, Chinese ceramics, it became clear that the subject itself had an interesting history as a collecting category. One name that consistently arose in references to collectors and exhibitions of Chinese ceramics was the Burlington Fine Arts Club. After putting it aside for many years, I decided recently that it was time to pay attention to this group and its archive in the National Art Library (NAL).

The archive is extensive and therefore both a blessing and a curse but I am grateful to the staff of the NAL for making it available to me and cheerfully answering my many questions about the material. In any archival study, decisions have to be made about how to manage, organize, and interpret the material so I am especially grateful to the anonymous readers of this manuscript who pointed me in a direction I had not considered and therefore made this a much more lucid and comprehensive study.

Finally, I wish to thank SOAS for the period of sabbatical that provided the time to concentrate on this study and the many people behind the scenes who support my work in general. In particular my sister, Dr Patricia Pierson, deserves special mention for bringing unusual yet vital sources to my attention, especially those on subjects that are far beyond my area of expertise, such as mummy culture.

Part 1

Introduction

Introduction

A New Gentlemen's Club for London

Chapter Contents

- History and a Description of the Club, its Activities, and Functions
- Location and Permanent Premises
- Exhibitions
- Membership
- Taste in Collecting and Display
- Conclusion

> Burlington Fine Arts Club, 17, Savile-row, W. — Is intended to bring together amateurs, collectors, and others interested in art; to afford ready means for consultation between persons of special knowledge and experience in matters relating to the fine arts; and to provide accommodation for showing and comparing rare works in the session of the members and friends. To provide in the reading room periodicals, books, and catalogues, foreign as well as English, having reference to art. To make arrangements in the gallery and rooms of the club for the exhibition of pictures, original drawings, engravings, and rare books, enamels ceramic wares, coins, plate, and other valuable works. To hold, in addition to the above, once in the year or oftener, special exhibitions which shall have for their object the elucidation of some school, master, or specific art. Members to have the privilege of introducing friends to these special collections. To render the club a centre where occasionally conversazioni may be held of an art-character. Members to have the power of introducing two visitors, ladies or gentlemen. To provide, in addition to the above art objects, the ordinary accommodation and advantages of a London club. The club possesses a valuable library of books of reference on art. The entrance fee is £5 5s., and the subscription £5 5s. The power of election is vested in the committee, and is by ballot.
>
> Charles Dickens (Jr.), *Dickens's Dictionary of London*, 1879

History and a Description of the Club, its Activities, and Functions

The Founding of a New Members' Club

In April 1866, a group of gentlemen got together to found a new club for art collectors.[1] It was modelled on their favourite gentlemen's clubs and was designed as a counterpoint to a group founded earlier, which was perceived as having lost its direction. Most of the founder members of the new club were members of the earlier group, which was called the Fine Arts Club and had been founded in 1856. The Fine Arts Club began as the Collector's Club and was founded by the first curator (called 'superintendent') for Art Collections at the new South Kensington Museum (later the Victoria and Albert Museum, V&A), John Charles Robinson (1824–1913), who was an instrumental figure in the Museum's early history, helping to define its collecting and display remit.[2] The Collector's Club was based in the museum and included among its members the V&A's founder, Henry Cole (1808–1882), as well as Baron Marochetti (1805–1867), a sculptor and diplomat,[3] and the Marchese d'Azeglio (Vittorio Emanuele Taparelli, 1816–1890), who had been the Sardinian Ambassador to London.[4] The formation of the Collector's Club was announced in the *Art Journal* in 1857:

> The Collector's Club. A new society of amateurs of *vertu* has just been formed under this title; consisting solely of such gentlemen as collect for their own tastes, objects of antiquity and are not dealers therein ... Baron Marochetti gave the use of his studio for the preliminary meeting, at which a large assemblage gathered and Sir A. Fountaine's antique majolica formed an important point of attraction.[5]

The new club stated that its purpose was: 'to hold regular conversazione where objects of art were to be exhibited'.[6] As its historian Ann Eatwell noted:

> These exhibitions would form unparalleled opportunities for viewing private collections that had rarely been seen before. The unlocking of specimens from rich private sources and the meeting of collectors at gatherings where information could be exchanged, comparisons drawn and expertise and knowledge of objects gained were the real if unspecified intentions, behind the club's formation.[7]

The term 'conversazione' was a peculiarly nineteenth-century one which in England at that time was used to describe society gatherings or 'soirées' associated with the arts and sciences.[8] One such event was depicted in a famous painting in the National Portrait Gallery: 'The Royal Academy Conversazione, 1891', by G. Grenville Manton which shows just how formal yet social such events were (Figure I.1).

The Fine Arts Club (FAC), as the Collector's Club was known from later in 1857 onwards, while clearly social, had two undeclared additional functions: to provide a venue for the development of interest in and knowledge of decorative arts (none such existed before its founding) and to support the development of the future V&A, as Robinson needed to cultivate collectors and promote the subject areas with which the museum was concerned.[9] The FAC should be seen as supporting these aims, even though its existence (and that of its successor) inherently contradicted the public educational aims of the new museum. Robinson, and Henry Cole, believed it was a national duty to encourage collecting and that museums were in the service of this, as well as education in taste.[10] The fulfilment of such aims required objects and collectors, so Robinson used the new club as a tool to support the museum. Through its successor, the club became much more than that, however.

To enhance its effectiveness, the FAC expanded rapidly to include around 100 members (up to 200 in the 1860s), mostly men, as was the custom at that time, and its programme of meetings and activities was established early on.[11] Members were expected to exhibit their objects for discussion where the meetings were held and many loaned them to other exhibitions, including at the South Kensington Museum, most notably the Loan Exhibition of 1862 which attracted over 900,000 visitors, thus

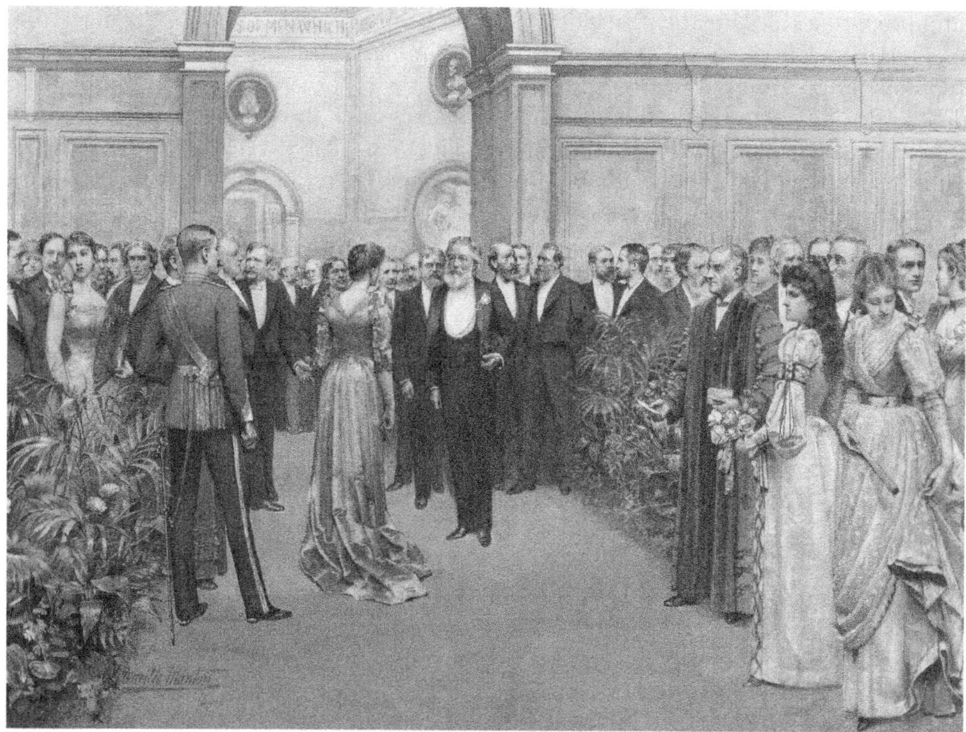

Figure I.1 The Royal Academy Conversazione, 1891, G. Grenville Manton, 1855–1932, Pen, ink and gouache. 45 × 61.4 cm, NPG 2820

Source: © National Portrait Gallery, London.

demonstrating the vital role of the club for Robinson. Members of the Club were on the exhibition committee and Robinson was its director and organizer.[12]

He was clearly not satisfied with the club's potential, principally because, as Eatwell noted, the FAC 'became a victim of its success'. Its meetings were very popular, took place during the London season, and were increasingly attended by large numbers of non-members, thus impeding its original stated purpose. It also had no permanent premises so members themselves were obliged to host the large-scale, fashionable events.[13] Along with Robinson, a number of key members of the FAC became dissatisfied and decided to set up a new, more focussed and 'serious' club with premises, using the gentlemen's club model. In 1866, therefore, in response to the seemingly frivolous and ineffectual nature of the FAC, a preliminary meeting was held in April to discuss the formation of a new club, which was agreed by those who attended.[14] A provisional committee was created at this meeting and this was followed by a first general meeting in June of 1866, at 49 Lower Grosvenor Street, London, the home of one of the members. The provisional committee consisted of five members, one acting as chair: J. C. Robinson, Ralph Wornum (1812–1877), the print collector Richard Fisher (1809–1890), who was then closely associated with the Print Room of the British Museum, and William Smith (1808–1876), who seems to have resigned shortly afterwards.[15] The chair was the Marchese d'Azeglio.[16] At the first general meeting in

June, a permanent committee was elected,[17] and was tasked with choosing a name and preparing rules for the new club.[18] Membership was stated to be 79 at that time.

Premises were discussed at the very first preliminary meeting in April of 1866, and the committee proposed leasing premises from a Mr Toovey who had a building at 177 Piccadilly. As the new club was to be located close to Burlington House, this location gave its name to the club: the Burlington Fine Arts Club (BFAC, hereafter also 'the Club').[19] The name was officially reported at a subsequent meeting, in July 1866, and a report was given which described Toovey's proposed terms as:

> rooms, supplies provided, refreshments, etc. Toovey to receive the amounts collected for entrance fees and annual subs (collected by him too); agreement with Toovey can be terminated if number of members falls below 100 in the 2nd year; if members exceed 150, then Toovey will only get the annual subscriptions.[20]

The acceptance of these terms was presented in a proposed circular to members that also included a description of the new Club's terms and conditions:

> **The Burlington Fine Arts Club**
>
> At a general meeting of the Members of the Club held at 177 Piccadilly, on the 20th of July, 1866, the Report of the Committee appointed at the meeting of the 5th of June, 1866, was read and it was unanimously resolved, -
>
>> First, to accept Mr Toovey's offer of his premises over the ground floor at 177 Piccadilly, and to establish the club therein.
>>
>> Secondly, that the rooms shall be opened for the reception of members, if possible, on the 1st of December next, or, at the latest, on the 1st of January, 1867.
>>
>> Thirdly, that the members be requested immediately to pay the entrance fee of five guineas, and the first year's subscription of five guineas, to the account of the Burlington Fine Arts Club, at the London and Westminster Bank, St. James Square.
>>
>> The above payment of ten guineas to entitle to all privileges of the club up to the 1st of January 1868.[21]

The objectives of the Club and the rules and regulations were defined and drafted by the committee over the summer. In the first printed set of Rules and Regulations (1866), it was stated that the new club 'is formed for the purpose of bringing together amateurs, collectors, and persons interested in the Fine Arts; and for the exhibiting and comparing the acquisitions made from time to time by the Members'.[22] This dual purpose, social gatherings and the display of members' collections in organized exhibitions, a development from FAC practice, was in fact pioneering and unique, as no other private members club was doing this, including those focussing on the arts.

The nineteenth century in London was a time when a number of private clubs, mostly restricted to 'gentlemen', were opened, including the Arts Club (1863), the Athenaeum (1834), the Garrick (1831), the Langham (1830), and the Savage (1857). Many of these declared an association with the 'arts', as defined in that period, but most also had a slightly different approach to activities than the BFAC. The Athenaeum, for example, was designed as a social club for leading artistic, literary and scientific men, and for patrons of the arts and sciences.[23] Its main activity was passive – to provide services for its members: a London address or premises, a library, dining rooms, smoking and drinking rooms, meeting rooms, etc.[24] Like the other clubs, the 'arts' in the Athenaeum's objectives were also mainly related to a description of members' interests or professions as artists or patrons, for example, rather than the 'fine arts' which were collected and subject to connoisseurship.[25]

The Burlington Fine Arts Club, in contrast, had the display and discussion of artworks as an active main focus, with services provided as a secondary but essential daily function. Thus, it was, essentially, a gentlemen's club for art collectors and it is collecting that was the driving force behind both its founding and its activity focus.

Location and Permanent Premises

The presentation of exhibitions and displays at the Club, as well as essential services, was facilitated by the acquisition of permanent premises in 1870 at 17 Savile Row.[26] This location would situate the Club in the centre of the London art world at that time. As Pamela Fletcher and Anne Helmreich have noted with reference to the mapping of the nineteenth-century London art market, the West End, as that part of London is known, was home to the Royal Academy and other exhibition societies such as the Royal Society of Painters in Watercolours and commercial galleries such as Colnaghi.[27] In addition, numerous antique dealers were located here, as well as the auction houses such as Christie's, an important source for many of the items collected and displayed by Club members.[28] Dealers, however, were prohibited from Club membership, an interesting condition that will be discussed later in this chapter.

After refurbishment by Club member Sir Matthew Digby Wyatt (1820–1877),[29] the Club's permanent premises had a grand Gallery for displays as well as a morning room, a committee room, a games room with a billiard table, a library, and other essential facilities for a gentlemen's club (Figure I.2). As images of the Gallery demonstrate, the design of the space was traditional and very much reflective of the period room phenomenon that was gaining pace at the time the building was opened.[30] While not necessarily aiming for a defining period style for this room beyond what Sparke *et al.* refer to as a 'representational device', the interior design was both reflective of the Club members' actual (the aristocrats) or aspirational home environments as well as a typical environment for the display of pictures and works of art in the nineteenth century both in the home and in commercial or institutional premises.[31]

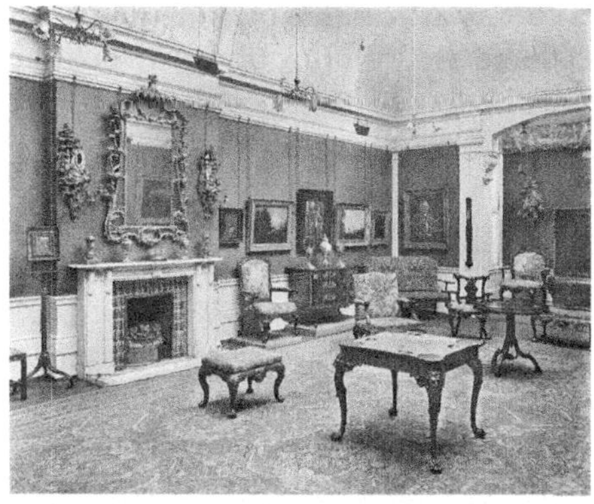

Figure I.2 Photograph: interior view of the Burlington Fine Arts Club at 17 Savile Row, London, February 1921, BL25311/001

Source: © Historic England Archives.

The other aspects of the premises should not be seen as unimportant, however, as these essentially were what encouraged members to join. The Club's focus on art collections was of course attractive but it was the functional rooms and services that members paid for and that justified their initial and annual fees. For many members, this was a London base, though without the overnight accommodation provided by some clubs. For wealthy men of the time, their club became a central part of their lives and 'functioned as a surrogate home'.[32] Having dedicated premises was an important aspect of the Club's identity. It therefore should be defined first and foremost as a gentlemen's club, with associated services and facilities, even though what made it different were its main activities. While minutes of the early meetings demonstrate that a discussion had taken place concerning the character of the premises, whether they should be devoted to dining or 'Art', ultimately it was always to be a gentlemen's club in form and an art club in practice. This structural function enabled and required the Club to charge both an entrance fee, as was and is traditional for private members' clubs, and an annual subscription, to pay for the services and premises.

In its first 50 years, the cost of membership and schedule was recorded as: 'The entrance fee is £5.5s payable on election; annual sub is £5.5 payable on election and then on 1st January each year.'[33] In 1901, this amount was equivalent to about £500 or £600 today, annually.[34] On joining, therefore, members were required to contribute more than £1000, which would in itself limit membership. Membership fees were increased in the twentieth century, due to rising costs associated with a new lease on the building. In 1924, new members were required to pay a subscription of £7.7 but also an additional guinea each for the Library and Exhibition Funds, which was requested from existing members as well.[35] These fees enabled members to have coffee and read newspapers, organize dinners on the premises, play billiards and cards (this under strict conditions, however[36]), read in the Library, and view each other's collections either in general displays or special curated exhibitions, where their works were presented alongside external, non-members' collections. There were also plenty of opportunities for the discussion of collections at regular events such as conversazione or 'Thursday Evening Gatherings'.

The tradition of hosting the conversazione was continued from Fine Arts Club practice. As noted previously, this earlier club was essentially founded for this specific purpose. The BFAC's conversazione were organized either for themselves or for the Fine Arts Club who would use the rooms at Savile Row for their own events, until they dissolved their club in 1874. Some descriptions of conversazione in the Club's meeting minutes and rules give a flavour of these events and their popularity:

> XXVII Exhibitions of Works of Art, and Conversazioni for artistic purposes may be held in the Rooms of the Club, with the sanction and under the control and regulations of the Committee.[37]
>
> At any Conversazione to be held at the Club each Member may introduce personally two friends (either ladies or gentlemen). In case of Special Exhibitions, members may introduce, in the daytime, personally or by ticket, a certain number of friends, the number to be determined by the Committee, and the tickets to be obtained from the Honorary Secretaries.[38]
>
> Two conversazioni have been held in the rooms of the Club, during the year. One just before the opening of the Water colour Exhibition on the evening of the 3rd of June 1871; the other by the Members of the Fine Arts Club, on the 25th

April last. The first was attended by 157 visitors and 43 members of this Club, in all 200; the second by 11 visitors, and 34 members of this Club, in all 147.[39]

In addition to conversazione, there were also 'Thursday Evening Gatherings', held monthly. These were also described in minutes and rules:

> VI Besides the formal Exhibitions, many objects of interest have as usual, been shown by the Members and their friends, especially at the Thursday Evening gatherings, which have been held monthly during this season.
>
> The Committee beg leave to call the attention of the Members to these monthly meetings, as having proved highly agreeable and well calculated to develop both the social and artistic character of the Club.
>
> The gatherings are preceded on these occasions by a house dinner, which owing to the want of more adequate accommodation is necessarily limited to twelve. The notice of the dinner is posted in the Reading Room, and such gentlemen as desire to dine, on any of these occasions write their names on the notice paper.[40]

As Club meeting minutes vary somewhat in their completeness and content, it is not clear how long such events continued to take place but the conversazione ceased to be noted in the twentieth century. Similar events for viewing and discussing objects as the Thursday Evenings were noted until the Club's effective closure in 1939.

Associated with these activities and the Club's general services was a requirement for proper management and staffing of the premises, which, in the case of the BFAC, also included staff who could assist with objects and their management. The Club was run by a management committee, with two key postholders:

> The general and pecuniary management and direction of the concerns of the Club, including the appointment and removal of all Officer and Servants, is vested in a Committee to be composed of not less than 12 Members, including a Treasurer and Honorary Secretaries, who are to be appointed by the Committee.[41]

There were also Trustees who were responsible for the lease on the premises and the Club's investments, which included debentures, irredeemable bonds (consuls), war loan stock, and Great Eastern Railway stock.[42] The Club's financial security has been attributed to the business acumen of one of its early members: John Malcolm (of Poltalloch, 1803–1893):

> [whose] business acumen made him a powerful and practical member of the Committee in securing the Club's financial fortunes. In 1871, to foot the bill of £2,500 for renovating the BFAC's newly acquired Savile Row premises, debentures were offered to Club members for £125, entitling the holder to an annual interest of four per cent. Robinson, Malcolm, William Mitchell (1820–1908) and Salting (George, 1835–1909) were among the 36 members who took out these debentures by 1876. Year after year Malcolm was appointed to the Club's Finance Sub-Committee and throughout the 1870s and 1880s both he and Mitchell are regularly found serving on the General Committee, with Mitchell taking the chair on various occasions after his election to the Committee in May 1875.[43]

Exhibitions

Such financial security underpinned the Club's main activity: exhibitions. The BFAC was in existence until 1951 and active until 1940. In that time they mounted over 110 formal exhibitions, with numerous other informal ones. (See Appendix A for a list of special exhibitions.) As stated in their earliest 'objects' (= objectives), the Club was founded not for dining or general meetings but for the display of collected art. This was certainly an unusual activity for a gentlemen's club as we have seen but it was in fact in keeping with the Club's location and situation in the art world terrain of West End London. The Club founders' desire for an organization that would display and facilitate the appreciation of collected objects in a more exclusive yet less private environment than was the case with the Club's predecessor, the Fine Arts Club, when meetings were held in the grand homes of members, was fulfilled by the acquisition of permanent, independent premises. Importantly, they selected a location in the heart of both clubland and the art market. Both the gentlemen's club and art aspects of the members' interests were equally accommodated therefore. The Club's location can also be seen as useful for the South Kensington Museum, which was, as we have seen, a crucial nexus for both members and their collections. The Museum was located away from the West End but the Club brought its expertise and approach to displays into the centre of London. It also enabled the Club, and John Robinson in particular, to pursue his notion of the additional function of the museum created for design education as the champion of decorative arts through encouraging connoisseurship and collecting.[44] Through the Club, therefore, Robinson, like several other members who will be discussed in this book, was able to function both within the institutional art world, through his museum, and outside it, with the Club facilitating and making possible such movement across boundaries.

With reference to the display space in the Club premises, its interior design and style deserve some consideration. As Figure I.2 demonstrates, the Gallery was designed as a luxurious domestic interior and for the ordinary exhibitions, the space was a suitable and conventional backdrop for a range of objects that usually included furniture, pictures, and various works of art. For the special exhibitions, however, display cases were used which presented objects in a museum style which was complemented by the professional catalogues produced for these shows (Figure I.3). Such displays were curated and arranged systematically, bringing the museum into the Club both visually and conceptually. A third space was created where the domestic and the professional and the private and public intersected. As this space was neither in the home nor the public museum, it also brought mainly privately collected objects into the open and together in a new way that would impact art historical analysis and connoisseurship, particularly with the special exhibitions.

In Club practice, exhibitions were defined as either 'ordinary' or 'special' displays. The former would most often be of miscellaneous art works 'from members and their friends'. A typical list of ordinary displays from the year 1871 consisted of:

> A series of Drawings + Etchings by Claude, of which a Catalogue was kindly prepared by Mr Julian Marshall:-
>
> A miscellaneous collection of China:-
>
> A choice selection of Limoges and other enamels, still on view in the Reading Room:-
>
> And a fine antique Bust from the Island of Cyprus, contributed by Mr. Malcolm.[45]

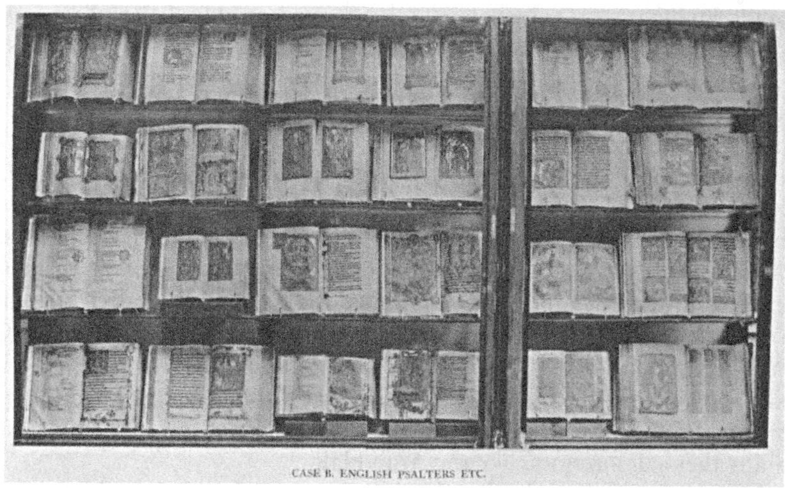

Figure I.3 Photograph of a display in the Illuminated Manuscripts exhibition of 1908, Case B

Source: Plate from Burlington Fine Arts Club, *Illustrated Catalogue of an Exhibition of Illuminated Manuscripts*, London, 1911.

The administration of these displays was managed by a member of staff known as the Registrar and Curator, who was also the assistant to the Honorary Secretary and for all Club administrative duties. The Registrar acted as an object manager, rather than a specialist with connoisseurship knowledge of the art works.

The 'special' exhibitions, however, were designed and managed by specialist committees. They were also more focussed and usually had a specific theme as described in an early committee meeting:

> The Committee propose, in addition to the ordinary exhibitions of the club, to form at least two special exhibitions, in illustration either of a particular master, or of a particular school of art, in the course of each London season.[46]

These exhibitions were organized by special member subcommittees formed for each one, with external advisors sometimes brought in as temporary members for the purposes of the exhibition. Lenders to the exhibitions also could be Club members or non-members, including institutions or individuals. Most often, committee members would approach lenders but very occasionally a call for contributions was published, as in the case of the Egypt exhibition discussed in Chapter 3. The lender profile was notably very wide-ranging. (For a list of active members and lenders, see Appendix B.) A random survey of external lenders reveals the names of Her Majesty the Queen and the Royal Palaces, the Archbishop of Canterbury, the national museums of France and Germany, Oxford and Cambridge university museums, Flinders Petrie, and Bernard Berenson. These lenders, and others who were notable, will be discussed in detail in the relevant exhibitions covered in the following chapters of this book.

The number of exhibits in the special exhibitions was often large, sometimes up to 500 pieces, with no obvious limits apart from space. The first of these special exhibitions was mounted by the Club in 1867 and the special exhibition of that year was 'Rembrandt Etchings', for which no catalogue was produced. Exhibitions were mounted regularly until 1939.[47] In keeping with the collecting interests of members, the subjects for exhibitions were wide-ranging (see Appendix A for a complete list of special exhibition titles). The only restrictions on exhibition subjects were that the work of living artists could not normally be presented.[48] With respect to paintings, for which this restriction would most apply, this was probably an attempt to distinguish the Club from other artist exhibition societies such as the Royal Academy which presented an annual exhibition of current work by Royal Academicians, or commercial premises like the Goupil Gallery.[49] Yet the Royal Academy, like the South Kensington Museum, was linked to the Club through members. For example, like Robinson, Frederick Leighton (1830–1896), a president of the Royal Academy, also used his membership of the Club to practise his other artistic interests. He did not, by prohibition (which he must have agreed to) exhibit his own work as a painter but he did exhibit his mainly 'Arab' objects as a collector. Leighton House, when it was his residence, would reflect this with its styled 'regionally themed' interiors, like the Arab Hall.[50]

While world arts were indeed displayed as an exhibition subject, as this book will demonstrate, generally speaking, the most popular subject area for Club exhibitions was paintings, prints, and drawings (50 per cent). This might well be a reflection of members' collecting tastes but it was also the easiest category of art to display in the Club's gallery space which might have been significant. In terms of visitor numbers, however, of the top eight exhibitions (more than 5,000 visitors, exclusive of members, see Appendix A), five were in this subject area as well, so this interest was not confined to the Club. In descending order, the most visited special exhibitions in the Club's history were:

1883	Pictures and Drawings by the late Dante Gabriel Rossetti (12,133)
1889	Portrait Miniatures (12,031)
1901	Silversmiths' Work of European Origin (11,501)
1903	Ancient Greek Art (11,346).

Such numbers are impressive for a private club but they do not indicate that the Club was popularly associated with any particular type of subject or art object.[51] All the subject areas are British or European in scope but successful exhibitions of non-western material were also mounted, from an early date, as will be discussed in the following chapters. The visitor numbers are also impressive, considering the limited access provided to the exhibitions. The main audiences for the Club's exhibitions were its members but also external visitors, who were invited to attend by members. The non-members who attended were therefore associates of members, revealing interesting social connections, as we will see. Visitors could either come with a printed invitation or accompany a member to enter the exhibitions. Objects were also viewed by large groups of visitors during conversazione or at Thursday evening meetings, which as we have seen, took place monthly for much of the Club's history and occasionally by other special interest groups such as members of the Royal Anthropological Institute (see Chapter 4).

Special exhibitions were also publicized and recorded by means of catalogues. Ordinary displays would sometimes have a dedicated catalogue but more often than not, they would simply have a printed record in the Gallery of the Club for visitors' use. For special exhibitions, however, from 1868 there was usually a dedicated catalogue with introductory remarks or a short preface. A number of these also had illustrated editions with introductory essays and additional material such as a catalogue *raisonné* of an artist's work. The illustrated editions were subscribed to but all catalogues were distributed to members as a matter of course. They were also shared with external contributors, other clubs, libraries, museums and membership groups such as the Liverpool Arts Club. Thus non-members could both view the exhibitions by invitation or they could read the catalogues. While this could hardly be called wide public access, it was in keeping with the Club's intention and desire to share works from members' collections among themselves and a wider viewership, but only with a desirable 'fraction of the public', particularly 'artists, men of letters, and other persons known to take a legitimate interest in Art', to whom access would be free.[52] Ladies, while not allowed to be members, could visit the exhibitions and a number were lenders to exhibitions throughout the Club's history, as the following chapters will demonstrate.[53] In this, the Club was reflecting common practice for gentlemen's clubs but it also acknowledged the role of women as art collectors and therefore participants in the art world at that time.

The special exhibitions did occasionally cause problems, however, and these were primarily financial. Exhibition costs were covered by the Club's own funds, including those raised on a case-by-case basis for special exhibitions. Much of these funds were generated from membership fees, subscriptions to illustrated catalogues, and subsequent sales. As the exhibitions were organized by semi-independent subcommittees, they often had undefined budgets and were not able to cover exhibition costs through catalogue subscriptions or sales. In many cases, the committees were fortunate because sometimes lenders would cover insurance costs themselves, but these costs were usually part of the exhibition budgets, along with 'carriage' (transportation), and security in some cases (police presence). Subcommittee members also gave their time free of charge, including those who were only honorary members for the purpose of the exhibition, for example, Flinders Petrie during the 1895 exhibition 'The Art of Ancient Egypt' (discussed in Chapter 3). Loan fees were not paid, or at least were not recorded as being paid, nor was conservation work listed, installation costs, or other common exhibition expenses. These exhibitions were therefore very much internal affairs and participation was considered part of being a member of the Club, which in itself is interesting. No member was too grand to serve on an exhibition committee.

What is more difficult to assess is the general impact of the Club's exhibitions, both at the time of display and subsequently. The specific impact of individual exhibitions will be discussed in subsequent chapters of this book but certainly members and lenders benefitted from having their works displayed at the Club and recorded in distributed catalogues. It is very likely, for example, that after such a provenance and exhibition history had been established, there would have been an impact on sales of objects. This is difficult to quantify but one example suggests a connection. The Club exhibited Egyptian art in 1921 and most of the exhibits came from the MacGregor Collection (see Chapter 3). This collection was sold by Sotheby's in 1922 and the sale was extremely successful. It is interesting that the Club's exhibition is cited numerous times in the catalogue, thereby having a legitimizing effect on the objects as well as confirming their authenticity, both attributes being attractive to buyers.[54] The Club's exhibitions and their catalogues, which are generally what remains of them, have also had an impact on art historical practice and historiography, as studies of specific exhibitions will show. The wider legacy of this will be considered in Part 3, the Epilogue of this book.

Membership

The exhibitions were essentially and primarily staged for the benefit of members, however, and like their collected objects, the Club's membership represents a wide cross-section of art collectors in Britain, and in some cases overseas. Like other gentlemen's clubs, the Club was certainly blessed with grand members and the membership profile was similar by design. The main categories of members included: aristocrats (or 'noblemen' as they were defined), politicians (who sometimes were also aristocrats), artists, other creatives such as writers or critics, businessmen, including bankers, museum professionals, foreign diplomats and honorary members by invitation, such as during a special exhibition, but strictly no women and no art dealers. As the general rules stated: 'From the beginning, as now, professional dealers were not eligible for membership. The rule is now interpreted to exclude any person who habitually makes profits out of transaction in works of Art in whichever capacity, principal or agent.'[55] This restriction on dealer membership is very interesting, not least because the Club's definition of 'dealer' is somewhat vague but also because commerce seems to be the excluding criterion. Members were of course participating in the art market, where they bought and sold their collections, and dealers were frequent lenders to exhibitions. It seems therefore that for the Club, 'dealer' was a professional designation and was different from occasional dabbling in sales. Yet dealers were crucial for underpinning the main activities of the Club and the Club was located in the heart of the art market in London. Some members of course inherited their objects but far more purchased them. Founder members of the Club, like Robinson, and later active members such as Benson, also acquired collections by purchase, disposed of items for members and, in Robinson's case, sold collections to members and worked in a museum where dealers were important suppliers of acquisitions and loans. Some of the first displays for the nascent museum were provided by dealers, at Marlborough House.[56] It seems therefore that the prohibition must not have referred to 'dealing activities' but rather to running a shop or being 'in trade'. Such a profession would in fact exclude one from most gentlemen's clubs, especially before 1900.[57] Exclusion of dealers from membership did not confer similar exclusion from Club activities, simply the use of Club premises, so in fact the prohibition was limited. Apart from this contradictory exclusion of one category of person, the Club's membership in fact brought together men across the upper and middle social and professional classes, from aristocrats and bankers to artists, writers, and 'foreigners'.

The definition of this latter category of member was also somewhat vague but as long as the membership committee agreed, persons living abroad – not resident in England specifically – could join in some capacity:

> Foreign artists, eminent collectors residing abroad, literary men and others distinguished in Art, may, on the recommendation of two members, and subject to the approval of the committee, be admitted by the committee as Honorary Members of the club during their stay in England, for a period not exceeding three months. Permanent non-resident Honorary Members may be admitted subject to the same regulations.[58]

> The Committee has the power to elect as Members of the Club gentlemen holding distinguished Art appointments in Scotland, Ireland, or the Continent on payment of the Entrance fee of £5.5s, and an Annual Subscription of £1.1s, such Annual Subscription, however, to be raised to £5.5s in case such Members should become permanently resident in England.[59]

In practice, this meant that museum directors in Ireland or Berlin could be members and several did take advantage of this membership concession.

The fees associated with membership, as noted above, including the later increases, were not a hindrance to the target members of the Club and the membership was therefore somewhat homogenous in its representation of the wealthier members of British society at that time, in keeping with other clubs. The full list of members runs in the thousands but it is worth taking a closer look at some of the founders and early members as these give a good overview of the member profile. Other members and contributors to exhibitions will be discussed in later chapters.

As we have seen, at the very first meeting of the Club, a provisional committee was created at this meeting which consisted of five members including a chair: J. C. Robinson, Ralph Wornum, Richard Fisher, William Smith, and the Marchese d'Azeglio.[60] Robinson was the prime force in the founding of the BFAC and was at that time a Keeper at the South Kensington Museum.[61] Wornum was also a Keeper, at the National Gallery, and like Robinson, had been active in the art and design education movement of the previous decades.[62] Thus there was a significant institutional affiliation in the early days of the Club and this would continue throughout the Club's history.

After the first meeting, the membership was quickly expanded. In July 1866, for example, original members proposed included Louis Huth (1821–1905) and his brother Henry, sons of the merchant banker, Frederick Huth, Alfred Morrison (1821–1897),[63] A. W. Franks (1826–1897),[64] John Ruskin (1819–1900), and Charles Schreiber (1826–1884).[65] Additional new members elected in 1866 to early 1867, were the artist, Dante Gabriel Rossetti (1828–1882) and his brother William, the art critic (1829–1919), Thomas Baring MP (1799–1873; MP for Huntingdon, the Earl of Northbrook), the collector, George Salting, the artist, Frederick Leighton (later Lord), and S. A. R. Le Duc d'Aumale, a French general (1822–1897, Duke of Orleans, owner of the Château de Chantilly).[66] There was, therefore, a cross-section of politicians, diplomats, art critics, museum professionals, artists, wealthy businessmen, and collectors. The designer Owen Jones (1809–1874) also joined in early 1867, thus reinforcing the early association of the Club with the South Kensington Museum.[67] J. M. Whistler (1834–1903) fatefully was elected in 1867 though his membership did not last very long. The 'Whistler incident', as it is commonly known, has been written about before but without recourse to the Club's archives, the events surrounding it have not been reported accurately. While somewhat sensational, it does reveal some of the personal tensions that could arise in the Victorian art world, and, by virtue of the fact of the Club's broad membership, also impact on its own activities. 'The Whistler incident' was recorded in the records of the Club in fairly dispassionate terms but was in fact related to seemingly bad behaviour on the part of Whistler against his son-in-law, the founding Club member Seymour Haden (1818–1910). Haden was a prominent surgeon who was also an etcher and print collector. He was married to Whistler's step-daughter and actively worked with Whistler on developing ideas for his work. However, as one biography puts it:

> Whistler and Haden's relationship was not trouble free. Haden objected to Whistler's relationship with Joanna Hiffernan in the early 1860s. On 23 April 1867 Whistler accused Haden of disrespect towards his late medical partner Dr Traer and knocked Haden through a plate-glass window in Paris. Haden and Whistler never spoke to each other again. On 18 December 1867 Whistler was expelled from the Burlington Club as a result of a complaint made by Haden concerning his behaviour in Paris.[68]

Another account explains the relationship between Haden and Whistler in terms of professional rivalry. They were both etchers, and had published sets of original prints in Paris:

> The two artists together planned to publish a set of *The Thames from its Source to the Sea*, but their powerful personalities clashed. Whistler resented Haden's overbearing behaviour and was jealous of ... praise of prints that the American regarded as inferior to his own. Haden's refusal to meet the costs of the funeral of his medical partner, James Traer, a friend of Whistler, who died in a Parisian brothel, proved to be the final straw for their difficult relationship.[69]

As the Club reported it, 'Mr Haden complained that he had, in a tavern in Paris, been grossly assaulted by Mr Whistler, a member of the Club'[70] and at the meeting at which this was reported, a letter was drafted to Whistler asking him to quietly withdraw his membership. While certainly unpleasant for all concerned, the only real consequences for the Club in this matter were the resignation of the Rossettis (D. G. and W. M.) in protest.[71] The Rossettis were of course prominent members of the London art world at that time, one as a critic and the other as a painter, and both were founder members of the so-called Pre-Raphaelite Brotherhood.[72] Dante Rossetti is representative of a core group of members of the Club in the nineteenth century: artists. The artist members were mainly part of a smaller group centred on the Pre-Raphaelite Brotherhood and the Aesthetic Movement as well as Holland Park in London. Yet within this category, there were also establishment artists such as Frederick Leighton and William Boxall (1800–1879). In later years members of the Bloomsbury Group were members, such as various Sitwells and the critic Lytton Strachey (1880–1932). The critics were a parallel group and equally diverse, from Ruskin to William Rossetti, Strachey, George Bernard Shaw, and Roger Fry. While their work may sometimes have been at odds, what unites the disparate members of the Club is their art-collecting activities rather than art patronage or production, because painters and print makers were not allowed to exhibit their work at the Club nor was the work of any contemporary artists permitted. The members, including the artists and critics, also were clearly united by wealth and a desire to be members of a fairly traditional gentlemen's club, a point worth noting.

Self-described collectors, who may or may not have had other occupations, were, of course, a major category of member. Some, like George Salting, who was elected in 1867, became significant figures in the history of art collecting in Britain. His life and activities were described in a recent history of print collecting as follows:

> [A]fter inheriting his fortune, ... George Salting found his vocation as a professional collector of art. Inspired by the beautiful objects he had studied in Rome and encouraged in his pursuits by the advice offered by his friend Louis Huth, and by Charles Drury Fortnum and Augustus Wollaston Franks of the British Museum, George Salting embarked on his chosen career with single-minded determination. Chinese porcelain was the focus of his first serious collection ... Salting received much encouragement from Louis Huth, himself a distinguished collector of Chinese porcelain. From 1874 Salting began the practice of depositing on loan his oriental porcelain and other collections of *objets d'art* at the South Kensington Museum, where they were put on public display ... While he was forming his oriental collections Salting began to move into the area of Renaissance bronzes and maiolica ... By 1896 Charles Drury Fortnum, in his authoritative book on maiolica, could describe Salting's maiolica collection as 'the richest private collection now in England' ...
>
> [He] kindly allows it to be exhibited, for the public benefit, at the South Kensington Museum.[73]

Salting's pattern of collecting, combining 'oriental' ceramics, prints, Renaissance bronzes and maiolica, as well as European paintings, in fact, reflects the complexion of the BFAC itself. A glance at the list of original members and the early activities of the Club demonstrates that it did not specialize in one particular area of art, even though its virtual predecessor, the FAC, has been interpreted as specializing in the decorative arts.[74] The BFAC, in contrast, did not specify a particular area of the arts that it would focus on in its initial 'objects' nor in its own histories (e.g. BFAC, 1895, 1925). Certainly the association with the South Kensington Museum and later the V&A was strong, and thus there was a significant interest among members in what were called the decorative arts,[75] but in fact the earliest members, who were also founders of the FAC, were mainly collectors or curators of prints and paintings, and these would continue to be a major interest for Club members. Among the earliest members for whom this was a focus were Ralph Wornum,[76] John Malcolm of Poltalloch, 'Holford' who was Robert Stayner Holford (1808–1892), father of the more prominent Sir George Holford (1860–1926), and Seymour Haden (discussed above). Wornum, in addition to being a National Gallery Keeper, was a portrait painter and a noted art critic. At the National Gallery, he worked under Director Charles Eastlake (1793–1865, himself a member of the FAC) and two of his successors, including Sir William Boxall, RA, who was also a member of the FAC and an original member of the BFAC.[77] Boxall had been proposed for membership of the FAC by future prime minister W. E. Gladstone (1809–1898),[78] a fellow member of the FAC, who appointed Boxall to the directorship of the National Gallery in 1866.[79] It was Boxall who had proposed Whistler for membership of the Club, possibly to his regret.

Malcolm of Poltalloch ('Malcolm', as he was usually referred to in the BFAC correspondence and meeting minutes), who was so important for the Club's early finances, was from a prominent landowning family and inherited the title of laird in 1857 upon the death of his older brother. The family seat was located near Argyll but the landholdings included plantations in the West Indies and a cattle station in Australia.[80] He began collecting in earnest when he purchased a Renaissance print collection of some 500 pieces from Robinson in 1860.[81] With Robinson's help, he built on this collection and by the time of his death, it consisted of around 1,000 examples. These were then sold with other items to the British Museum for a nominal sum after his death in 1895.[82] Malcolm's good friend, William Mitchell, also a print collector, donated his own collection of German woodcuts to the British Museum in the same year. They were both guided in their collecting by Robinson and all three had been members of the FAC and subsequently joined the BFAC. Several of the early exhibitions of the Club were filled with items from the Malcolm and Mitchell collections, including the Raphael and Michelangelo show of 1870 and the Rembrandt etchings show of 1877, both of which are discussed in Chapter 1.

Taste in Collecting and Display

While it is true that prints and paintings were among the most prominent areas exhibited by members, a survey of the contents of the exhibitions they presented, and the informal displays, demonstrates that the members' collecting tastes were very wide-ranging but nevertheless reflective of their time, place, and social position. The general areas collected by members as represented in the exhibitions include the following:

British and European Painting including portraits/portrait miniatures

Prints: drawings, sketches, etchings, woodblocks, architectural studies

Ceramics, from around the world

Metalwork: bronzes, silver, coins

Enamels: e.g. Limoges

Books and Manuscripts (English and European)

Ivory carving

Heraldic objects

Embroidery/textiles

Greek and Roman objects, including jewellery

Terra cottas (small sculptures)

World objects: Persian, Egyptian, Chinese, Japanese, 'Oriental', 'American', African, Pacific/Polynesian

The last area of collecting on this list, referred to here as 'world objects', is difficult to classify but might best be described as primarily miscellaneous craft items like ceramics and archaeological material, including what was considered archaeological material at the time but might not be today, as well as in some cases (Japan) prints and paintings. Several exhibitions featured archaeological objects (discussed in the chapters that follow), and a number of members were also members of archaeologically inclined groups such as the Society of Antiquaries, the Royal Anthropological Institute, and the Egypt Exploration Society (or Fund as it was originally named). In other subject areas, Club members were also members of associated fine art-related special interest groups and institutions, such as the British Institution, the Royal Academy, the Royal Society of Arts, the Fine Art Society and the Liverpool Arts Club. The Fine Art Society is an interesting link because it was founded in 1876 as a gallery specializing in British art and design. They presented the work of a number of artists who were also members of the Club, including Whistler, for whom the first one-man show was devised in 1880.[83] One of the founders of the FAS was Marcus B. Huish (Marcus Bourne, 1843–1921), also a member of the Club but somehow also a dealer, who collected ceramics and was a lender to the 'Coloured Chinese Porcelain' exhibition (see Chapter 2).

This intersection between Club members and other special interest groups is particularly notable and significant in the insight it gives into the collecting worlds of the nineteenth and early twentieth centuries. Several special interest groups were founded in the eighteenth century but it was in the nineteenth century that groups associated with collecting in every sense were founded, from traditional art objects to ethnographic material. As Westgarth has noted, it was in the second half of the nineteenth century that collectors began to concentrate on single object categories more than ever before and special interest groups can be said to reflect this.[84] The Club itself did not specialize but its exhibitions both facilitated specialization and reflected the trend.

Private collecting was the driving force behind the development of not just these groups but also the scholarly fields associated with them such as Archaeology, Anthropology, and Art History.[85] Traditionally these are considered to be separate developments,[86] but when viewed through the lens of art collecting, and the wide networks of Club members as collectors, it is clear that both scholarship and the practice of art collecting were not just interrelated, as has been noted before, but also interdependent, with universities and museums a beneficiary of these relations. All three disciplines owe their existence to collecting but the perception is that it is only Art History that was driven by art collecting. Anthropology, for example, is widely linked with ethnographic collecting,[87] but, in fact, the collectors may not necessarily have been collecting the objects as scientists but rather as art collectors, and the same is true for Archaeology. The practice of art collecting thus informed and framed other types of collecting.

The specific areas of collecting identified for the Club members are therefore reflective of nineteenth-century collecting practices and the complexion of the art market at that time. Histories of art collecting tend to focus on one area or one individual but even broader studies, such as by Susan Pearce, who theorizes collecting practices, tend to look at the activity of collecting rather than the objects and their availability.[88] If we examine the Club as an integral part of the London art world in the second half of the nineteenth century and the first decades of the twentieth century, then the members' seemingly diverse collecting tastes in fact are not so unusual, apart from in one area: contemporary art. There is a distinctly antiquarian bias present in both the Club's exhibitions and its members' collections but that is only indicated by what was exhibited at the Club. If we look at members who also belonged to other groups, we can see that a number were straddling two worlds with their collecting and consumption of art. For example, a number of members were patrons of contemporary artists, including W. C. Alexander, a patron of Whistler, who painted one of the Alexander daughters and decorated his house in Holland Park. Alexander also collected ceramics, especially Chinese ones, which he exhibited at the Club (see Chapter 2). His interested in Asian ceramics paralleled that of Whistler and Rossetti, who used them as props in their paintings. Whistler bought many of his ceramics in the Netherlands when they were cheap and other members bought similar wares from dealers such as Murray Marks, who would hire Whistler to illustrate the sale catalogue of the Thompson Collection (see Chapter 2). Ceramics was an area of collecting that was driven by dealers, yet another significant intersection with the art market that the Club reveals.[89]

Conclusion

These linked networks and activities, brought together through the Club and underpinned by private collecting, as argued here, will become more apparent in the following case studies of categories of exhibition subjects presented by the Club throughout its history. These exhibition subjects have been selected as particularly representative of Club activities, approaches and perspectives, as well as for their impact on respective fields. While not a comprehensive survey of all the exhibitions mounted by the Club, the selection is perhaps more valuable for its in-depth examination of both people and objects. As a gentlemen's club, the Burlington Fine Arts Club is an interesting phenomenon in its own right but it is its exhibitions focus that sets it apart. Upon close study, these exhibitions, the objects displayed within them, their lenders and critical responses can help to further illuminate the collecting and display worlds of London in the nineteenth and early twentieth centuries.

Notes

1 General Committee Minutes, vol. 1: 1866–1870, NAL (not paginated), BFAC Draft History, 1895, NAL 200.B.110.
2 In 'A Grand Design', www.vam.ac.uk/vastatic/microsites/1159_grand_design/essay-an-encyclopedia-of-treasures_new.html (accessed 11 Aug. 2014). See also: Helen Davies, 'John Charles Robinson's Work at the South Kensington Museum, Part II. From 1863 to 1867: Consolidation and conflict', *Journal of the History of Collections*, vol. 11, no. 1 (1999), pp. 95–115; 'John Charles Robinson's Work at the South Kensington Museum, Part I: The Creation of the Collection of Italian Renaissance Objects at the Museum of Ornamental Art and the South Kensington Museum, 1853–62', *Journal of the History of Collections* vol. 10, no. 2 (1998), pp. 169–188; Jacqueline Yallop, *Magpies, Squirrels and Thieves: How the Victorians Collected the World* (London: Atlantic Books, 2011).
3 A comprehensive biography, with sources, can be found at: www.victorianweb.org/sculpture/marochetti/biography.html (accessed 18 Dec. 2015).
4 'Minister of Sardinia to the Court of St James's'. He was also a co-founder of the St James Club in London in 1857 with Earl Granville after a dispute at the Traveller's Club, according to their own history. See www.stjameshotelandclub.com/history (accessed 18 Dec. 2015). For biographical information in English, see: www.whistler.arts.gla.ac.uk/correspondence/biog/display/?bid=D_Az_Mq (accessed 11 Aug. 2014),
5 Cited in Ann Eatwell, 'The Collector's or Fine Arts Club, 1857–74: The First Society for Collectors of the Decorative Arts', in *The Decorative Arts Society 1850 to the Present, Journal Number Eighteen, Omnium Gatherum* (Suffolk, 1994), p. 25.
6 Ibid., p. 25.
7 Ibid., p. 25.
8 From Merriam-Webster dictionary: see www.merriam-webster.com/word-of-the-day/2011/12/15/#i0SYHelD3eUOpZQv.99 (accessed 11 Aug. 2014).
9 Eatwell (1994), p. 26.
10 See Rebecca Wade, 'Pedagogic Objects: The Formation, Circulation and Exhibition of Teaching Collections for Art and Design Education in Leeds, 1837–1857', unpublished PhD thesis, University of Leeds, 2012, pp. 18–19 for discussion.
11 Ibid.
12 Ibid, p. 28. In another source, Eatwell has described this exhibition as the Club's 'finest hour', 'Borrowing from Collectors: The Role of the Loan in the Formation of the Victoria and Albert Museum and its Collection (1852–1932)', *DAS: The Decorative Arts Society 1850 to the Present, Journal Number Twenty-four, Omnium Gatherum* (Suffolk, 2000), p. 5. Lenders' and Committee members' names can be seen in the catalogue: Science and Art Department of the Committee of Council on Education, *Catalogue of the Special Exhibition of Works of Art of the Mediaeval, Renaissance and More Recent Periods on Loan at the*

South Kensington Museum, June 1862. Note that one member of the Committee is W. E. Gladstone, M.P.

13 Ibid, p. 29.

14 27 April 1866, General Meeting minute book, V&A 86.KK.37 (not paginated).

15 This is possibly because he was a print dealer, a category of Club member that was not permitted in the bye-laws. For a biography, see Anthony Griffiths, ed., *Landmarks in Print Collecting: Connoisseurs and Donors at the British Museum since 1753* (London: British Museum Press, 1996), pp. 90–112.

16 27 April 1866, General Meeting minute book, V&A 86.KK.37 (not paginated).

17 The members of the committee were as follows: '1. The Marquis d'Azeglio, 2. Mr. Richard Fisher, 3. Mr. J. C. Robinson, 4. Mr. R. N. Wornum, 5. Mr. William Smith [note in pencil - 'resigned'], 6. The Baron Ferdinand de Rothschild, 7. Sir Coutts Lindsay Bart., 8. The Baron Marochetti, 9. Mr. Alexander Barker, 10. Mr. Alfred Morrison, 11. Mr S. Addington, 12. Mr. John Webb'. General Meeting minutes for 5 June 1866.

18 5 June 1866, General Meeting minute book, V&A 86.KK.37 (not paginated).

19 177 Piccadilly is next to Fortnum and Mason department store in the French Railways building (now Cath Kidston) and diagonally across from the Royal Academy, in Burlington House. Mr Toovey was James Toovey who ran a publishing house from the premises until 1894. See British History Online: www.british-history.ac.uk/report.aspx?compid=40571 (accessed 19 Sept. 2014). The BFAC took over the ground floor of the building initially.

20 General Meeting minutes, 20 July 1866.

21 Ibid.

22 BFAC Rules and Regulations, I, 1866, NAL archives, 200.b.110.

23 F. R. Cowell, *The Athenaeum, Club and Social Life in London 1824–1974* (London: Heinemann, 1975), p. 41.

24 Amy Milne-Smith, *London Clubland: A Cultural History of Gender and Class in Late Victorian Britain* (Basingstoke: Palgrave, 2011), pp. 118–119.

25 Anthony Lejeune, *The Gentlemen's Clubs of London* (London: Stacey International, 1979).

26 According to the General Meeting minutes, 17 January 1871:

> [T]he Committee were able to conclude an agreement for taking the present premises 17 Savile Row, which they have secured on lease for a term of 31 years from the 29th of September 1870 at an annual rent of £315 with the option of terminating the same at the expiration of/or of 20 years, upon six months notice. The lease will be granted to Sir William Drake, Mr Fisher, Mr Malcolm and Mr Vaughan, as Trustees for the Club.

27 www.mapping-the-london-art-market (accessed 9 May 2016).

28 Christie's was (and still is) located at 8 King Street from 1823 and Westgarth notes that antique and curiosity dealers began to move into the West End from the 1820s. M. Westgarth, 'Introduction', in *A Biographical Dictionary of Nineteenth-Century Antique and Curiosity Dealers*, Regional Furniture XXIII (Glasgow: Regional Furniture Society 2009), p. 9.

29 Wyatt was the architect and historian Matthew Digby Wyatt (1820–1877). He was the first Slade Professor of Fine Art at Cambridge. See https://dictionaryofarthistorians.org/wyattm.htm (accessed 6 Oct. 2015).

30 John Harris, *Moving Rooms: The Trade in Architectural Salvages* (New Haven, CT: Yale University Press, 2007), Chapter 7 'The Period Room in European Museums', p. 119.

31 Penny Sparke, Brenda Martin, and Trevor Keeble, eds., *The Modern Period Room: The Construction of the Exhibited Interior, 1870–1950* (London: Routledge, 2006); Harris (2007), p. 120.

32 Milne-Smith (2011), p. 109.

33 Rules and Regulations, General Meeting minutes 17 Jan. 1871.

34 Using the historic inflation rate calculation: www.thisismoney.co.uk/money/bills/article-1633409/Historic-inflation-calculator-value-money-changed-1900.html (accessed 17 Dec. 2015). In terms of purchasing power, it would be about £500. See www.measuringworth.com/ukcompare/relativevalue.php (accessed 17 Dec. 2015).

35 General Meeting minutes for 29 May 1924.

36 In the rules and regulations adopted at the General Meeting of 17 Jan. 1871, it is noted that: 'XL – No account shall be opened by any Member of the Club with any of the servants. XLI — No dice are to be used, and no games of chance are to be played in the Club.' This is probably in response to changes in the perception of gambling in the nineteenth century, after the excesses of the eighteenth. 'Gambling continued to be an attraction of club life into the nineteenth century, but such excesses became increasingly unacceptable' (Milne-Smith, 2011, p. 23).
37 Rules and Regulations, General Meeting minutes, 17 Jan. 1871.
38 Rules and Regulations, General Meeting minutes, 17 Jan. 1871.
39 General Meeting minutes, 14 May 1872.
40 General Meeting minutes, 27 May 1873.
41 Rules and Regulations adopted at meeting, 17 Jan. 1871.
42 The assets varied over time and are listed in the minutes of General Committee meetings, which were quarterly as opposed to the AGM minutes, but summaries of the year's assets, income, and outgoings can also be found here.
43 Griffiths (1996), p. 164.
44 Yallop (2011), pp. 68–69.
45 General Meeting minutes, 14 May 1872, point VII. But the rules about leaving objects at the Club were strict: 'That any members of the Club may be at liberty to bring works of art and leave them for a period not exceeding a fortnight in the rooms on the 2nd floor of the Club, for inspection and discussion.' (amendment to the Bye Laws 19 Feb. 1872, in GM minutes for 14 May 1872).
46 General Meeting minutes, 15 January 1867.
47 In 1940, during the Second World War, the Club premises had to be vacated. After the war, there were no further special exhibitions before the Club's dissolution in 1951. The details of the demise of the Club are provided in Chapter 5.
48 'The main object of the Club being the exhibition of Works of Art of past ages, the works of living artists will be admitted only upon special application to the Committee.' (Rules and regulations adopted at General Meeting, 17 Jan. 1871.)
49 The Royal Academy of Arts was founded in 1768 by William Chambers to promote art production (called 'Design' at the time) through an annual exhibition and an associated school. It moved to its Burlington House premises in 1867, shortly after the BFAC was founded. See www.royalacademy.org.uk/about-the-ra#our-story (accessed 22 Jan. 2016). On artist exhibition societies and the Goupil gallery, see Anne Helmreich, 'The Socio-Geography of Art Dealers and Commercial Galleries in Early Twentieth-Century London', in Helena Bonett, Ysanne Holt, and Jennifer Mundy, eds, *The Camden Town Group in Context* (London: Tate Research Publication, May 2012), see www.tate.org.uk/art/research-publications/camden-town-group-/anne-helmreich-the-socio-geography-of-art-dealers-and-commercial-galleries-in-early-r1105658 (accessed 9 May 2016).
50 I would suggest that such interiors are another aspect of period rooms that could be explored, both through notions of Orientalism and authenticity.
51 The visitor numbers recorded are for non-members. It is not known how many members regularly attended the exhibitions.
52 General Meeting minutes, 18 May 1869.
53 For example: 'Amongst the visitors to the Exhibitions it may be mentioned that the Club was honoured by the presence of HRH the Princess of Wales' (General Meeting minutes for 27 May 1879).
54 For example, lots 697; 1418-27, Sotheby, Wilkinson and Hodge, *Catalogue of the MacGregor Collection of Egyptian Antiquities*, London, June 26–July 6 1922.
55 Burlington Fine Arts Club, *History, Rules, Regulations, and Bye-laws*, 17 Savile Row, London, W.1, 1925, p. 19.
56 Eatwell (2000), p. 22.
57 Milne-Smith (2011), p. 37.
58 General Meeting minutes, 9 May 1868.
59 Rules and Regulations adopted at General Meeting 17 Jan. 1871.
60 27 April 1866, General Meeting minute book, V&A 86.KK.37 (not paginated).
61 Robinson's biography is covered in Yallop (2011), pp. 51–121. His background as an artist is perhaps relevant here, as is his view that much of the great art in Britain was hidden and

should be shared. Robinson was also a collector, but of limited means. However, he visited a number of private and public collections in Europe and this background gave him, in Yallop's view, a connoisseur's approach to art, in contrast to the education one promoted by Henry Cole (ibid., p. 68). Hence Robinson's founding of the FAC, and later the BFAC.

62 See Wade (2012, p. 127) where he is described as a 'significant figure to the practice and pedagogy of art and design education'.

63 Morrison's biography is covered in Caroline Dakers, *A Genius for Money: Business, Art and the Morrisons* (New Haven, CT: Yale University Press, 2011), which is mainly about his father James, but Alfred is best known for his collections and connoisseurship, the 'Victorian Maecenas' according to Dakers (ibid., p. 3). He was an active member of the Club.

64 Franks was an influential keeper at the British Museum from 1851. For a biography of Franks, who later became 'Sir Wollaston', see Marjorie Caygill and John Cherry, eds., *A. W. Franks: Nineteenth Century Collecting and the British Museum* (London: British Museum Press, 1997).

65 BFAC General Committee minutes, vol. 1, meeting 17 July 1866. Ruskin was of course the great critic, historian and philanthropist who was actively involved in both the writing of painting history and the shaping of genres. For a recent biography, see Robert Hewison, *John Ruskin* (Oxford: Oxford University Press, 2007).

66 See www.asce-chantilly.com/portraits/aumale.html (accessed 25 June 2016). For a complete listing of members, see the Index to Candidate Books, NAL.

67 Ibid., 12.31.1866; 2.12.67. Owen Jones was an architect and designer who was a close associate of Henry Cole. He was therefore involved in the establishment of the South Kensington Museum (later the V&A) and is best known for his seminal text, *The Grammar of Ornament* (1856). For an overview of his life and work, see Carol Flores, *Owen Jones: Design, Ornament, Architecture and Theory in an Age in Transition* (New York: Flores, 2006).

68 See http://etchings.arts.gla.ac.uk/catalogue/biog/?nid=HadeFS (accessed 12 Aug. 2014).

69 Martin Hopkinson, *No Day Without a Line: The History of the Royal Society of Painter-Printmakers 1880–1999* (Oxford: Ashmolean Museum, 1999), p. 10.

70 General Committee minutes, 11 June 1967.

71 GM, 19 December 1867, and 'Editorial: the Burlington Fine Arts Club', *The Burlington Magazine*, vol. XCIV, April 1952, p. 98.

72 Dinah Roe, *The Rossettis in Wonderland: A Victorian Family History* (London: Haus Publishing, 2011); Julie L'Enfant. *William Rossetti's Art Criticism: The Search for Truth in Victorian Art* (Lanham, MD: University Press of America, 1998).

73 Griffiths (1996), p. 190. See Stacey Pierson, *Collectors, Collections and Museums: The Field of Chinese Ceramics in Britain, 1560–1960* (Bern: Peter Lang, 2007), pp. 95–96, for a brief discussion of the significance of Salting's Chinese ceramics collection in this field in Britain. Brief biographies can also be found on the V&A and National Gallery websites, as Salting was also a collector of paintings and gave 192 to the National Gallery: www.nationalgallery.org.uk/content/conWebDoc/2194 (accessed 13 Aug. 2014); www.vam.ac.uk/content/articles/g/george-salting/ (accessed 13 Aug. 2014).

74 Eatwell (1994).

75 The concept of a distinction between decorative and fine arts did already exist but 'decorative arts' was not a term used by the Club, apart from 'decorative furniture'. For the Club, all objects, fine or otherwise, were for the most part classified as 'art' but sometimes 'works of art' functioned as signalling 'not painting'. For a somewhat controversial history of the term and concept of 'decorative arts', see Isabelle Frank, ed., *The Theory of Decorative Art: An Anthology of European and American Writings, 1750–1940* (New Haven, CT: Yale University Press, 2001).

76 *Oxford Dictionary of National Biography*, online edition: Charles Sebag-Montefiore, 'Holford, Robert Stayner (1808–1892)', rev. first published 2004 http://dx.doi.org/10.1093/ref:odnb/37559 (accessed 18 Dec. 2015).

77 www.dictionaryofarthistorians.org/wornumr.htm (accessed 13 Aug. 2014); Thomas Seccombe, 'Wornum, Ralph Nicholson (1812–1877)', rev. David Carter, in *Oxford Dictionary of National Biography* (Oxford: Oxford University Press, 2004); online edn, first published 2004. See http://dx.doi.org/10.1093/ref:odnb/29978 (accessed 18 Dec. 2015). Interestingly, Wornum was also a member of the Swedenborg Society, whose primary focus is the works

and ideas of Emanuel Swedenborg. See Richard Lines, *A History of the Swedenborg Society, 1810–2010* (London: the Swedenborg Society, 2012), p. 43. Also see Christopher Whitehead, *The Public Art Museum in Nineteenth Century Britain: The Development of the National Gallery* (London: Routledge, 2005) for Wornum in the history of the National Gallery.

78 On Gladstone as a collector and member of the FAC, see Eatwell (1994) and Marcia Pointon, 'W. E. Gladstone as an Art Patron and Collector', *Victorian Studies*, vol. 19, no. 1 (Sept., 1975), pp. 73–98.

79 See www.dictionaryofarthistorians.org/boxallw.htm (accessed 13 Aug. 2014).

80 Stephen Coppel, 'Malcolm, John, of Poltalloch (1805–1893)', in *Oxford Dictionary of National Biography* (Oxford: Oxford University Press, 2004); online edn, May 2005.www.oxforddnb.com/view/article/62981 (accessed 18 Dec. 2015).

81 Griffiths (1996), p. 162.

82 Ibid., p. 159.

83 Available at: http://faslondon.com/fas/about-us/about-us (accessed 7 June 2016).

84 Westgarth (2009), p. 10.

85 Pierson (2004b), pp. 7–8.

86 For example, Christopher Gosden, *Anthropology and Archaeology: A Changing Relationship* (London: Routledge, 1999); George W. Stocking, *Victorian Anthropology* (New York: Free Press, 1987); Udo Kultermann, *The History of Art History*, rev. edn (New York: Abaris Books, 1993); Nigel Llewellyn, 'The History of Western Art History', in Michael Bentley, ed., *The Routledge Companion to Historiography* (London: Routledge, 1997), pp. 828–848.

87 For example, James Clifford's *The Predicament of Culture: Twentieth-Century Ethnography, Literature and Art* (Cambridge, MA: Harvard University Press, 1988); and *The Cultures of Collecting* (London: Reaktion, 1994).

88 *Investigation into Collecting in the European Tradition* (London: Routledge, 1999).

89 The role of Whistler and Murray Marks in the ceramics field in England is discussed in Pierson (2007).

Part 2
Exhibitions

1 Paintings and Prints in Europe and Britain

Chapter Contents

- Introduction
- *'Netherlandish' Prints and Painting*
- 1877 Etched Work of Rembrandt
- 1892 Pictures by Masters of the Netherlandish and Allied Schools
- *Italian Regional Painting*
- 1894 Pictures of the Ferrara School: School of Ferrara-Bologna
- 1898 Milanese Masters: Pictures by Masters of the Milanese and Allied Schools of Lombardy
- 1919 Florentine Painting before 1500
- Conclusion

Introduction

This chapter examines the Club's approach to the exhibiting of European painting and prints, what were (and still are) defined as 'old masters'. Members of the Club collected widely, as we have seen, and within the category of paintings and prints, those produced by British artists were also exhibited at the Club. Some of these were made by artist members and associates, such as Burne-Jones and Rossetti, but only displayed after their deaths for reasons noted in the Introduction.[1] The Club also exhibited British prints and paintings collected by members such as the works of Cozens, Blake, and Turner. It was with their displays of European prints and paintings, however, that the Club both carried on established traditions of presentation and interpretation and innovated new ones, in some cases, making a lasting impact on approaches to the subject in the field. In order to illustrate this, the chapter will begin with the Club's exhibitions of Rembrandt Etchings (1877) and Early Netherlandish Painting (1892), which can be seen as reflective of the traditional art collecting approaches of the eighteenth and nineteenth centuries, but with a new display strategy. This will be followed by a discussion of exhibitions of Italian regional schools of painting, from 1893–1919, where innovative approaches to display and categorization were used.

'NETHERLANDISH' PRINTS AND PAINTING

1877 Etched Work of Rembrandt

The idea for an exhibition of the Etched Work of Rembrandt was proposed by Seymour Haden in late 1876. The minutes of the Club's General Committee meetings record that this was approved along with the recommendation by the exhibition subcommittee for the inclusion of two additional members:

> 11.4.1877
> Read recommendation of the Rembrandt Etchings Exhibition Subcommittee and their meeting on the 9th inst and resolved that Mr Charles Blanc of Paris be elected an Honorary Member of this Club, and that Dr Strater [sp?] of Aix la Chapelle be elected an Honorary Visitor for the period of the Rembrandt Etchings Exhibition.
> (Note III of minutes)

After the exhibition closed, the minutes further note the visitor numbers which indicate a successful and popular show:

> 17.7.1877
> III It was reported that the Rembrandt Etchings Exhibition which was opened on 15th May, was closed on Saturday 7th inst. having been attended by 3379 visitors exclusive of members of the Club.[2]

An earlier exhibition of 'Rembrandt Pictures, Drawings and Etchings' had been mounted in 1867, and was the first major exhibition of the Club at its Piccadilly premises, but no catalogue was produced at that time. It is referred to in the catalogue for the second exhibition of Rembrandt etchings mounted by the Club in 1877, which was seen by its participants as a departure from the usual method of presenting such material. As the catalogue author, Seymour Haden, noted:

> On the occasion of a former Exhibition of the Etchings of Rembrandt, in the Old Club House in 1867, it was suggested to the Committee that the arrangement according to *Subject*, then universally adopted, was fatal to the comprehensive study of such works, and that it might be with advantage be discarded for the more rational order of *date of production*; that an arbitrary method, by which works of the latest were mixed up with works of the earliest period, confused the sense, perverted the judgment, and rendered critical examination and comparison impossible; and, generally, that such a system might satisfy the Cataloguer, was unworthy of the Biographer and useless to the Student. The Art work of a lifetime, it was contended, should not be looked at as a series of haphazard disjointed efforts, but as the continuous expression of a prolonged chain of logical sequences depending for their coherence on the due maintenance of the order of their production; and only to be properly understood when studied in that order.[3]

Haden then suggested that such an approach would lead to new works coming to light and more accurate attributions of known works. He described the Committee's full backing of such an approach and the significance of it as follows:

> To these representations – novel and revolutionary as they no doubt felt them to be – the Committee were good enough to listen, and hence it came to be conceded not only that there should be a second Exhibition of the Etched Works of Rembrandt in the rooms of the Club, but that that exhibition, in accordance with one of the fundamental objects for which the Club was established, should be made subservient to a directly useful purpose. Discarding therefore, the methods of the Catalogues from Gersaint downwards, we have now, for the first time, what may be called the Natural History of Rembrandt before our own eyes, and may be read, ... with the events of his life, the motives of that Art of which those events were, after all, but the proximate cause.[4]

While this does sound somewhat hyperbolic, it was indeed a new approach to the display of such material.[5] To put Haden's views into context, they come at a time when Rembrandt etchings had been the subject of a wave of critical popularity in France. During the nineteenth century, the critic Charles Blanc (1813–1882) and the collector Eugène Dutuit (1807–1886) – both of whom were made honorary members of the Club for the exhibition, as well as Haden – wrote catalogues of Rembrandt etchings, which

> took a turn at classifying and describing Rembrandt's etchings and they positioned their catalogues either following or counter to the tradition of subject groupings set by the Parisian dealer Gersaint [cited by Haden] who wrote the first catalogue of Rembrandt's etchings, published in 1751.[6]

Haden thus used the Club's exhibition and its catalogue to apply a counter-Gersaint methodology of classifying and interpreting etchings from a biographical perspective, as he called it – a 'natural history of Rembrandt'. Today this is a standard approach in art history but in 1877, if the artist was considered at all in the interpretation of his work, it was through his 'genius' rather than his life history, as Haden proposed here. What follows in the catalogue essay is a biography of Rembrandt that is framed by the concept of genius nonetheless. There is also a plea for the categorization of engraving as 'art', which is in keeping with the author's own professional interests as an engraver as well as his collecting of engravings. For example: 'to this Club [is due] no less the credit of proving, by its splendid demonstration of to-day, that it is *par excellence*, a Painter's Art'.[7]

The Lenders

Haden, the catalogue author and exhibition instigator, who was so important in the early days of the Club, was an influential figure in the world of printmakers in the later nineteenth century and the most significant lender to this exhibition. He was instrumental in setting up what became the Royal Society of Painter-Printers and in gaining recognition for original printmakers.[8] It is not surprising, therefore, that he should have had such strong feelings about the way Rembrandt's etchings were classified, dated, and authenticated. He founded the Society of Painter-Printers in 1880, to redress the exclusion of original etchers from membership of the Royal Academy, and the consequent lack of recognition experienced by printmakers compared with painters.[9] As we saw in the Introduction, the Club was founded by a group of mainly print collectors, demonstrating that among these collectors, the print was held in high esteem. For this category of art, as well as others that will be explored here, the development and status of the category were driven and defined by collectors. In fact, we can see that in the nineteenth century and first half of the twentieth century, it was private collectors who held much of the power in the art world, not the institutions, and the Club provides good evidence for this.

Nonetheless, in mounting the 1877 exhibition, Haden was also promoting his personal interests as a collector. Indeed, Haden 'ranked as one of the foremost collectors of Rembrandt etchings'.[10] Not surprisingly, it was his own classification of the material that was being presented. In addition to Haden, Dutuit was also a lender, and the list of lenders to the exhibition noted at the beginning of the catalogue also includes a number of established collectors of prints and paintings who were early Club members such as Richard Fisher, R. S. Holford MP, Alfred Morrison, as well as Henry Vaughan (see Chapter 3). Three men who are not well known today but who have been described as the 'generation of collectors that followed [Slade] in the third quarter of the century [who] were even more selective in forming their collections',[11] also contributed to the exhibition: Henry Broadhurst (1840–1911, MP, collection published 1872), St John Dent (d. *c.* 1884, collection sold 1884), and Rev. J. Griffiths (1806–1885, ex-Warden of Wadham College, Oxford, collection sold 1883).[12] The rest of the contributors on the list, including Club members and non-members, are equally diverse in both background and collecting tastes, as the following biographical sketches will demonstrate.

Samuel Addington (*c.* 1807–1886), for example, was a wool merchant and original member of both the Fine Arts Club and the Burlington Fine Arts Club.[13] He collected porcelain, coins, and prints. Edward Cheney (1803–1884) was a collector of Renaissance art, especially the Tiepolo family, and was based at Badger Hall in Shropshire. He seems to have known Ruskin (Club member) and his wife.[14] 'Lady Eastlake', not a member due to her gender, was probably Elizabeth Rigby (1809–1893), wife of Sir Charles Eastlake (1793–1865) who was the painter, writer, and Director of the National Gallery (not his nephew of the same name, who was a Club member). Rigby, described as a 'pioneer woman art writer', was an active and very opinionated member of the London art and literary worlds and a proto-feminist.[15]

The Rev. J. J. Heywood was John James Heywood (1827–1887), an MP from a prominent banking family who knew Whistler and was an active Club member in its early days.[16] William Bell Scott (1811–1890) was a poet, artist, and engraver. He was also a close friend of the Rossettis, which is possibly his connection to the Club.[17] H. Danby Seymour (Henry, 1820–1877) was an MP for Poole, and Committee member of the Nineveh Fund, which was established in 1851 to fund further work by Layard in 'Babylonia'.[18] With respect to the Club, he was a patron of G. F. Watts (1817–1904) and a friend of Gustave Waagen (d. 1868, see Chapter 3), whose work on great British art collections inspired the Club's founders.[19] Seymour was also co-founder of the India Reform Society in 1853.[20] These biographical sketches represent a typical cross-section of lenders and members which encompasses artists and their patrons, politicians, merchants, and female relations of members. This latter category of lender, along with women who were lenders in their own right, would continue to be significant throughout the Club's history, thus reflecting the typical gender politics of the time. Women could participate in but not be full members of a number of organizations and institutions. It also in some ways challenges the common characterization of women as partners of collectors, or secondary collectors, rather than as primary collectors, particularly as participants in exhibitions of collections.[21]

Exhibits and Interpretation

Another major lender was R. S. Holford of Westonbirt, who was Robert Benson's father-in-law (see biography in Appendix B). An MP, art collector, and founder of the Westonbirt Arboretum, Holford was the lender of one of the prints that Haden singled out as significant in his catalogue introduction, 'Portrait of Rembrandt in a Turned Up Hat and Embroidered Mantle' (cat. p. 55, no. 7) (Figure 1.1), versions of which are now in the French national collection,[22] the British Museum and the Morgan Library, New York, which interestingly has the provenance of another Club exhibition lender, Kennedy and Co (probably Sydney Kennedy, see Chapter 2).[23] The Morgan Library also has a print previously owned by exhibition contributor John Webster, of a crucifixion, which is a theme also singled out by Haden in his catalogue text as significant.[24] The provenances of older collections are noted in this catalogue but the lenders themselves became significant provenance sources for later collectors,

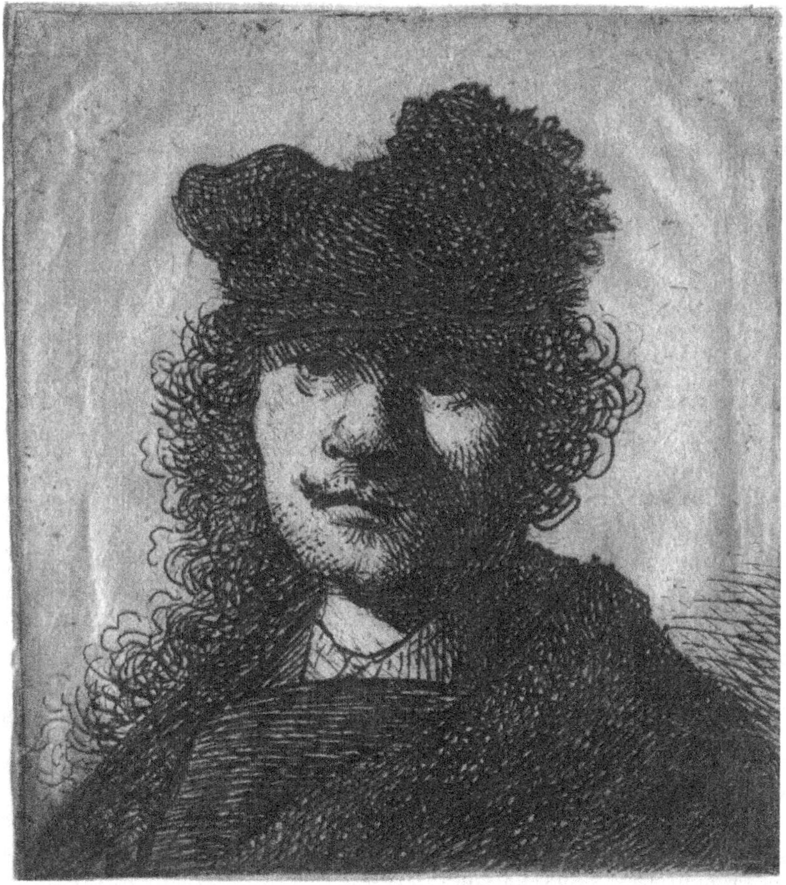

Figure 1.1 Self-portrait in cap and dark cloak: bust, Rembrandt van Rijn, 1606–1669, reworked by a pupil. Etching on paper, *c.* 1631, 66 × 60 mm. The Morgan Library, B 001-015, purchased from Kennedy and Co, February 1926.

Source: © The Morgan Library & Museum, New York.

such as Morgan (see Chapter 2). One such pre-1877 provenance was the 'Aylesford Collection', which refers to that assembled by the 5th Earl, Heneage Finch (1786–1859), who inherited his father's small collection and then expanded it into what has been described as 'amongst the finest ever assembled'.[25] Holford's prints in exhibit no. 7 are ex-Aylesford, for example.[26]

In addition to setting out his methodology and singling out key prints in the catalogue, Haden also helpfully describes stylistically the display itself, which is very much of its time and place, reflecting the opinions of the author as well. He notes:

> [A] single tour of the gallery, in the direction, of the arrow of indication, will show us much that this article is meant to indicate. Manifest differences of style and treatment marking the dawn, growth and maturity of Rembrandt's genius will probably strike us first; then a certainly inequality of the work of the first ten years, as if different hands had been employed upon it – coarse publications like the "Ecce Homo," coming in incongruous apposition with refined plates like the "Death of the Virgin," melodramatic efforts like the "Raising of Lazarus," with timid representations like the "Good Samaritan", – and so forth. These once passed, a greater homogeneity of design and handling will become apparent, and then Landscape will be seen not only to have a place, but to become so predominant as nearly to fill the wall space devoted to the next ten years. Then, at last, these, in their turn, will give way to portraits, compositions and Biblical subjects of such transcendent power and beauty that we shall need no more to convince us that the apogee of this form of art has been reached.[27]

The arrangement was thus by subject but within a developmental chronology, as Haden promised the Club's exhibitions committee. Through this could be shown, in Haden's view, the artist's own development as a maker. The exhibition itself was designed by a maker/collector, who by framing Rembrandt as a maker rather than the author of independent artworks, elevated his own status. To some extent, this was somewhat brave as it risked demoting the works, even though Haden wished to elevate the craft.

As stated previously, at this time it was private collectors as the owners of the objects defined as 'art' who wielded much of the power in the art world. In the nineteenth century they were sometimes employed by museums to catalogue their collections. Two lenders to the Club's exhibition, Fisher and Willshire, were both authors of British Museum catalogues of prints, and worked for the museum in some unofficial capacity. Richard Fisher wrote the catalogue of early Italian engravings, and Willshire that of German prints mentioned previously. Fisher's was never published and he was by all accounts difficult to work with.[28] Yet both men had been commissioned as outside authors on the basis of their collections and connections as collectors. Today this would be an unusual practice in a national museum.

After 1877, the Club continued to mount exhibitions of a wide range of prints and drawings up to the time of its closure, including Dutch Masters (1878), Rossetti (1883), Early French (1891), and Japanese (1933). A number of themed exhibitions also included drawings. This was to be a solid category of object collected and presented by the Club, therefore. It would also lead to exhibitions of paintings, with the prints appearing to be the most familiar medium among the founder members, and therefore a starting point for visual material. Once paintings or 'pictures' began to be exhibited, these exhibitions too would provide an insight not only into the character of collecting in that field but also its interpretation. As the exhibitions in this chapter will demonstrate, in the category of prints and paintings, while there was a continued interest among members in 'Netherlandish' art, such as the work of Rembrandt, it was Italian painting which was the most popular among members and their associates, and the most frequently exhibited.

Before the first Italian exhibition in 1894, in the Netherlandish category, there was an exhibition after the first Rembrandt show of 1867 of the work of Dürer and Lucas van Leyden, which consisted of prints and drawings (1869) and was accompanied by a catalogue. At this stage, the catalogues were not illustrated and did not include interpretative essays or material. There was another exhibition of 'Drawings by Dutch Masters' in 1878 but the first paintings exhibition in this category was staged in 1892. This was a much broader exhibition in terms of its regional definition, a practice which would be abandoned when it came to exhibiting Italian art.

1892 Pictures by Masters of the Netherlandish and Allied Schools

The General Committee minutes concerned with this exhibition demonstrate an evolving focus and title, and also reveal some of the practical arrangements:

> 5.1.1892
> V A suggestion for an Exhibition of Pictures by Dutch Masters was discussed and Mr Vaughan kindly undertook to communicate with Mr Walter Armstrong on the subject and report to a future meeting of the Committee.
>
> 1.3.1892
> V The following gentlemen were appointed a Subcommittee to make the necessary arrangements for an Exhibition of Paintings by Dutch Masters Mr Walter Armstrong, Mr Cock, Mr Benson, Mr Monkhouse.
>
> 31.5.1892
> X It was agreed that the Exhibition of Early Netherlandish Pictures now in the Gallery be open to visitors on Sunday from 2 to 7, and that this be indicated on the invitation forms.
>
> 14.6.1892
> III The Subcommittee of the Netherlandish Pictures Collection reported that it was proposed to print an Illustrated Edition of the Catalogue with 26 plates, and undertook at the request of the Committee to obtain estimate of cost for the next meeting.
>
> 2.8.1892
> VI It was ordered that the Exhibition of Early Netherlandish Pictures be kept open until the 13th of August.[29]

As the minutes indicate, an exhibition that was proposed as one of 'Dutch masters' eventually became one of 'Early Netherlandish Pictures', which may have been a refinement agreed by the subcommittee for the exhibition, perhaps based on the availability of loans or perhaps for art historical classificatory reasons, but surviving records do not make reference to this. The exhibition subcommittee was composed of three collectors and one museum professional, a pattern that would be maintained for much of the Club's exhibiting history.

Lenders and Exhibits

As there was clearly a connection between print and painting collectors, many of the lenders to this paintings exhibition were also involved in the earlier drawings shows. Holford, for example, was a lender but through his son, Captain Holford (Sir George Lindsay Holford), who loaned paintings on behalf of his father who died that year. Captain Holford had inherited his father's estates and property, including the family seat, Westonbirt.[30] Another lender common to both the 1877 and 1892 exhibitions was Alfred Morrison, who was an equally prolific collector. He is best known in the paintings field for his triptych, now known as 'the Morrison Triptych', in the Toledo Museum of Art, Ohio.[31] This was exhibited in the Club's exhibition as no. 42 (see Plate 1). This painting is a good example of the way in which scholarship on such works has developed since the late nineteenth century. In 1892, it was firmly attributed to Jan Gossaert (known as Mabuse). By 1927, the Club itself had reattributed it to Hans Memling[32] and then by 1955 it was thought to be by Simon van Herlam.[33] Since then, it has been attributed to an anonymous 'master', 'Master of the Morrison Triptych' who nonetheless has a distinct identity, such that other works have been attributed to him.

The exhibition's catalogue author, Walter Armstrong (1850–1914), that year appointed Director of the National Gallery of Ireland,[34] says of the attributed artist of this triptych: 'In 1508 [he] went to Italy, after which only his portraits are interesting.'[35] He does not mention Morrison's triptych at all. This is fairly typical of the Club's catalogue essays which are often about the exhibition's topic in general, with some consideration of actual exhibits, rather than an essay specifically about those exhibits. Accordingly, Armstrong notes the following in the Introduction, reflecting the current thinking about early Netherlandish art:

> The school of art which flourished in the Netherlands between 1400 and about 1550 was only the most brilliant development from the Gothic school of the Lower Rhine.
>
> ... Some Flemish writers contend that these works prove the great movement of the early fifteenth century to have had a purely national origin, ... This seems to be a patriotic opinion ... Perhaps the fairest way to put it will be to say that, so far as it was ecclesiastical, the early art of the Netherlands was affiliated directly upon the Art of mediaeval Germany ...; and so far as it was secular that its determining cause was the remarkable personality of Jan van Eyck ...[36]

This is based on the work of Waagen, who was associated with a number of collectors in Britain, as we will see in Chapter 3, but who was also the first to write an art-historical treatise on early Netherlandish art, with his *Ueber Herbert und Johann van Eyck* of 1823.[37] Waagen's book, *Treasures of Art in Great Britain* (1854), an important record of private collecting at the time, was translated from the German by Lady Eastlake, wife of the Director of the National Gallery, who was a lender to the 1877 exhibition noted above.[38] The Morrison painting also reminds us of the manifold connections between Club members and their collections. Morrison had the triptych displayed at Fonthill in rooms designed for him by Club member Owen Jones.[39]

While Morrison was a Club member, a number of loans to the exhibition came from non-members, including the Duke of Devonshire, the Earl of Crawford and Balcarres, the Earl of Pembroke, Earl Spencer, and the Earl of Verulam. However, these were typical owners of Netherlandish pictures, which decorated the great houses, and of course they had to have been known to members so that they could be persuaded to participate. The Duke of Devonshire (the 7th), for example, had loaned a Rembrandt print to Haden's 1877 exhibition and he was based at Chatsworth, which possessed a significant collection of 'old master pictures'. The Duke in 1892 would have been the 8th Duke, Spencer Cavendish (1833–1908), a prominent statesman who was asked but declined to be prime minister three times.[40] The Duke loaned Jan van Eyck's *The Consecration of Thomas a Becket* to the exhibition (no. 7) and Waagen mentions seeing this picture on his visit to Chatsworth.[41]

The Earl of Crawford and Balcarres was the 26th Earl, James Lindsay (1847–1913), whose father had built up a significant art collection at Balcarres. He loaned no. 46, a Virgin and Child attributed to 'Geeraert David'. This is one of a series of paintings attributed by Friedlander to the 'Master of the Embroidered Foliage'.[42] A recent exhibition presented research that suggested strongly that all the paintings in this series were not by the same hand, however, and most borrowed heavily from the earlier work of Rogier van der Weyden.[43]

The Earl of Pembroke was the 13th Earl, George Herbert (1850–1895), and like the others, a politician. His family seat was Wilton House, near Salisbury, and he loaned no. 59, a Lucas van Leyden called *A Card Party* (today called *The Card Players*, Wilton House)[44] (Figure 1.2). Earl Spencer would have been the 5th Earl, John Poyntz Spencer (1835–1910), also a Member of Parliament, like the other Earls who were lenders. He loaned no. 32, *Portrait of Lady Jane Grey* by Lucas de Heere, which is at Althorp. The Earl of Verulam was James Walter Grimston (1809–1895), the 2nd Earl. He was also a politician and loaned no. 12, the portrait of Edward Grimston by Petrus Christus, which would have come from the family seat, Gorehambury House near St Albans. There was one further Earl who, unlike the others, was actually a member of the Club, the Earl of Northbrook, who was Thomas Baring, as noted in the Introduction. He was the first Earl of Northbrook and a distinguished politician who was Viceroy of India under Gladstone. He loaned several paintings to the exhibition, including no. 14, *Virgin and Child Enthroned* by Rogier van der Weyden, from Stratton Park. This is today in the Thyssen-Bornemisza Collection in Madrid, and may have been sold at the Earl of Northbrook collection sale at Christie's, in December 1919.[45]

The fact that all of these lenders were aristocrats but also politicians is significant but also reflective of the time. As collectors, however, they are a more interesting group. For example, they may have perceived themselves as custodians of inherited art and estate furnishings, rather than specifically art collectors, like many other Club contributors. The Club itself changed the identity of their objects by presenting their works similarly to other collected art, in a new space, thus removing the objects from the sphere of luxurious household furnishings and the country house. This is a form of art collecting and of display which the study of the Club's exhibitions brings to light, and which merits further study.

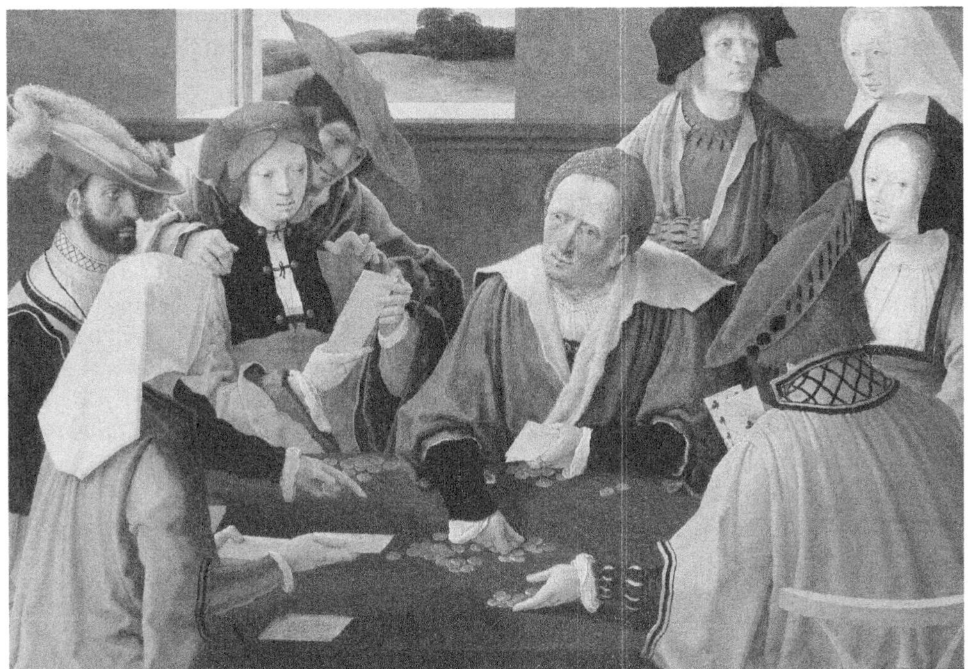

Figure 1.2 The Card Players, Lucas van Leyden (*c*. 1494–1533). Oil on panel, Wilton House.
Source: © Collection of the Earl of Pembroke, Wilton House, Wiltshire/Bridgeman Images.

Another lender, Sir Francis Cook (1817–1902), a Club member, can perhaps be seen as a dedicated art collector whose collection was formed through the Club, rather than simply presented by it. His renowned paintings collection, dispersed in the mid-twentieth century but containing a number of what are considered to be great masterpieces, was built up with the guidance of Club founder, J. C. Robinson, over a period of 30 years, starting with the purchase of a number of paintings from Robinson's own collection in the 1860s.[46] This is arguably a form of trade that might be seen as contrary to the Club's prohibition on 'dealers' as it is entirely possible that Robinson, who was also a museum professional, profited from the Cook acquisitions. In fact, sales were an issue for one of Cook's masterpieces that was loaned to the Club's exhibition – no. 11, *Three Marys at the Sepulchre* (entitled *Holy Women at the Sepulchre* in the catalogue), attributed in the catalogue tentatively to Jan van Eyck but now to Hubert. This is now in the Museum Boijmans van Beuningen in Rotterdam and was the subject of much anxiety when it was sold off by Cook's great-grandson Francis (1907–1978):

> In the 1920s Herbert Cook and other trustees of the National Gallery had established a 'Paramount Pictures List', which included those 'supreme masterpieces' that 'must be acquired for the nation at any cost'. Among these was Van Eyck's Three Marys. The government had committed to spend up to £100,000 to save it and was prepared to do so even in wartime. Robert Witt of the National

> Art-Collections Fund, knowing the high sums that could be attained for Old Masters, appealed to the trustees: letting the Van Eyck or any masterpiece leave the country was the 'last thing [Francis's] father would have approved or allowed.' Yet he and Clark were unable to convince the trustees or Francis to accept any sum under £150,000 for the Van Eyck. When in April 1940 D. G. van Beuningen offered an astronomical £250,000, the painting was swiftly sold.[47]

The painting thus went from one private collection to another and was sold by Cook's family, yet the sale was one that was framed as something the original collector 'would not have approved'. The painting's identification as a 'national' art work is interesting as well. It was not by a British artist but its ownership by a British collector defined it as a 'national' masterpiece. With the regular appeals to 'save art for the nation' that still take place, the circumstances of Cook's painting point to a concept of art 'nationality' and cultural stewardship that is increasingly being explored.[48] The National Art Collections Fund (NACF), founded in response to the perceived inadequacy of the National Gallery, has been involved in such efforts since its foundation.[49] Herbert Cook (1868–1939, later Sir, the 3rd Baronet) was a founder of the NACF (today the Art Fund), along with several other Club members, including Roger Fry and Robert Witt.[50] The Fund represents a twentieth-century art organization that intersected with the Club and reflected some of its early aims, yet it is frequently characterized as a middle-class organization.[51] Cook, not middle class, had been an active member of the Club, serving on the committee of several exhibitions during his membership, including that of the Ferrara-Bologna School show, which will be considered later in this chapter.

Robinson himself was also a lender, as was George Salting, who, as we have seen, was a prolific collector of a wide range of material from Renaissance bronzes, to ceramics, including Chinese ones, prints, and paintings. When Salting died in 1909, he left a large bequest of works of art to the nation, including Chinese ceramics, Renaissance bronzes, and sculpture to the V&A, prints and drawings to the British Museum and a number of important paintings to the National Gallery. As Patricia Rubin noted in a recent study of Salting's bequest to the National Gallery, 'The range, as well as the quantity and quality of the works remains astonishing. They include such iconic masterpieces as Nicholas Hillard's miniature of the *Young Man Among the Roses* at the V&A and Vermeer's *Woman Seated at a Virginal* in the National Gallery.'[52] An early member of the Club, Salting loaned no. 48 to the 1892 exhibition: *Holy Family* by 'The Master of the Death of the Virgin'. This is now in the National Gallery in London and is attributed to the 'workshop of Joos van Cleve'.[53] Salting can therefore be seen as a representative member of the Club, in his wide-ranging tastes, wealth, and public philanthropy.

The Club mounted only one more exhibition on the theme of 'Dutch' or 'Netherlandish' pictures: 'Pictures by Dutch Masters of the Seventeenth Century' (1900) which was organized by Armstrong, Benson, and Captain Holford. It included 59 paintings by a wide range of famous artists including: Rembrandt, Cuyp, Dou, Hals, Hobbema, de Hoogh, Metsu, van Ruisdael, Steen, and Vermeer. Two paintings by the latter were included: *Lady Playing a Clavichord* (no. 15) (Figure 1.3) and *The Music Lesson* (no. 23). The first picture was loaned by George Salting and is now in the National Gallery, London (as *Young Woman Seated at a Virginal*).[54] The latter example is now in the Frick Collection, New York, where it is entitled *Girl Interrupted at her Music*.[55] It was

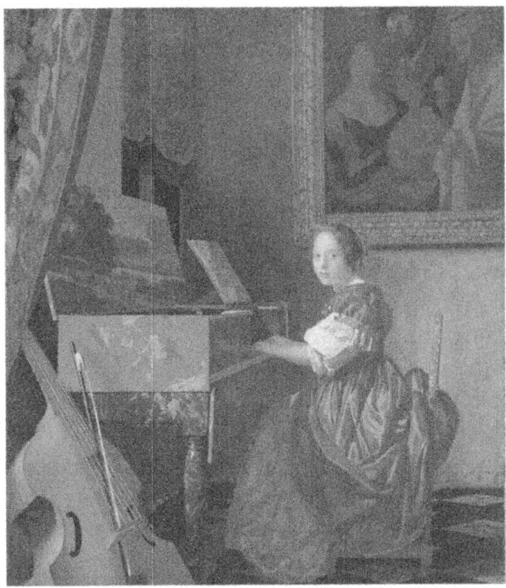

Figure 1.3 *A Young Woman Seated at a Virginal*, Johannes Vermeer (1632–1675), *c.* 1670–1672. Oil on canvas, 51.5 × 45.5 cm, George Salting Bequest, 1910. The National Gallery, London, NG2568.

Source: © The National Gallery, London.

loaned to the Club by Lewis Fry (1832–1921), who was a member of the chocolate manufacturing family and therefore a Quaker, but also a Liberal MP for Bristol and an art collector. He too had intersecting interests that are typical of Club members, including education. His self-portrait can be seen at the University of Bristol, which he was instrumental in founding, for example.[56]

ITALIAN REGIONAL PAINTING

While there were several exhibitions of prints and paintings from the Netherlands, the Club members' main interests lay not in Northern European works but rather in Italian paintings. There were a number of exhibitions dedicated to different aspects of Italian painting, mainly focusing on regional schools. The earliest Italian exhibition mounted by the Club was one which focussed on the engraved work of Marc Antonio Raimondi in 1868. In the General Committee minutes, it was noted:

> The Committee have the pleasure of reporting that an Exhibition was held in the rooms of the Club in the year 1868, consisting of Engravings of Marc Antonio Raimondi; also they wish to call attention to the fact that the Club is indebted to Mr G. W. Reid for the preparation of a catalogue of the Collection, it is under like obligations to Mr. R. Fisher for a critical essay on the genius of Marc Antonio – likewise they have to state that Mr Fisher made advantageous arrangements for taking photographs from the Collection, and that a copy of a published volume consisting of such Catalogue, essay and Photographs is in the possession of the Club, and serves as a record of an Exhibition which was generally deemed of great interest and value. The thanks of the Club were conveyed to the gentlemen through whose kindness the Exhibition was indebted for its success.[57]

Fisher's introductory essay to the catalogue is one of the first such published in a Club catalogue and it gives a biography of the artist as well as a survey history of his work.[58] The exhibition was not arranged chronologically, however, as it pre-dated the 1877 Rembrandt show that was the first to do this. The Italian exhibition which followed it, 'Raphael Sanzio and Michel-Angelo Buonarroti' (1870), was also an exhibition of prints. The first Italian paintings exhibition also included drawings, as was often to be the case later. This was 'The Work of Luca Signorelli and His School' (1893), an exploration of attribution and influences, as discussed in the catalogue essay.[59] It may also have been the inspiration for the approach to Italian paintings at the Club thereafter – presentation by regional school. Like Dutch paintings, therefore, Italian paintings were presented after initial exhibitions of prints and drawings, the collecting 'comfort zone' of the Club's founder members.

1894 Pictures of the Ferrara School: School of Ferrara-Bologna

In the General Committee minutes for this exhibition, its organization was noted in some detail. Its juxtaposition with proposed exhibitions on other, very different subjects is very much in keeping with Club exhibition practice:

> 1.8.1893
> The Subcommittee appointed to consider and report upon suitable subjects for the Winter and Summer Exhibitions for the years 1893–1894, submitted the following subjects for consideration of the General Committee, viz:-
>
> For the *Winter* Exhibition,
> Japanese Metal and Lacquer Work
> Historical Lace and Embroidery.
>
> For the *Summer* Exhibition,
> Pictures of the Ferrara School
> English Landscape Painting Before Turner.
> ...

It was decided that the subject for the next Summer Exhibition shall be Pictures of the Ferrara School and the following Subcommittee was appointed for this Exhibition: Mr Benson, Mr Poynter and Professor Venturi; with the power to add to their number. Mr Benson was authorized to expend £15 upon photographs for this Exhibition.

> 6.3.1894
> V A draft of the Preliminary Notice prepared by the Ferrara Exhibition Subcommittee was read and ordered to be printed and sent to the members of the Club and other possessors of Pictures.
>
> 15.5.1894
> VIII It was agreed that the Exhibition of Pictures of the Ferrara-Bologna School be opened on Monday evening 28th May and closed on Saturday 28th July.
>
> 26.6.1894
> VII The Ferrara Exhibition Committee reported the cost of an Illustrated Catalogue containing 20 pictures at about £225 for 250 copies. It was agreed that such Catalogue be issued to members at the price of £1-11-6 per copy.[60]

The minutes provide evidence of exhibition planning practices, including invitations to lend that were sent out to both Club members and potential lenders. They also indicate that exhibition subcommittees evolved, with the final exhibition committee, as noted in the catalogue, including: 'Cavaliere Professore Adolfo Venturi*, Walter Armstrong, R.H. Benson*, Sidney Colvin, Herbert F. Cook*, Edward J. Poynter.' Those with an asterisk were Club members at that time. The catalogue essays were provided by Venturi and Benson. Adolfo Venturi (1856–1941) was a Club member and a noted Italian art historian. At the time of the exhibition, he was general inspector of the *Belle Arti* at the Ministry of Public Instruction in Rome and two years later would be appointed Professor of Art at the University of Rome. As an art historian, he is best known as a pioneer of the modern school of art history in Italy.[61] Benson was from the Benson banking dynasty and therefore very wealthy. He was an active member of the Club, a prolific collector and the son-in-law of Holford, as noted earlier.[62] Not surprisingly, a number of the same committee members (and lenders) were involved in both the previous Dutch and future Italian paintings exhibitions, including Robinson, Cook (Francis), Holford (Captain), and Salting.

Lenders, Contributors, and Exhibits

While Dutch old masters, particularly their attributions, were seen still to be in need of scholarship before 1900, Italian paintings were a well-established category in 1894. The Club, therefore – or the catalogue authors – decided specifically to classify groups of Italian paintings into subcategories of national schools, or regional schools, as was the practice in art history at the time. The Ferrara-Bologna exhibition was the first of these regionally classified Italian painting shows for the Club and thus is representative of what would come to be the Club's usual approach, one informed by scholarly connoisseurship, but also utilizing what Haskell described as 'the most ambitious contribution to specialized art history that had yet been made anywhere'.[63] This would be the provision of photographs in the exhibition of what were considered to be key paintings that could not be included. The comparative photographs approach was a first for the Club but one which is standard practice today.[64] This approach was praised by several authorities of the time,[65] including Bernard Berenson (1865–1959), early in his critical career. Berenson, a contributor of photographs to the exhibition but not a lender of paintings, was the well-known art critic and scholar of Italian Renaissance art. Originally from Lithuania, he emigrated with his family to America, where he studied art history at Harvard under Charles Norton, one of the founders of the field in the United States.[66] Berenson met Venturi in England and was greatly influenced by Morelli in his connoisseurship approach to the subject (but then rejected some of his claims). He also bought the Florentine villa I Tatti which is today the Harvard University Center for Italian Renaissance Studies.[67] He has been described as 'the single-most influential art historian in the United States for most of the twentieth century',[68] and thus it is interesting to see some of his early work in relation to the Club's exhibition. Berenson, of course, was already involved in the art market at that stage, through both curatorship and collection development.[69] As he was not a Club member, his dealing activities were not prohibited, or even perceived as such if Robinson's similar activities can be taken into account. Herbert Cook, for example, was a client of

Berenson's, as well as a supporter of some of his critical works.[70] Berenson praised the Club's exhibition catalogue which included a catalogue *raisonné* of works by masters of the school, but not unequivocally as he felt there were some errors of attribution.[71]

Nonetheless, Haskell, in his history of old master exhibitions, summed up the significance of the Club and this particular exhibition as follows:

> Their exhibition of 1894 was especially remarkable. It was devoted to a field of Italian Renaissance art that had only recently attracted any attention from scholars ... It was organized by a leading Italian art historian, Adolfo Venturi, and it was described by the young Bernard Berenson ... as 'one of the finest retrospective exhibitions that has ever been seen in London.' [fn 41] The only substantial features surviving from the past were that nearly all the objects on view were borrowed from private collections in Great Britain.[72]

Haskell also notes that the two most significant pictures in the show were loaned by Robert Benson, Dosso Dossi's *Circe* (no. 54) and Correggio's *Christ Taking Leave of his Mother* (no. 50). Benson, a driving force behind the exhibition, began collecting Italian paintings in 1884, and from then on developed what has been described as a collection 'of outstanding importance', but which was dispersed by sale in 1927 and is therefore not associated with him in most of the provenance literature.[73] Benson's approach to collecting such pictures was slightly different from his contemporaries, however:

> From the 1880s onwards, a major trend in private collecting was to form a collection representative of all schools, periods, and subjects, rather like a miniature national collection. The principal British collector along those lines was Sir Francis Cook of Doughty House, Richmond ... Benson stands at the opposite end, choosing out of the whole those schools with which he had the most sympathy. The fact that the names of the artists of the fourteenth- and fifteenth-century pictures were less certain than, say, seventeenth-century Dutch pictures, or not known at all, testifies to his connoisseurship and signifies that he was a discriminating collector.[74]

Benson benefitted from a close study of his father-in-law, R. S. Holford's collection of old masters and he was active in public life as well, serving as

> a trustee of the National Gallery from 1912 and as a trustee of the Tate Gallery (founded 1897[75]). He was a member of the Council of the Victoria and Albert Museum and he joined the Executive Committee of the NACF in 1903, the year it was founded, thus becoming associated with the acquisition of many works of art for the national collections.[76]

Benson thus combined in the way of so many Club members public support for the arts with private collecting, a formative association that needs to be acknowledged in the history of London's art institutions.

In addition to Benson, as noted in the exhibition catalogue, the full List of Lenders is very interesting and is therefore printed in full here:

> HM the Queen, Irish National Gallery, Corporation Galleries of Art Glasgow, Royal Institution Liverpool, University Galleries Oxford, Arundel Society London, Lord Ashburton, Sir Hickman Bacon, Bt*, Herr von Beckerath of Berlin, R. H. Benson*, Bernard Berenson of Florence, the Earl Brownlow, the Duke of Buccleugh, KT, Charles Butler*, Signor Cavalieri of Ferrara, Miss Cohen, W. Martin Conway*, Sir Francis Cook*, Herbert F. Cook*, Robert Crawshay, Sir William J. Farrer*, C. Drury E. Fortnum, DCL*, Dr Gustavo Frizzoni of Milan, Henry Hucks Gibbs*, W. H. Grenfell, Dr Fritz Harck of Berlin, J. P. Heseltine, Captain Holford CIE, Mrs Horner, James Knowles*, the Right Hon. Sir Henry Layard, GCB*, the Earl of Leicester, KG, Ludwig Mond, FRS*, J. Wingfield Malcolm of Poltalloch, C. Fairfax Murray, the Earl of Northbrook, GCSI*, the Marquis of Northampton, KG, Mrs Oman, Claude Phillips, Edward J. Poynter, RA, Sir J. C. Robinson*, J. Ruston, George Salting*, the Lord Sempill, Charles Eastlake Smith, J. Stogdon, Sir Charles Turner*, Cavaliere Prof. A. Venturi*, Henry Wagner, J. Hanson Walker, the Lord Wimborne. (*denoting Club members)

Thus the lenders were a wide-ranging mix of major institutions, Club members, collectors who were not members (including women), artists, aristocrats, and politicians. Many were associated with other Club exhibitions, including those not related to paintings, as subsequent chapters will demonstrate.

Benson, as the instigator, was naturally a key lender to the exhibition, including two paintings he cited as 'masterpieces' in his somewhat florid Introduction: no. 6 Cosme (Cosimo) Tura, *The Flight into Egypt*, 'from the Collection of William Graham', and no. 50, Antonio Allegri da Correggio, *Christ Taking Leave of His Mother Before the Passion*, loaned by Benson. The Tura was mentioned on p. xiv of the Introduction and is now in the Metropolitan Museum of Art, New York (49.7.17).[77] At the time of the exhibition, Tura was considered one of the great masters, but yet Benson says of the example in the National Gallery at that time that it both 'repels and attracts'.[78] Today Tura is still recognized as one of the great painters attached to the court of the Estes.[79] Another Tura, which was loaned by Francis Cook (no. 5), is now in the National Gallery in Washington, DC[80] (Figure 1.4). The Benson Correggio, perhaps accorded greater status today as one of the most important Renaissance painters, as opposed to just part of the Ferrara School,[81] is now in the National Gallery in London.[82]

The National Gallery is yet another institution that was linked to the Club through its members and like the Club, the National Gallery was indebted to collectors. Founded in 1824 with a gift of pictures from the collector John Julius Angerstein (1735–1823), its first Director was Eastlake, whose widow, as we have seen, loaned etchings to the Club's 1877 exhibition. The director at the time of the exhibition was the newly appointed Sir Edward Poynter (1836–1919), also a lender to the 1894 exhibition, another intersection between the private and public that, as we have seen, would not have been considered improper at that time. In fact, Poynter could be said to be typical of many of the artists who were associated with the Club, in that he was a painter, who trained with Club member Frederick Leighton, and he knew Whistler. He had his own collection, yet he was director of the national collection and later a president of the Royal Academy.[83] Sidney Colvin (1845–1927), another contributor to the Ferrara-Bologna exhibition, was also a prominent museum

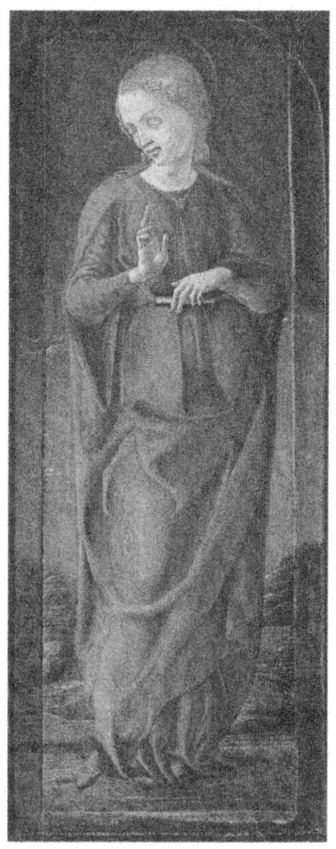

Figure 1.4 *The Annunciation with Saint Francis and Saint Louis of Toulouse* (middle right panel), Cosmè Tura, Ferrarese, *c.* 1433–1495, *c.* 1470/1480. Tempera and distemper on panel, overall (middle right panel): 31 × 12.4 cm (12 3/16 × 4 7/8 in.) framed: 43.5 × 16.8 × 4.4 cm (17 1/8 × 6 5/8 × 1 3/4 in.). Samuel H. Kress Collection, 1952.2.6.c.

Source: Courtesy National Gallery of Art, Washington, DC.

professional, being Keeper of Prints and Drawings at the British Museum from 1883. He is credited with establishing the department on a more steady and respectable course and for attracting key collections from Malcolm, Mitchell, and Salting, all Club members.[84] Like them, Colvin was a Club member from an early date, and as will be apparent through subsequent Club exhibitions discussed in this book, the British Museum was a key agent in the history of the Club as well as a beneficiary.

Another picture singled out by Benson in the Introduction was loaned by the Earl of Northbrook, Thomas Baring (discussed above): no. 42, Ludovico Mazzolino's *Christ Disputing with the Doctors*. This painting is also now in the National Gallery, having been purchased not long after this exhibition in 1897, and it is possible that its display by the Club may have positively affected its value.[85] Northbrook loaned only the one painting but a major lender was the Queen, demonstrating that the palace was quite willing to lend to exhibitions mounted by a private members' club at that time. Among the palace loans were: no. 17, Lorenzo Costa, *Portrait of a Lady* ('To Mr. Berenson of Florence is due the suggestion that the portrait is of Isabella d'Este.'); no. 51, Correggio, *Holy Family with S. James* ('from the Collection of King Charles I'); no. 61, Dosso Dossi, *San Guglielmo* ('From the collection of King Charles I, where it seems to have been described as "The picture of Charles Audax, the last Duke of Burgundy"'). All of these are significant pictures in their own right but they also possess a most prestigious provenance.

Two other contributors are noted in the catalogue list, but they were not lenders. Instead they are cited in attributions and for contributing photographs, as in the case of Bernard Berenson, or were more closely involved in planning the exhibition and contributing to the catalogue preface like Venturi. As we have seen, Venturi was on the exhibition committee, along with Walter Armstrong, Benson, Sidney Colvin, Herbert F. Cook, and Edward J. Poynter. He thus contributed to an interesting combination of individuals which included an academic, three museum professionals, and a private collector. As the author of the catalogue preface, Venturi set the tone for the exhibition, noting that while Ferrara is 'now so squalid and thinly inhabited', in the fifteenth century,

> Ferrara ... became a centre of art. Painting especially flourished, but it was painting of a severe style, sharp and bold in outline, and wonderfully true in minuteness of detail and expression. History, perhaps, has failed to render justice to the skill of Ferrarese artists, their dramatic sentiment, their exuberant life, and their warmth of colour and effect.[86]

Venturi was from Modena and thus felt a more personal connection to the locus of the school of painting.

Equally personal was the fact that for Robert Benson, it is clear that his own collecting preferences inspired the research and probably the idea for the exhibition in the first place. As he stated in the main catalogue essay:

> The Art of the Emilia ... has been unduly neglected in the past. Vasari ... did not like Ferrarese drawing, colour or romance, and his prejudice and carelessness have extended even unto the last generation. Ferrara, the capital, ... now lies off the beaten track. Its archives have been left comparatively unexplored, till within the last fifteen years, Cavaliere Adolfo Venturi of Modena ..., and others, have made their secrets accessible, and furnished a surer basis of criticism ... And, in fact, with the exception of Correggio, and, perhaps, Dosso, it must be admitted that Ferrarese painters were not colourists of the first rank, popular at first sight like Perugino, Ghirlandaio or Titian.[87]
>
> In England, we have somehow overlooked until recently the fact there once dwelt here a vigorous and gifted race ... who found means of self-expression in form and colour under the political security of the Court of the Este, and whose art forms an organic whole with stages of development and decay, characteristically differing, like their dialect, from that of other parts of Italy.[88]

He argues for a uniqueness yet also a developmental pattern that was more fully illustrated in the exhibition and the catalogue through comparative photographs. It is hard to say whether Benson himself was responsible for the innovative inclusion of comparative photographs in the exhibition but he does put forth his own ideas about connoisseurship in the catalogue which suggests that he may have at least contributed to this approach:

> To a gifted and trained eye technique is as unmistakable as physiognomy, and colour is distinctive like the timbre of a voice. In the opinion of the present writer, an analysis of the rhythm of the composition, the scale of colour, the impasto, the brushwork, the penitmenti – in a word, an analysis of the *painting*, wherever time and the restorer have spared it – is less liable to lead to confusion, and goes deeper than the anthropometrical method ...[89]

Understanding technique is essential to connoisseurship, yet understanding the idea behind the work is also important.

> No analytic method will serve beyond a certain point. The highest criticism must start from the idea in the mind of the artist and end with the details of his

> embodiment thereof, not *vice versa*, else it is liable to fail to distinguish between good and bad, between masterpiece and schoolpiece, between original and copy. For every true work of art, whether expressed in stone, colour or sound, is, in the verdict of Beethoven prefixed to an eternal masterpiece of his own, 'mehr Ausdruck der Empfindung als Malerei'.[90]

This was the typical art historical bias of the period, where the genius of the artist, the 'idea of the mind', was at the forefront of analysis and technique should follow. To some extent, this is also what Haden was trying to do with Rembrandt, as a way of elevating engraving beyond mere technique and thus into the realm of 'art'. Not surprisingly, since Benson was involved again, the same bias would inform the interpretation of the next Italian region exhibited by the Club: Milan and Lombardy.

1898 Milanese Masters: Pictures by Masters of the Milanese and Allied Schools of Lombardy

In contrast to the previous exhibition, the General Committee minutes concerning this exhibition reveal a somewhat flexible and disorganized approach to exhibition schedules, which appears to have been characteristic of the Club. As can be seen below, the 'Milanese' exhibition was intended originally to follow soon after the 'Ferrarese' but other exhibition plans and unforeseen events got in the way, reminding us that Club exhibitions were planned and organized voluntarily by individuals, not in or by professional organizations:

3.12.1895

III The Exhibitions Committee reported upon various subjects which had been suggested for the next Exhibition, and they were requested further to consider the suggestion for an Exhibition of Enamels.

21.1.1896

VI It was decided to postpone the proposed Enamels Exhibition to next year.

VII It was agreed to hold the proposed Exhibition of the Milanese School during the coming Season, and Mr Robert Benson, Mr Herbert Cook and Mr Cock were affirmed a subcommittee with that object.

4.2.1896

II Milanese School exhibition postponed 'until after the Enamels Exhibition agreed upon for next year'.

7.7.1896

IV Mr Cock read a letter from Mr Robert Benson on the subject of the Exhibition of the Milanese School, and it was agreed that the Exhibition should take place in 1898, and the Secretary was directed to write to Mr Herbert Cook accordingly.

5.10.1897

VI It was proposed, seconded and resolved that it is desirable that the forthcoming Milanese Exhibition should be opened in the month of April next, as soon after the middle of the month as might be found convenient to the Exhibition Committee.

3.5.1898

VII The Milanese Exhibition Committee reported that in consequence of the death of Mr Cock and the absence from England of Mr Herbert Cook, there had been delay in the revision of the Catalogue, and Mr Waterfield was invited to join the Exhibition Committee in the place of Mr Cock.

14.6.1898

IV It was agreed to issue an Illustrated edition of the Milanese Exhibition Catalogue, and to order 150 copies, with option to extend the order to 250, or to 200 at the same rate as 250.

V It was agreed to keep open the Exhibition a fortnight longer than the time originally named, + to close on Sunday 10th July, notice to be given to the contributors accordingly.[91]

The text of Robert Benson's letter noted in the minutes of 7.7.1896, does not survive but he also collected Italian paintings by masters from other regions than Ferrara, so it is not surprising that he should have been actively involved in a subsequent Italian exhibition of 1898. The catalogue notes that he was on the exhibition committee along with: 'The Late Alfred Cock; Herbert F. Cook, S. Arthur Strong, [and] The Late O. C. Waterfield'. Some of these committee members are obvious choices for this exhibition theme, whereas one, Waterfield, is somewhat surprising. Cook, for example, was an obvious choice as he had provided an inventory of paintings and lenders, a 'catalogue *raisonné*', in the catalogue for the previous Italian exhibition, and was also a lender to it and this present exhibition. Alfred Cock (1848–1898) had been a lender to the Netherlandish pictures exhibition, discussed above, as well as both the Blue and White and the Coloured Porcelain exhibitions that are discussed in Chapter 2. He is best known today for his book and manuscript collections, however. Sandford Arthur Strong (1863–1904) was both an Orientalist scholar and librarian/curator for the Duke of Devonshire, the Earl of Pembroke, and the House of Lords.[92] He translated texts in a number of languages including Arabic, Chinese, Pali, and Assyrian, while holding the position of Professor of Arabic at University College London.[93] In addition to his language skills, however, Strong had a lifelong interest in paintings and was encouraged by Sidney Colvin to work for and catalogue the collections at Chatsworth, no doubt facilitating loans to the Club from the Duke of Devonshire.[94] O. C. Waterfield seems only to have had a personal connection to members of the Club. He was Ottiwell Charles Waterfield (1831–1898), headmaster of Temple Grove School from 1863 till 1880. He had taught the Bensons, including Robert, and was a lender to the Club's Greek ceramics exhibition where his interests seem to fit more comfortably (see Chapter 2).

In spite of the mixed interests of committee members, their social connections were vital for loans and support of the Benson-led approach. Probably through the efforts of Benson and Cook, this exhibition was designed along similar principles as the Ferrarese one, also utilizing photographs to provide comparative material and focussing on pictures in English collections. The perspective and selection were also informed by the work of Frizzoni, who is cited in the catalogue introduction and is listed as a contributor (but not a lender). As the catalogue author (anonymous but originally attributed to Cook and possibly revised by Benson[95]) notes:

> In defining the scope of the present Exhibition, it has been considered advisable to be guided not so much by geographical or historical considerations as by the affinities, natural and elective, of the art of this wide region.[96]
>
> The district of Italy, then, with which the present Exhibition is concerned, may be said to lie between the Alps on the north and the Po on the south, between the Adda on the east and the further boundary of Piedmont on the west.
>
> Knowledge of the art-history of this region is singularly defective. No other section of Italian art has been so strangely neglected by writers and students; ... Vasari was the earliest delinquent, and his careless account of the school found ready repetition with the later writers. ... Only in recent times has any serious attempt been made to grapple with and sift the material to hand ... Morelli followed in 1877 ...
>
> [p. xii] To Morelli we owe the first systematic account of the Milanese school, so far as it depends upon L. da Vinci, and to Dr. Gustavo Frizzoni, his successor ... It is as well, however, to remember that Leonardo was a Florentine by birth, habits and training, and should always be classed with the Florentine school. That he happened to pass twenty-five years of his life in Milan, and thereby profoundly modified the natural development of the local school, in no way affects the character of his art, which was Florentine in its aims and principles, and totally unlike the older Lombard style.[97]

For Benson and Cook, regional identification was about geography of production as well as residence of producers, thus enabling da Vinci to be claimed for Milan.

Gustavo Frizzoni (1840–1919) had also been a contributor to the Ferrarese exhibition and was clearly well known to the Club's members. He was famed for his association with Giovanni Morelli (1816–1891), who had been Berenson's mentor and a pioneer of connoisseurship studies in Italy. He also knew both Charles Eastlake and Henry Layard (1817–1894), thus contributing to the connected network that drove the Club's activities and influence.[98]

Lenders and Exhibits

The profile and list of lenders to this exhibition are also very similar to that of the previous one, with a number of aristocrats included as well as the Cooks, Benson, Salting, Holford, Morrison (through his wife), and Robinson. The aristocrats included Northbrook, Devonshire, Crawford and Balcarres, Buccleuch,

Carysfort, and Spencer. Two such lenders who seemingly appear for the first time are Lord Aldenham and the Earl of Elgin. Aldenham was actually Henry Hucks Gibbs (1819–1907), who became Baron Aldenham in 1896, and was a lender to several ceramics exhibitions (see Chapter 2) as well as the Ferrarese one.[99] The Earl of Elgin was Victor Bruce (1849–1917), the 9th Earl, and son of James Bruce who had been Governor-General of Canada. Victor Bruce had served as Viceroy to India and loaned no. 47 to the exhibition, *Portrait of a Young Man Holding an Arrow*, which was attributed to Leonardo. In the catalogue entry, the attribution is questioned by Waagen, who suggests that it might perhaps be by Boltraffio, 'one of Leonardo's best and rarest scholars'.[100] This is now firmly attributed to Boltraffio and is in the Timken Museum of Art, San Diego, California[101] (see Plate 2).

The different opinions about exhibits that often appear in Club catalogues can strike the present-day reader as somewhat contradictory but in the context of Club interpretative practice, it was fairly common and represents what they would have seen as active connoisseurship – something to be debated. Berenson, for example, published quite a few works which challenged attributions, often because of flawed connoisseurship methods, as he saw it, such as in a pamphlet he published in May 1895 which criticized exhibits in a show presented by the New Gallery.[102]

Works by Leonardo are a good example of this. Two other contributors loaned works by or attributed to him, the Earl of Carysfort, Club member: no. 17, *La Vierge au Bas Relief* ('Attributed to Leonardo da Vinci') and the Marquis of Lansdowne: no. 35, *Portrait of a Lady Holding a Vase* ('Attributed to Leonardo da Vinci, Exhibited at Burlington House, 1876'). The former painting is illustrated in the exhibition catalogue, but labelled there as by Cesare da Sesto, thus there are two attributions in the Club's catalogue. It is now believed still to belong to the same family, the Probys of Elton Hall, Peterborough. The Earl of Carysfort at the time of the exhibition was William Proby (1836–1909), the fifth and last Earl. The latter painting, listed in the catalogue under Luini and 'attributed to Leonardo', is now in the National Gallery, Washington, DC, entitled *The Magdalen*.[103] As we have seen, works attributed to Leonardo are included in this exhibition because he spent 25 years in Milan and thereby had a strong influence on local style, according to the catalogue author.[104] The author (following Moretti) also divides the painters of this region into several groups: (1) individuals, such as Foppa, influenced by no other; (2) those influenced for a time by Leonardo but not 'permanently affected'; and (3) finally those permanently and apparently sadly forever changed by the impact of Leonardo.[105] Foppa was 'considered to be the father of the Lombard school' by the catalogue author,[106] and today still maintains such status in the field. His style is usually described as 'late Gothic'.[107] Paintings attributed to Foppa loaned to the Club's exhibition include numbers 3 and 4, a virgin and child and a dead Christ with symbols of the passion.[108] Both of these paintings were lent by Sir Martin Conway (1856–1937), a typical polymath of the type associated with the Club: prominent art historian and professor of art, mountaineer, politician, museum director, and trustee.[109] In an autobiographical study of collecting, he discussed his purchases in Italy, including what turned out to be a fake Foppa. In this chapter, he also noted his acquaintance with Morelli:

> It was in the early part of the month of May, 1887. I was spending two or three months in Milan. The famous Giovanni Morelli, the great connoisseur of Italian Art, was then living.
>
> One day, when I was in his apartment and he was discoursing upon painting ..., he suddenly broke off to say:
>
> 'The only way really to get a thorough knowledge of the old painters is to collect pictures ..."
>
> 'Collect pictures,' I said: 'that's easy to recommend; but how am I going to pay for them?'
>
> 'That's not difficult,' he replied: 'they are cheap enough, if you know how to look for them and where to find them. It's not so much money as an educated eye that a collector needs. If you were to find a previously unknown Raphael, the chances are you could buy it for a hundred francs.'
>
> 'And please, where and how am I to begin?' I asked.
>
> 'You have been studying the Milanese School very closely during the last few weeks, and by now you know the paintings and style of most of the artists. There is Vincenzo Foppa, for instance. Very few pictures by him are known, and yet he must have painted plenty, and probably several exist which have not yet been identified. Begin by going to all the small dealers' shops in Milan, and see if you can't find a forgotten Foppa in some dark corner ...'[110]

Conway was not a member of the Club at that time but clearly was known to those who organized the exhibition. As Director of the Imperial War Museum, and trustee of the National Portrait Gallery, he was part of the London art world network that encompassed the Club.

The regionalist approach to classifying Italian paintings referred to by Conway in his study of collecting and utilized by the Club seems to begin with Luigi Lanzi (1732–1810), a Jesuit priest who published *Storia Pittorica dell'Italia* in 1795–1796, which 'focused on regional schools rather than on single artistic personalities'.[111] Thus the artists populating the Club's exhibition were grouped by their region, which was said to have contributed to a distinctive style. Within this, the Club defined certain stylistic sub-categories which were represented by specific artists. For example, in contrast to Foppa, Solario is an artist who, according to the Club, is representative of the second style of Milanese painting, as defined in the catalogue – those artists influenced for a time by Leonardo, but whose work was not 'permanently affected'. There are several pictures attributed to him in the exhibition, including an Annunciation loaned by Arthur Kay, now in the Louvre.[112] In the Club's catalogue it is considered a masterpiece: 'a work of the greatest brilliance of colour, and high finish',[113] but it is the *pietà* at Rossie Priory that is singled out as the finest work in Britain. It was too large to lend but was represented by a photograph taken specially for the exhibition.[114]

Boltraffio would be representative of the third type – influenced and forever changed by Leonardo. He is described as coming 'under Leonardo's spell'[115] and 'not a great artist, and entirely lacking in imagination and dramatic power', but he nonetheless exhibits 'a singular refinement'.[116] His portraits are praised, however, including the one loaned by Ludwig Mond (1839–1909, a distinguished chemist, whose son Sir Alfred would be the first Baron Melchett, see below), no. 48, *Portrait of a Man*. This is now in the National Gallery in London and was part of the Mond bequest to that museum in 1924.[117] The catalogue author says of Boltraffio's portraits that there is a 'tendency to attribute all Milanese portraits whatsoever – particularly those in profile – to this refined artist',[118] suggesting that the artist's high birth may have been seen as an appropriate social status for that type of subject matter and more noteworthy than his talent. In fact, another portrait loaned to the Club's exhibition, no. 44, lent by Mrs. Alfred Morrison, was previously attributed to Boltraffio but in this exhibition it is assigned to Bernardino de Conti. The author notes: 'Mrs. Alfred Morrison's portrait of a lady, exhibited at the New Gallery Early Italian Exhibition in 1894, under Boltraffio's name, is admittedly one of the finest of Bernardino de Conti's works.'[119] The catalogue entry notes that it was assigned to de Conti by Morelli.[120] This is a further demonstration of the Club's form of connoisseurship. Attributions for a number of these artists were still tenuous at the time of the Club's exhibition and this supported the justification for mounting such a show. Mrs Morrison's painting was last sold by Christie's in 1993 and is now in a private collection.[121]

The New Gallery and the British Institution

The reference to the New Gallery exhibition in 1894 that Mrs Morrison's painting appeared in is an important one, as this was considered a benchmark exhibition for 'early' Italian painting, which was a fashionable sub-category of collecting in that field. It was also the exhibition that was criticized by Berenson. Early Italian painting was not a new field of collecting, however, and in Britain its emergence is attributed to Eastlake:

> By the 1880s, ... the enthusiasm for early Italian pictures had taken a firm hold. Sir Charles Eastlake, the Italophile director of the National Gallery between 1855 and 1866, had bought an altarpiece by Mantegna in 1855 for £1,125 12s, and then achieved a coup in 1857 with the purchase of 30 pictures from the Lombardi-Baldi collection in Florence for £7,035 (an average of £235 each) which gave the National Gallery, at a stroke, pictures by or attributed to Duccio, ... Botticelli, ... and most famous of them all, *The Battle of San Romano*, painted in the 1450s by Paolo Uccello.[122]

In this particular case, a new fashion in collecting was created by one of the national museums and then emulated by private collectors.

The display of this category of painting was new in the 1890s, however. Of the exhibition at the New Gallery, one critic at the time said:

> The display of Italian pictures at the New Gallery is certainly, so far as London is concerned, without a precedent among the exhibitions of this kind. In fact, within its limits of time and territory – for all works later than 1550 and all pictures by Venetian artists have purposely been excluded – it may justly be regarded as the best possible supplement to the National Gallery that Art students could require. In the first place a whole room, containing about eighty pictures, has been devoted to the Trecento Art, that is the Art of Giotto, his pupils and followers, and the quaint and naïve productions of the Sienese ...[123]

The New Gallery was a commercial gallery founded in London in 1888 by former employees of the Grosvenor Gallery (founded 1877)[124] and it featured a number of prominent members of society who were on its Committee, many of which overlapped with the BFAC, either as Club members or exhibition lenders.[125] For example, at the time of the Club's exhibition, the list of General Committee members of the New Gallery included:

> President: The Earl of Carlisle, The Lord Battersea, R. H. Benson, The Lord Balcarres, Charles Butler [whose collection was purchased by Benson], Dr. W. Bode, Royal Museum, Berlin, Sir Edward Burne-Jones, Bart., Sidney Colvin, Herbert F. Cook, The Earl of Crawford, Sir William Farrer, Wickham Flower, A. W. Franks, 'President of the Society of Antiquaries', Captain George L. Holford, Right Hon. Sir Henry Layard, Prof. J. H. Middleton, Director South Kensington Museum, C. Fairfax Murray, The Earl of Pembroke, Charles H. Read, George Salting, Henry Vaughan, The Lord Wantage, Henry Willett and The Lord Windsor.[126]

This is an example of an intersection between the commercial art world and the Club that, yet again, challenges their prohibition on dealer members but suggests that the prohibition was a class-based one related to running a shop as opposed to participating in the art market, as proposed in the Introduction.

Northampton and Mond were lenders to the New Gallery exhibition and one of Butler's exhibits is still garnering attention today: no. 27, four small panels by Masaccio which have been identified as being part of the Pisa altarpiece, which are now in Berlin, having been acquired by von Bode (a Club member) after the National Gallery passed on them.[127] Thus, there is much overlap not just with members but also with the New Gallery exhibition and the Club's slightly later one, demonstrating that, unlike the Ferrarese exhibition, the Milanese one was perhaps less innovative, in terms of its content. It certainly was less controversial but the Club's exhibition is still cited as a provenance and exhibition history for a number of the pictures that have come on the market since 1898. It was also a regionalist gathering of works, rather than a more widely chronological one.

The New Gallery was not the only exhibiting and sale venue that was closely associated with Club exhibitions in the nineteenth century. As an exhibition, the Milanese show can be seen generally, like its predecessor, as an 'old masters' display and the precedent for all old master exhibitions in Britain was set by the British Institution. Founded in 1805 to exhibit the work of living and dead artists, it was the first such institution to stage regular temporary exhibitions of pictures, which were also for sale. It was similar to the Royal Academy but not run by artists. Instead, its directors were all collectors and connoisseurs.[128] Another aim was to stage private exhibitions for artists, who would be permitted to copy some or parts of borrowed 'old master' pictures from members, thus contributing to artist training, like the RA.[129] In 1814, the British Institution resolved to stage an intentionally themed old master paintings exhibition, the first of its kind: 'Pictures of the Old Flemish and Dutch Masters'.[130] The exhibition, which opened in May 1815, included pictures by Rembrandt, Rubens, and Van Dyck.[131] This was followed by an exhibition in 1816 of pictures from the 'Italian and Spanish Schools'.[132] The parallels with the BFAC are numerous, not least in the Club's later desire to merge with the British Institution and take over its premises when the British Institution's lease expired in 1867.[133] The membership to some extent was similar (in some cases with actual overlap) and of course its main activity was similar, thus suggesting that the origins of the BFAC were not just in the FAC but also in the British Institution though the link is not well known. It also provided a means of trading works of art without resorting to 'dealers'. As Haskell noted:

> That the primary aims of the British Institution in mounting Old Master exhibitions had been to raise the standards of British taste and to promote the talents of British artists had been well enough understood (and endorsed) by the Institution – and was constantly being flung back at its organisers by their enemies whenever there seemed to be any risk of its being neglected. But, as has so often been the case with later Old Masters exhibitions, there appeared to be no reason to restrict all aims to this primary one. It became clear very soon that such exhibitions offered an excellent opportunity for buying and selling works of art without the distasteful need of having to do so through dealers or to the accompaniment of publicity. A picture lent to the exhibition one year would, in the following one, be recorded in the collection of another owner. Thus an important Rembrandt portrait and Lotto's celebrated *Lady Holding a Drawing of Lucretia* (then believed to be by Giorgione) exhibited at the British Institution in 1854 by Sir James Carnegie (Lord Southesk) were acquired privately, shortly before the exhibition closed, by Robert Holford for Dorchester House ... it was not only private individuals who were alert to the opportunities that these exhibitions provided. The trustees of the National Gallery had purchased Van Eyck's *Arnolfini Double Portrait* after it had been shown by Major James Hay in 1841 ...[134]

Perhaps this was the specific origin of the Club's dealer prohibition.

The lease on the British Institution's premises expired in September 1867. This was then turned into a separate gentlemen's club but there was concern that the established exhibitions of old masters would cease as well, after having become 'firmly rooted in the social calendar'.[135] Alternative sites for these exhibitions were sought, and some support was found in the Royal Academy but it was the BFAC that made the formal suggestion to take over the organization of the exhibitions but using rooms of the Royal Academy. The RA agreed but then decided it would organize the exhibitions itself, which it did from 1870 in its new premises at Burlington House, thus moving into the display of the work of deceased artists which continues in much expanded form today alongside its traditional remits.[136]

Nonetheless, the Club continued to organize exhibitions of Italian paintings thereafter and the connection seems clear. The Ferrarese and Milanese exhibitions were followed by five regional Italian shows, starting with Siena (1904), then Umbrian (1910), Venetian painting of the 18th Century (1911 – the catalogue includes an Introduction by Roger Fry), Early Venetian Painting (1912), and the Venetian School, including Titian (1914). The final Italian regional painting exhibition was Florentine Painting before 1500.[137] It would be this final exhibition of early Florentine pictures in 1919 that would prove to be a more ground-breaking show for the Club than some of the preceding ones, in spite of its opening after the First World War.

1919 Florentine Painting before 1500

Perhaps because of the timing of this exhibition and its preparation, the General Committee minutes only briefly note the following:

> 28.5.1918
> (no numbering) Exhibitions subcommittee consisted of: Mr R H Benson, Dr Borenius, Mr Campbell Dodgson, Mr H Harris, Col Lyon, Mr Maclagan, Lord Plymouth, Sir C H Read, and Mr R C Witt.
>
> 10.12.1918
> It was agreed to have an Exhibition of Florentine pictures in the ensuing Summer and Messrs Fry, Borenius, Clifford Smith, Harris and Witt were appointed as the Exhibition Committee, with power to add to their number.[138]

In contrast to its earlier predecessors discussed above, this exhibition is entitled 'Florentine Painting' but it includes objects other than paintings or visual material, a fairly common practice in ordinary Club exhibitions.[139] Nonetheless, for this exhibition, paintings are still the primary focus. The reason for the inclusion of other objects might be conformity to a wider kind of 'house style' for exhibitions that developed after 1900. As noted in the Introduction to this book, the Club mounted annual 'special' exhibitions as well as less formal 'ordinary' ones and the latter were almost always a mixture of pictures and objects. Some of the later special exhibitions were more inclusive in terms of exhibits, yet there is no discussion of this as a formal policy in Committee minutes. Most likely it relates to the organizing committee's personal interests and those of potential lenders. In this particular case, it might also relate to the subject area, early painting, which might appear not only on traditional formats such as panel or canvas, but also furniture, for example.

As can be seen from the minutes extracted above, the exhibition of Florentine painting was planned during the First World War, demonstrating that there was little interruption to Club activities at that time. New members were still joining, including both George Bernard Shaw and Osbert Sitwell in 1918. In that year, the exhibitions committee agreed the topic of the Summer exhibition and formed an exhibition subcommittee which ultimately included Roger Fry (1866–1934), Tancred Borenius (1885–1948), Harold Clifford Smith (1876–1960), Herbert Cook, Henry Harris (*c.* 1870–1950), and Robert Witt (1872–1952), who planned it as a continuation of the series of exhibitions of Italian regional painting, with Pictures of the Early Venetian School (1911/12) preceding it.

Roger Fry was the critic, painter, and Bloomsbury Group member, who joined the Club in 1902.[140] He wrote the Introduction to the exhibition catalogue, which was also reprinted as a chapter in his book *Vision and Design* of 1920. Borenius would later be on the exhibition committee for the Club's Art of Primitive Peoples exhibition of 1935 but his area of expertise made more sense for an exhibition of Italian paintings (see Chapter 4 and Appendix B for biographical details). He was close to Fry and at the time of the Club's exhibition, was a lecturer at University College London, in Fry's former position. Fry was also a friend of Henry Harris, who, according to Kenneth Clark (another Club member), 'did nothing and said nothing'.[141] In a biographical sketch of Harris, he is described as socially very well connected, including to the Prince of Wales and Ramsay Macdonald (the first Labour Prime Minister, 1931–1935). After losing money through gambling, he moved to a villa in Florence and it was there that he built up a collection of Italian paintings,[142] some of which he loaned to the Club's exhibition. He also knew Bernard Berenson and apparently reconciled the estranged Berenson and Fry at a dinner party in 1927.[143] Unlike Fry, who loaned only a couple of brocades to the exhibition (p. 44 of catalogue, 'on table opposite recess'), Harris loaned five pictures and one piece of furniture. Two of the pictures are notable: no. 4, *The Crucifixion* by Bernardo Daddi (Figure 1.5) and no. 37, di Giovanni's *St Catherine*. Of the former, Fry notes in the catalogue of the exhibition, 'In Mr Harris' Bernardo Daddi we get nearer perhaps to Giotto as a composer ...',[144] relating to his lament

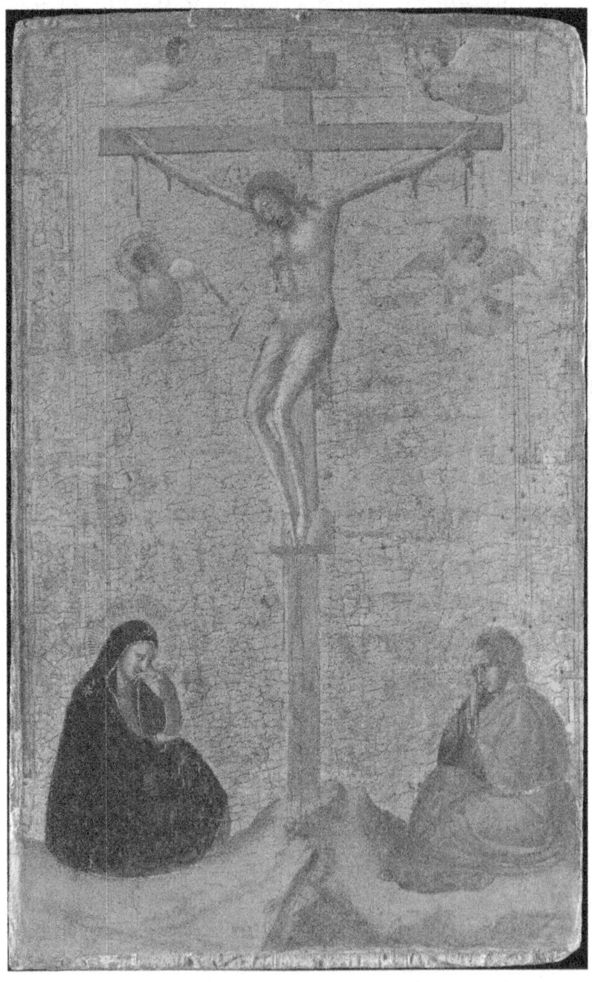

Figure 1.5 *The Crucifixion*, Bernardo Daddi, (Italian, Florence (?) *c.* 1290–1348 Florence), *c.* 1325–30. Tempera on wood, gold ground, overall 18 1/4 × 11 3/8 in. (46.4 × 28.9 cm); painted surface 17 1/2 × 11 3/8 in. (44.5 × 28.9 cm). Gift of Asbjorn R. Lunde, 1999. The Metropolitan Museum of Art, New York, 1999.532.

Source: Courtesy of the Metropolitan Museum of Art, New York.

about there being very few Giottos in England at that time. The painting in question, exhibit no. 4, was described as 'a thing of beauty' in *The Burlington Magazine* review of the show.[145, 146] Only one painting in the exhibition was attributed to Giotto, the *Salvator Mundi* in no. 2, loaned by Lady Jekyll.[147] It was described in the review of the exhibition in *The Burlington Magazine* as 'The most important Trecento picture in the collection.'[148] The second picture loaned by Harris was no. 37, *Saint Catherine of Alexandria* by Bartolomeo di Giovanni, which, as noted in the catalogue, was published by Fry in *The Burlington Magazine* in 1916. Interestingly, Harris also loaned a piece of furniture, and this exhibition included sections on 'Furniture' and 'Works of Art', as well as paintings.

Furniture was also loaned by the next member of the exhibition committee, Harold Clifford Smith, who would briefly work as a Keeper at the V&A in the 1930s. He seemed to specialize in works of art and furniture, publishing books on jewellery, the furnishings and interiors of Buckingham Palace and other related topics.[149] Herbert Cook, also on the committee, loaned *Christ, the Angel of the Annunciation and the Virgin* by Agnolo Gaddi, the son of Taddeo Gaddi, who trained with Giotto (no. 8 – now in a private collection). Robert Cleremont Witt, the final member of the exhibition committee, was primarily a collector of prints and drawings, left by bequest to the Courtauld Institute in London, which he had co-founded with Samuel Courtauld (another Club member) and Lord Lee of Fareham. He and his wife collected many reproductions and photographs of paintings that he also left to the Institute, forming the core of the Witt Library there. Accordingly, he loaned 'a collection of reproductions of pictures and drawings by masters represented in the Exhibition', which was displayed 'on the table opposite the recess' in the exhibition rooms, continuing the comparative approach the Club pioneered earlier.[150]

General Lenders and their Exhibits

A key lender to the exhibition who was not on the committee was Benson, and he was joined by several other members who frequently loaned paintings to exhibitions (and others): F. Cook, Holford (by now Lt.-Col Sir George), Messel (see Chapter 2) and the Monds, in this case Ludwig's son Sir Alfred Mond (1868–1930), first Baron Melchett. Like his father, Sir Alfred was a financier, politician, and businessman, forming ICI in 1926.[151] At the time of the exhibition, Mond was the First Minister of Works, and involved in the plan (abandoned) to use the British Museum for Air Board accommodation in the First World War.[152] He loaned both works of art and furniture to the Club's exhibition. A collector who had only recently joined the Club also loaned to the exhibition: Henry Oppenheimer (1859–1932), who was a partner in the bank Speyer Brothers and instrumental in securing storage for the National Gallery collections during the First World War.[153] He collected widely and loaned a couple of bronzes to the exhibition. His wife, however, is credited with the loan of a painting by Piero di Cosimo, *Minerva and the Flute*, no. 30. A reviewer of the exhibition had somewhat harsh words to say about this picture, however: 'There is no valid reason for assigning to Piero di Cosimo the tame and uninteresting "Minerva and the Flute" (Mrs. Henry Oppenheimer).'[154] It is interesting that her loan was a much more significant work of art than the bronzes loaned by her husband. She is deliberately listed as its lender and is not lending it after his death, as Mrs Morrison did.[155] She left another painting by bequest to the National Gallery (NG 4826) and thus may have been an active collector in her own right.

By the time of the exhibition, Captain E. G. Spencer-Churchill (1876–1964) had also joined the Club. He was an enthusiastic collector (and cousin of Winston), who loaned a significant picture to the exhibition, no. 13, attributed here to Fra Angelico, *A Miracle of SS Cosmas and Damian*, which like several others, is noted to be reproduced in the 'Arundel Club Portfolio' (see Plate 3). In this version the imagery is that known more frequently today as 'the miracle of the black leg', a theme Fra Angelico painted in the frescoes of San Marco.[156] It is a popular image in medical history literature as it appears to record an early attempt at transplantation. The attribution of this seemingly amateur painting was questioned at the time of the Club's exhibition, in the review in *The Burlington Magazine* where the author suggests that it might better be ascribed to 'the earliest time of Fra Filippo'.[157] Another painting featuring these two saints was accorded higher praise and a confirmed attribution in the same review: the piece of a predella from San Marco that was loaned by the National Museum of Ireland to the Club (no. 18).[158] 'Hardly in any other instance has Fra Angelico realized a composition so frankly, so powerfully dramatic, or so boldly ventured upon representation of the human figure in violent action.'[159] According to the exhibition catalogue, this painting was acquired from the sale of William Graham's collection in 1886[160] and had been exhibited in the Old Masters exhibition at 'Burlington House' (aka the Royal Academy) in 1877.[161] As noted previously, Benson also acquired a number of paintings at Graham's sale, and he is noted to have been a friend of Graham.[162]

Generally speaking, the lender profile for this exhibition was very similar to that of previous Italian ones, and in fact for most Club exhibitions. This one also included the royal collections, through H.M. the King (no. 14, Benozzo Gozzoli's *Fall of Simon Magus*, still in the Royal Collections; plus 12 drawings by Leonardo, 'in the writing room downstairs', 'twelve of his finest and most celebrated drawings'),[163] numerous country house collections, for example, those of the Marquess of Bath, Viscount Lascelles, Lord Carmichael of Skirling, etc. (the latter two being Club members), as well as several institutions. In this case, the institutional lenders included the National Gallery of Ireland, as noted above, and the Ashmolean, which loaned its most famous Italian painting, Uccello's *The Hunt in the Forest* or *The Hunt by Moonlight* as it was called in the Club's catalogue (no. 22) (see Plate 4). This had been acquired by gift in 1850 from the Earl of Ilchester and is still recognized today as innovative in its use of perspective.[164] At the time of the exhibition, it was already famous, and was seen as the highlight of the show:

> Nothing in the exhibition gives quite such a shock of delight as the *Hunt by Moonlight* by Paulo Uccello .... Owing perhaps to certain minor differences of technique, and above all to the unwonted buoyancy of mood expressed, that master of iconoclastic criticism, Signor Adolfo Venturi, has preferred to assign the Oxford panels to the school of Uccello. So far as I know, he is alone among competent critics of Italian art in taking this view. Whatever this *Hunt by Moonlight* is ..., it makes the heart of the spectator leap responsively in his breast ...[165]

Venturi was not associated with this exhibition but his critical work was still being cited, demonstrating a continuing debate about attributions that persisted (and still persists) well into the twentieth century.

The Royal Academy was involved as an institution, through its loan of its Leonardo cartoon of 'The Virgin and Child with St. Anne', which was displayed 'over the fireplace' in the exhibition. This was the subject of some controversy when it was put up for sale in 1962. It was later 'saved for the nation' and featured in the Leonardo show of 2011 at the National Gallery, where it now resides.[166]

As with other Club exhibitions, artists were also lenders, whether members or not. In the present exhibition, two artists loaned several exhibits together. Charles Ricketts (1866–1931) and Charles Shannon (1863–1937) were artists, partners, friends of Oscar Wilde, art collectors, and founders of the Vale Press in 1894. As collectors, they are said to have 'formed one of the most magnificent collections of old master drawings and paintings, Egyptian and Greek antiquities, Japanese woodblock prints and Persian miniatures'.[167] Their collection entered the Fitzwilliam Museum, Cambridge, by bequest in 1937. Other pieces were donated to the National Gallery, including the small picture attributed to Masaccio which they loaned to the Club's exhibition (no. 5). This is now said to be simply 'Florentine'[168] but it was seen as revelatory when displayed in 1919. 'One starts back, incredulous at first at the very mention of a new Masaccio, so rare and precious are the works of the young master, who, … changed the whole current of art …'[169] They also loaned another painting that is now in the National Gallery (by bequest from Shannon), Piero di Cosimo's *The Fight Between the Lapiths and the Centaurs*, still attributed to Piero and said to be part of a piece of furniture from the palace.[170] It was included in the pictures section of the exhibition, however, suggesting that the Club's definition of 'painting' was somewhat fluid, and perhaps associated with authorship. Unlike the Oppenheimer 'Piero', discussed above, the exhibition reviewer was full of praise for this one: 'The real Piero di Cosimo, a painter swayed by every passion, by every impression, is seen in the tremendous "Battle of the Centaurs and Lapiths" (Mr. C. Ricketts and Mr. C. Shannon).'[171]

Other works singled out in the review include no. 26, an *Adoration of the Magi* by Fra Filippo Lippi, loaned by Sir Frederick Cook. The reviewer described it as a 'beautiful tondo', 'probably his earliest extant work, and certainly one of his finest?'[172] It had been exhibited several times by then, in both the Burlington House (RA) Old Masters exhibition and at the Grafton Galleries. The Grafton Galleries opened in London as a commercial space in 1893 and Roger Fry became an advisor, yet another intersection with the Club.[173] The Cook Lippi is now in the National Gallery, Washington, DC, and is attributed to both Fra Angelico and Fra Filippo Lippi.[174] The other picture accorded high praise was loaned by Sir George Holford, no. 19, a *Virgin and Child with Saints* by Pesellino. This is now in the Metropolitan Museum in New York and is still attributed to Pesellino.[175]

The reviewer of the exhibition, Sir Claude Phillips (1846–1924),[176] praises much that is included but quite a few of the pictures are seen as second rate, with the exhibition being somewhat of a mixed bag, in his opinion:

> This is perhaps as beautiful an exhibition as any of the long series which, for the instruction and delight of students and art lovers, have been brought together in the gallery of the club. At the same time it is not, indeed it does not profess to be, an illustration of Florentine painting – still less of Florentine art – during the great period which the title covers. You cannot in dealing with Florence treat the sculpture and the painting separately – the two are inextricably interwoven …
>
> It would, indeed, be unsafe (?) for the student of the 15th century to assume that he could derive an adequate idea even of Florentine painting even from a study of these beautiful examples, and these alone …

> If we judged Florentine painting of the Quattrocento by the exquisite pictures now hung upon the walls of the club, and by these alone, we should run the risk of entirely missing its true meaning.[177]

He also says of a Pollaiuolo that it is a 'second-rate and repulsive example'. [178]

The exhibition was therefore both too biased towards 'exquisite pictures' and not comprehensive enough. In fairness, in his Introduction to the exhibition catalogue, Roger Fry does not make any attempt to reconcile or justify the selection of exhibits. In fact, the essay does not even need to be attached to the exhibition for it is a general survey and discussion of the value and impact of early Florentine art. While this might seem more scholarly than Benson's earlier painting essay, it is in fact just as personal in its perspective. This is reflective of the Club's approach to writing art history in that the individual collector or 'expert' expresses his opinion generally but in many cases, apart from Fry, setting this against the opinions or work of others. For example, after a long discussion about the 'intellectual' in art, and the role of it in Italian painting, Fry finally begins to refer to exhibits, but not as exhibits, simply as examples of this art in England. These are examples chosen to populate his history of Florentine painting, with digressions about the 'scientific' and 'psychological' in art. At the end, he sums it up by saying:

> In Florentine art, then, one may see at happy moments of equilibrium the supreme advantages of intellectual art and at other and less fortunate moments the dangers which beset so difficult an endeavour. It was after all a Florentine who made the best prophesy of the result of modern aesthetic when he said, 'Finally good painting is a music and a melody which intellect only can appreciate and that with difficulty.'[179]

The Florentine artists were not purely emotional, therefore, or possessed of an 'artistic temperament'.[180] Rather, 'an aesthetically intelligible principle' combined with curiosity make up Fry's definition of the intellectual with regard to early Florentine painting.[181] This of course reflects his formalist approach to aesthetics which he outlined in 'An Essay in Aesthetics', *New Quarterly*, 1909 (reprinted in his *Vision and Design*, 1920) that would seem to be somewhat of a contrast to the usual connoisseurship-driven studies published by the Club. Yet Fry's emphasis on the intellectual has echoes of the 'mind of the artist' noted by Benson in his essay for the 1894 exhibition. Fry's reference to a 'modern aesthetic' further situates his views in the beginnings of the Modernist movement, in which he played such a significant role.

Interestingly, the Club might also have inspired Roger Fry in another way, in his co-founding of *The Burlington Magazine*, possibly in the name for the journal but also in its initial remit. In the first editorial of March 1903, the magazine's editor, Robert Dell (1865–1940), stated:

> Finally, then, we may hope – or at least endeavour – to remove a curious and shameful anomaly, this namely, that Britain, alone of all cultured European countries, is without any periodical which makes the serious and disinterested study of ancient art its chief occupation. The anomaly is the more surprising in that the great English aristocratic collectors of the last two centuries showed an independence of judgement, a subtlety of taste, such, that even now, in spite of recent depredations, England remains a place of pilgrimage for lovers of the finest creations of past times.[182]

Many, if not most, of these 'great English aristocratic collectors' were members or associates of the Club and quite a few members of *The Burlington Magazine*'s consultative committee were also affiliated with the Club, including Lord Balcarres, Herbert Cook, von Bode, Campbell Dodgson, Sidney Colvin, and of course Fry. In a history of Fry and *The Burlington Magazine*, the author notes this connection:

> While a certain careless type of British dilettantism was to be avoided, another more serious aspect of that tradition may have been influential, even on the choice of name for the new publication. In addition to the location of the Magazine's offices at New Burlington Street, London, and the association with Lord Burlington and Burlington House (seat of the Royal Academy of Arts and the Society of Antiquaries), the Burlington Fine Arts Club (founded 1857) was surely important: its focused annual exhibitions of works largely drawn from private collections aroused the interest and admiration of scholars and collectors throughout Europe and America, and its large-format, beautifully illustrated scholarly catalogues with their goldish-green buckram bindings provided a model to be emulated. Its supporters included a striking mix of very rich collectors, noble amateurs and scholars.[183]

Fry, therefore, through his membership and work for the Club, was instrumental in continuing to present such art works to viewers and readers through the art literature of the twentieth century.

Conclusion

The exhibitions of prints, drawings, and paintings discussed in this chapter represent the prevailing and continuous tastes of the founders and early members of the Club but also their personalized approaches to the interpretation of the exhibition themes. On the one hand, these reflect contemporary approaches to the subject matter but on the other, they also demonstrate the unconstrained and therefore sometimes innovative methods that a private group can utilize when unrestricted by institutional processes and politics. This was further enhanced by the wide-ranging backgrounds and perspectives of exhibition committee members, such as Benson and Fry. Not surprisingly, this unusual context for art displays nurtured a similarly wide range of exhibition topics, as the next chapters will demonstrate.

Notes

1 The work of living painters was excluded from exhibition. See page 12.
2 General Committee minutes, 17.7.1877.
3 Burlington Fine Arts Club, *Catalogue of the Etched Work of Rembrandt Selected for Exhibition at the Burlington Fine Arts Club* (London, 1877), p. 6.
4 Ibid., pp. 6–7.
5 Anthony Griffiths (ed.), *Landmarks in Print Collecting: Connoisseurs and Donors at the British Museum since 1753* (London: British Museum Press, 1996), p. 164.
6 Alison McQueen, *The Rise of the Cult of Rembrandt: Reinventing an Old Master in Nineteenth-Century France* (Amsterdam: Amsterdam University Press, 2003), p. 223.
7 BFAC (1877), p. 14.
8 Martin J. Hopkinson, *No Day Without a Line: The History of the Royal Society of Painter-Printmakers 1880–1999* (Oxford: Ashmolean Museum, 1999), p. 9.

9 Ibid. The authors note on p. 10 that Haden may also have been driven by the breakdown in his relationship with Whistler, that clearly had fairly wide-reaching consequences (e.g. the expulsion from the Club).
10 Griffiths (1996), p. 206.
11 Ibid., p. 118.
12 Ibid., p. 182. None of the three was a Club member at the time of the exhibition.
13 See www.whistler.arts.gla.ac.uk/correspondence/biog/display/?bid=Addi_S (accessed 2 Nov. 2015).
14 Tim Knox, 'Edward Cheney of Badger Hall: Forgotten Collector of Italian Sculpture', *Sculpture Journal*, vol. 16, no. 1 (2007), pp. 5–20. Available at: www.historywebsite.co.uk/articles/Albrighton/Ruskin/Ruskin.htm (accessed 2 Nov. 2015).
15 See https://dictionaryofarthistorians.org/rigbye.htm (accessed 11 Feb. 2015).
16 See www.whistler.arts.gla.ac.uk/correspondence/people/biog/?bid=Heyw_JJ&firstname=J&surname=Heywood (accessed 2 Nov. 2015).
17 John Batchelor, 'Scott, William Bell (1811–1890)', in *Oxford Dictionary of National Biography*, first published 2004; online edn, Oct 2007. Available at: http://dx.doi.org/10.1093/ref:odnb/24938 (accessed 22 Dec. 2015).
18 Mogens Trolle Larsen, *The Conquest of Assyria: Excavations in an Antique Land* (London: Routledge, 2014), p. 287.
19 Barbara Bryant, *G. F. Watts Portraits: Fame and Beauty in Victorian Society* (London: National Portrait Gallery, 2004), p. 28.
20 Bill Cash, *John Bright: Statesman, Orator, Agitator* (London: Tauris, 2011), p. 184.
21 This latter aspect is not well studied, if at all, but there are numerous studies of individual women art collectors as well as an important survey of aspects of women's participation in the art world, Clarissa Campbell Orr, ed., *Women in the Victorian Art World* (Manchester: Manchester University Press, 1995). There is also a useful chapter on collecting in Patrizia Di Bello's *Women's Albums and Photography in Victorian England: Ladies, Mothers and Flirts* (London: Routledge, 2007).
22 McQueen (2003), p. 191.
23 See http://corsair.themorgan.org/cgi-bin/Pwebrecon.cgi?BBID=161984 (accessed 11 March 2016).
24 See http://corsair.themorgan.org/cgi-bin/Pwebrecon.cgi?BBID=179962 (accessed 11 March 2016).
25 See www.britishmuseum.org/research/search_the_collection_database/term_details.aspx?bioId=133800 (accessed 4 Nov. 2015).
26 'The Aylesford collection was acquired en bloc for £3,000 in 1846 by Woodburn, who sold some thirteen (or seventeen according to Lugt) Rembrandt sheets to R. S. Holford for £3,500 (Holford bought others later on).' Ibid., note 25 above. The British Museum also acquired a number of ex-Aylesford prints.
27 BFAC (1877), p. 30.
28 Griffiths (1996), p. 13.
29 General Committee minutes, January to August, 1892.
30 See www.holfordtrust.com/textonly.asp (accessed 11 Dec. 2015).
31 See http://classes.toledomuseum.org:8080/emuseum/view/objects/asitem/People$00402996/0?t:state:flow=7c1703b3-d942-4708-b76b-d3b2727b661c (accessed 11 March 2016).
32 BFAC, *Burlington Fine Arts Club, Catalogue of the Loan Exhibition of Flemish and Belgian Art, a Memorial Volume* (London: BFAC, 1927), p. 28, no. 60 (as 'attributed to Hans Memling'), repr. plate XXXII. The 'artist' was named by M. J. Friedländer, *Zeitschrift für bildende Kunst*, vol. I (Leipzig, 1915), p. 12.
33 W. R. Valentiner,'Simon van Herlam, the Master of the Morrison Triptych', *Gazette des Beaux-Arts*, vol. XLV (Jan. 1955), pp. 7, 10.
34 See www.nationalgallery.ie/en/aboutus/History/NGI_Directors/Walter_Armstrong.aspx (accessed 4 Nov. 2015).
35 Burlington Fine Arts Club, *Exhibition of Pictures by Masters of the Netherlandish and Allied Schools of XV. and Early XVI. Centuries* (London, 1892), p. xix.
36 Ibid., pp. v–vi.
37 Bernhard Ridderbos *et al.*, eds., *Early Netherlandish Paintings: Rediscovery, Reception and Research* (Amsterdam; Amsterdam University Press, 2005), p. 187.

38 Carola Hicks, *Girl in a Green Gown: The History and Mystery of the Arnolfini Portrait* (London: Vintage, 2011), p. 178.
39 Caroline Dakers, *A Genius for Money: Business, Art and the Morrisons* (New Haven, CT: Yale University Press, 2011), p. 230.
40 Jonathan Parry, 'Cavendish, Spencer Compton, marquess of Hartington and eighth duke of Devonshire (1833–1908)', in *Oxford Dictionary of National Biography*, first published 2004; online edn, Jan 2008. Available at: http://dx.doi.org/10.1093/ref:odnb/32331 (accessed 11 Dec. 2015).
41 Gustav Waagen, *Treasures of Art in Great Britain*, 4 vols, 1854. Repr. (Cambridge: Cambridge University Press, 2015), p. 226.
42 M. Friedlander, *Early Netherlandish Painting* (New York: Springer, 1969), p. 86, Supp. 128, p. 82.
43 See www.clarkart.edu/exhibitions/mystery/index.cfm (accessed 4 Nov. 2015).
44 Reginald Herbert Pembroke (15 Earl of), *The History and Treasures of Wilton House: Home of the Earls of Pembroke and Montgomery for over 400 years* (Andover: Pitkin Pictorials, 1957), p. 6.
45 See www.museothyssen.org/en/thyssen/ficha_obra/55 (accessed 5 Nov. 2015).
46 Elon Danziger, 'The Cook Collection, Its Founder and Its Inheritors', *The Burlington Magazine*, vol. 146, no. 1216, Collectors and Patrons (July 2004), pp. 444–458.
47 Ibid., p. 456.
48 A recent study of the politics of saving art was published in Christine Sylvester, *Art/Museums: International Relations Where We Least Expect It* (London: Routledge, 2009), Chapter 3.
49 Andrea Geddes Poole, *Stewards of the Nation's Art: Contested Cultural Authority, 1890–1939* (Toronto: University of Toronto Press, 2010), pp. 197–198.
50 Danziger (2004). He was also a founder of *The Burlington Magazine*.
51 Poole (2010), p. 198.
52 Patricia Rubin, '"The Outcry": Despoilers, Donors, and the National Gallery in London, 1909', *Journal of the History of Collections*, vol. 25, no. 2 (2012), pp. 253–275.
53 See www.nationalgallery.org.uk/paintings/workshop-of-joos-van-cleve-the-holy-family (accessed 5 Nov. 2015).
54 See www.nationalgallery.org.uk/paintings/johannes-vermeer-a-young-woman-seated-at-a-virginal (accessed 24 Nov. 2015).
55 See http://collections.frick.org/view/objects/asitem/search@/1/primaryMaker-asc/title-asc?t:state:flow=651bc66b-fbe9-4d48-84be-01f4875d240b (accessed 24 Nov. 2015).
56 See www.bbc.co.uk/arts/yourpaintings/paintings/the-right-honourable-lewis-fry-pc-mp-185181 (accessed 24 Nov. 2015); www.bristollawsociety.com/lewis-fry/ (accessed 24 Nov. 2015).
57 General Meeting minutes, 18.5.1869.
58 Burlington Fine Arts Club, *Marc Antonio Raimondi* (London, 1868), pp. 1–19.
59 Burlington Fine Arts Club, *The Work of Luca Signorelli and his School* (London, 1893).
60 General Committee minutes 8.1893–6.1894.
61 See https://dictionaryofarthistorians.org/venturia.htm (accessed 11 Nov. 2015).
62 See Grove Art Online, Oxford Art Online, Oxford University Press, 'Benson, R. H.'. Available at: www.oxfordartonline.com/subscriber/article/grove/art/T007959 (accessed 26 Nov. 2015).
63 Francis Haskell, *The Ephemeral Museum: Old Master Paintings and the Rise of the Art Exhibition* (New Haven, CT: Yale University Press, 2000), p. 96.
64 It seems possible that this exhibition innovation may have been the impetus behind the founding of the Arundel Club in 1904 'for the purpose of photographing pictures and other works of art in private collections or galleries not easy of access, and of supplying the members with prints of the photographs'. The provisional committee includes many of the BFAC members/associates: Balcarres, Conway, Colvin, Armstrong, Fry, and H. Cook. 'The Arundel Club', *The Burlington Magazine for Connoisseurs*, vol. 4, no. 12 (March 1904), p. 203.
65 Haskell (2000).
66 C. Hugh Smyth and P. M. Lukehart, eds., *The Early Years of Art History in the United States: Notes and Essays on Departments, Teaching, and Scholars* (Princeton, NJ: Princeton University Press, 1993).

67 See http://itatti.harvard.edu/ (accessed 11 Nov. 2015).
68 See https://dictionaryofarthistorians.org/berensonb.htm (accessed 11 Nov. 2015).
69 Rachel Cohen, *Bernard Berenson: A Life in the Picture Trade* (New Haven, CT: Yale University Press, 2013).
70 Ernest Samuels, *Bernard Berenson: The Making of a Connoisseur* (Cambridge, MA: Harvard University Press, 1979), p. 222.
71 Burlington Fine Arts Club, *Exhibition of Pictures, Drawings and Photographs of the School of Ferrara-Bologna, 1440–1540* (London, 1894), pp. 31–56; Bernard Berenson, 'Burlington Fine Arts Club, Exhibition of Pictures, Drawings and Photographs of Works of the School of Ferrara-Bologna', *Revue Critique d'Histoire et de Littérature*, vol. 29, no. 18 (May 6, 1895), pp. 348–352.
72 Haskell (2000), p. 94.
73 Simon Sebag-Montefiore, 'R. H. Benson as a Collector', Appendix 3 in Jehanne Wake, *Kleinwort Benson: The History of Two Families in Banking* (Oxford; Oxford University Press, 1997), p. 480.
74 Ibid.
75 See www.tate.org.uk/about/who-we-are/history-of-tate (accessed 24 Nov. 2015).
76 Sebag-Montefiore (1997), p. 483.
77 See www.metmuseum.org/collection/the-collection-online/search/437849?=&imgno=0&tabname=object-information (accessed 9 Nov. 2015).
78 BFAC (1894), p. xiv.
79 See www.oxfordartonline.com/subscriber/article/grove/art/T086559?q=cosme+tura&search=quick&pos=1&_start=1#firsthit (accessed 9 Nov. 2015).
80 See www.nga.gov/content/ngaweb/Collection/art-object-page.41587.html (accessed 24 Nov. 2015).
81 For example, Alessandra Buccheri, *The Spectacle of Clouds, 1439–1650: Italian Art and Theatre* (Farnham: Ashgate, 2014), p. 64.
82 See www.nationalgallery.org.uk/paintings/correggio-christ-taking-leave-of-his-mother (accessed 9 Nov. 2015).
83 See www.nationalgallery.org.uk/paintings/history/directors/sir-edward-poynter (accessed 9 Nov. 2015).
84 Griffiths (1996), pp. 14–15.
85 See www.nationalgallery.org.uk/paintings/lodovico-mazzolino-christ-disputing-with-the-doctors (accessed 9 Nov. 2015).
86 BFAC (1894), p. v.
87 Ibid., p. xi.
88 Ibid., pp. xi–xii.
89 Ibid., p. xxxvi.
90 Ibid., p. xxxv.
91 General Committee minutes, 12.1895–6.1898.
92 https://dictionaryofarthistorians.org/strongs.htm (accessed 11 Dec. 2015).
93 Notes of the Quarter, January, February, March, 'J. Arthur Strong', *Journal of the Royal Asiatic Society of Great Britain and Ireland for 1904*, RAS 1904, pp. 387–394.
94 https://dictionaryofarthistorians.org/strongs.htm (accessed 11 Dec. 2015).
95 The General Committee minutes note that Cook asked for his name to be removed 'from the foot of the Milanese catalogue' and to be removed from the committee. He appears to have disagreed strongly with suggested revisions. General Committee minutes, 26.7.1898, note II.
96 Burlington Fine Arts Club, *Illustrated Catalogue of Pictures by Masters of the Milanese and Allied Schools of Lombardy; Exhibited May, June, and July, 1898* (London, 1899), p. ix.
97 Ibid., p. xi.
98 See https://dictionaryofarthistorians.org/morellig.htm (accessed 11 Nov. 2015).
99 Quite a few members became titled during their time at the Club and this was duly and correctly noted in Club correspondence and publications. It can lead to some confusion therefore.
100 BFAC (1899), p. 13 in exhibit section of the catalogue.
101 See www.timkenmuseum.org/collection/italian/portrait-youth-holding-arrow (accessed 11 Nov. 2015).

102 Ernest Samuels, *Bernard Berenson: The Making of a Connoisseur* (Cambridge, MA: Harvard University Press, 1979), pp. 221–222.
103 See www.nga.gov/content/ngaweb/Collection/art-object-page.46155.html (accessed 11 Nov. 2015).
104 BFAC (1899), p. xi.
105 Ibid., p. xv.
106 Ibid., p. xiv.
107 Andrea Bayer and Mina Gregori, *Painters of Reality: the Legacy of Leonardo and Caravaggio in Lombardy* (New York: Metropolitan Museum of Art, 2004), p. 27.
108 The first painting is now in the Philadelphia museum: see www.philamuseum.org/collections/permanent/102013.html (accessed 12 Nov. 2015).
109 Peter H. Hansen, 'Conway, (William) Martin, Baron Conway of Allington (1856–1937)', in *Oxford Dictionary of National Biography*, first published 2004. Available at: http://dx.doi.org/10.1093/ref:odnb/32536 (accessed 13 Nov. 2015).
110 Martin Conway, *The Sport of Collecting* (London: F.A. Stokes, 1914), pp. 8-9.
111 Laura Iamurri, 'Art History in Italy: Connoisseurship, Academic Scholarship and the Protection of Cultural Heritage', in M. Rampley, *et al.*, eds., *Art History and Visual Studies in Europe: Transnational Discourses and National Frameworks* (Leiden: Brill, 2012), p. 393.
112 See http://cartelen.louvre.fr/cartelen/visite?srv=car_not_frame&idNotice=13898 (accessed 13 Nov. 2015).
113 BFAC (1899), p. lxii.
114 Ibid., p. lxi.
115 Ibid., p. lvii.
116 Ibid., p. lviii.
117 See www.nationalgallery.org.uk/paintings/giovanni-antonio-boltraffio-portrait-of-a-man-in-profile/*/key-facts (accessed 13 Nov. 2015).
118 BFAC (1899), p. lix.
119 Ibid., p. lix.
120 Ibid., p. 12 of exhibit section.
121 See www.christies.com/lotfinder/LotDetailsPrintable.aspx?intObjectID=3041641 (accessed 13 Nov. 2015).
122 Sebag-Montefiore (1997), p. 481.
123 Jean Paul Richter, 'Italian Pictures at the New Gallery and at Burlington House', *The Art Journal*, new series (1894), p. 62.
124 The Grosvenor Gallery displayed the work of several artist members of the Club, including Whistler and Burne-Jones. For a history, see Colleen Denney, *At the Temple of Art: The Grosvenor Gallery, 1877–1890* (Madison, NJ: Fairleigh Dickson University Press, 2000).
125 Incidentally, the New Gallery also hosted a visit from Club members in 1896. As the General Committee minutes of 31.3.1896 note: 'IV. An Invitation from the Directors of the Exhibition of Spanish Art at the New Gallery, to the Members of the Club to spend an evening there was accepted with thanks.'
126 The New Gallery, Regent Street, 'Exhibition of Early Italian Art, from 1300-1550', 1893–1894, preliminary pages.
127 Eliot Woodridge Rowlands, *Masaccio: Saint Andrew and the Pisa Altarpiece* (new York: J. Paul Getty Museum, 2003), p. 90.
128 Haskell (2000), pp. 47–48.
129 Ibid., p. 48.
130 Ibid., p. 63.
131 Ibid., p. 64.
132 Ibid., p. 69.
133 General Committee minutes 27.2.1869.
134 Haskell (2000), p. 71.
135 Ibid., p. 73.
136 Ibid., p. 74; James Fenton, *School of Genius: A History of the Royal Academy of Art* (London: Royal Academy, 2006), p. 255.
137 'Italian art of the Seventeenth Century' (1925) was more broad in scope.

138 General Committee minutes, 5.12.1918.
139 As well as some special ones. The Ferrarese exhibition included medals and this was noted in its title.
140 BFAC Candidate Book, vol. VI, entry no. 937.
141 Robert Cumming, ed., *My Dear BB…' The Letters of Bernard Berenson and Kenneth Clark, 1925–1959* (New Haven, CT: Yale University Press, 2015), p. 527.
142 Ibid.
143 Ibid.
144 Burlington Fine Arts Club, *Catalogue of an Exhibition of Florentine Painting Before 1500* (London, 1919), p. 10.
145 Claude Phillips, 'Florentine Painting Before 1500', *The Burlington Magazine for Connoisseurs*, vol. 34, no. 195 (June 1919), p. 210.
146 See www.metmuseum.org/collection/the-collection-online/search/438423 (accessed 15 Nov. 2015).
147 Lady Jekyll was Dame Agnes (1861–1937), artist and daughter of William Graham (1817–1885), patron of the Pre Raphaelites, whose collection was sold in 1886. She was also the sister-in-law of the garden designer. Like a number of the Pre-Raphaelite painters, she owned old master pictures. See Elizabeth Prettejohn, *Cambridge Companion to the Pre-Raphaelites* (Cambridge: Cambridge University Press, 2012), pp. 37–38.
148 Phillips (1919), p. 210. This painting could not be traced.
149 For example, H. Clifford Smith, *The Danny Unicorn Jewel* (London, 1914); *Victoria and Albert Museum: Catalogue of English Furniture & Woodwork* (London: V&A, 1930); *Some Mid-Georgian Furniture from the Royal Collections* (London, 1935).
150 BFAC (1919), p. 35.
151 Fred Aftalion, *A History of the International Chemical Industry*, second edn (Philadelphia, PA: Chemical Heritage Foundation, 2001), p. 140.
152 Gaynor Kavanaugh, *Museums and the First World War: A Social History* (London: Bloomsbury, 1998), reprint, p. 50.
153 See www.britishmuseum.org/research/search_the_collection_database/term_details.aspx?bioId=93105 (accessed 14 Nov. 2015).
154 Phillips (1919), p. 216.
155 Mrs Morrison was known to have collected lace, as was noted in Margaret Jourdain, 'Lace in the Collection of Mrs. Alfred Morrison at Fonthill', *The Burlington Magazine for Connoisseurs*, vol. 2, no. 4 (June 1903), pp. 95–97, 99, 101, 103.
156 Laurence Kanter and Pia Palladino, *Fra Angelico* (New York: Metropolitan Museum of Art, 2005), Chapter VI.
157 Phillips (1919), p. 210. This painting is today in the Kunsthaus, Zurich.
158 See www.nationalgallery.ie/en/Collection/Collection_Highlights/Painting_and_Sculpture/Fra_Angelico.aspx (accessed 15 Nov. 2015).
159 Phillips (1919), p. 210.
160 BFAC (1919), p. 24 of objects section.
161 Ibid., p. 24 of exhibits section.
162 Sebag-Montefiore (1997), p. 481.
163 See www.royalcollection.org.uk/collection/403372/the-fall-of-simon-magus (accessed 15 Nov. 2015); Phillips (1919), p. 210.
164 See www.ashmolean.org/ash/objects/makedetail.php?pmu=730&mu=732>y=qsea&sec=&dtn=15&sfn=Artist%20Sort,Title&cpa=1&rpos=0&key=WA1850.31 (accessed 15 Nov. 2015).
165 Phillips (1919), p. 210.
166 See http://hansard.millbanksystems.com/commons/1962/mar/28/royal-academy-of-arts-sale-of-works-of (accessed 15 Nov. 2015).; referred to as 'the Burlington House cartoon', see exhibition labels, no. 73: see www.nationalgallery.org.uk/leonardo-da-vinci-painter-at-the-court-of-milan-exhibition-guide (accessed 11 Nov. 2015).
167 See www.fitzmuseum.cam.ac.uk/gallery/hiddenhistories/biographies/bio/friendship/ricketts shannon_biography.html (accessed 15 Nov. 2015).
168 See www.nationalgalleryimages.co.uk/Imagedetails.aspx?q=NG3627&ng=NG3627&frm=1 (accessed 15 Nov. 2015).
169 Phillips (1919), p. 210.

170 See www.nationalgallery.org.uk/paintings/piero-di-cosimo-the-fight-between-the-lapiths-and-the-centaurs (accessed 15 Nov. 2015).
171 Phillips (1919), p. 217.
172 Ibid., p. 210.
173 Helmreich (2012). The Galleries were incorporated in 1891.
174 See www.nga.gov/collection/gallery/gg4/gg4-41581.html (accessed 15 Nov. 2015).
175 See www.metmuseum.org/collection/the-collection-online/search/437276?=&imgno=0&tabname=object-information (accessed 15 Nov. 2015).
176 Phillips was the first Keeper of the Wallace Collection and a critic for various publications. His father founded the *Daily Telegraph* newspaper. See https://dictionaryofarthistorians.org/phillipsc.htm (accessed 24 Nov. 2015).
177 Phillips (1919), p. 208.
178 Ibid.
179 BFAC (1919), p. 14.
180 Ibid., p. 7.
181 Ibid., p. 8.
182 *The Burlington Magazine for Connoisseurs*, vol. 1, no. 1 (March 1903), pp. 3–5, at p. 5.
183 Caroline Elam, '"A More and More Important Work": Roger Fry and *The Burlington Magazine*', *The Burlington Magazine*, vol. 145, no. 1200, Centenary Issue (Mar. 2003), p. 146.

2 Ceramics East and West

Chapter Contents

- Introduction
- 1873 English and Continental Porcelain
- 1888 Greek Ceramic Art
- 1895 Blue and White Oriental Porcelain
- 1896 Coloured Chinese Porcelain
- 1910 Early Chinese Pottery and Porcelain
- Conclusion

Introduction

Roger Fry, whose work was instrumental in the Florentine exhibition discussed in Chapter 1, also contributed to an earlier exhibition of ceramics mounted by the Club. Not normally associated with ceramics, Fry is nevertheless representative of the fact that the members of the Burlington Fine Arts Club possessed wide-ranging tastes and expertise in artworks, as demonstrated through their exhibitions. One specific tendency that is notable is a more serious interest in ceramics, almost equal to that of prints and painting, yet many members who collected ceramics, or like Fry contributed to ceramic exhibitions, were not especially known as ceramic collectors or experts. The general popularity of ceramics among Club members is, however, consistent with the taste for ceramics that had been prevalent in Britain from the sixteenth century onwards and which continued throughout the twentieth century.[1] During the nineteenth century, ceramics became a significant aspect of the art market in Britain, particularly from the 1860s when the Club was founded. Partly in consequence, by the second half of the nineteenth century, ceramics were represented in the museum collections of Britain. As we have seen, the Club was founded by a museum professional, J. C. Robinson, and had a number of museum professionals as active members throughout its history. They provided ready access to public ceramic collections and Club members in turn donated ceramics to these institutions. Like paintings and the National Gallery, there was a symbiotic relationship between private collectors of ceramics at the Club and public collections in museums. We should remember too that the founding group of members of the Club, including Robinson, were also core members of the BFAC's predecessor club, the Fine Arts Club, which specialized in decorative arts, including ceramics.

Nonetheless, the Club was unusual in treating ceramics as 'art' for themed exhibition purposes. There had been public displays of ceramics prior to this, for example, in the Great Exhibition of 1851, where ceramics were presented as examples of manufacture and the 1862 loan exhibition at the South Kensington Museum, organized by Robinson, which featured ceramics in a wider 'works of art display'.[2] There were also dealer displays from the likes of Duveen and Murray Marks (discussed below), which were designed to cultivate collecting by highlighting specific collections, but none of these was designed as a themed display dedicated to ceramics as an art medium. This highlights the unusual emphasis on ceramics in quite a few of the Club's exhibitions throughout its history, some of which were specifically dedicated to ceramics. One of their earliest exhibitions of any art was entitled 'Oriental Porcelain' (1868), for which a catalogue was not produced so there is no record of what was displayed. However, it appears that it may have been an exhibition of the collection of one of the founder members, the Marquis d'Azeglio:

> 12.6.1866
> 1st general committee meeting: various business; present: Marquis d'Azeglio chair, A. Barker, R. Fisher, C. J. Palmer, J.C. Robinson, R. H. Wornum; 19.12.1867 'Resolved that the Marquis d'Azeglio be requested to oblige the Committee by allowing his collection of China to be exhibited in the rooms of the club.'[3]

Of all ceramic types, it was 'oriental' ceramics that were the most prominent in the exhibition schedule over the years, both in dedicated ceramics exhibitions and in exhibitions of other themes that featured ceramics. Within this category it was particularly but not exclusively Chinese ceramics that were the most popular among members. This too is not surprising as Asian ceramics in general and Chinese, in particular, were the type increasingly collected more than any other for much of the late nineteenth century in Britain, a form of specialization that was encouraged and to some extent driven by the Club's exhibitions.[4] The popularity of ceramics generally among Club members is indicated by the fact that in a number of the exhibitions mounted by the Club, regardless of the specific topic, ceramics were a dominant medium, suggesting that many art historical topics, in the eyes of the Club, also could be illustrated through this medium, apart from those specifically dedicated to a painter or a school of painting. The following survey of a range of ceramic-themed exhibitions mounted by the Club will characterize the Club's approach to ceramic connoisseurship and interpretation, which is usually reflective of prevailing taste and current scholarship in that field but in some cases responsive to developments in other areas of art history practice.

1873 English and Continental Porcelain

The first ceramics exhibition mounted by the Club, for which a catalogue was produced, was 'English and Continental Porcelain' of 1873.[5] The catalogue is descriptive, without an introductory essay, but the tone is clear from the didactic points made at the outset. Each type of ware, arranged by place of production, is described, and often the 'best period' is noted. As would become standard practice, the exhibition subcommittee is noted at the beginning of the catalogue and it featured two prominent ceramics collectors, including one from the British Museum, A. W. Franks, as well as Charles Schreiber, whose involvement was deemed to be necessary for fulfilling the exhibition aims. As noted in the General Committee minutes:

18.2.1873

IV Resolved that an Exhibition of European porcelain be held in the gallery; the subcommittee for such Exhibition to be Sir D Wyatt, Mr Haden, Mr Fisher, Mr Franks and Mr Schreiber; vide 5th Resolution 12 Nov 72 – repairs in the gallery nearly completed … it was thought desirable to reopen the Gallery with a collection of British china to be exhibited in the existing cases or in such further cases as may be needed, that the Secretaries be requested to write to Mr Franks and Mr Schreiber, asking them to join Sir D Wyatt Mr Haden Mr Fisher as a subcommittee for carrying out the above object.[6]

As noted in Chapter 1, Franks was a Keeper at the British Museum, but Charles Schreiber's history has not been explored yet. He was quite an influential collector and member of the Club at the time of the exhibition. Schreiber was an academic (Trinity College, Cambridge), then an MP (Cheltenham; Poole) and a collector of ceramics and other objects, along with his wife, Lady Charlotte (1812–1895).[7] The Schreibers collected mainly English ceramics and this was what was given to the V&A after his death.[8] The other committee members such as Haden and Fisher were all early Club members or founders, and generally they are seen as painting or prints specialists, as indicated in Chapter 1. Their membership of a ceramics exhibition subcommittee is surprising in that respect, but not in the context of the Club. Here those with experience of working with art, whether as collectors, artists, curators, or critics were typically the members who organized the exhibitions. They may have had relevant specialist knowledge but often did not except when it came to writing the catalogues, which generally was done by specialists, either members or not.

Lenders and Exhibits

In this exhibition, in spite of its title, most of the exhibits were European porcelain, not English, and the list of lenders (including Schreiber) includes collectors of a wide range of continental European wares. Boddam Castle (1819–1891) of Bristol (not the place Boddam Castle of the same name), was one of them.[9] A barrister descended from a long line of East India Company employees, he is listed as a collector of Bristol porcelain (along with the Schreibers) in Chaffers' handbook of 1874.[10] William Chaffers (1811–1892) was a dealer and pawnbroker, who, according to various sources, sold coins, 'china' and antiques.[11] He is best known in the ceramics field for his book, *Marks and Monograms on Pottery and Porcelain of the Renaissance and Modern Periods …*, which was first published in London in 1863. Through this book, and its multiple editions, he actively contributed to the development of the market for ceramics through publications such as handbooks which listed types, identifying features and owners. In doing so, Chaffers contributed to collecting knowledge structures (Westgarth 2009) and promoted collecting as well as collectors. As a dealer, he could not be a member of the Club but he was part of the network that supported Club members and Club activities associated with art. For example, he was an advisor to both Club member William Holburne (1793–1874) on his private collection and the South Kensington Museum, on whose behalf he is known to have purchased works of art and organized exhibitions.[12]

Also mentioned on the same page as Chaffers, with reference to collectors of 'Maiolica, Siena' was O. Coope, i.e. Octavius E. Coope (1814–1886), Club member and MP (Great Yarmouth; Middlesex), who loaned two pieces of Sèvres porcelain for the exhibition.[13] Sir William Drake (1817–1890) was also a Club member and a prominent lawyer, who collected etchings and ceramics, a combination that is not unusual in the Club context. He wrote about both, including the etchings of Seymour Haden of the BFAC, who was discussed in Chapter 1.[14] For the porcelain exhibition, he loaned Italian ceramics from Venice, a subject on which he also published.[15] He was further a member of the Royal Society of Painter-etchers and Engravers, co-founded by its first president, Seymour Haden, and representative of typical owners of ceramics who were not on the surface specialists in that area.[16] Alfred Seymour MP (1824–1888) was MP for Totnes and then Salisbury, and also was noted as a collector of prints and drawings.[17] His participation in the exhibition demonstrates that he clearly also collected some European porcelain, which he loaned to the show.

These men were all part of the London business and political worlds centred on the City and at Westminster. As were Francis Fry and Henry H. Gibbs. Francis Fry (1803–1886) was the grandson of the founder of Fry's chocolate and known as both a 'china' and book collector.[18] His particular interest was in early bibles, on which he published several studies. As a ceramics collector, Fry specialized in Bristol wares, which he loaned to the Club's exhibition, but he was not a Club member.[19] Henry H. Gibbs was Henry Hucks Gibbs, who was a lender to the Ferrara exhibition discussed in Chapter 1, and would be made 1st Baron Aldenham in 1896, a name under which he is sometimes listed. Gibbs was a director and Governor of the Bank of England, then an MP for the City of London.[20] He loaned examples of Worcester porcelain to the exhibition,[21] yet was better known for his library. Like Fry and several other lenders and members of the Club, he was a prominent book collector,[22] with books seeming to be another parallel interest for a number of members throughout the Club's history. 'Charles Luard' also was not known as a ceramics collector. He was probably Maj.-Gen. Charles Edward Luard (1839–1908), made famous today for the story of the murder of his wife, Caroline, and his own suicide.[23] He loaned Vienna and Italian porcelain to the exhibition.[24]

Two people associated with Whistler were lenders. Lady Dorothy Nevill (1826–1913) was a plant collector, writer, and friend of Whistler and Disraeli. She wrote memoirs and corresponded with Darwin, to whom she supplied rare plants.[25] Not able to be a member of the Club, she nonetheless knew men who were. She loaned 11 pieces (with her husband).[26] Robert W. Edis (later Sir, 1839–1927) was a prominent architect and member of the Club. Whistler lived in rooms designed by Edis in Tite Street, London,[27] and Edis seems to have collected some Dresden porcelain, as evidenced by his participation in the exhibition.[28]

Some lenders were dedicated ceramics collectors, however. J. E. Nightingale, for example, was possibly James Nightingale (1838–1908), who was noted as a collector of Worcester porcelain[29] and published his own works on *Early English Porcelain* (1881) and church plate. He loaned about 15 pieces to the exhibition, the bulk of which was Worcester porcelain. Other lenders supplied porcelains that were likely part of their household goods, and might be seen as part of what are now called country house collections. Baron Mayer de Rothschild MP (Mayer Amschel, 1818–1874), of the banking family and a Liberal MP for Hythe in Kent,[30] loaned seven Sèvres jardinières to the exhibition[31] and was a member of the Club. The 'Marquis of Westminster' was probably Hugh Grosvenor (1825–1899), who was made Duke of Westminster in 1874. Apart from inheriting the great family landholdings, he was an MP for Chester and then later entered the House of Lords.[32]

These selected lenders were representative of Club membership and Club associates in that period. Their ownership of ceramics is also characteristic, representing a special interest for some, but also non-specialist ownership for others. Their different social, professional, and collecting backgrounds confirm not only that Club members' interests were wide ranging but also that owners of ceramics were equally diverse. It seems that ceramics, at least in Britain, were an extremely common object type to possess and collect in the second half of the nineteenth century. Several lenders to this exhibition likely inherited porcelains that perhaps were once (and still) used as household objects but others clearly collected them intentionally.

As the sources of the exhibits demonstrate therefore, in the 1870s, ceramics occupied an interesting conceptual space, moving between the functional and the decorative, often at the same time. The question we need to ask here, then, is, when did ceramics begin to transcend this space, becoming collectibles, as opposed to functional items in Britain? When could this be called collecting as opposed to consumption or a sub-category of consumption? It has been argued elsewhere that the porcelain rooms of the early seventeenth century might be the place to start, representing as they do presentations of collected and therefore transformed functional ceramics. In these rooms, ceramics were grouped en masse and displayed on the walls, becoming part of the interior decoration. This is one reason why ceramics are a common feature in period room displays.

The ceramics presented in porcelain rooms before 1750 were made in China and later Japan, and thus this practice itself can be seen to begin with Chinese porcelain (made earlier than the Japanese). Such ceramics, generally in vessel form, represented both exotica and the quotidian at the same time.[33] Their conceptualization and classification as exotica can be traced back even further in Britain to the sixteenth-century displays of mounted Chinese ceramics, often presented alongside other 'curiosities', a process that was itself transformative but also associated with a dedicated space. This type of display, and the later massing of ceramics in dedicated rooms, can be interpreted as helping to re-categorize Asian ceramics as performing a decorative function, but it is only one form of collecting. The conceptualization of Asian ceramics as non-functional, collectible objects beyond interior display probably begins with their transformation into antiques, an early nineteenth-century phenomenon. Prior to this, a certain type of ceramic became collectible in a different way, through associations with Classical art and archaeology in the eighteenth century. This was the period of 'Greek vase mania' that will be discussed with reference to the next exhibition in this chapter.

For Asian ceramics, their transformation came on the heels of this mania and the consequent Neoclassical revival in design which signalled the end of Chinoiserie. It was at this time, in the early nineteenth century, that Asian ceramics came to be called 'old china', as can be seen in the catalogue of Joseph Banks' collection of 1807.[34] Subsequently, there was the sale of Queen Charlotte's collection in 1819, a resale of ceramics that then were no longer household goods, giving these transformed collectibles a collection provenance. From the 1850s, specialist ceramic literature began to emerge, contributing to the identification of ceramics as a collectible medium. Survey texts on world ceramics and specialist types such as 'English porcelain' became commonplace, with one of the most important (and the first) being Joseph Marryat's *Collections towards a History of Pottery and Porcelain in the 15th–18th Centuries* (London, 1850) which, along with Chaffers' *Marks and Monograms on Pottery and Porcelain* (London, 1863), became a manual for collectors. A typological standardization developed where ceramics as objects were then given their own vocabulary. Marryat (Joseph II, 1790–1876) was not a dealer like Chaffers, but rather a banker, a Member of Parliament and advocate for plantation owners in the West Indies. He was the son of a prominent plantation owner who had holdings in Trinidad, Jamaica, Grenada and St Lucia[35] and began to write about ceramics, among other topics, after his retirement from politics.

In the 1860s and 1870s, thanks to artists like Whistler and Rossetti, a new Chinamania, associated with the Aesthetic Movement, would follow on from this, encouraged by the art market at that time. The dealer Murray Marks was a main player in this, for example. By the time of the Club's first major ceramic-themed exhibition, therefore, ceramics were perceived as objects that could perform on several levels, at once both as decorative objects and increasingly as 'art', unlike paintings and prints. There was a desire expressed in 1873 to include ceramics in the wider category of objects of art and to define a classificatory system for them as art objects with a history. Displays like the Club's exhibition and accompanying publications contributed to this activity and led to a developing specialist field of ceramic collecting and ceramics in art history, particularly for non-western wares.

The Catalogue

It can be argued that, in 1873, the Club was a driving force in this move towards specialist ceramic collecting and scholarship. The catalogue for its exhibition, while clearly somewhat basic, was nonetheless detailed and prescriptive. Unlike in later Club exhibition catalogues, few of the objects are singled out and there is no introductory essay which would help to determine what the Club's perspective on the subject was, but the catalogue did serve a connoisseurship function, as it gave a list of contents and lenders as well as providing names for wares, histories of their production, and a vocabulary for shapes, designs, and colours. As noted previously, a number of pieces are described as 'fine examples' of their type, giving the reader (and viewer) a guide to what to aim for. In two cases, the rarity or understudied nature of certain exhibits is briefly mentioned. For example, in the section on 'Dresden (Meissen)', the author (unknown – presumably one of the subcommittee members) states: 'Special notice should be taken of two figures ... Lent by Mr Seymour Haden, of great rarity and of the finest quality.'[36] And in the section on Bristol, 'Very fine examples of this important but comparatively little known fabric have been most kindly lent for exhibition ...',[37] indicating that scholarship on this ware was not well developed at that time. Indeed, the first publication on Bristol porcelain was only printed in 1873: Hugh Owen's *Two Centuries of Ceramic Art in Bristol. Being a History of the Manufacture of "The True Porcelain" by Richard Champion ...*' (London, 1873). Bristol porcelain is mentioned in earlier publications, such as the first edition of Chaffer's *Marks and Monograms* (1863: 137–138) and even earlier in Marryat (1850: 187) but in the exhibition catalogue, it is clear that very little still was known about the ware.

The exhibition itself is also an early example of a ceramics display which included both English and 'Continental' porcelain. In fact, it is the earliest non-institutional exhibition of collected porcelain in Britain. There had been an earlier show on a similar subject at the Department of Science and Art, the precursor to the South Kensington Museum, but this was not from multiple private collections, only that of the Queen, with a catalogue written by Robinson.[38] As noted above, porcelain was also exhibited at the Great Exhibition in 1851 – all types, including vessels, raw materials, and objects – from many regions, representing ceramic manufacture.[39] The South Kensington Museum exhibited porcelains in its own collections (loaned or otherwise) of various types after this but it was the Club's exhibition that was the first dedicated survey exhibition of that ceramic subject. In its identification and presentation as a Club exhibition theme, therefore, British and continental porcelain was presented as well as interpreted as 'art', physically removing the objects from the product or craft categories in which other public exhibitions tended to situate ceramics.

This form of art historical presentation and reclassification was adopted in other specialist ceramic areas in a way that was more seamless because of pre-existing art historical frameworks for the subject area concerned. This is particularly notable with the subject of the next exhibition, Greek ceramics.

1888 Greek Ceramic Art

In the eighteenth century, Greek 'vases' (the most popular terminology) began to be collected, as we have seen, but not necessarily as ceramics. They became collectible ceramics for other reasons. As the texts concerned with Greek vases of the time demonstrate, particularly the catalogues of William Hamilton's collection, Greek ceramics were collected as a form of Classical art.[40] This was representative of the context of the time, when the Neoclassical fashion in design, Classical archaeology, and the collecting of Classical (Greek and Roman) art was in full swing, and ceramics contributed to this. Nonetheless, as Greek 'vases' became a singular type of Classical art to collect, this brought ceramics into the art collecting milieu.

Greek vase collecting fell out of favour somewhat by the mid-nineteenth century but by then, ceramic collecting in general had started to become more popular, as we have seen. Nonetheless, Greek vases were still conceptualized as 'art' rather than 'ceramics'. By the late nineteenth century, there was a resurgence of interest in Greek vases and the Club would mount an exhibition that neatly situated these objects into the collecting category of 'ceramics'. The Club's exhibition was instigated by a collector and unusually for the Club, focussed on a single collection. As noted in the General Committee minutes for this exhibition:

31.1.1888

VII It was agreed that an Exhibition of Greek Art be held in the Gallery as early as practicable after the close of the Japanese Exhibition, and that the offer of Mr Van Branteghem's Collection be accepted, and that he be informed that arrangements would be made for his personally placing his Collection in the Gallery during the first fortnight in April.

7.2.1888

III The following gentlemen were appointed the Subcommittee for the forthcoming Exhibition of Greek Ceramic Art, viz: Sir William Drake, Mr Tebbs, Mr Waterfield, and Mr Van Branteghem. [Mr Tebb's name was subsequently erased by his request.][41]

21.2.1888

W Bode elected honorary member of the Club.

5.5.1888

IX The Chairman on behalf of the Exhibition Subcommittee reported the arrangements which had been made for the opening of the Exhibition and the … of an Illustrated Catalogue of the Greek Ceramic Collection, by which Mr van Branteghem had undertaken its cost, and to take himself any copies not subscribed for, handing over to the Club any surplus of the subscriptions, after deduction of his expenditure. Copy of circular provided.[42]

The amount of organizational information surviving for this exhibition is unusual in that we are told specifically why the topic was chosen – because it was offered by the collector, a Club member. Possibly that is also why the final title selected by the Club for the exhibition was chosen: 'Greek Ceramic *Art*' (my emphasis). This title is different from that of the other ceramic exhibitions in that it describes the ceramics as 'art'. In this it is, however, in keeping with the traditional classification of decorated Greek ceramics as fine art, where it is their decoration that is therefore of primary interest, rather than the material. The Club, however, described these ceramics as representative of ceramic art, thus retaining an overt association with the medium that is normally elided with the 'Greek vases' category. In the previous ceramics exhibition of 1873, the Club attributed ceramic types to location of production, such as Dresden, Bristol, Buen Retiro, in the manner in which ceramics were typically classified and identified at the time (and still are today). Thus, for the Club, 'Greek vases' became 'Greek Ceramic Art'.

As the emphasis on the pictorial in Greek ceramics had become commonplace by the later nineteenth century, the Club's exhibition appears to be the first to apply a more refined, ceramic-centred version of it. It is also incidentally the first dedicated exhibition of a collection in private hands of Greek vases in Britain, reflecting a general resurgence of interest in Greek vases in the late nineteenth century. The first public exhibition of Greek vases in Britain was at the British Museum in 1772, the Hamilton collection,[43] where the first Greek vases had arrived with the Sloane Collection in 1753.[44] In 1832, an exhibition of vases excavated from Vulci by Secondiano Campanari was displayed at his home in London, but the intention was to sell the pieces.[45]

As we will see, the same could be argued for the collection on which the Club's exhibition was based. The cataloguing of the objects and the content of the introductory essay to the Club's exhibition catalogue are directly linked to the collector van Branteghem and his collection on display, and reflect the recent development of the 'authorship' approach to classifying Greek ceramics, that is, by named painter. This approach can be said to have been inspired by van Branteghem's collection, as it started with the work of A. Furtwangler and W. Klein, German scholars who both published important works in the 1880s.[46] Some of this work was based on the van Branteghem collection, which was in fact one of the major private collections on which much scholarship was based at the time.[47] Alphonse van Branteghem (d. 1911), who served on the exhibition committee, was a Belgian lawyer and collector of mainly Greek objects.[48] His collection was sold in 1892, and thereafter became a major provenance for Greek vases, with the Club's exhibition of it also cited. The author of the Club's exhibition catalogue, honorary Club member 'Dr. W. Fröhner, Conservateur des Musées Impériaux' was also friends with the collector, reflecting the close relationship between scholarship and the market at the time.[49] The work of Paul Hartwig (1859–1919), particularly *Griechische Meisterschalen* (1893), was informed by his first-hand knowledge of the van Branteghem collection (Hartwig also acted as the collector's agent in Rome),[50] and J. D. Beazley's (1885–1970) seminal work on vase painters would be indebted to this collection, which he visited, and its classification.[51]

Frohner's framing of Greek vases through authorship thus reflected contemporary scholarship but it also retained their fine art status. The 'star' pieces in the Club's show therefore included examples by 'famous' painters, such as Euphronios, and the cup in catalogue no. 8 (see Plate 5). The cup is now in the MFA Boston (95.27) and was purchased from the 1892 Drouot sale of the van Branteghem collection by Edward Perry Warren (1860–1928), from whom the museum purchased it.[52] Van Branteghem himself had purchased it as late as 1887 from Mrs Hamilton Gray (Elizabeth, *c.* 1801–1887), who has been described as 'the female pioneer of Etruscology in Britain'. A published author of numerous texts, including *History of Etruria*, she was an antiquarian of some repute, whose objects were acquired during tours of Italy, visiting newly opened tombs at the invitation of local antiquities dealers.[53] This type of provenance was considered appropriate and even ideal at that time.

Other Lenders and Exhibits

While Mrs Hamilton Gray was not a lender, the Club's committee minutes indicate that the purpose of the exhibition was essentially the showcasing of this one private collection, an unusual approach for the Club whose exhibitions tended to involve many different lenders.[54] Indeed, objects nos 1–82 are all from van Branteghem's collection with just a small number of other pieces supplied by a range of Club members and associates of members. Sir William Drake, Club and exhibition committee member, for example, contributed four pieces, none by named painters, but he was also a contributor to the previous exhibition of ceramics in 1873 (see above). Another Club member and contributor was C. Drury Fortnum, who will be discussed with reference to his Middle Eastern ceramics collection (see Chapter 3). Henry H. Gibbs contributed to this as well as the 1873 exhibition, as we have seen, and a Charles Butler contributed one piece. This may be Charles Butler (1821–1910), Justice of the Peace, a committee member for the New Gallery discussed in Chapter 1. J. Stewart Hodgson (James, 1827–1899) was a banker and close friend and patron of Lord Leighton (a Club member) who painted a portrait of Steward Hodgson's daughters.[55] He contributed five pieces, two of which were published by Klein in *Meistersignaturen*.[56] C. Brinsley Marlay (Charles, 1831–1912) was a major benefactor to the Fitzwilliam Museum, Cambridge.[57] He loaned three pieces to the exhibition. Henry Vaughan we will look at with reference to the Persian Art exhibition in Chapter 3 and O. C. Waterfield was the Bensons' headmaster who was discussed in Chapter 1. Waterfield loaned 12 small terracotta figures to the exhibition.[58]

The next contributors named in the catalogue were not members but clearly were associated with them. Alfred Lawson (?–1921), for example, was a collector of coins and classical antiquities, including Greek jewellery, much of which was purchased by the British Museum. Lawson was based in Smyrna, as director of the Ottoman Bank there, and had corresponded with Franks, a founder member of the Club.[59] According to the Club's exhibition catalogue, Lawson was asked to send a few pieces from Smyrna.[60] The Marquis of Northampton was possibly the 4th Marquis, Admiral William Compton (1818–1897), who had also been a lender to the 1894 exhibition discussed in Chapter 1.[61] He loaned nos 101–117 in the catalogue, including three pieces that were described as 'magnificent' in the introductory essay.[62] One object loaned by a W. Paton (n.d.) was described as 'one of the most beautiful in existence'.[63] This was exhibit no. 120, an 'attic Lekythos' that is now in the Museum of Fine Arts, Boston (00.359) (Figure 2.1). This was also acquired from the collection of Edward Perry Warren.[64] Indeed, in the catalogue entry, the skill and beauty of the painting are said to be only equalled by that of 'the greatest masters of the Renaissance'.[65] Such language reinforces the association of the exhibits with the fine arts and painting, rather than ceramics.

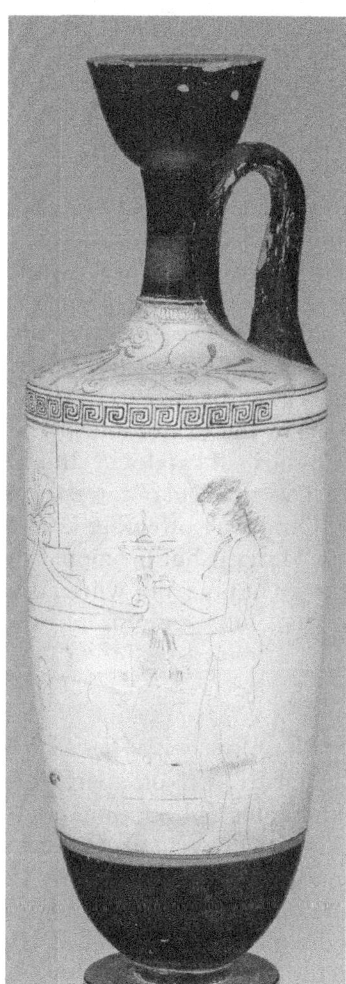

Figure 2.1 Oil flask (*lekythos*), the Thanatos Painter, Greek, Classical Period, about 440–430 BC. Ceramic, Height: 40 cm (15 3/4 in.), Museum of Fine Arts, Boston, Henry Lillie Pierce Fund 00.359.

Source: Photograph © 2016 Museum of Fine Arts, Boston.

W. S. Salting (William Severin, 1837–1905) was the brother of Club member George Salting (see Chapter 1).[66] He loaned two terracotta figurines. 'The Right Hon. W. H. Smith, MP' was William Henry Smith (1825–1891), of the bookseller and newsagent family, who held several prominent government offices, including Leader of the House of Commons.[67] He loaned four terracotta figures to the exhibition. The final contributor was Hermann D. Weber, MD (1823–1918), who was a prominent physician whose patients included several prime ministers.[68] He also clearly collected Greek ceramics as he loaned nos 125–141 to the exhibition.

The contributor profile is similar to that of other Club exhibitions but the presentation and interpretation of the material displayed in the exhibition are notable as they are at once innovative in their application of current scholarship approaches and yet also representative of the connoisseurship style of writing usually adopted by the Club. This exhibition was also more specialized in its focus than the previous one discussed in this chapter but in fact, for ceramics, this specialization would become the standard approach used by the Club thereafter, as the next three ceramics exhibitions will demonstrate.

1895 Blue and White Oriental Porcelain

After the exhibition of Greek Ceramic Art, the next ceramics-themed exhibition was 'Blue and White Oriental Porcelain' in 1895. In the minutes of the General Committee meetings, it is briefly stated that:

17.7.1894

IV It was agreed to have an Exhibition of Blue China in the Winter, and a Subcommittee was appointed for arranging the same, viz:

Mr W. G. Rawlinson, Mr Monkhouse and Mr Cock[69]

5.3.1895.

II Upon the application of the Blue and White Exhibition Committee for an extension of time it was agreed to keep the Exhibition open a week longer than originally arranged, and to close on Sunday 24th instant.[70]

The casual reference in the minutes to the exhibition topic as 'Blue China' situates it in the older collecting movement known as 'Chinamania' mentioned above that was prevalent in the second half of the nineteenth century.[71] There would naturally be an association with this trend and the group that championed it through the Club's Pre-Raphaelite connections.(see Chapter 1). However, this was not the first exhibition of 'Oriental' ceramics presented by the Club, as we have seen (that was 'Oriental Porcelain' of 1868), but it was the first to focus on China, even though this is not reflected in the final title of the exhibition. It was also the first 'Oriental' ceramics exhibition to have a published catalogue and be focussed on a single style category – blue and white. This particular category is one that was first developed in the commercial world and was often associated with 'Nankin porcelain', a style category mentioned in Marryat but promoted by dealers in association with their invented 'revival' of taste in blue and white, discussed below. It was still a popular theme in 1895 as the Club's extension of the display period for a further week demonstrates.[72]

Lenders and Exhibits

This exhibition was more personal for the committee members as most, apart from one, loaned pieces from their own collections to the exhibition. Cosmo Monkhouse (discussed below) was joined on the committee by Richard Mills (who prepared the catalogue entries), Walter Armstrong (who did not lend), Alfred Cock and W. G. Rawlinson. It was Armstrong who had written the catalogue for the exhibition of Masters of the Netherlandish School (1892), which was discussed in Chapter 1. W. G. Rawlinson (1840–1928) was a Turner scholar and collector and primarily responsible for the Club's earlier Turner exhibition and reproduction of Turner's *Liber Studiorum* (1872) (see Chapter 1).[73] Richard Mills (d. 1901) was a solicitor[74] and had been a member of the short-lived Hogarth Club, founded in 1858 as an alternative space for artists like Rossetti to display their work.[75] He was a collector of a number of the Club members' works, including those of Rossetti and Burne-Jones, and these were sold after his death by Christie's in the Modern Pictures and Drawings sale of 13 April 1908. His Chinese porcelain collection, much of which had been displayed in the Club's exhibitions, was sold three days earlier, with the Club's exhibitions prominently noted to promote the sale.[76] This is a good example of how the Club's exhibitions came to be part of the art historical infrastructure of the art market, a notable seal of approval for the works sold.

Another lender to the exhibition played an even more prominent role in both the wider art world and also the ceramics collecting field. Cosmo Monkhouse (William, 1840–1901) was a prominent Victorian art critic.[77] A painting specialist, he nonetheless wrote the introductory essay to the Blue and White catalogue, as well as that for the subsequent exhibition of Coloured Chinese Porcelain.[78] As we have seen, Club members' expertise was rarely seen as confined to one type of art or region of art production and Monkhouse's essay on blue and white can therefore be seen as informative on several levels. It focuses on China and it begins historiographically with a survey history of the collecting and study of the subject. It then continues with a history of production in China, thus situating his essay in the encyclopaedic literature of ceramics as pioneered in English by Marryat. He also treats blue and white as a collecting fashion, noting that at the end of the eighteenth century and up to the middle of the nineteenth century, blue and white was out of favour in Britain.[79] But he then states that this had changed in recent years:

> Of recent years blue-and-white has had its revenge in England, the taste for it having risen almost to a mania. Pieces which, forty years ago, could have been purchased for a few sovereigns, perhaps for a few shillings, have sold for hundreds of pounds ...
>
> Amongst the most famous collections are, or were, those of the late Dante Gabriel Rossetti, Mr. Whistler, Mr. Louis Huth, Sir Henry Thompson and Mr Alfred Morrison.[80]

Each of the collectors mentioned above was a member of the Club and each is associated with a 'collection' of blue and white, a unifying treatment that membership of the Club enabled and conferred. Monkhouse later mentions Salting and the fact that Huth's collection was still intact at the time of the exhibition. (This would later be sold in the early twentieth century.) He also noted that: 'the British Museum [had] what is probably the most complete collection (historically considered) in the world', which he attributes to Franks. In 1895, Monkhouse believed that Franks's catalogue of his own collection (1876) was 'still the most complete and trustworthy summary of existing knowledge of the subject'.[81] With the revival of interest in blue and white around 1860–1870, the Club's exhibition seems to be taking place at the right time in that it was following on from recent developments in the field, similarly to the Greek ceramic exhibition, albeit slightly later. It was also organized by and contributed to by most of the main collectors of Chinese porcelain at that time in England, as identified by the Club. To some extent, therefore, the Club's exhibition and catalogue fuelled the revived taste for blue and white and extended interest in it, as there were no similar non-commercial exhibitions of the subject at that time. Thus, there is a suggestion of promoting the topic to justify collecting as clearly practised by the exhibition committee members. The role of dealers in this and the initial revival (or construction) of taste in blue and white will be discussed below.

As noted, the title of the exhibition is 'Oriental' but the focus of Monkhouse's essay, and indeed the exhibition itself, is *Chinese* blue and white. There was one case in the exhibition that featured Japanese blue and white (case J) and most of this material was lent by two collectors: W. C. Alexander and R. Phene Spiers.

William Cleverly Alexander was the wealthy banker, art patron, and collector noted in the Introduction, whose daughters were painted by Whistler, and who was a great patron of the artist (and a Club member).[82] He also collected Japanese woodblock prints and Chinese ceramics. His ceramics collection is interesting from our perspective because it included what was fashionable, for example, Qing porcelains and Japanese blue and white, but also Song ceramics, which were only just gaining popularity at that time.[83] Richard Phene Spiers (1838–1916) was a prominent architect,[84] who had worked for Club member Digby Wyatt. He was also clearly a ceramics collector, as his many loans to the blue and white exhibition attest. He was not a Club member, however.

The exhibition contents also demonstrate that it was up to date with developments in both collecting and knowledge in the field of Chinese ceramics. It includes Chinese sherds, for example, that were excavated at Fostat in Egypt and lent by Franks (Case A). Fustat (old Cairo) was first formally excavated in 1912 but bits and pieces were coming out after 1867 and the advent of autonomous rule in Egypt.[85] Sherds are commonly exhibited today but their early display by the Club can be seen to represent their parallel interest in archaeology, as will be discussed in Chapter 3. Also current in the blue and white exhibition was the inclusion of information about what are known as 'reign marks' which are emphasized in the catalogue essay. By that stage, reign marks were a standard way of classifying Chinese ceramics, e.g. 'Ming, Chenghua period'. This began around 1875 in English-language texts and is still a widely used form of classification today.[86] At the time of the Club's exhibition, it was thought that reign marks had started to appear much earlier than they are known to have appeared today, so the essay erroneously mentions Hongwu (1368–1392) reign marks, for example.[87] Nonetheless, it was known by 1895 that earlier reign marks were to be found on later pieces and even on export wares. In one example, Monkhouse states that the Chenghua (1465–1487) reign mark found on no. 304 is 'ludicrous' (cat. p. xv – it is clearly an eighteenth-century piece), but this is part and parcel of 'the difficulties of determining the age of Chinese porcelain ... ([as]...date marks are no certain indication of the period in which the piece was made'[88] (see Plate 6).

Monkhouse does not include a bibliography but it is clear that his essay is informed by the work of Stephen Bushell (1844–1908), who translated Chinese texts on porcelain, starting in 1886 ('Chinese Porcelain Before the Present Dynasty') and by Stanislas Julien (1797–1873) whose *Histoire de la Fabrication de la Porcelaine Chinoise* was published in 1856. This was a translation of the Chinese text *Jingdezhen taolu* of 1815.[89] The Chinese texts provided information about production, including cobalt and its sources, different techniques of decoration, etc. which Monkhouse has noted (e.g. p. xv, on 'imported blue'). There are also certain quotations which clearly came from Chinese sources such as:

> In the list of the china furnished for the Emperor we read of '31,000 dishes with flowers; 16,000 white plates with blue dragons; 18,400 cups for flowers or wine, with two dragons in the midst of clouds; 11,250 dishes, white ground with blue flowers ...'.[90]

This would likely have come from Julien's translation of the *Jingdezhen taolu*. Citing the quotation above, Monkhouse notes that blue and white was probably made in the

Yuan period (1279–1368) but also suggests that it was made long before. At the time of the exhibition, no Yuan blue and white was known in England so this is also indicative of the extent of knowledge at the time.

None of the exhibits is singled out by Monkhouse as a masterpiece but the overall composition of the exhibition is of blue and white vessels in a wide range of forms but mainly dishes and bowls. Some designs were singled out, however, indicating their popularity among collectors of the time. The most notable is the so-called 'hawthorn' pattern which is actually a prunus and appeared on mass-produced blue and white 'ginger jars' such as the famous one owned by Louis Huth, which was sold in 1905 for £6,000, a record price.[91] It does not appear to have been lent to the exhibition. Monkhouse mentions the hawthorn design in his Introduction, and in the main catalogue a whole paragraph is given over to it on page 14 to introduce an entire section of Case C devoted to it.[92] This pattern was popularized by the likes of Rossetti who featured it in the background of one of his portraits.[93] Rossetti and members of the Aesthetic Movement were also responsible for the popularity of the 'aster' design which is also given its own section in Case C.[94] Whistler can perhaps be attributed with the popularization of Chinese porcelain decorated with seemingly languid female figures (usually court ladies in fact), whom he imitated in his paintings and described as 'long Elizas'. Some of the mainly seventeenth-century porcelains with this design served as props in his paintings.[95]

A final note about the contents of the exhibition, which is also indicative of its time, is the inclusion of 'powder blue' wares in an exhibition of blue and white. These would today be classified as monochromes, not blue and white, but in the late nineteenth century, they were extremely popular (Case H). Just as this ware would not today be called 'blue and white', an exhibition of that title would also be unlikely to include mounted porcelains, as this one does. One example was even loaned by Franks, from his own personal collection, but it did enter the British Museum shortly afterwards (exhibit no. 15) (Figure 2.2).

In addition to Franks, the list of lenders in general is informative, as it includes, as usual, both members and non-members of the Club. The members of the exhibition committee we have already looked at and others, such as Franks, Huth, Read, and Salting have been covered in other chapters (respectively, Introduction, Chapter 3, and Chapter 1). 'Tebbs', however, is interesting. He was Henry Virtue Tebbs (1833–1899) who was a solicitor and collector of a wide range of objects, including works by his close friend D. G. Rossetti. Tebbs was married to Emily Seddon, and according to William Rossetti, was 'well known in the legal world and as a collector of many objects of art'.[96] Tebbs wrote the catalogue for the Club's posthumous exhibition of D. G. Rossetti's work in 1883 and sold a large collection of Japanese *tsubas* to the V&A in 1888.[97] After his death, his collections of books and objects were sold at Sotheby's in 1900. Other contributors to the Club's exhibition of blue and white are interesting for the revelation that they were ceramics collectors, which is not usually mentioned in their biographies. William Agnew (1825–1910), for example, was the founder of Agnews art dealership in Mayfair and is best known for paintings. He was created a baronet in the same year as the exhibition, but was not a member, of course.[98] The Lord Battersea was Cyril Flower (1843–1907), Whistler's patron and Liberal MP.[99] George H. Boughton, A.R.A (1833–1905), Club member, was the painter and friend of Whistler and Henry James.[100] J. Annan Bryce (1841–1923)

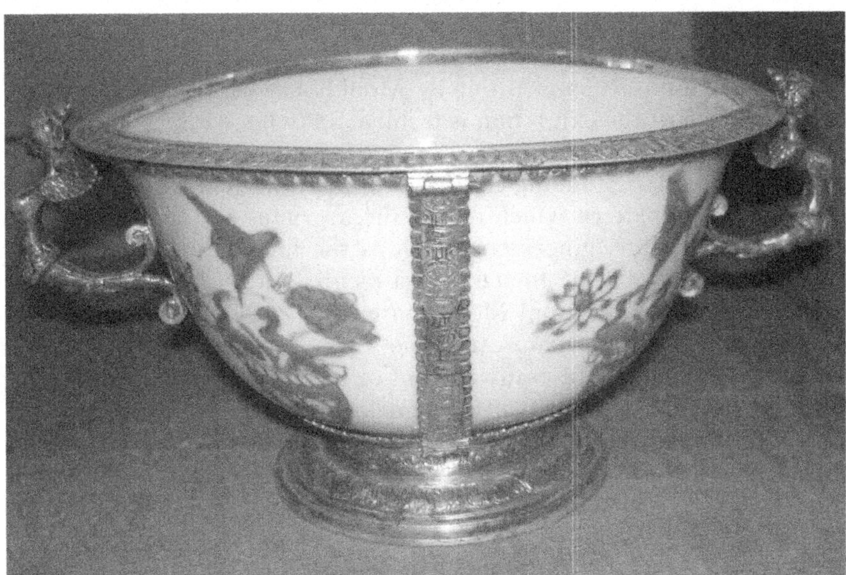

Figure 2.2 Bowl with silver gilt mounts, China, Wanli period, 1573–1619; mounts 1580, probably English. Porcelain decorated with underglaze cobalt blue. Height: 9.6 cm, width: 15.7. Bequeathed by Sir Augustus Wollaston Franks, AF.3131.

Source: © Trustees of the British Museum, London.

was a businessman, MP, and Director of the Burma railway,[101] and a Club member. Wickham Flower (b. *c.* 1836) was also a friend and patron of Whistler, as well as a Club member.[102] Frederick Wedmore (1844–1921) was an art critic and Club member who had a somewhat contentious relationship with Whistler, even though he greatly admired his work and published books about his etchings.[103] J. P. Heseltine (John Postle, 1843–1929), was a stockbroker, etcher, and collector, primarily of old master pictures.[104] He was also a trustee of the National Gallery and a good friend of Whistler, like so many of the other lenders, but was not a Club member at the time of the exhibition.

Sir Henry Thompson (1820–1904) was yet another friend of Whistler and a prominent surgeon. He collected Chinese blue and white with the help of the dealer, Murray Marks (1840–1918) and Whistler illustrated a catalogue of the collection, published in 1878 in time for its display and sale.[105] This collection and catalogue then became a provenance for subsequent collectors, as no. 284 in the Club's exhibition catalogue notes: 'A PAIR OF PRECISELY SIMILAR DISHES (in bottom shelf), purchased at the sale of Sir Henry Thompson's in 1878, and shown in Mr. Whistler's Illustration to that catalogue, plate XVII.'[106]

Along with Whistler, Marks can be said to have played a leading role in initiating a 'revival' of interest in blue and white, using that category name several times in his published catalogues. A leading figure in the Aesthetic Movement, Marks has been the subject of several studies.[107] For our purposes, he was the agent behind several of the collections from which loans were contributed to the Club's exhibition and therefore part of the commercial infrastructure of the Club's main activity, yet was personally excluded from membership. Joel Duveen (1843–1908) would also fall into this category and was instrumental in fuelling the revival of taste or in fact creating a new taste for blue and white, particularly 'Nankin' in the 1860s with sales of Dutch collections that were then being broken up.[108] The influence of these dealers in this collecting and ceramics category needs to be highlighted, particularly as they seem to have invented it, while packaging it cleverly as a 'revival'. From a wider perspective, the role of dealers here and the number of non-member contributors to Club exhibitions suggests too that membership was not a prerequisite for participation in the wider Club sphere or to benefit from it.

Other members were not so closely connected to Whistler but were associated with other artists and artistic movements, including as makers and patrons. Val. C. Princep, R.A., for example, was not a member of the Club at the time of the exhibition but he had been in the past.[109] Princep (Valentine Cameron, 1838–1904) was the artist and member of the Pre-Raphaelite Brotherhood. His painting, *A Nautch Girl* (1878) was widely admired at the time and is today in the Royal Collection.[110] Another lender, Major General R. Mackenzie, Club member, is listed as the owner of the painting by George Romney of *Lady Hamilton as Titania* (1793; Folger library today, FPa48) in a book published in 1903.[111] T. Humphry Ward (Thomas, 1845–1926), was a Club member, author, and journalist. He was married to the writer Mary Augusta, aka Mrs Humphry Ward, author of *Robert Ellsmere* (1888).[112]

Not surprisingly, this Club exhibition therefore was populated by a number of members of the Pre-Raphaelite and Aesthetic Movements, key artist circles that intersected with and supported the work of the Club. A significant further connection between many of the lenders to this exhibition was the artist Whistler, and his own association with blue and white porcelain. As an artist, he collected blue and white for a specific purpose, but he influenced other collectors by raising interest in this ware and promoting it through his paintings, illustrations in catalogues, and interior design work. Collectors of Whistler's own work became part of this porcelain network, as is demonstrated by a study of the lenders to the Club's show in 1895. It is therefore somewhat ironic that Whistler had been so spectacularly expelled from the Club in its early days.

1896 Coloured Chinese Porcelain

Blue and white was not the only type of Chinese (sometimes Japanese but often undifferentiated) porcelain collected by members and associates of the Club. As a subsequent exhibition demonstrates, taste in Chinese ceramics was significantly broader than just blue and white but the material was also quickly being defined specifically as 'Chinese'. This is the first Club exhibition specifically to do so for ceramics. There had been earlier exhibitions of specifically Chinese and Japanese art (1878) and Japanese engravings (1888) (see Appendix A), thus signalling an early regionalizing approach to non-western material by the Club, but for ceramics, this exhibition of 1896 was the first.

The General Committee minutes for this exhibition do not give an indication why and are brief, noting simply that:

11.2.1896

III It was decided to organize an Exhibition of Coloured Oriental Porcelain to be opened in the Club Gallery in May next, and the following gentlemen were appointed a Subcommittee to carry out the arrangement: Mr Cock Mr Mills Mr Monkhouse Mr Rawlinson and Mr Salting.[113]

The exhibition of 'coloured Chinese porcelain' mounted in May of 1896 was generally seen as a sequel to the blue and white exhibition, as both its timing and the introductory essay to the catalogue indicate. This second category of Chinese porcelain was defined as anything with colour, e.g. enamelled wares and monochromes. This exhibition had more lenders than the blue and white one, and two more people on its subcommittee, now including George Salting (see Introduction and Appendix B for biographical details).[114] The introductory essay to the catalogue states that the exhibition is confined to Chinese works because Japanese porcelain needed a whole exhibition to itself, which ultimately never transpired. Monkhouse, the author, also stated that he did not want to duplicate the essay in the previous catalogue but the result is that this one essentially is only a list.

Nonetheless, it is instructive for its use of the terminology of the time, both descriptive and technological, e.g. 'baking' for firing, and 'Naples yellow' for pale yellow; puce (cat. no. 12) for dark red or purple, and 'self glaze' for monochromes. The latter is further said to be the highest class of Chinese porcelains: 'In no class of porcelain is the supremacy of the Chinese more complete than in that of the single coloured glazes',[115] reflecting the prevailing taste of the time in England. The style categories in which the porcelains are divided, such as *famille verte* and *famille rose* are attributed to Albert Jacquemart,[116] and Marryat is cited as a source where an exhibit was previously illustrated.[117] The essay also reveals what styles of porcelain were popular at that time, including 'sang de bœuf' which has a mottled dark red glaze, and what is today called *fahua*, which has a dark blue base glaze and is decorated with other colours confined to raised slip lines:

> Amongst the most curious pieces to be found in these cases are a few in which the surface has been modelled so as to raise an edge round the decorative compartments, thus allowing several colours to be used without running into one another in the kiln, a device similar to that of *cloissons* in enamel.[118]

Two *sang de bœuf* pieces are singled out as masterpieces: 'the most celebrated of all these colours is that named by the French "sang de bœuf." The examples in the exhibition which nearest approach perfection are Mr. Manchester's bowl (No. 271) and Mr. Davies' splendid jar (No. 217).'[119] But in spite of the praise for monochromes, Monkhouse states that most of exhibition consists of polychrome wares. Interestingly, 'Egg shell' is considered a separate category at that time, referring to very thin-bodied wares but not a particular colour or glaze. Other types are less conveniently categorized, including wares with black base glazes, which even in 1896 were more commonly called *famille noire*, but not here. One related piece, with white flowers on a black ground, was, however, identified as unique: 'Mr Louis Huth whose bottle (No. 378), decorated with a white floral pattern on a black ground, has the reputation of being unique.'[120] In fact, there are quite a few anomalies in the catalogue and essay, which suggest that the Club's definition of 'coloured wares' was somewhat individual, likely a result of drawing together disparate items from various lenders, rather than intentionally representative of wider scholarship of the time, like the blue and white exhibition. It may also have resulted from the fact that this exhibition was a last-minute replacement (see note 114).

For example, on page 14 of the main catalogue, it is said, erroneously, that green was the 'dynastic' colour for the Ming dynasty, which changed to yellow in the Qing (called 'Tai Tsing'). And several export items were included which do not seem to contribute to a wider narrative, such as no. 164 which has a Dutch coat of arms in the middle, and no. 266 which is red kinrande ware with blue and white inside and English silver mounts. In fact, on p. xii, Monkhouse assumes most of the exhibits were made for the western or foreign markets, whereas his characterization of blue and white wares had a domestic Chinese focus. This reflects a bias towards blue and white by collectors and consumers of blue and white outside China, one that was not shared by Chinese consumers, however. Monkhouse's emphasis on export is interesting because it is in one way innovative. He mentions with reference to numbers 180–182 something described as 'Siamese ware'. These are likely to be examples of what today is known as 'Bencharong' ware, made for the Thai court in the eighteenth and nineteenth centuries.[121] This is still a fairly obscure ware in terms of scholarship so its inclusion here is a surprisingly early appearance (Figure 2.3).

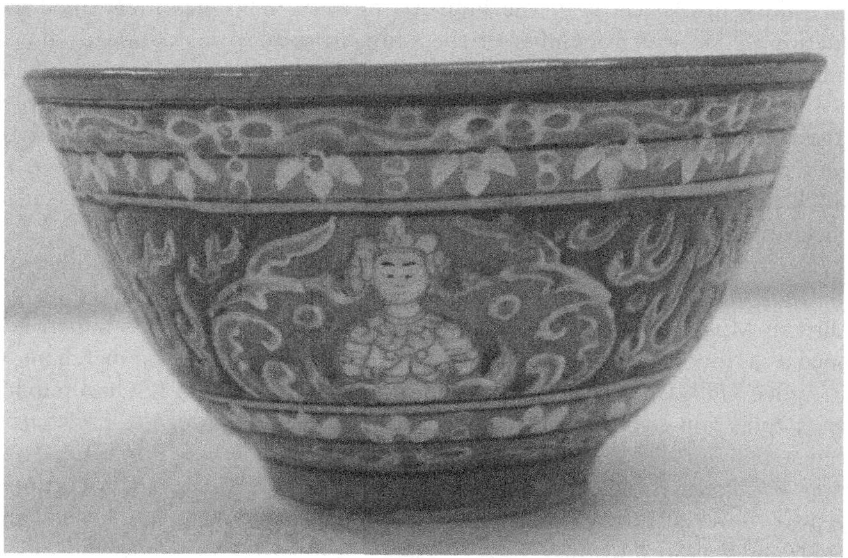

Figure 2.3 Bowl, Qing dynasty, eighteenth century, China, porcelain decorated with overglaze enamels. Height: 22.5 cm, diameter: 4.5 cm, Franks.572.

Source: © Trustees of the British Museum, London.

As with the previous catalogue, the entries here were separately written by Richard Mills, whose collection of ceramics was sold by Christie's after his death, and at the end of the catalogue a table of date marks was included, something which became standard in books on 'oriental' ceramics post-Chaffers. Thus, both the Blue and White and the Coloured Chinese Ceramics catalogues had standard contents for ceramic collectors' books at that time but in the latter case, the exhibits, contents and interpretation were somewhat disconnected and not reflective of the trend towards specialization in the wider field. This itself might be a reflection of the size of the exhibition and the number of exhibits.

Lenders

The Coloured Chinese Porcelain show was a very large exhibition, with 549 exhibits, and more lenders than the previous exhibition. Many of the lenders overlapped but there were others appearing here for the first time. For example, 'W. Arkwright, Esq.' was possibly William Arkwright Esq. (b. 1857), 'a descendant of the famous Sir Richard Arkwright of Spinning Jenny fame. He was a very keen dog breeder and published "The Pointer and His Predecessors".'[122] He does not seem to be noted as a ceramics collector and nor does the next lender, Sir Hickman (Beckett) Bacon (1855–1945), who loaned the 'Siamese' pieces and was a lender to the Ferrara exhibition discussed in Chapter 1. Bacon was the 11th/12th Baronet Redgrave/Mildenhall, High Sheriff of Lincolnshire and a JP.[123] He is best known today for his collection of prints and English watercolours.[124] Marcus B. Huish was the barrister, art dealer, editor of the *Art Journal*, and the first Managing Director of the Fine Art Society, who was mentioned in the Introduction.[125] He was a member of the Club, in spite of his commercial activities, and is not known as a ceramics collector. Nor was S. E. Kennedy (Sydney Ernest, 1855–1933), lender to the Rembrandt etchings exhibition (see Chapter 1) and a trustee of the London Stock Exchange. He was a partner in the family firm of Sydney Kennedy and Co. and is listed in the *Stock Exchange Gazette* of 1914 as a 'stock jobber', market-makers who specialized in certain types of securities. His collection was sold in 1916.[126]

Mrs Edward Bloxam is associated with ceramics, as she may be the mother of the Rev J. F. Bloxam (d. 1928), collector of blue and white. His heirs donated his pieces to the British Museum and the V&A. Edward Bloxam (d. 1891), his father, is also mentioned as a donor.[127] George R. Davies (1844–1918) was a cotton merchant, who lived at Agden Hall, Cheshire. The dealer Edgar Gorer (1872–1915) had purchased the Davies collection two years before perishing in the sinking of the *Lusitania* and produced a catalogue of the collection: *Collection of Old Chinese Porcelains Formed by George R. Davies, Esq., …* (London: Gorer and Son, 1913). Davies' collection was displayed by Gorer at Dreicer and Co in New York City where the dealer Duveen criticized it and was sued for this.[128]

Other more familiar contributors included William Mitchell, Alfred Morrison, Val Princep, W. G. Rawlinson, Charles Read, George Salting, and Henry Virtue Tebbs, who, with the exception of Read, have all been discussed previously but demonstrate the wide interests and professional connections of lenders to a ceramics exhibition.

As usual, therefore, the lender profile for this exhibition is diverse but unusually the exhibition theme and organization were somewhat broad and undefined, even more so than its predecessor. After this exhibition, however, it would seem that at least for the collectors in the Club and their associates, their knowledge of Chinese ceramics, and of China itself, would develop quite considerably over the next 14 years, a development in scholarship and collecting that is related to exposure, a circumstance that is reflected in the third exhibition of Chinese ceramics mounted by the Club in its history.

1910 Early Chinese Pottery and Porcelain

With reference to this exhibition, the General Committee minutes of the Club are detailed and state:

> 6.7.1909
>
> 4 [the numbering changed in the minutes] It was Resolved that the Summer Exhibition consist of Early Chinese Porcelain, Han, Sung and Ming, and that Mr Read and Mr Hobson be appointed a subcommittee with power to add to their number.
>
> 4.1.1910
>
> 4 It was agreed to add to the Summer Exhibition (Chinese Ceramics) Sub Committee the names of Sir Arthur Church, Edward Dillon, Geo. Eumorfopoulos and Col. Lyon.
>
> The Exhibition Committee are empowered to obtain estimates for an Illustrated Catalogue and submit them to the General Committee as soon as practicable. The Exhibition to be opened on Sunday 1st May.
>
> 8.2.1910
>
> IX The Committee approved the invitation to Mr R L Hobson to use the Club as an Honorary Member until the close of the Chinese Ceramics Exhibition.
>
> The Exhibition Subcommittee were authorized to remunerate Mr Hobson at their discretion up to £50.
>
> X It was agreed to invite H E The Chinese Minister to join the Chinese Exhibition Committee.
>
> 3.5.1910
>
> X It was agreed to send invitations to the Exhibition, to the members of the National Art Collections Fund.
>
> 31.5.1910
>
> IV Exhibitions subcommittee consisted of: Lord Balcarres, E Dillon, Sir C Holroyd, Col. Lyons, C H Read, R H Benson, R E Fry (Roger), L C. Lindsay, Earl of Plymouth, W G Rawlinson, Frederick Wedmore.[129]

A number of significant and familiar names appear above, along with the National Art Collections Fund which, as we have seen, had links to a number of Club members and would ultimately be a recipient of the Club's final assets (see the Epilogue). Interestingly, this is also the first mention that any non-members who contributed to Club exhibitions, such as Hobson above, were to be remunerated for this service. It is also notable that the Chinese Minister was invited to join the committee. Unlike the earlier exhibitions of Chinese ceramics, this one was altogether a much more professional project. It was seen as the third in a series, with blue and white plus coloured Chinese porcelain but the subject of the third exhibition was perceived as being less familiar to members than the other two: 'An attempt has been made ... to show the classes of ware that preceded and inspired the later and better known types of Chinese ceramic productions.'[130]

Committee member Charles Read (1857–1929; after being knighted in 1912, he was commonly known as Sir Hercules Read) succeeded Franks at the British Museum and was affiliated with other societies concerned with objects, such as the RAI (see Chapter 4).[131] As the author of the catalogue Preface, Read notes that one of the reasons 'early' Chinese ceramics were less familiar is that dating was uncertain and the quality was 'crude'.[132] But he also notes that due to railway building in China, more examples of the early wares were coming into Europe and this enabled chronological classifications.[133] To put this into context, collectors in the late nineteenth century would have used fine porcelain as their benchmark for quality and this would include export and armorial wares, as seen in the previous two exhibitions. Thus, in comparison, earlier stonewares and earthenwares, of the likes that were increasingly coming out of China, would have seemed crude. This is of course in great contrast to traditional Chinese connoisseurship of ceramics, which for the most part possessed the opposite opinion of stonewares. Nonetheless, Read makes several common assumptions about Chinese consumers in the Preface which result in a conclusion that 'the ancestor-worshipping Chinaman' will appreciate these early wares, even though most came out of tombs.[134] This is evident in the following passage:

> This influx of hitherto little-known specimens is mainly due to the making of railways in China, the necessary excavations disclosing tombs which range in date from about the beginning of the Christian era onwards. The ancestor-worshipping Chinaman has always had a deeply-routed respect for graves, and a strong prejudice against disturbing them. In addition, his respect for antiquity for its own sake, is equally strong, and it may be taken for granted that these ancient vases will be fully appreciated by the Chinese collector. We are fortunately not entirely dependent on the native exporter for all our information with regard to these remains. Lieut. Brooke, whose murder by Lo Lo brigands last year cut short a promising life, had found in caves in South-West China a large quantity of similar wares, which came safely home and have since been presented by Mrs. Brooke to the British Museum as a memorial to her son. The caves in which these vessels and figures were discovered were regarded as haunted by the natives of the district, who avoided their vicinity as being altogether uncanny, a belief pointing to considerable antiquity.[135]

At the time of the exhibition, there was still distrust of China and Chinese dealers of goods, which had been reinforced by the story of Lt. Brooke's murder. This is a reference to the death of John Weston Brooke (1880–1908), British military officer and Fellow of the Royal Geographical Society, in 1908 during an expedition to Eastern Tibet, where he was apparently killed by members of the Yi minority group, which lived in an area known in the nineteenth century as 'Lolo land'.[136] It should be noted that this is also the age of what was perceived as protective plunder so that Brooke's early ceramics collections would have been viewed as 'rescued'. [137]

Read later mentions 'Sung' ceramics (e.g. Song dynasty, 906–1279) and states that these have been imitated by potters (in China) since the eighteenth century.[138] However, knowledge of Song ceramics was still in its infancy outside of China: 'For a western eye to distinguish with certainty between the true Sung and some of the later imitations is not easy, nor indeed always possible.' Read follows this with a mention of wares that would today seem out of place in the 'early' classification: mounted Ming and Qing ceramics, such as those from Burghley House, Stamford. These were loaned by J. Pierpont Morgan (1837–1913), of the prominent American banking family, who was a prolific collector of a wide range of art works and books, including Chinese porcelains.[139] Morgan was a member of the Club and well known internationally at that time.[140] Read thanks another prominent member of the Chinese culture community in London at that time: Lionel Giles (1875–1958), who seems to have translated the Chinese inscriptions and marks for the catalogue. Giles was at that time a Keeper at the British Museum and son of the sinologist Herbert Giles, famous for co-inventing the Wade-Giles system of Romanization.[141] Lionel Giles was not a member of the Club but his assistance with the catalogue of the exhibition is yet further evidence of the Club's standing in society and the art world of the time, as well as the social and professional reach of its members. What is clear from this exhibition is that the collaboration with museums that was notable in earlier exhibitions continued into the twentieth century.

To that end, the introductory essay in the catalogue was written by R. L. Hobson, a colleague of Giles (and Read) at the British Museum, where he would work from 1897 till 1938.[142] A specialist in ceramics, he wrote numerous catalogues of English, European, and Chinese ceramics, including what is still cited today, the two-volume *Chinese Pottery and Porcelain* of 1915. In his essay for the Club's exhibition, he takes a more objective approach than Read and essentially presents a chronological history of Chinese ceramics from the Han period to the seventeenth century. The essay is interesting as a state-of-the-field narrative. For example, the earliest wares presented, those of the Han period (206 BC–220 AD) are at that time a great mystery because, as Hobson states: 'Chinese literature is all but silent on the subject of Han pottery.'[143] Hobson, like other specialists at that time, was increasingly familiar with Chinese texts on ceramics that were being translated by the likes of Bushell, as noted previously. But Han pottery is significant because: 'Almost all our examples are mortuary objects, models of the possessions with which the sacred dead had been surrounded in life. As such, they rank in archaeological importance with the models found in Egyptian tombs.'[144] This is an interesting comparison to make because it too is indicative of the time of the exhibition. As we will see in Chapter 3, Egyptian objects were very popular at that time and Egypt was essentially the focus of archaeological activity by British and Europeans throughout the nineteenth century. The Club had also presented a popular Egyptian exhibition in 1895 (see Chapter 3). It is interesting that there is no comparison with Greek ceramics but this would actually be made later by Herbert Read (1893–1968, no relation to C. H. Read) in *Art and Industry* (1934) when he compared a Song vessel with a Greek vase.[145] It seems that Modernism was the framework for such a comparison and perhaps a way to move away from archaeology, which dominated perceptions of the 'East' in the later nineteenth century.

Hobson further noted a big gap between the Han and the Song periods in terms of representation in the exhibition. At that time, almost nothing was known about the somewhat culturally diverse period of Chinese history from the third to the seventh centuries, which encompassed the Period of Disunion and the Sui dynasty. Knowledge of the arts of these periods would not really develop until later in the twentieth century. Even the Tang period (618–906) was unfamiliar, although much of the tomb art that was leaving China at that time consisted of Tang burial figurines.[146] The Yuan period (1279–1368) is mentioned in the essay but almost nothing is said about it as it too was somewhat unfamiliar to both Chinese and Western scholars and collectors at that time.

Lenders and Exhibits

The exhibition concludes with Ming (1368–1644) wares which would not today be considered 'early' and the catalogue includes the lists of reign marks, marks, and inscriptions that had become standard by that date. It is also one of the illustrated catalogues produced by the Club so that it includes a number of black and white and some colour illustrations. The total number of exhibits was 491, which is large, even by the Club's standards. There were also a large number of lenders: 47. As noted above, the final committee consisted of seven individuals, some of whom were members of the Club and others who were not, including the Chinese Minister and a prominent chemist, Sir Arthur Church (1834–1915). Church was a member of the Club and clearly a ceramics collector and enthusiast. He was the Professor of Chemistry at the Royal Academy and a painter himself, known for technical studies of art and pottery.[147] The committee also included Edward Dillon, George Eumorfopoulos, and Read, whom we have previously discussed. Edward Dillon (d. 1914) wrote several connoisseurship books including one on *Porcelain* which was published in 1904 (by Methuen). In this, he made a plea for more technical information and less emphasis on marks, citing much of the familiar literature but also 'Professor Church's little handbook'.[148] The technical plea is not surprising as Dillon trained as a chemist and worked for both the Royal Mint and the mint in Osaka, where he also developed expertise in Japanese art.[149] Six chapters of his book on porcelain are devoted to the porcelain of China, however, more than any other region and he illustrates a number of pieces that were in the V&A, the British Museum and the Salting collections (he cites Salting as his friend in the Preface, p. viii). Dillon is related to the Victorian Orientalist painter Frank Dillon (1823–1909), who specialized in views of Egypt and was also a member of the Club. (Edward donated his works to the V&A.)

George Eumorfopoulos (1863–1939) would become a prominent collector of Chinese art and British studio ceramics in the first half of the twentieth century.

His collection was widely admired in his lifetime and much of it ended up shared between the British Museum and the V&A after his death.[150] In the Preface to the catalogue of his ceramics collection, published in 1925, Eumorfopoulos gave an interesting summary of his own involvement in the field but which also situates it in the time of the exhibition:

> It was in 1891 that I first became interested in ceramics as a collector ... began by collecting English and Continental porcelain. To these a few pieces of Oriental came to be added, and as these grew in number it soon became clear that the European had to go.
>
> In those days – the last decade of the nineteenth century – 'Oriental' meant Chi'ing (Qing) porcelain, with just a few pieces of Ming thrown in. The Ming we knew then was a little blue and white and some of the coarser enamelled wares.
>
> Our knowledge of the more delicate enamelled Ming wares ... is quite recent. It is only within the last few years that specimens have reached the West.
>
> So far as my own collection goes it will, I think, be found that the Ming period is adequately represented.
>
> ...
>
> The main strength of the collection lies in the early wares. It was in 1906 that I saw for the first time a few specimens of the tomb wares, and I was at once attracted to them. Archaeological appeal alone, however, has never induced me to acquire an object: to enter my collection it was indispensable that it should at the same time appeal to me aesthetically in some way or another. For this reason it will be found that the number of pre-Han pieces is restricted.[151]

Pre-Han ceramics were never very popular in Britain, and were superseded by Tang dynasty funerary figurines, which featured prominently in Eumorfopoulos's collection. In reference to these, he also cited the Club's 1910 exhibition:

> From 1908 onwards these tomb wares appeared in increasing numbers, and collections were gradually being formed. By the end of 1909 they were exciting sufficient interest and discussion for the Committee of the Burlington Fine Arts Club to decide to hold in the summer of 1910 an exhibition of 'Early Chinese Pottery and Porcelain'.[152]

More importantly, if one is considering the impact of the 1910 exhibition on the collecting field, Eumorfopoulos noted: 'It was subsequent to, and one might say consequent on, our acquaintance with the T'ang wares that our knowledge of the Sung widened.'[153] He loaned to the Club's exhibition what was then seen to be a Song piece and which is still dated Song or Liao today, but its identification has changed (Figure 2.4). In the exhibition catalogue, it was thought to be an example of the famous but mysterious Ru ware or its Southern imperial equivalent, Guan ware.[154]

It was in fact from the time of this exhibition that 'Sung' became not just a time period but a style of ceramics to be collected. As Hobson noted in a review of the exhibition in *The Burlington Magazine*:

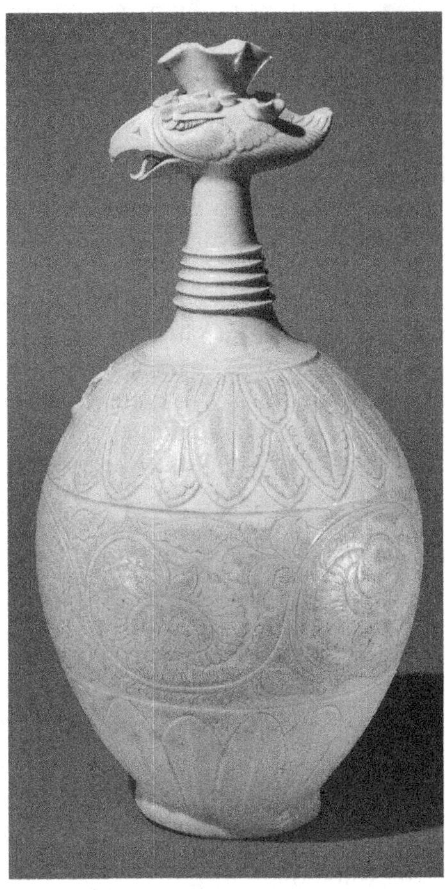

Figure 2.4 Ewer, Song or Liao, tenth–eleventh century, China. Porcelain with carved decoration. Height: 13.5 cm. BM 1936,1012.206.

Source: © Trustees of the British Museum, London.

> For the last two years [1909–1910] the attention of collectors has been attracted more and more to a large and varied group of Chinese wares which had previously been almost unknown and certainly quite misunderstood in Europe. A fairly representative series of these was exhibited at the Burlington Fine Arts Club in the spring of last year, and since then many more examples and some fresh varieties have reached this country.[155]

Indeed, a wide variety of what were considered to be Song ceramics were featured in the exhibition, and by 1915, when Hobson published his definitive two-volume survey of Chinese ceramics, he would state: 'The Sung wares are true children of the potter's craft, made as they are by the simplest processes, and in the main decorated by only genuine potter methods.'[156] The Club's exhibition would therefore signal the beginning of a shift in taste away from highly decorated porcelains, to seemingly more authentically crafted stonewares, at least among the members of the Club and local potters. Among these members was Roger Fry, also a committee member, who, in a review of the exhibition for *The Nation* (23 July 1910) rhapsodized about the qualities of 'Sung' pots.

> Nothing could, however, be more convincing that the pottery of that time shown recently at the Burlington Fine Arts Club. The specimens of Sung pottery there collected were a revelation of the utmost possibilities of the potter's craft. The fascination of pottery is made up of many and varied appeals to the imagination, and all these seem at their highest in this Sung ware. There is the purely plastic quality, the evidence of the most perfect control over matter, the impress of will without let or hindrance, and in that alone these Sung bowls, in spite of their extreme simplicity of form, are perfect examples. One needs to take one of them in the hand (impossible, alas! in museums and exhibitions) and feel with two fingers the inside and outside to realise how perfectly the two planes are related, with what subtle

> co-ordination and variety, how the structure is at once massive and delicate. All the astounding skill of hand of the potter is here devoted to the refinement of the rough, primitive pot, not to its elaboration into something quite different, as happened in later ceramics.[157]

The apotheosis of this would be Bernard Leach's championing of 'the Sung standard' in his *Potter's Book* of 1940.[158]

A final exhibition committee member who needs to be discussed is Lt-Col. G. B. Croft Lyons, FSA (1855–1926). His fellow committee member Read would write in his obituary:

> My first recollection of him must have been in the early nineties when he not infrequently came to the Museum [the British Museum] bringing some prize for comparison, a piece of English china or an heraldic seal. As Sir Wollaston Franks was keenly interested in both subjects he and Lyons soon became intimate.[159]

This might also have been how he became associated with the Club. The V&A has noted that he collected widely, including ceramics, sculpture, metalwork, textiles, and woodwork and in his lifetime loaned 978 objects to the museum, which later were bequeathed.[160]

Thus, Croft Lyons, Eumorfopoulos, Hobson, and Read loaned pieces to the exhibition but the other committee members did not. As we have seen with other museum-professional members of the Club and contributors, Hobson's lending from his own collection would not have been seen as a conflict of interest at that time, even though he was employed by the British Museum. Other lenders were individuals who loaned frequently to Club exhibitions including Alexander, Benson (see Chapter 1), and Rawlinson. Less familiar lenders included La Comtesse de Bearn, who appears to have been Martine-Marie-Pol de Béhague (1869–1939), an art patron and collector best known for her paintings collection.[161] She also collected Islamic art.[162] She loaned several pieces to the exhibition, including B57, a Jun flowerpot (illustrated in the 1911 edition) (Figure 2.5), but her connection to the Club is not known. Another new and interesting lender, not a Club member, was Dr. Justus Brinckmann (1843–1915), a museum director in Hamburg, who was a 'champion of Modern Art'[163] and clearly a ceramics collector.[164]

Alfred Trapnell (1838–1917), not a Club member, was a well-known ceramics collector, however. He was from Bristol and specialized in English porcelain but his collection of Chinese ceramics was published in 1906, by Gorer, *The Trapnell Collection of Old Chinese Porcelain*. He earned a living in the metal smelting business.[165] The Veitch collection, from which several pieces were loaned, is one that appears as a provenance in sales of ceramics but little is known about its owner. G. T. Veitch (n. d.) appears to have worked for Jardine Matheson in Asia for five years in the 1880s.[166] This would explain how his collection was mainly acquired in China, according to reviews of an exhibition of his collection at the Birmingham Art Gallery in 1904.[167]

In spite of what appears to be a long list of lenders,[168] in examining the exhibits as a whole, it is clear that for the most part they belonged to just three lenders:

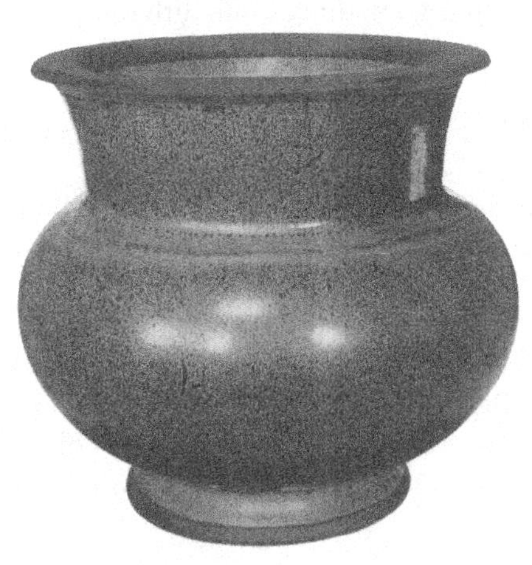

Figure 2.5 Jun ware *zhadou*. Plate XIX from Burlington Fine Arts Club, *Illustrated Catalogue of Early Chinese Pottery and Porcelain*, London, 1911

Eumorfopoulos, Alexander, and Benson. Benson's objects tended to be later but all three contributed early and late objects to the exhibition. The exhibits generally are very wide-ranging, demonstrating that a canon of 'early' pieces, which today would not include Ming and Qing, had yet to be developed among collectors in Britain. Many of the pieces tend to be sculptural as well, and architectural ceramics are included in the show, probably because of their sculptural nature. As they were made of ceramic, however, they were readily included in an exhibition which today would likely consist primarily of vessels and burial figurines. To a large extent, the exhibition contents also reflect the collections of members and lenders in its eclecticism. Thus, what members collected and owned was the starting point for the exhibition, in conjunction with a suggested theme. This appears to be the same pattern followed for all other Club exhibitions and is to be expected as the Club generated its own exhibitions. The range of objects also suggests that much of it was decorative, being supplied by either owners of grand homes (e.g. the Duke of Devonshire) or collectors of other material on which ceramics might be placed (e.g. Henry Hirsch; see Chapter 4). Only a few lenders seemed to specialize in ceramics as collectors, or in China as a location for objects in their collections. This is important because this exhibition is often seen as representative of a new taste in Chinese ceramic collecting that is reflective of a new relationship with China that provided access to hitherto unfamiliar wares. This was not an exhibition about China as expressed through ceramics, but rather 'Chinese' as a category for ceramics, unlike the Greek exhibition where ceramics were seen to represent Ancient Greece, and a subsequent Club exhibition on Chinese art (1915), where the art enabled a definition of Chinese culture and society (see Appendix A). Within this it is also notable that several lenders to the 1910 exhibition were medical doctors and collectors who specialized in other things so this indicates that in 1910 Chinese porcelain was still considered decorative among mainstream collectors, not representative of a more scholarly taste in ceramics, which is how specialist collectors in the field would later characterize them.[169] For specialist collectors, however, this exhibition did help to raise the profile of their area of interest and begin to refine it so that a collecting canon could be developed. At the same time, perhaps even in response to the exhibition, in a reversal of previous patterns, dealers began to champion earlier wares, such as Gorer and Blacker in whose *Chinese Porcelain and Hard Stones* of 1911 the Han and Song periods are mentioned as being the source of 'purer forms'.[170] The exhibition, devised to highlight members' interests and objects, seems to have inspired the market, rather than the other way around.

Where this exhibition also had a significant impact was in aesthetics, through the display of genuinely 'early' Chinese ceramics to wider audiences, including potters. As noted in the Preface to this book, this exhibition was seen by several potters and was inspirational in the design of their own work. The most influential pieces were those defined as 'Song', stonewares which were perceived as the antithesis of more industrial porcelain and representative of a new more handmade aesthetic in ceramics.[171] The perception of Song wares as the work of individual 'artists' made them seem modern but also representative of 'art', a status they still retain today, which can be directly connected to the Club's exhibition.

Conclusion

Through the two 'western' and three 'oriental' ceramics exhibitions discussed here, one can see how knowledge in the ceramics field developed to become more specialized in terms of regional attribution (Greek; Oriental to Chinese) and subject knowledge, but also for the Chinese ceramics in particular how this increasing knowledge was dependent on increased exposure to new material. Chinese ceramics initially had been provided by the local art market but then subsequently were coming directly out of China from the late nineteenth century onwards, creating not only a direct connection to the source of the objects but also encounters with hitherto unseen types. The fact that the exhibitions in this chapter were five of several that focussed exclusively on ceramics reflects a widespread taste for this material among members of the Club, even though it was founded by what were essentially print collectors (see Chapter 1) but also the popularity of ceramics in Britain. However, this is less telling than the overwhelming presence that ceramics played in exhibitions that ostensibly were not focussed on that material, such as the Egypt one of 1895, discussed in Chapter 3. The progression in ceramic exhibition topics from English and Continental ceramics to specifically 'early Chinese' further reflects the trajectory of the collecting field of ceramics towards the non-western, returning in a way to the origins of ceramic collecting. As Eumorfopoulos noted, he began with England and 'progressed' to Chinese and this was a pattern exhibited by a number of collectors, but not all of course. Many continued to collect English and European as well as Qing, after the Song turn. For example, a major donation of mainly Qing ceramics was made by bequest to the V&A after the death of George Salting. This was published at the time and stimulated taste among a wide range of collectors. But Salting, as we have seen, was not a dedicated ceramics collector, nor was his main area of interest China. As seen in Chapter 1, and as Chapter 3 will demonstrate, Salting collected almost every area that was represented by the Club, and some of his non-Chinese ceramics came to be seen as a material that represented 'Islamic art' for a number of public and private collections. He is a collector with many identities, claimed for many fields, yet his pluralism was typical of his peers in the Club, as this study demonstrates.

Notes

1 Stacey Pierson, *Collectors, Collections and Museums: The Field of Chinese Ceramics in Britain, 1560–1960* (Bern: Peter Lang, 2007).
2 Science and Art Department of the Committee of Council on Education, 1862.
3 General Committee minutes, 12.6.1866.
4 Pierson (2007).
5 Burlington Fine Arts Club, *A Short Description of the English and Continental Porcelain, Exhibited June 1873* (London, 1873).
6 General Committee Minutes, 18.2.1873.
7 Pierson (2007), pp. 78–79; Ann Eatwell, 'Private Pleasure, Public Beneficence: Lady Charlotte Schreiber and Ceramic Collecting', in Clarissa Campbell Orr, ed., *Women in the Victorian Art World* (Manchester: Manchester University Press, 1995), pp. 125–145.
8 See www.vam.ac.uk/content/articles/c/charlotte-schreiber/ (accessed 13 Sept. 2015).
9 There is a stained glass window dedicated to him in a church in Clifton, Bristol. See Dr Rhona Beare, *A Guide to Our Stained Glass Windows* (Clifton: Christ Church, 2015).
10 William Chaffers, *Marks and Monograms on Pottery and Porcelain of the Renaissance and Modern Periods ....* (London, 1874), p. 856.
11 Mark Westgarth *A Biographical Dictionary of Nineteenth Century Antique and Curiosity Dealers*, Regional Furniture, vol. XXIII (Glasgow: Regional Furniture Society, 2009), p. 11; Virginia Hoselitz, *Imagining Roman Britain: Victorian Responses to a Roman Past* (Woodbridge: Boydell and Brewer, 2007), pp. 70–71, fn 45; Charles Dawson, 'In Search of the Marksman – William Chaffers', *English Ceramic Circle Transactions*, vol. 24 (2013), pp. 195–222 and http://sculpture.gla.ac.uk/view/organization.php?id=msib1_1234176170 (accessed 14 June 2016).
12 Ann Eatwell 'Borrowing from Collectors: The Role of the Loan in the Formation of the Victoria and Albert Museum and Its Collection (1852–1932)', *DAS: The Decorative Arts Society 1850 to the Present, Journal Number Twenty-four, Omnium Gatherum* (Suffolk, 2000), pp. 21–29; Nicholas Smith, 'A Stitch in Time. The V&A and the Bayeux Tapestry, I', V&A blog, May 14, 2013; available at: www.vam.ac.uk/blog/tales-archives/stitch-time-va-and-bayeux-tapestry-1 (accessed 13 June 2016); Lisa White, 'A Collector of Distinction: Sir William Holburne (1793–1874)', *Apollo Magazine*, September 2003, pp. 46–54; Dawson (2013).
13 BFAC (1873), p. 6.
14 William Richard Drake, *A Descriptive Catalogue of the Etched Work of F. S. Haden* (London, 1880) and *Notes on Venetian Ceramics* (London: J. Murray 1868).
15 BFAC (1873), p. 7; Sir William Drake (1868).
16 Martin J. Hopkinson, *No Day Without a Line: The History of the Royal Society of Painter-Printmakers 1880–1999* (Oxford: Ashmolean Museum, 1999), and see Chapter 1.
17 He was mentioned in an article by Campbell Dodgson, 'Una Vilana Windisch', *The Burlington Magazine*, 1930. Reprinted in M. Levey, ed., *The Burlington Magazine: A Centenary Anthology* (New Haven, CT: Yale University Press, 2003), p. 40.
18 David J. Hall, 'Fry, Francis (1803–1886)', *Oxford Dictionary of National Biography* online, 2004, http://dx.doi.org/10.1093/ref:odnb/10209 (accessed 30 Dec. 2015).
19 BFAC (1873), e.g. p. 11.
20 Martin J. Daunton, *State and Market in Victorian Britain: War, Welfare and Capitalism* (Woodbridge: Boydell, 2008), Chapter 8.
21 BFAC (1873), p. 20.
22 See http://edmondhoyle.blogspot.co.uk/2011/12/from-pen-and-library-of-henry-hucks.html (accessed 6 Oct. 2015).
23 Minette Walters, *A Dreadful Murder: The Mysterious Death of Caroline Luard* (London: Pan, 2013).
24 BFAC (1873), p. 21.
25 M. B. Olgilvie and J. D. Harvey, eds., *The Biographical Dictionary of Women in Science*, vol. 2, L–Z (London: Routledge, 2000), pp. 936–937.
26 BFAC (1873), p. 22.

27 See www.whistler.arts.gla.ac.uk/correspondence/biog/display/?bid=Edis_RW (accessed 21 Sept. 2015).
28 BFAC (1873), p. 17.
29 Aileen Dawson, *The Art of Worcester Porcelain: 1751–1788: Masterpieces from the British Museum Collection* (Lebanon, NH: University Press of New England, 2007), pp. 24–25.
30 William D. Rubinstein, ed., *Palgrave Dictionary of Anglo-Jewish History* (Basingstoke: Palgrave Macmillan, 2011), p. 250.
31 BFAC (1873), p. 23.
32 Gervase Huxley, *Victorian Duke: The Life of Hugh Lupus Grosvenor, First Duke of Westminster* (Oxford: Oxford University Press, 1967).
33 Pierson (2007), pp. 28–29.
34 Joseph Banks, 'Collections on the subject of Old China and Japan wares with Some Remarks on these interesting manufactures made in Lady Banks's Dairy at Spring Grove', manuscript, 1807. Published by Rose Kerr, 'Chinese Porcelain at Spring Grove Dairy: Sir Joseph Banks's Manuscript', *Apollo* (January 1989), pp. 30–34.
35 David R. Fisher, 'MARRYAT, Joseph II (1790–1876), of Wimbledon House, Surr. and 6 Richmond Terrace, Whitehall, Mdx.', in D. Fisher, ed., *The History of Parliament: The House of Commons 1820–1832* (2009). Available at: www.historyofparliamentonline.org/volume/1820-1832/member/marryat-joseph-1790-1876 (accessed 19 June 2016); Legacies of British Slave Ownership database, 'Joseph Marryat. Profile and Legacies Summary', available at: www.ucl.ac.uk/lbs/person/view/11416 (accessed 19 June 2016).
36 BFAC (1873), p. 9.
37 Ibid., p. 11.
38 A catalogue was published: J. C. Robinson, *A Descriptive Catalogue of a Collection of Oriental and Old Sèvres Porcelain, the Property of Her Majesty the Queen: Deposited for Exhibition in the Museum of the Department* (London: HMSO, 1853).
39 See the official catalogue of 1851: *Official Catalogue of the Great Exhibitions of the Works of Industry of All Nations, 1851* (London: Spicer Brothers, 1851).
40 Michael Vickers, 'Value and Simplicity: Eighteenth-Century Taste and the Study of Greek Vases', *Past and Present*, no. 116 (1987), pp. 98–137.
41 There appeared to have been an issue with the authenticity of some of the proposed exhibits:

> 24.4.1888
> III Mr Tebbs having informed the Committee that he had received a letter from a correspondent at Athens stating that some of the Terra Cottas found in Asia Minor were modern fabrications, he (Mr Tebbs) renewed his previous suggestion that it might be desirable by some note prefaced to the Catalogue to indicate that the Club was not responsible for the authenticity of any of the objects exhibited. The subject having been discussed and it appearing that the general feeling of the members present was against the insertion of the suggested note in the Catalogue It was moved by Dr Hamilton seconded by Mr Tebbs and unanimously Resolved that this Committee having delegated to a Subcommittee the power of making the Exhibition Arrangements it is inadvisable to interfere with the discretion of the Subcommittee in any matter relating thereto.

42 Letter of May 1888:

Burlington Fine Arts Club
17 Savile Row, W.,
May, 1888

It is proposed to issue to Subscribers an ILLUSTRATED Edition of the CATALOGUE of the Collection of objects of GREEK CERAMIC ART now exhibited in the Gallery of the Club.

The Illustrations will consist of about Fifty-two Plates, and will be issued with the letterpress on *large* paper only. Specimens of the Illustrations can be seen at the Club.

The number of copies printed will be 125 on large paper, at £2 12*s* 6*d*., and 25 copies numbered 1 to 25 on Japan paper (with a double set of Plates) at £10 10*s* each.

As it is necessary, in order to cover the cost of production, that all the above copies should be subscribed for, Members of the Club who desire to secure copies, are requested to notify the same by filling up and returning to me the enclosed form, without delay.

J. BEAVAN,
Secretary

43 Vickers (1987), p. 104.

44 Vinnie Norskov, *Greek Vases in New Contexts* (Aarhus: Aarhus University Press, 2002), p. 116; E. Moignard, *Greek Vases: An Introduction* (Bristol: Bristol Classical Press, 2006), p. 95.

45 Norskov 2002, p. 89. For the catalogue, see P. O. Bronsted, *A Brief Description of Thirty-Two Ancient Greek Painted Vases, Lately Found in Excavations Made at Vulci, in the Roman Territory, by Mr. Campanari and now Exhibited by Him in London, no. 15, Leicester Place* (London, 1832).

46 As cited in Athena Tsingarida, 'The Search for the Artist. The van Branteghem and Bourquignon Collections and the Connoisseurship of Greek Vases', in S. Schmidt and M. Steinhardt, eds., *Sammeln und Erforschen: Griechische Vasen in Neuzeitlichen Sammlungen* (Munich: C.H. Beck, 2014), note 3, pp. 115–122; A. Furtwängler, *Beschreibung der Vasensammlung im Antiquarium* (Berlin: Königliche Museen zu Berlin, 1885); W. Klein, *Euphronios. Eine Studie zur Geschichte der griechischen Malerei* (Wien, 1886); W. Klein, *Die griechischen Vasen mit Meistersignaturen* 2 (Wien, 1887).

47 Tsingarida (2014).

48 S. R., 'A van Branteghem', *Revue Archéologique*, Quatrième Série, T. 18 (JUILLET-DÉCEMBRE 1911), pp. 362–363.

49 Fröhner 'was the former curator of the Department of Antiquities at the Musée Napoléon (later Musée du Louvre) and van Branteghem's adviser and friend'. According to Tsingarida (2014), pp. 115–116: An acknowledged expert in epigraphy, who certainly influenced van Branteghem's interest for vascular inscriptions. W. Fröhner, himself, owned a small but important collection of inscribed objects, now in the Cabinet des Médailles in Paris. According to several letters addressed to Fröhner, van Branteghem's concern for vascular inscriptions occurred at least 1887 when he settled in London for a year.

50 Ibid., p. 118.

51 Ibid., pp. 115, 119.

52 See www.mfa.org/collections/object/drinking-cup-kylix-153673 (accessed 7 Oct. 2015). Warren was a colourful collector and Beazley was part of his circle. See David Sox, *Bachelors of Art: Edward Perry Warren and the Lewes House Brotherhood* (London: Fourth Estate, 1991).

53 Dyfri Williams, 'Etruscan Production and Interpretation: The Hamilton Gray Vase', in J. Swaddling and P. Perkins, eds., *Etruscan by Definition: The Cultural, Regional and Personal Identity of the Etruscans; Papers in Honour of Sybille Haynes* (London: British Museum Press, 2009), pp. 10–12.

54 Note: when 'Collection' is mentioned in an exhibition title, it does not normally mean one that belongs to a particular collector. The name of the collector is given in those cases. See Appendix B.

55 See http://theesotericcuriosa.blogspot.co.uk/2013/03/shaking-family-tree-of-lord-romsey-art.html (accessed 7 Oct. 2015).

56 BFAC, *Catalogue of Objects of Greek Ceramic Art, Exhibited in 1888* (London, 1888), nos 92–96; Wilhelm Klein, *Die griechischen Vasen mit Meistersignaturen* (C. Gerold's Sohn, 1887).

57 See www.fitzmuseum.cam.ac.uk/gallery/cockerell/pigstytopalace/marlay.html (accessed 7 Oct. 2015).

58 See BFAC (1888), catalogue, p. 102. Note: these may be the ones that Tebbs objected to, see note 41.

59 Dyfri Williams and Jack Ogden, *Greek Gold: Jewelry of the Classical World* (London: British Museum Press,1994), p. 92. For a biography of Franks, see Marjorie Caygill and John F. Cherry, eds. *A. W. Franks: Nineteenth Century Collecting and the British Museum* (London: British Museum Press, 1997).

60 BFAC (1888), p. 68.
61 See www.thepeerage.com/p3027.htm#i30267 (accessed 10 Dec. 2015).
62 BFAC (1888), p. 3, re: 111–113.
63 BFAC (1888), Introduction, p. 6.
64 See www.mfa.org/collections/object/oil-flask-lekythos-153982 (accessed 7 Oct. 2015).
65 BFAC (1888), p. 54.
66 Daunton (2008), p. 168; see http://adb.anu.edu.au/biography/salting-severin-kanute-2626 (accessed 10 Dec. 2015).
67 *Sir Herbert, Bart., M.P. Maxwell, (1894). Life of the Right Honourable William Henry Smith M.P. (New edn) (London: William Blackwood and Sons), repr. (Cambridge: Cambridge University Press, 2010).*
68 See http://munksroll.rcplondon.ac.uk/Biography/Details/4672 (accessed 7 Oct. 2015).
69 General Committee minutes, 17.7.1894.
70 General Committee minutes, 5.3.1895.
71 Pierson (2007), pp. 62–67.
72 Total visitor numbers were: 2408. It is possible that the extension was also due to other factors.
73 See https://dictionaryofarthistorians.org/rawlinsonw.htm (accessed 7 Oct. 2015).
74 Probate notice: www.thegazette.co.uk/London/issue/27370/page/7098/data.pdf (accessed 27 Nov. 2015).
75 Deborah Cherry, 'The Hogarth Club: 1858–1861', *The Burlington Magazine*, vol. 122, no. 925 (Apr. 1980), pp. 236–244, at p. 242.
76 *Catalogue of the Collection of Old Nankin Porcelain Whole Coloured & Old Chinese Enamelled Porcelain Formed by Richard Mills,... Many of the Pieces Were Exhibited at the Burlington Fine Arts Club in 1895 and 1896* (London: Christie, Manson and Woods, 10 April 1908). Some biographical information can be found at: www.invaluable.com/auction-lot/sir-edward-coley-burne-jones-bt.,-a.r.a.,-r.w.s.-17-c-lmjd4wzz4y (accessed 27 Oct. 2015).
77 Dana Garvey, 'Cosmo Monkhouse: A Conservative Reconsidered', *Nineteenth-Century Art Worldwide*, vol. 14, issue 2 (Summer 2015). Available at: www.19thc-artworldwide.org/summer15/garvey-on-cosmo-monkhouse-a-conservative-reconsidered (accessed 7 Oct. 2015).
78 BFAC, *Catalogue of Coloured Chinese Porcelain, Exhibited in 1896* (London, 1896).
79 BFAC, *Catalogue of Blue and White Oriental Porcelain, Exhibited in 1895* (London, 1895), pp. v–vi.
80 BFAC (1895), p. vi.
81 A. W. Franks, *Catalogue of a Collection of Oriental Pottery and Porcelain* (London, 1876); BFAC (1895), p. vii.
82 See http://etchings.arts.gla.ac.uk/catalogue/biog/?nid=AlexWC (accessed 8 Oct. 2015).
83 Pierson (2007), p. 70.
84 See http://collections.vam.ac.uk/item/O179344/richard-phene-spiers-plaquette-lanteri-edouard/ (accessed 8 Oct. 2015).
85 Tasha Vorderstrasse and Tanya Treptow, eds., *A Cosmopolitan City: Muslims, Christians, and Jews in Old Cairo*, Oriental Institute Publications 38 (Chicago: The Oriental Institute of the University of Chicago, 2015).
86 Pierson (2007), p. 60. Reign marks are an inscription which notes the dynasty and emperor's reign period in which they were produced. A typical one from the Ming dynasty would read: 'Made in the reign of Xuande in the Great Ming dynasty' 大明宣德年製.
87 BFAC (1895), p. xiii. Reign marks began to be used systematically in the Xuande period, 1426–1435.
88 BFAC (1895), p. xiv.
89 Lan Pu,景德镇陶录, 1815. For a discussion of this text and its many additions and translations, see Ellen Huang, 'China's China: Jingdezhen Porcelain and the Production of Art in the Nineteenth Century', PhD dissertation, University of California, San Diego, 2008.
90 BFAC (1895), p. xii.
91 Pierson (2007), p. 65.
92 BFAC (1895), pp. xiii, xx, xxi.

93 Pierson (2007), p. 64.
94 BFAC (1895), pp. 13–14.
95 Pierson (2007), p. 63.
96 William Michael Rossetti, *Some Reminiscences,* vol. I (Cambridge: Cambridge University Press, 2013 [1906]), p. 144.
97 See http://collections.vam.ac.uk/item/O77413/sword-guard-michitoshi/ (accessed 28 Nov. 2015).
98 A. D. Nicholl, 'Agnew, Sir William Gladstone (1898–1960)', rev. Marc Brodie, *Oxford Dictionary of National Biography*, first published 2004; online edn, Jan 2011. http://dx.doi.org/10.1093/ref:odnb/30349 (accessed 10 Dec. 2015).
99 See www.whistler.arts.gla.ac.uk/correspondence/people/biog/?bid=Flow_C&firstname=cyril&surname=flower (accessed 10 Dec. 2015).
100 See www.whistler.arts.gla.ac.uk/correspondence/people/biog/?bid=Boug_GH&firstname=george&surname=boughton (accessed 10 Dec. 2015).
101 See www.irishartsreview.com/island-paradise/ (accessed 10 Dec. 2015).
102 See www.whistler.arts.gla.ac.uk/correspondence/biog/display/?bid=Flow_W (accessed 8 Oct. 2015).
103 See http://etchings.arts.gla.ac.uk/catalogue/biog/?nid=WedmF (accessed 10 Oct. 2015).
104 See www.liverpoolmuseums.org.uk/walker/collections/works-on-paper/watermark/explore.aspx?coll=4&per=69017&rdir=/walker/collections/works-on-paper/watermark/&page=1 (accessed 10 Oct. 2015).
105 Murray Marks, *A Catalogue of Blue and White Nankin Porcelain Forming the Collection of Sir Henry Thompson* (London, 1878); on Thompson, see Pierson (2007), pp. 68–69.
106 BFAC (1895), p. 38.
107 For example, Clive Wainwright, "A gatherer and disposer of other men's stuffe': Murray Marks, Connoisseur and Curiosity Dealer', *Journal of the History of Collections*, vol. 14, no. 2 (2002), pp. 161–176; Pierson (2007), pp. 64–65, 68–70.
108 Meryl Secrest, *Duveen: A Life in Art* (Chicago: University of Chicago Press, 2004). The Dutch connection was noted by Lady Schreiber in her diaries. See for example, The Earl of Bessborough, ed., *Lady Charlotte Schreiber, Extracts from her Journal, 1853–1891* (London: John Murray, 1952), p. 182.
109 He was member no. 259 and had resigned in 1879.
110 Malcolm Allbrook, *Henry Prinsep's Empire: Framing a Distant Colony* (Canberra: ANU Press, 2014), p. xviii; T. J. Barringer, *Reading the Pre-Raphaelites* (New Haven, CT: Yale University Press, 1998), p. 48; Caroline Dakers, *The Holland Park Circle: Artists and Victorian Society* (New Haven, CT: Yale University Press, 1999), pp. 207–208.
111 'Romney', *Masters in Art. A Series of Illustrated Monographs, Issued Monthly*, vol. 4, part 37 (Boston: Bates and Guild Company, 1903), p. 41.
112 He was author of *The English Poets*, multiple vols, vol. 1 (London, 1911).
113 General Committee minutes, 11.2.1896.
114 It was, however, a subject that was decided upon quite late in the year, as an original exhibition proposal for Enamels was repeatedly postponed until an alternative subject had to be decided. General Committee minutes (1895–96).
115 BFAC, *Catalogue of an Exhibition of Coloured Chinese Porcelain* (London, 1896), p. viii.
116 Albert Jacquemart, *Histoire de la céramique: étude descriptive et raisonné des poteries de tous le temps et de tous les peuples* (Paris, 1873).
117 BFAC (1896), p. xii.
118 Ibid., p. viii.
119 Ibid., pp. viii–ix.
120 Ibid., p. xi.
121 For a recent study of this ware, see Anne Håbu and Dawn Rooney, eds., *Royal Porcelain from Siam: Unpacking the Ring Collection* (Oslo: Hermes Publishing, 2013).
122 See www.the-saleroom.com/en-gb/auction-catalogues/woolley-and-wallis/catalogue-id-srwo10018/lot-cd8937dd-05bf-44ba-946d-a401007831bd (accessed 19 Oct. 2015). This appears to be the only source.
123 See www.thepeerage.com/p12774.htm#i127740 (accessed 10 Dec. 2015).
124 For example, The Arts Council, *English Watercolours from the Hickman Bacon Collection* (London: The Arts Council, 1946); Eric Shanes, *The Golden Age of Watercolours: The*

Hickman Bacon Collection (London: Dulwich Picture Gallery, 2001), declares it to be the best in the world. Bacon also donated several hundred Japanese prints to the British Museum in 1907. See www.britishmuseum.org/research/search_the_collection_database/term_details.aspx?bioId=133681 (accessed 10 Dec. 2015).

125 See www.whistler.arts.gla.ac.uk/correspondence/biog/display/?bid=Huis_MB (accessed 10 Dec. 2015). See also Fine Art Society, *125 Years of Exhibitions at the Fine Art Society PLC, 1876–2001* (London: The Fine Art Society, 2001).

126 See www.history.ac.uk/projects/research/jobbing (accessed 1 Nov. 2015); *Stock Exchange Gazette*, 'Directory of Directors....' (London: Thomas Skinner and Co, 1914), p. 591. See www.liverpoolmuseums.org.uk/ladylever/collections/chinese/dealersessay/page2.aspx (accessed 19 Oct. 2015).

127 See www.britishmuseum.org/research/search_the_collection_database/term_details.aspx?bioId=142038 (accessed 19 Oct. 2015).

128 See www.bidamount.com/chinese-qing-porcelains-the-george-davies-collection/ (accessed 28 Nov. 2015); also www.liverpoolmuseums.org.uk/ladylever/collections/chinese/noiressay/page3.aspx#_ftn15 (accessed 19 Oct. 2015); 'Chinese Porcelain in the Davies Collection', *The Burlington Magazine for Connoisseurs*, vol. 23, no. 123 (June 1913), pp. 162–167; 'Chinese Porcelain. Purchase of a Well-Known Collection', *The Times*, 20 February 1913, p. 9.

129 Extracted from General Committee Minutes for 6.7.1909; 4.1.1910; 8.2.1910; 3.5.1910; and 31.5.1910.

130 BFAC, *Exhibition of Early Chinese Pottery and Porcelain* (London, 1910), Preface, p. xvii.

131 David M. Wilson, 'Read, Sir (Charles) Hercules (1857–1929), Museum Curator', *Oxford Dictionary of National Biography*, available at: http://dx.doi.org/10.1093/ref:odnb/35693 (accessed 1 Dec. 2015).

132 BFAC (1910), Preface, p. xvii.

133 Ibid.

134 Ibid., p. xviii.

135 Ibid., pp. xvii–xviii.

136 Denise M. Glover, Stevan Harrell, Charles F. McKhann, and Margaret Byrne Swain, *Explorers and Scientists in China's Borderlands, 1880–1950* (Seattle, WA: University of Washington Press, 2012), p. 113, fn. 8. An account of Brooke's travels, recreated from his diaries, was published by W. N. Fergusson, *Adventure, Sport and Travel on the Tibetan Steppes* (London, 1911).

137 James Hevia, 'Loot's Fate: The Economy of Plunder and the Moral Life of Objects "From the Summer Palace of the Emperor of China"', *History and Anthropology*, vol. 6, no. 4 (1994), pp. 319–345.

138 BFAC (1910), p. xviii.

139 Louise Auchincloss, *J. P. Morgan: The Financier as Collector* (New York: Harry N. Abrams, 1990).

140 Jean Strouse, *Morgan: American Financier* (New York: HarperCollins, 2000).

141 John Minford, 'Sinology, Old and New', *China Heritage Quarterly*, no. 13 (March 2008). Available at: www.chinaheritagequarterly.org/articles.php?searchterm=013_giles.inc&issue=013 (accessed 29 Nov. 2015).

142 See www.britishmuseum.org/research/search_the_collection_database/term_details.aspx?bioId=85528 (accessed 10 Dec. 2015).

143 BFAC (1910), p. xxi.

144 Ibid., p. xxii.

145 According to Herbert Read:

> The Greek vase is based on exact measurements, and its proportions are regular ... The Chinese vase does not obey any such exact rules ... I do not think that there is any doubt that the average sensitive person, the 'man of taste', would find the Chinese vase superior as a work of art ...
>
> (*Art and Industry*, London, 1934, pp. 21–23)

146 The exhibition features several, all loaned by Eumorfopoulos: the camel M4; the *sancai* jar A66; and the *tianwang* figure, B1.

147 Frank Greenaway, 'Church, Sir Arthur Herbert (1834–1915), chemist', *Oxford Dictionary of National Biography*, available at: http://dx.doi.org/10.1093/ref:odnb/51472 (accessed 29 Nov. 2015).

148 A. H. Church, *Cantor Lectures on Some Points of Contact Between the Scientific and Artistic Aspects of Pottery* (London: Trounce, 1881), p. vi in Exhibition catalogue Preface.

149 Jessica Harrison-Hall, *Ming Ceramics in the British Museum* (London: British Museum Press, 2001), p. 588.

150 Pierson (2007), p. 91.

151 George Eumorfopoulos, 'Preface', in R. L. Hobson, *The Eumorfopoulos Collection*, vol. I (London, 1925).

152 Ibid.

153 Ibid.

154 BFAC (1910), p. 8.

155 R. L. Hobson, 'Some Old Chinese Pottery', *The Burlington Magazine*, vol. xix (1911), p. 262.

156 R. L. Hobson, *Chinese Pottery and Porcelain* (London, 1915), p. 46.

157 Roger Fry, 'The Chinese Exhibition', *The Nation*, vol. VII, no. 17 (23 July 1910), pp. 593–594.

158 Stacey Pierson, 'The Sung Standard: Chinese Ceramics and British Studio Pottery in the 20th Century', in S. Pierson, ed., *Song Ceramics: Art History, Archaeology and Technology*, Colloquies on Art and Archaeology in Asia, no. 20 (London: School of Oriental and African Studies, 2004), pp. 81–102.

159 Hercules Read (1926) 'Lieut.-Colonel George Babington Croft Lyons', *The Antiquaries Journal*, vol. 6, pp. 451–452. doi:10.1017/S0003581500057024.

160 See www.vam.ac.uk/content/articles/l/lt-col-george-babington-croft-lyons/ (accessed 27 Oct. 2015). For an obituary, see C. T. Bailey, 'Colonel Croft Lyons', *The Burlington Magazine for Connoisseurs*, vol. 49, no. 284 (Nov. 1926), p. 240.

161 Robert Cumming, ed., *'My Dear BB...' The Letters of Bernard Berenson and Kenneth Clark, 1925–1959* (New Haven, CT: Yale University Press, 2015), pp. 515–516.

162 See, for example, G. Contenau, 'Les nouvelles salles d'art musulman au Musée du Louvre', *Syria*, T. 3, Fasc. 3 (1922), pp. 251–260.

163 See https://dictionaryofarthistorians.org/brinckmannj.htm (accessed 27 Oct. 2015).

164 He loaned A29, a Tang ox and cart.

165 See http://carp.arts.gla.ac.uk/image.php?id=pe_193&t=1&urltp=search.php%3Fstart%3D0%26end%3D6%26what%3D%26who%3D1089020817%26where%3D%26when%3D%26period%3D%26search%3D99 (accessed 1 Nov. 2015).

166 See http://janus.lib.cam.ac.uk/db/node.xsp?id=EAD%2FGBR%2F0012%2FMS%20JM%2FF11%2F176;sib0=180, for a copy of his contract with the firm. (accessed 29 Nov. 2015).

167 W, 'Notes on the Veitch Collection of Chinese Porcelains in the Birmingham Art Gallery', *The Burlington Magazine*, vol. iv. (1904), p. 232. He was also probably related to the Veitch horticultural family, as is suggested by surviving letters in the Jardine Matheson archives.

168 Other interesting lenders included the following: Walter Behrens (1861–1913), Sir William H. Bennett, KCVO (1852–1931), the Bloxams, 'Mrs Bushell' (Florence Matthews, n.d.), Joseph H. P. Chitty (1861–1942), the Duke of Devonshire – most likely the 9th duke, Victor Christian William Cavendish (1868–1938), W. S. Halsey (n.d), Wilson Crewdson (1856–1918), Henry Hirsh (d. *c.* 1934), J. A. Holms (John Augustus, 1866–1938), Sir John Kirk (1832–1922), Sir Trevor Lawrence (1831–1913), L. C. R. Messel (1872–1953), Max Rosenheim (1849–1911), 'Lady Stern' and E. J. Wythes (d. 1949). (see Appendix B for biographical information).

169 Pierson (2007), pp. 94–95.

170 Edgar Gorer and J. F. Blacker, *Chinese Porcelain and Hard Stones*, vol. 1 (London: Gorer and Son, 1911), p. ix.

171 Pierson (2007), pp. 96–97.

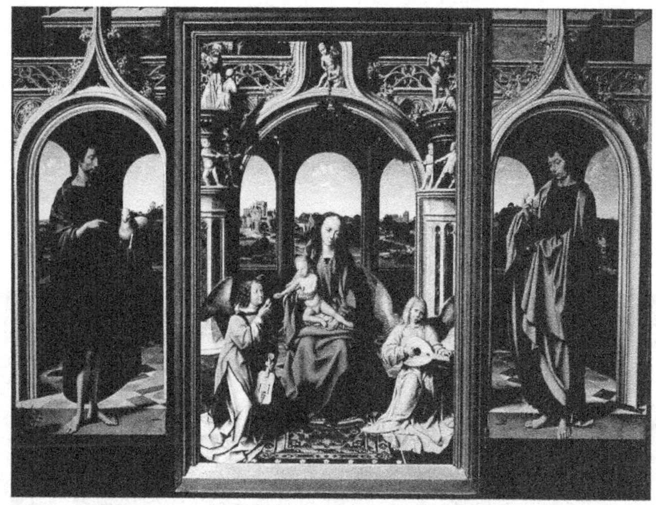

1 The Morrison Triptych, Master of the Morrison Triptych (Flemish, active about 1500). Oil on wood panel, 38 3/8 × 23 ¾ in. (97.5 × 60.4 cm). Toledo Museum of Art Toledo, Ohio. Purchased with funds from the Libbey Endowment. Gift of Edward Drummond Libbey, 1954.5.

Source: © Toledo Museum of Art, Toledo, Ohio.

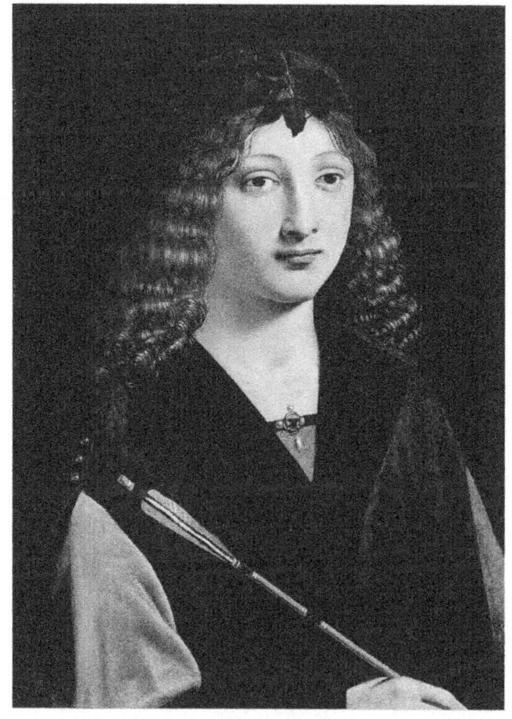

2 *Portrait of a Youth Holding an Arrow*, Giovanni Antonio Boltraffio, 1467–1516. Oil on wood panel *c.* 1500–1510, 49.7 × 35.4 cm.

Source: The Putnam Foundation, Timken Museum of Art, San Diego, USA/Bridgeman.

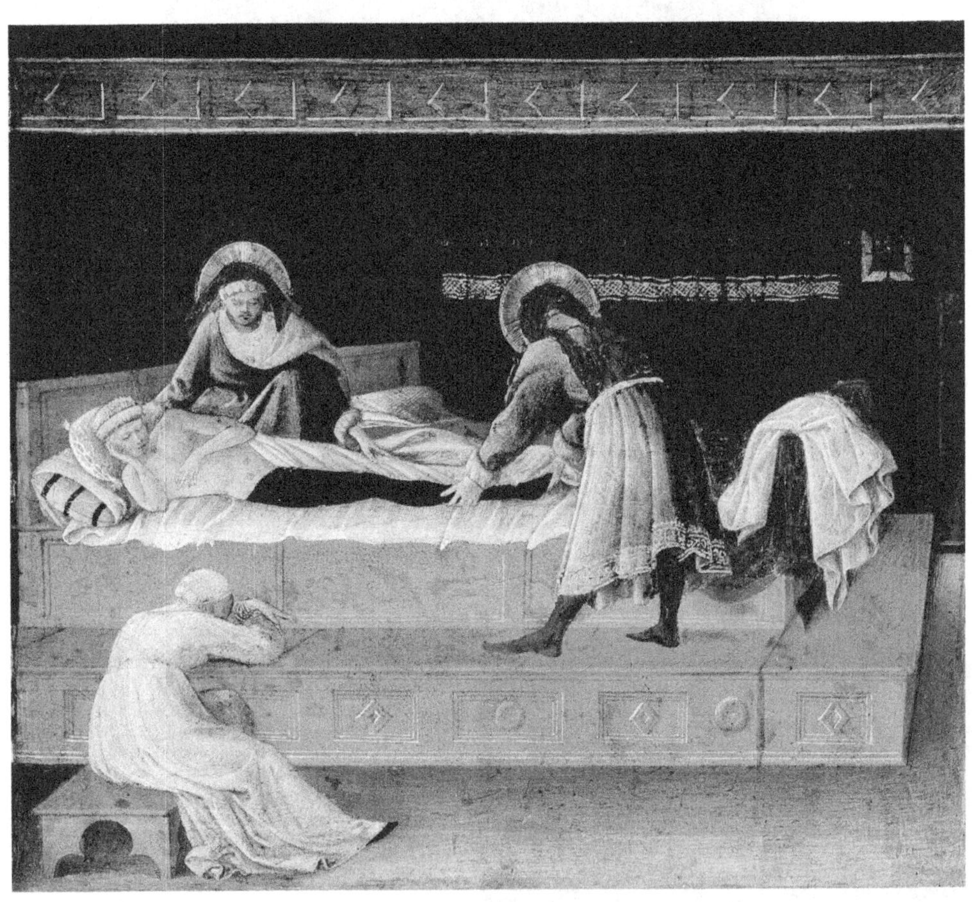

3 *Miracle of the Deacon Justinian*, Fra Angelico (Guido di Pietro), *c.* 1395–1455, 1438–1440. Wood, 20 × 22 cm.

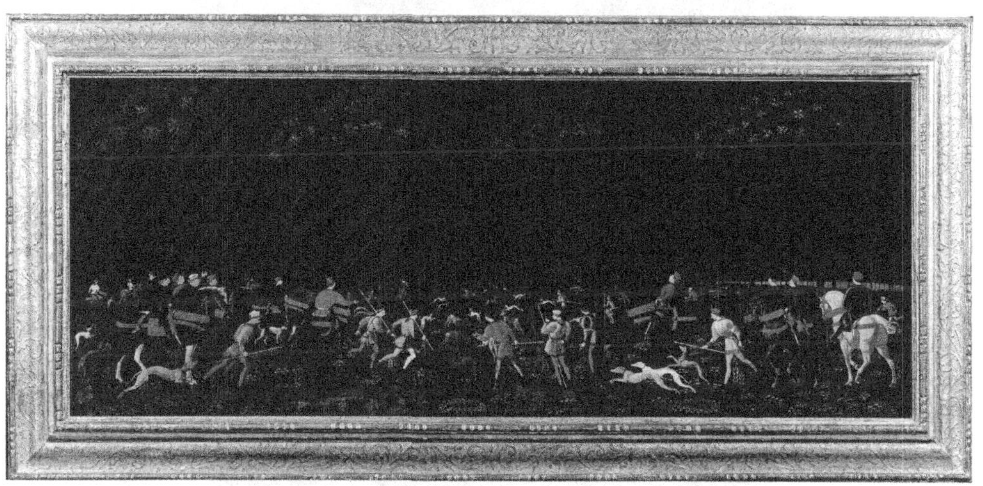

4 *The Hunt in the Forest*, Uccello (Paolo di Dono), 1397–1475, *c.* 1470. Tempera and oil, with traces of gold, on panel, 73.7 × 177 cm. WA1850.31.

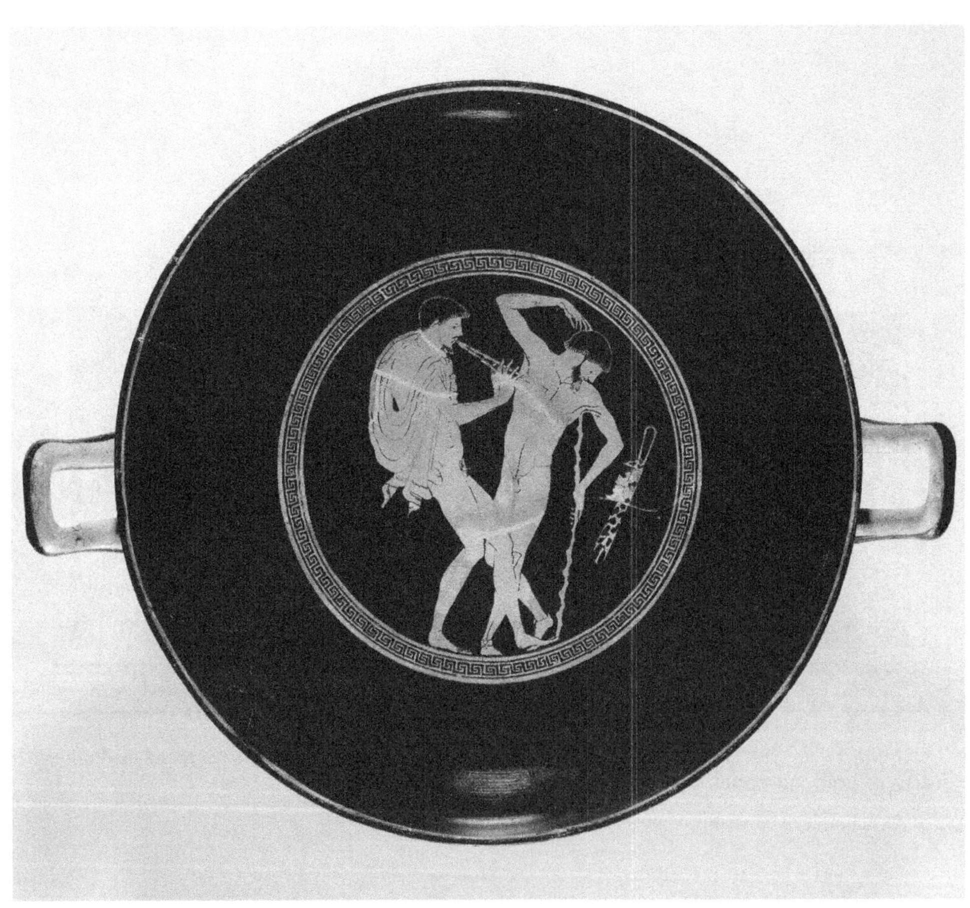

5 Drinking cup (*kylix*), painter: Onesimos, potter: Euphronios. Greek, Late Archaic Period, 490–480 BC. Ceramic. Height: 11.7 cm (4 5/8 in.), diameter: 36.5 cm (14 3/8 in.), Museum of Fine Arts, Boston. Catharine Page Perkins Fund, 95.27.

Source: Photograph © 2016, Museum of Fine Arts, Boston.

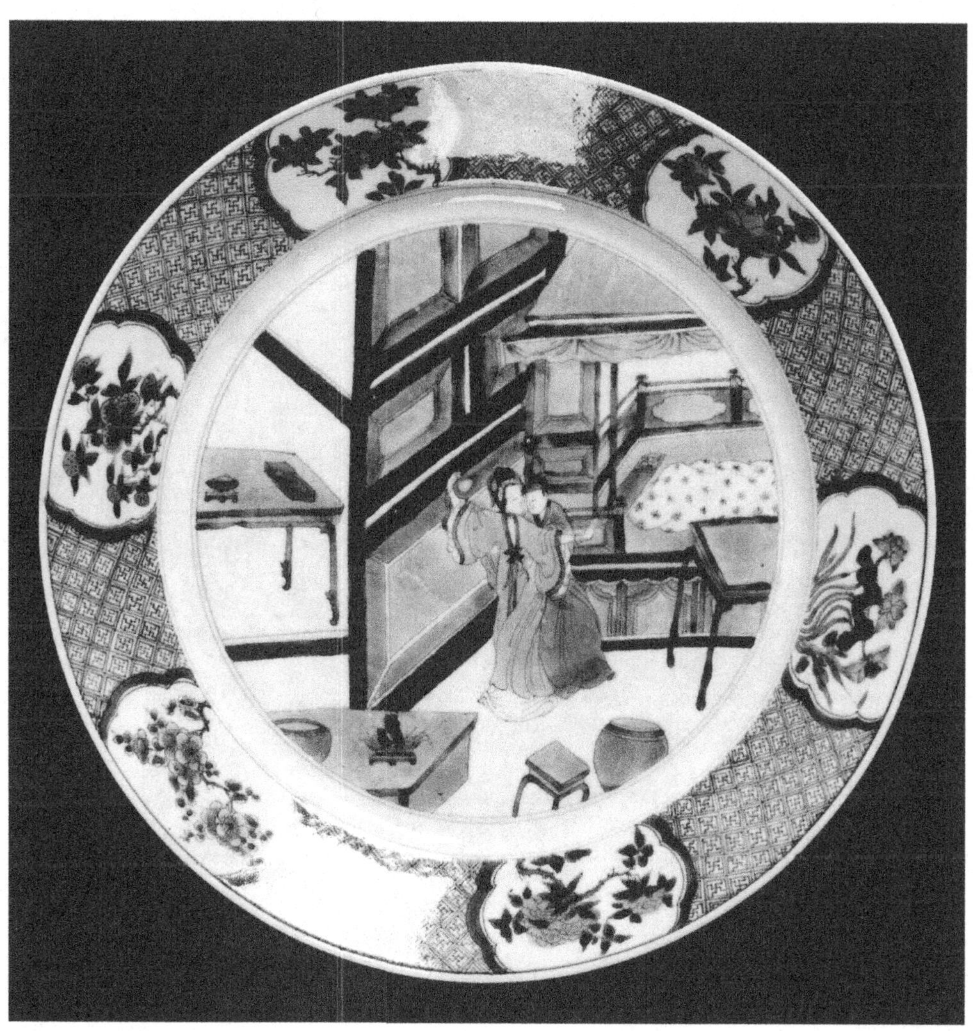

6 Dish, Qing dynasty, Kangxi period, 1662–1722, with Chenghua mark. Porcelain painted in underglaze cobalt blue, Jingdezhen. Diameter 26.4 cm. George Salting Bequest, *c.* 727–1910.

Source: © Victoria and Albert Museum, London.

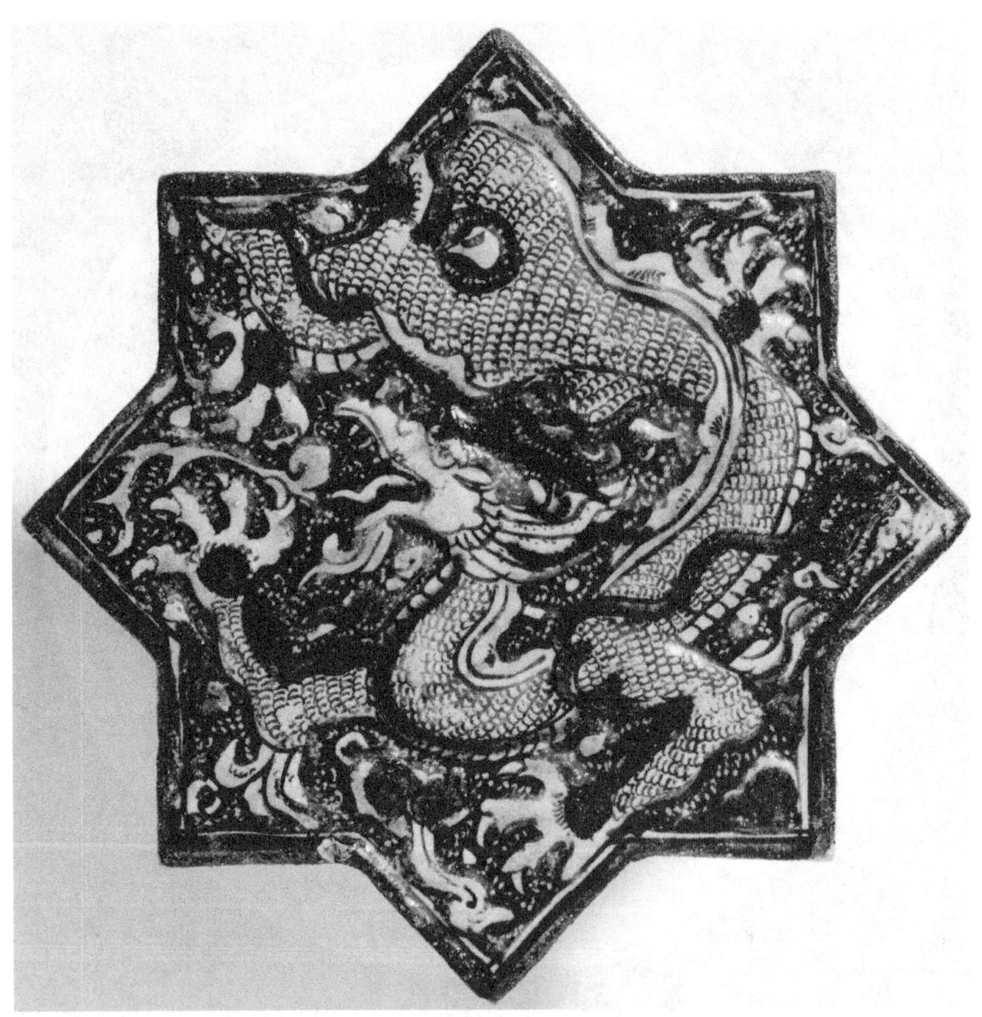

7 Tile, Kashan (Iran), *c.* 1270–1275. Fritware with moulded, painted, and lustre decoration. Width: 20.4 cm, depth: 1.5 cm. George Salting Bequest, *c.* 1870–1910.

Source: © Victoria and Albert Museum, London.

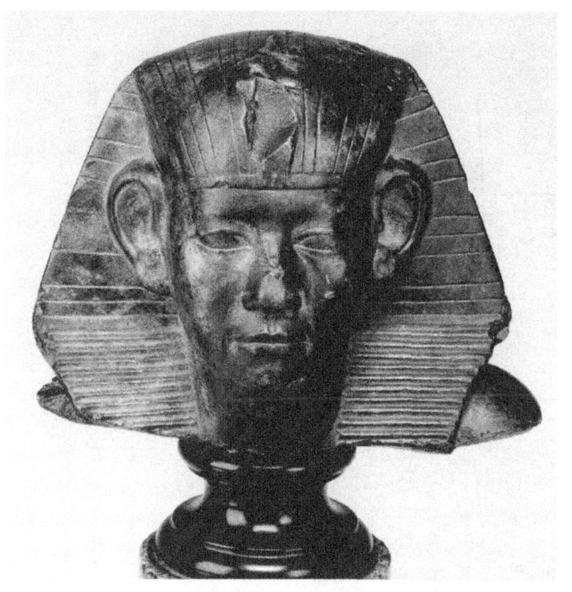

8 Statue of Amenenhat II, Egypt, Aswan, reign of Amenenhat III, *c.* 1831 BC–1786 BC. Shelly limestone. Length: 12 cm, width: 14.3 cm. Oscar Raphael Bequest. E.2.1946.

Source: © Fitzwilliam Museum, Cambridge.

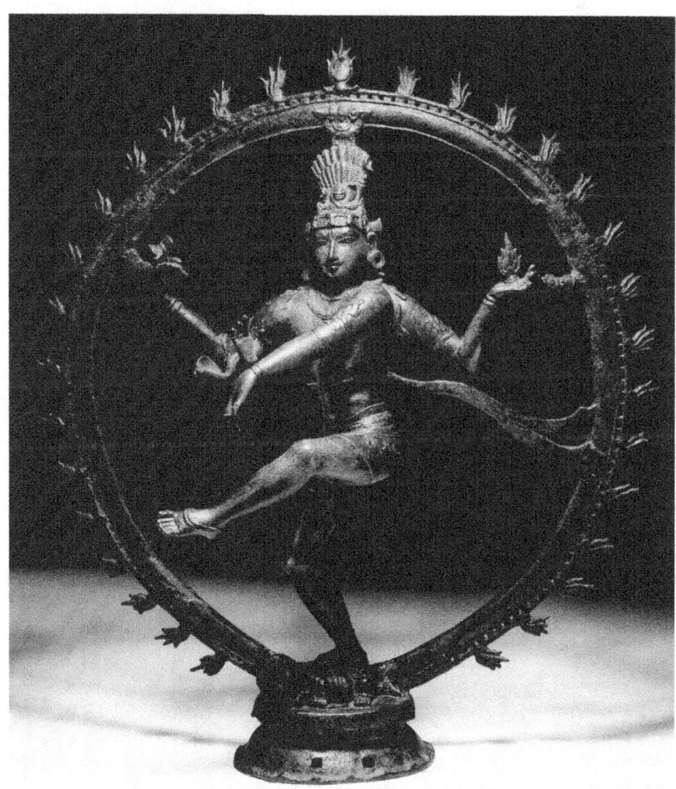

9 Shiva Nataraja, Madras, India, Chola period, 1100–1200. Copper alloy. Height: 85.2 cm, width: 75 cm. Bequeathed by Lord Ampthill. IM.71-1935.

Source: © Victoria and Albert Museum, London.

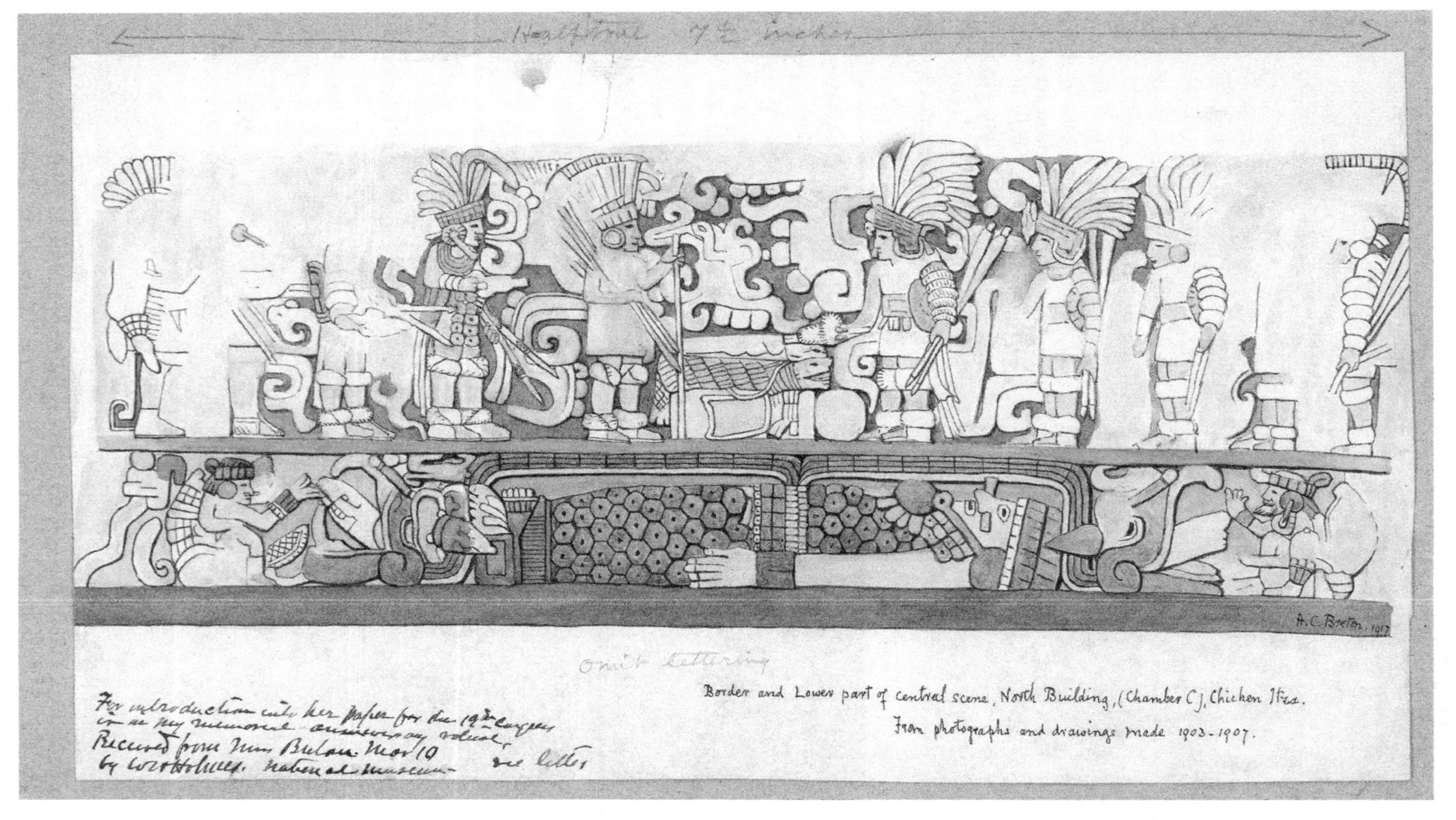

10 Copies of frescoes at Chichen Itza, 1902; 1917, Adela Breton (1849–1923). Watercolour drawing, 'border and lower part of central scene, North Building, Chamber c'. NAA MS 7462.

Source: © National Anthropological Archives, Smithsonian Institution, Washington, DC.

3 Persia, Egypt, and India

Chapter Contents

1885 Persian and Arab Art

As the exhibitions discussed in Chapter 2 demonstrate, many members of the BFAC shared an interest in non-Western arts, an interest that was also shared among a surprisingly large number of art collectors and artists in London in the second half of the nineteenth century and the first quarter of the twentieth. As will be demonstrated, the members' interest in global objects also tended to centre upon the decorative arts, rather than the fine arts. With few exceptions, members collected paintings and prints from Europe and Britain, not those of other countries. The exceptions reflect what was available in Britain at the time, such as Japanese prints, Indian miniatures, and some Chinese paintings. Members who collected these areas of prints and painting tended to do so after 1900, when they became more available on the market. Percival David (1892–1964, a Club member), for example, purchased his most famous Chinese painting, Han Gan's *Night Shining White* (now in the Metropolitan Museum, New York) while he was in Shanghai in the 1930s and members of the imperial family were liquidating their collections.[1] The decorative arts of these regions were collected from an early date, however, as demonstrated in an exhibition staged by the Club in 1885. The 'Exhibition of Persian and Arab Art' opened on 18 March 1885 and was the first temporary, dedicated exhibition of what was called specifically 'Persian art' in Britain. As noted in Blair and Bloom,]'[it] gathered for the first time objects belonging to a large number of private collectors in Britain'.[2] Like all Club exhibitions, it was organized by a committee of members (called here a 'committee of arrangement') and was open to the public by invitation. Some 4,198 visitors viewed the show, not counting members, a successful exhibition by Club standards.[3] The exhibition committee included two key members who would be important for several exhibitions in this chapter: Henry

Wallis (1830–1916) and C. D. E. Fortnum (aka Charles Drury, 1820–99). As noted in the General Committee minutes, it was Fortnum who proposed the exhibition:

> 4.12.1884
>
> VII The Committee considered a letter from Mr Fortnum suggesting an Exhibition of Damascus Rhodian Persian and other kindred wares, as also a suggestion that Mr Pullen's [*sic*] collection of photographs of excavations in Asia Minor should be exhibited at the same time on the walls of the gallery, and it was agreed to adopt these suggestions ... and the following gentlemen were appointed a Subcommittee to make the necessary arrangements vis: ... Tebbs; Vaughan, and Fortnum, with power to add to their number.[4]

The genesis of the exhibition would seem to be ceramics, a material through which many cultures and art historical fields could be interpreted by the Club. As noted in the previous chapter, ceramics such as those mentioned above were a key area of interest for Club members and the subject of special exhibitions (see Plate 7). It is notable, however, that many of the Club's exhibitions of other subjects, particularly non-Western material, began with ceramics and other vessel-based decorative arts. This was also combined with an interest in the archaeology of the regions being considered for exhibition, as the above minute and the catalogue of the 1910 Early Chinese Pottery and Porcelain exhibition confirm. Thus is it not surprising that it should have been Fortnum who proposed what would become a somewhat broader 'Persian and Arab' exhibition. C. D. E. Fortnum was a 'gentleman-connoisseur' who was 'the last of the Fortnums of Fortnum and Mason, grocers of Piccadilly'.[5] He travelled in Europe and the Middle East and became an expert on both maiolica and what we now call Islamic ceramics, creating important collections of both ceramic types which are now in the Ashmolean, the V&A, and the British Museum. The archaeological photographs mentioned in the minutes above were taken by Richard Popplewell Pullan (1825–1888), who had led 'expeditions to Asia Minor' (according to the Club minutes) and is most famous today for his 'discovery' of the so-called Lion of Knidos in 1858, which is now on display in the British Museum.[6] Pullan was a prominent architect and the brother-in-law of the Victorian architect-designer William Burges (1827–1881). He worked in Knidos with the Royal Engineer Robert Murdoch Smith (1835–1900), who would spend a lot of time in Persia and was instrumental in helping the South Kensington Museum develop its collection of Persian art in the years 1875–1889.[7] For much non-Western material, museums such as the South Kensington used the services of buying agents who were active in the countries where the objects originated. Bushell, who was discussed in Chapter 2, performed this function while in China, and Murdoch Smith performed a similar function in what was then Persia.

The Lenders

The main exhibition subcommittee: Henry Tebbs, Henry Vaughan, Wallis, and Fortnum, persuaded a long and illuminating list of lenders to participate in the exhibition, but not all the lenders were members of the Club. This was a pattern followed for most of the larger exhibitions at the Club, as we have seen. Fortnum's loans were mainly ceramics, as might be expected of a specialist collector of this material. Henry Virtue Tebbs who was discussed in Chapter 2, was a friend of W. Holman Hunt (also a lender) and D. G. Rossetti. His loans to the Persian exhibition were a little more diverse than Fortnum's as they included glass, a 'book cover', and carpets.[8] In fact, Tebbs was known as a book collector with a special interest in book bindings, which he also lent to exhibitions at the Club. One important example, dating to the late fifteenth century, is now in the Royal Collection.[9] Henry Vaughan (1809–1899) is also perhaps best known for his collections of Western art and objects. He gave Constable's *Haywain* to the National Gallery, for example, and other significant bequests to both the British Museum and the V&A.[10] In spite of being on the exhibition subcommittee, Vaughan only loaned one object: a wall tile (cat. no. 95) but this demonstrates again that for the Club, exhibitions and their organization were not confined to members with specific expertise in the exhibition topic.

Both Vaughan and Tebbs were associated with Pre-Raphaelite members and non-members of the Club who participated in Club exhibitions, including this one. William Holman Hunt (1827–1910), for example, loaned an interesting range of primarily metalwork vessels to the exhibition.[11] No. 261, for example, was a 'Syrian Circular Tray .... Obtained by the owner direct from the Mosque of Omar, or "Dome of the Rock", in Jerusalem', thus providing evidence for Hunt's travels.[12] Hunt had founded the Pre-Raphaelite Brotherhood with Rossetti in 1848 and is most famous for his religious paintings and domestic scenes such as *The Awakening Conscience* 1853, now in the Tate Collection.[13] As a lender to the Persian exhibition, Holman Hunt was joined by William Morris (1834–1896) and Burne-Jones, thus confirming the taste, and some would say expertise, among this artist group for what would later be called 'Islamic art'.[14] Morris, for example, was consulted about the design merits of the 'Ardebil carpet' and its proposed acquisition by the South Kensington Museum.[15] Not surprisingly, his loans to the Persian exhibition consisted of several carpets and textiles but also ceramics, metalwork, and manuscripts[16] (Figure 3.1). Morris, Hunt and Burne-Jones were not members at the time of the exhibition, or indeed ever, yet they were involved in its exhibitionary activities. Along with Owen Jones, they also brought the art and design worlds into the Club, and vice versa, similar to Whistler and Rossetti with ceramics and prints.

Some artists associated with the Club were, however, also members and prominent lenders to this exhibition and several others. Sir Frederick Leighton, for example, was a founder member of the BFAC, as we have seen, and possessed a large collection of what were then called Persian and Rhodian ceramics. He loaned over 20 of these to the exhibition and of course created fantastic 'Islamic' rooms at his home, Leighton House in Holland Park, London. At the time of the Persian exhibition, the 'Arab Hall' extension to Leighton's house had recently been completed.[17] In this room, the 'Arab' nature of the design is almost entirely created through ceramics. Thus, like other lenders and members, Leighton's primary interest was in the ceramics of the Middle East, rather than other materials. These were also what was most available on the market at that time. Leighton's social position, association with the Royal family and presidency of the Royal Academy placed him in somewhat of a different category than some of the other artist-members, who more often than not, were RAs. Leighton also lived quite grandly, in Holland Park, an area of London which was populated by several other artists, patrons, and members of the BFAC.[18] Burne-Jones, for example, lived nearby as did G. F. Watts, W. C. Alexander and Val Princep. Several collectors and Club members also lived in the area, including the prominent Ionides family. The son of Constantine Ionides (1833–1900), 'Aleco' was a lender to the Persian exhibition, a friend of Whistler, and a client of the dealer Murray Marks.[19] Another lender to the

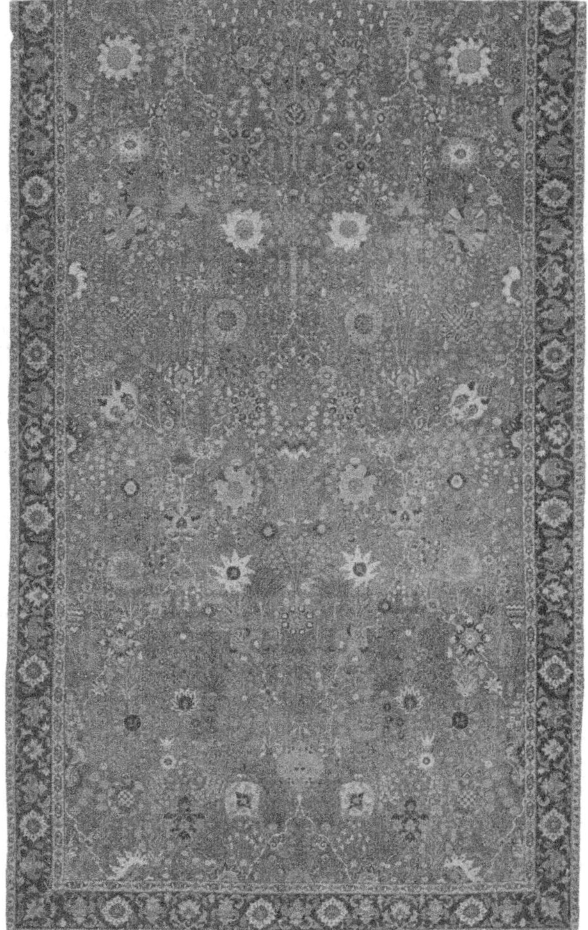

Figure 3.1 Carpet, Kerman province, Iran (possibly), 1600–1700. Cotton warp, silk and cotton wefts, wool pile. Length: 523 cm, width: 330.5 cm.

Source: © Victoria and Albert Museum, London.

Persian exhibition was 'Mrs Coronio', aka Aleco's sister, who was not a Club member but was closely associated with it through family.[20]

A number of collectors who were patrons of Leighton, the Pre-Raphaelite painters, and William Morris were lenders to the Persian exhibition, demonstrating not only shared interests in art but also a social connection that the Club facilitated. Their membership of a gentleman's club in London also equalized their status and interests. Louis Huth, for example, came from a banking family and was a member of the Club along with his brothers Charles and Henry. Louis was a patron of several contemporary artists and architects, including Whistler (who painted Mrs Huth) and G. F. Watts (who rebuilt the family estate, Possingworth Park).[21] Like Fortnum, Huth was also primarily interested in ceramics and his 19 loans to the Persian exhibition were primarily of this material, apart from one metalwork vessel (Figure 3.2).[22] By the time

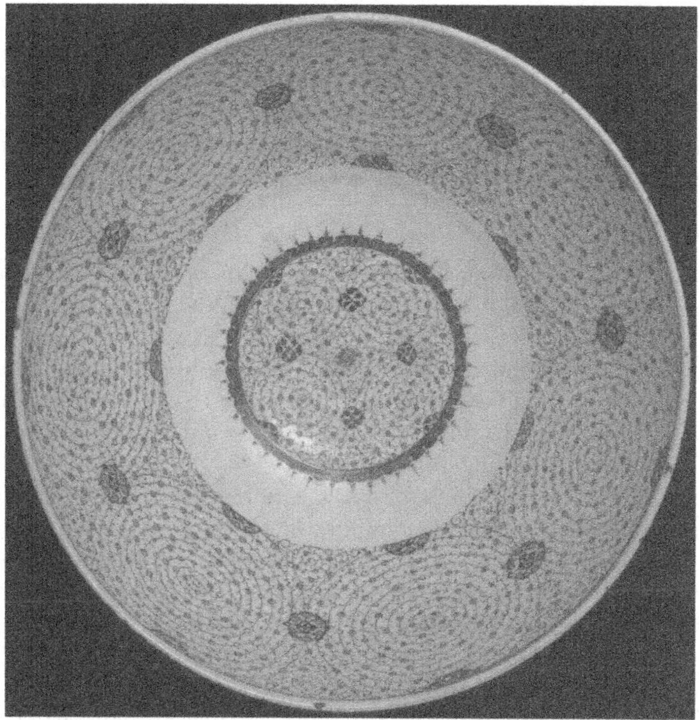

Figure 3.2 Bowl, Iznik, Turkey (probably), *c.* 1545–1550. Fritware with polychrome underglaze decoration. height: 19.1 cm, diameter: 44.2 cm. George Salting Bequest, *c.* 1880–1910.

Source: © Victoria and Albert Museum, London.

of the exhibition in 1885, Huth had already gained some recognition for his collection of Chinese porcelain, and was included in a catalogue by his fellow Club member A. W. Franks.[23] Huth also appears to have been instrumental in encouraging the Asian ceramic collecting of his fellow Club member and Persian exhibition lender, George Salting, who was also friendly with Fortnum and Franks, another example of the close links between collectors and different groups facilitated by the Club. This relationship, and his ceramic collecting, were described thus:

> George Salting found his vocation as a professional collector of art. Inspired by the beautiful objects he had studied in Rome and encouraged in his pursuits by the advice offered by his friend Louis Huth, and by Charles Drury Fortnum and Augustus Wollaston Franks of the British Museum, George Salting embarked on his chosen career with single-minded determination. Chinese porcelain was the focus of his first serious collection. Many of the pieces he bought came from Dutch collections formed in the seventeenth and eighteenth centuries which were being broken up in a series of major sales in the late 1860s and early 1870s. In his acquisition of blue and white porcelain, the highly regarded *famille verte* and *famille rose* and the rare black enamelware, Salting received much encouragement

> from Louis Huth, himself a distinguished collector of Chinese porcelain. From 1874 Salting began the practice of depositing on loan his oriental porcelain and other collections of *objets d'art* at the South Kensington Museum, where they were put on public display. Because he was frequently exchanging pieces from his collections for better examples there was no certainty that particular objects would always be on view. The Salting collections began to acquire an organic character as pieces were added or replaced before the eyes of admiring visitors and collectors.

In contrast to other ceramics collectors, his interest in Asian examples preceded an interest in European ceramics, much of which was acquired in the Paris art market:

> While he was forming his oriental collections Salting began to move into the area of Renaissance bronzes and maiolica … By 1896 Charles Drury Fortnum, in his authoritative book on maiolica, could describe Salting's maiolica collection as 'the richest private collection now in England' …
>
> '[He] kindly allows it to be exhibited, for the public benefit, at the South Kensington Museum.' Many of his most important pieces were acquired at the famous Fountaine sale of 1884, where he spent thousands of pounds on well-known documented examples from Gubbio and Castel Durante. A few Urbino pieces which had eluded him at the Fountaine sale were secured by Salting at later sales. By far the most important of these was the Frederic Spitzer art sale in Paris held at the late collector's house … from April 1893. Here Salting astounded the collecting world by his daily appearances in the saleroom over the course of seven weeks; he bid in person large sums of money for the Renaissance objects … Salting was reported to have spent more than £35,000 at the Spitzer sale.[24]

Salting's 28 loans to the Persian exhibition were all ceramics, apart from one carpet (cat. no. 592). A number of the ceramics are examples of what is now called Iznik ware but in the exhibition were referred to as 'Rhodian ware'.[25] For example, no. 365, a 'Rhodian jug' was lent by Huth (Figure 3.3) and then purchased by Salting at the Huth sale at Christie's in London, in May 1905. It was then donated to the V&A by bequest from Salting in 1911.[26] The biography of this object reminds us of how interconnected the different aspects of the art world were (and still are). In this case, one collector purchased from another collector at auction and then gave the purchase to a museum by bequest. The private object became public through the intervention of the art market.

At the time of the Club's exhibition, it was thought possible to distinguish 'Rhodian' wares from 'Persian' ceramics, which was the single general category used for all similar ceramics by Robinson in his 1862 exhibition catalogue essay.[27] Thus, progress in identification was seen to have been made during the Club's show, and this was attributed to Franks.[28] A number of these were presented in 'cabinet 9 – Rhodian ware' and were loaned by Leighton, Huth, Tebbs, Fortnum, Godman, and Salting, among others.

The leading authority on Asian ceramics in the 1880s can be said to be Franks, a Keeper at the British Museum from 1851, and author of one of the earliest texts to distinguish Asian ceramics geographically (Franks 1876). The debt to Franks' catalogue of 1876 was acknowledged by the Club in its 1896 exhibition of Coloured Chinese Ceramics (see Chapter 2). As we have seen, Franks was also a founder member of the Club and instrumental in advising other members on their collections and collecting

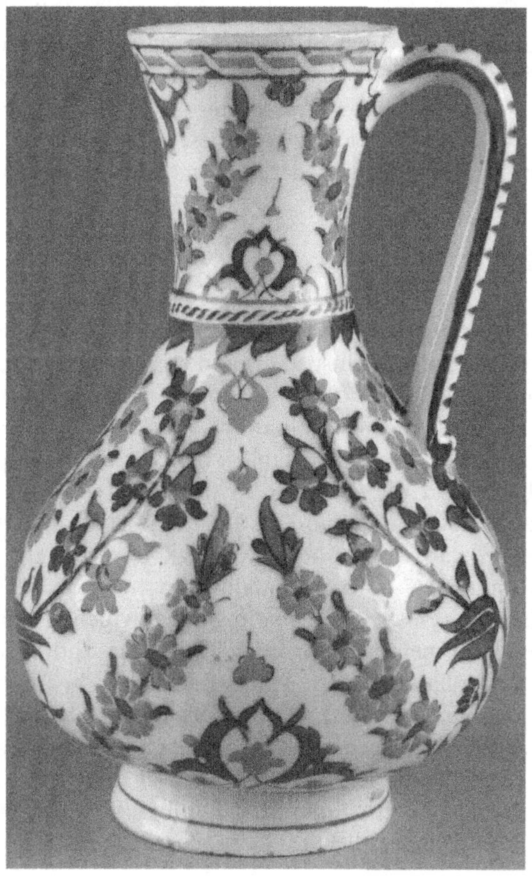

Figure 3.3 Jug, Iznik, Turkey (probably), 1560–1590. Fritware with polychrome underglaze decoration. height: 25.1 cm, diameter: 15.9 cm. George Salting Bequest, *c.* 1898–1910.

Source: © Victoria and Albert Museum, London.

strategies. Franks himself had a substantial collection, most of which has ended up in the British Museum, and from this he loaned three pieces to this exhibition (catalogue numbers 434, 547, 652), as well as many other shows. He is cited numerous times in the catalogue essay, which was written by Club member, Henry Wallis.

Henry Wallis has been described as 'one of the first true experts in Persian art' but he was better known in his time as a painter and associate of the Pre-Raphaelite Brotherhood.[29] His fellow painters were most impressed with his now most famous work, *Death of Chatterton*,[30] which caused a sensation when it was first exhibited at the Royal Academy in 1856. It was universally praised, including by Ruskin, a fellow Club member.[31] After coming into an inheritance, Wallis later in life became a collector of ceramics, both Italian and Islamic.[32] He studied and wrote extensively about ceramics, particularly Islamic ceramics, becoming an authority on the subject and chief cataloguer of famous collections such as that of Frederick du Cane Godman (1834–1910), also a member of the Club and lender to the Persian exhibition.[33] Godman was a scientist and Fellow of the Royal Society, demonstrating the broad appeal of 'Persian' and 'Arab' art at the time of the exhibition. Much of his collection was donated to the British Museum through his daughter. Wallis had experience of travel to both Italy and Egypt and made numerous acquisitions for himself and others on these trips, including William Bode (1845–1929) in Berlin.[34] These activities, along with his personal collection and interest in archaeology, informed the text of his introductory essay for the Persian art exhibition.

The Main Catalogue Essay

In the introductory remarks at the beginning of the exhibition catalogue, Wallis starts by clearly stating the aims of the exhibition: 'To illustrate the more important phases of the art of Persia, and its effluent arts, of Damascus and Rhodes.'[35] The focus is on material in British collections, which therefore consists mainly of ceramics. Thus, like any exhibition, it is a construct, limited by specific variables, which have an impact on the conceptualization of the theme and the structure of the narrative. There is much discussion of ceramics in the catalogue essay and of the literature of ceramics, to ground the exhibition in the current state of that field. What were seen as the key survey texts are mentioned: 'De Brongniart, Marryat, Jacquemart mention Persian ceramics'[36] but Wallis notes that in these texts there are some errors which are being corrected by current scholarship by Club members Fortnum, Robinson, and Franks, who is attributed with inventing the Rhodian category. Wallis then notes the multiple published sources on Persian art, valuable, as he said, mainly for illustrations but not content, but it should be noted that not one of these carries the name 'Persian art', as this category was still somewhat fluid and not fully established at the time of the Club's exhibition. Significantly, the role of Murdoch Smith's handbook for the South Kensington Museum is emphasized, though the collection he procured for the museum was considered badly displayed.

> It must never be forgotten that students of Persian Art are deeply indebted to Colonel Smith. To his promptitude, energy, and sound taste the country owes the large collection of Persian Art objects at South Kensington. Purchased in 1876, it has not yet been fairly displayed. It is a singular illustration of the irony of fate which has relegated the art of the land of the sun to rooms where the direct light of day never enters, and where the brilliant lustre tiles and vases reflect the muddy tints of a dull brick wall.[37]

Robert Murdoch Smith had worked in Persia as an engineer for about ten years when he contacted the South Kensington Museum offering to acquire objects for its collection.[38] At the same time, Smith also acquired the prominent French collection formed by Jules Richard (1816–1891) for the Museum which received over 2000 objects in late 1875. They had been shipped via the new Suez Canal and were put on display in April 1876.[39] Smith also wrote the accompanying handbook which was a key text for many collectors: *Persian Art* (1876).

At the time of writing the exhibition catalogue essay, Wallis considered the South Kensington collection to be a work in progress, ten years after it was first acquired through Murdoch Smith. The Museum's collection was still not representative, in his opinion, but nor was the art of Persia well understood generally. 'The time may be distant when the secret of Persian art stands open and revealed.'[40] However, it is clear that generalizations could still be made, some of which persisted and still persist in the analysis of 'Islamic art' today. For example, 'Persian art is essentially symbolic …', and there is a 'prohibition to represent the human figure …'. [41] Yet Wallis notes that in the exhibition, this is not rigorously enforced, nor is it in some famous architectural sites in Persia, such as the 'Royal Palace at Ispahan' where there are paintings of Shah Abbas, which are poor quality and probably European.[42] Wallis also grounds the study of Persian art in 'her architectural monuments',[43] thus accounting for the large number of tiles present in the exhibition. Yet it was monuments, and the associated archaeology of such monuments that essentially stimulated interest in the objects of the region.[44]

If the British fascination with Persia and the Arab world can be given a starting point, it may be the experiences of travellers and of the design theorist Owen Jones, a Club member (see the Introduction). Jones had travelled to Italy, Greece, Egypt, Turkey, and Spain where he was inspired by the Alhambra Palace and architecture in Cairo, particularly the use of colour and pattern.[45] What he saw on this Grand Tour was incorporated into his monumental *Grammar of Ornament*, published in 1856. This coincided with new ideas about design education, which what we now call Islamic art became an important part of, through the appreciation of architectural ornament. Leighton's Arab Hall, for example, is a study in tile arrangement.

Thus, while clearly influenced by personal experience and social acquaintance, Wallis's essay gives an interesting picture of the state of the field of 'Persian Art' at the time of the exhibition, in which ceramics are firmly situated.

Context for the Exhibition

The South Kensington Museum was a key locus for the development of a specific field of Persian art at that time. The first-ever dedicated Persian art display in London was presented at the South Kensington Museum (later the V&A) in 1876 to display the newly acquired collection purchased for the Museum by Murdoch Smith. Its first-ever display of what was described as 'Persian' material, however, was the ceramics in their 1862 loan exhibition, which, as we have seen, was possibly a formative influence on the Club (see the Introduction). However, the Club's exhibition of 1885 was the first non-institutional exhibition of Persian art and is therefore seen as pioneering. It was also more comprehensive than the South Kensington Museum exhibition of 1876 in that it consisted of loans from multiple contributors and therefore presented material that was not normally on display in public. It was therefore very much in keeping with the Club's intention to bring to light as much privately collected art as possible. This exhibition, like several of the ceramics ones, is also significant for the participation of so many members of the Pre-Raphaelite Brotherhood, whose interest in Islamic art is widely noted but their collections have yet to be the subject of a dedicated study. This Club exhibition therefore would seem to be a significant record of a moment in the history of collecting, as well as the display and classification of Islamic art in London. The next major exhibition of Persian art in London was the 1931 International Exhibition of Persian Art, at the Royal Academy, which was indebted to the Club's earlier attempt, but is usually credited with being the first.[46] The Club's exhibition also demonstrates and highlights the fact that ceramics were the material that underpinned the collecting and scholarly fields of Islamic art in Britain. For this field, ceramics were a pre-existing interest among collectors but ceramics are also a primary material for archaeology, which is another interest among Club members, as the next exhibitions demonstrate.

1895, 1921 The Art of Ancient Egypt, The Art of Egypt

The author of the Persian and Arab Art catalogue, Henry Wallis, was also largely responsible for another exhibition concerned with the Middle East, which followed the Persian art exhibition, in 1895. This exhibition was agreed in a Club General Committee meeting the year before:

> 26.6.1894.
>
> VIII It was resolved that the next Summer Exhibition shall consist of Egyptian Art, and that Mr Henry Wallis and Mr Hilton Price be the Subcommittee for carrying out the Exhibition, with power to add to their number.[47]

At a subsequent meeting, a press release was also drafted and agreed which solicited exhibits, a fairly unusual step for the Club which indicates that this exhibition was seen as more unusual than some of the others recently displayed:

> 17.7.1894.
>
> III It was agreed that the following paragraph be forwarded to the Editors of the London daily papers, and the Athenaeum & Academy, with a request for insertion:-
>
> Exhibition of Egyptian Art & Antiquities
>
> The Burlington Fine Arts Club proposes holding an Exhibition of Egyptian Art and Antiquities in the Spring of next year. The Committee of Arrangement has been promised contributions by well known collectors; but there are many persons possessing collections or single objects of interest who may not be personally known to the members of the Committee. The Committee would doubtless be happy to receive any communications relating to such collections or objects from their possessors.[48]

At the time of the exhibition planning, not many members would have claimed to have been collectors of Egyptian objects but two members who could make this claim were on the initial exhibition committee: Henry Wallis (who would write the catalogue) and Frederick Hilton Price (1842–1909). Wallis was, of course, instrumental in organizing the Persian art exhibition and was an acknowledged expert on ceramics. As it happens, he was also very interested in Egyptian antiquities. Along with several of his fellow Pre-Raphaelite painters, he founded the Society for the Preservation of the Monuments of Ancient Egypt (SPMAE) in 1888.[49] According to Thompson (2015), British artists became interested in Egyptian archaeology after the discovery in the same year of the Roman panel paintings at Hawara, popularly known as the Fayyum Portraits.[50] They were discovered by Flinders Petrie (1853–1942) who was working as an excavator for the Egypt Exploration Fund (EEF, est. 1882) at the time.[51] Petrie would also join the Club exhibition committee, along with several other eminent Egyptologists, but Wallis's co-organizer, Hilton Price, also had links to the EEF, becoming its president in 1905. The EEF, today known as the Egypt Exploration Society, was founded by Amelia Edwards (1831–1892), responsible for Petrie's professorial post at UCL and much of the Petrie Museum's collection, and a coin specialist from the British Museum, Reginald Poole, to 'raise a fund for the purpose of conducting excavations in the Delta, which up to this time has been very rarely visited by travellers'.[52] Its members included Egyptologists but also collectors, who helped to fund its excavations. Both Wallis and Hilton Price were collectors, the latter publishing a catalogue of his collection in 1897.[53] Wallis even paid for his trips to Egypt through collecting. He apparently bought antiquities in Egypt and then sold them in England when he returned, supplying the art market through primary acquisitions. As collectors were needed to fund the archaeology, this was not seen as unethical.[54] Unlike Wallis, however, Hilton Price was a banker and a keen amateur archaeologist who worked on excavations in England and Wales.[55] Both were also lenders to the exhibition. Wallis and Price were joined on the exhibition committee by one more Club member, the Reverend William MacGregor (1842–1937), also a fellow member of the EEF. As the discussion of this exhibition will demonstrate, the EEF was of prime importance not only in the field of Egyptology and excavations but also for the participants in the exhibition, as well as the objects, whose collecting it enabled.

Rev. William MacGregor, from a very wealthy Scottish family, ventured to Egypt in 1885 to recover from a lung illness that may have been contracted during his charitable works, to which he devoted much time and energy at both Tamworth and his Liverpool parish.[56] MacGregor joined the EEF in the same year and became an important benefactor for the Fund. His status as a benefactor entitled him to a share of the antiquities found and he became a passionate collector thereafter. He even built his own museum in 1903 at his estate, Bolehall Manor in Staffordshire (now a private members club, Bolehall Manor Club). The museum was visited by both Wallis and Hilton Price, in addition to such significant figures as Lord Carnarvon[57] who would later find fame with the discovery of the tomb of Tutankhamun in 1922. Wallis went on to write a catalogue of MacGregor's ceramic collection, *Egyptian Ceramic Art: The MacGregor Collection, a Contribution towards the History of Egyptian Pottery* (1898).

Wallis, Hilton Price, and MacGregor were joined on the Exhibition committee by three non-Club members who were eminent in the field of Egyptology. Flinders Petrie, as noted above, was at that time just three years into the newly-created post of Edwards Professor of Egyptian Archaeology at UCL. Petrie was also a lender to the Exhibition, contributing nearly 40 objects to the show.[58] The other external members of the committee were not lenders but they were among the most prominent Egyptologists of their time: Professor Gaston Maspero (1846–1916) and Professor Dr Adolf Erman (1854–1937). Both Maspero and Erman were philologists and Egyptologists at respective universities in Paris and Berlin. They worked on hieroglyphics, using different methodologies. Maspero worked in Egypt as Director General of Excavations and Antiquities, introducing partage terms favourable to foreign excavators and Erman presided over what would become known as the 'Berlin School' of Egyptology.[59] With Petrie, this meant that the three most important names in the field were involved in the Club's exhibition.

The Lenders

The involvement of these Egyptologists also no doubt aided the unusually heavy participation of institutional lenders in the Exhibition. Normally most Club exhibitions consisted of members' objects, with occasional external loans from private collectors who were known to members, including the Queen in some cases (see Chapter 2, 'Pictures of the School of Ferrara-Bologna'). For the Egypt exhibition, however, five museums and institutions were persuaded to participate, including: the Royal Museum, Berlin, the South Kensington Museum, University College London, Liverpool Museum, and the Butler Museum, Harrow. The latter was located at Harrow School and had been named after the former Head Master Rev. Henry Montagu Butler (1833–1918). Butler had persuaded the Old Harrovian Sir Gardner Wilkinson (1797–1875) to leave his various collections to the School as a bequest. These included his collection of Egyptian antiquities.[60] More pieces were lent by the Royal Museum, Berlin, including the entire contents of one case, Case O, which featured a range of figures in bronze, wood, and faience and information about their excavation, where provided, for example:

> 12 Found at Memphis, probably in the tomb of Sarobian, prophet of Astarte in the reign of Amenophis IV (1882).[61]

The Berlin Royal Museum was responsible in the nineteenth century for the Egyptian collection that was housed in the Neues Museum from 1850. Their most famous object, the bust of Nefertiti, was not featured in the Club's exhibition as it was only discovered in 1912 by German excavators. However, the loans from Berlin were singled out in the exhibition catalogue for their quality and representativeness:

> For the high quality of their execution, and their representative character, the objects contained in the Case contributed by the Berlin Museum form a typical representation of Egyptian art which will long cling to the memory of the visitor to the Gallery.[62]

The other two institutional lenders to the Club's exhibition were University College London, which housed the Edwards collection, and Liverpool Museum, which loaned from the Mayer collection. The Edwards Collection was formed by Amelia Edwards, one of the founders of the EEF, discussed previously, and funder of Flinders Petrie's professorial post at UCL by bequest. Edwards had been a writer who travelled to Egypt, publishing a successful account of her trip in 1877.

> As part of the bequest, Edwards left her collection, the core of what is today the Petrie Museum. Numerically it is overshadowed by the quantity of finds from Petrie excavations, and the collection that Petrie himself formed from his purchases in Egypt and Europe.[63]

The loans from Liverpool were also associated with a private collection, that of the Liverpool jeweller and 'antiquary', Joseph Mayer (1803–1886). After being housed in his own Egyptian Museum, Mayer's collection was donated to Liverpool Museum in 1867. At this time, the Museum also began to sponsor excavations in Egypt and acquire additional objects.[64]

The Mayer collection loans consisted mainly of small everyday and funerary items, similar to many of the other exhibits, as well as a mummy hand with rings (Figure 3.4).[65] While presented here as 'art', such displays of human remains were common in Egyptological practice at that time. For example, another private collector

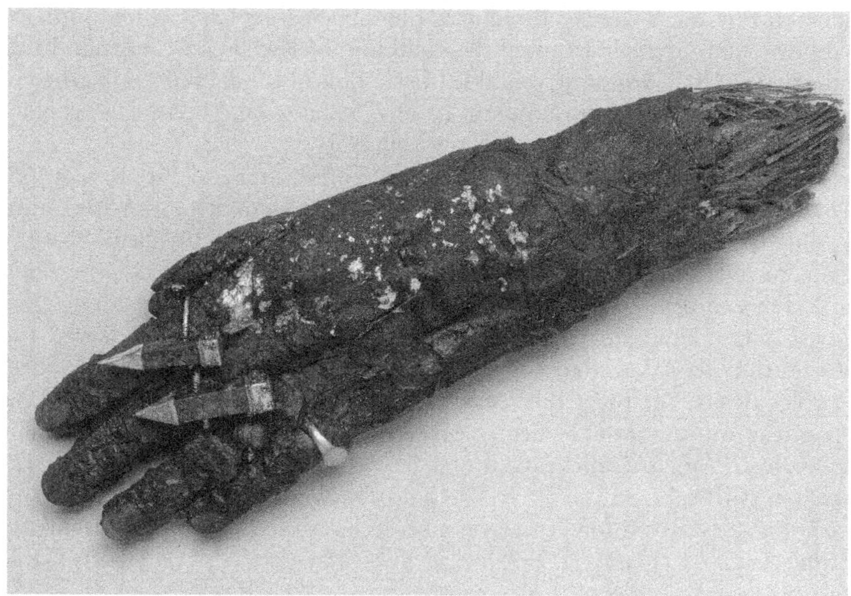

Figure 3.4 Left hand of a female mummy with rings, Saqqara, Egypt, Roman period. Rings of gold and lapis lazuli. M11438.

Source: © National Museums Liverpool, World Museum.

who was singled out for thanks in the catalogue essay loaned a group of temple objects from one site. 'Dr Fouquet, of Cairo' was the French medical doctor Daniel Fouquet (1850–1914) who lived in Cairo and was an early paleopathologist. He participated in the mummy 'unrollings' organized by Maspero when he was Director of the Egyptian Museum and Antiquities service.[66]

An object loaned by a more distinguished (at the time) private owner illustrates the scale and class of object featured throughout the exhibition. This object, a 'serpentine head of Amenemmes III' was owned by Field Marshal Francis Wallace (Lord) Grenfell (1821–1945).[67] It was acquired after the exhibition by Club member, Oscar Raphael (1874–1941), who bequeathed it to the Fitzwilliam Museum collection, where it now resides[68] (see Plate 8). Lord Grenfell had loaned it to the exhibition in 1895 and it was described as a masterpiece in the exhibition catalogue:

> The present Exhibition contains a masterpiece in the head of a King of the XIIth Dynasty (Case D, no. 16), contributed by General Sir Francis Grenfell, a work which would add lustre to any museum, and wherein is concentrated all the skill and refinement of the art of the epoch ...[69]

The Fitzwilliam has identified it as being carved from shelly limestone and originating from a tomb in Aswan.[70] Grenfell had a distinguished military career, having served in Africa and Egypt, and was in active service at the time of the exhibition. He later went on to become Governor of Malta and Commander-in-Chief of Ireland. He was made a peer in 1902 (1st Baron Grenfell).[71] Not much is known about his collecting activities but some of his ceramics were featured in Wallis's book *Egyptian Ceramic Art* (1900), and it appears that Grenfell acquired the collecting bug while on campaign in Egypt during the war in 1882, where he was able to use some of the art skills he learned while a student at the Slade School in London. Later Grenfell would become a president of the EEF (EES), like some of his other fellow collectors.[72]

Another distinguished military official and lender, General Pitt Rivers (1827–1900) had visited Egypt the year before (1881) and collected a wide range of objects. He was invited to participate in the Club's exhibition by Hilton Price, who appears to have known the General and his wife personally.[73] Thus, the range of lenders to the exhibition reflects the state of Egyptology and British engagement with Egypt at that time, not an obvious Club connection. The EEF played a critical role and thus so did archaeology, which was developing as a practice through Egypt explorations but the Club's exhibition was clearly not an archaeological one. From the outset, its title firmly placed the objects and the subject matter within the realm of 'art' and positioned it within an art history of the region, rather than a cultural one.

The catalogue essay reinforces this yet also declares that the objects within are not at that time classified as 'art':

> The present Exhibition is the first attempt to bring together a loan collection of examples of the art of Ancient Egypt. Such an undertaking has, indeed, until now been scarcely possible. The difficulties of collection in this case are exceptionally great. The opportunities of acquisition are rare and uncertain. Also, since the objects lie without the range of the departments of art hitherto claiming the attention of the connoisseur, a certain special knowledge is required to judge their artistic importance, and even to declare their authenticity. But the Burlington Club – which in the thirty years of its existence, has displayed in its Gallery so many phases of the Arts of various races and diverse periods – has considered that it may, at length, essay the exposition of the art of the race that founded the most ancient civilization of which we possess historical record.[74]

This ambiguous classification of ancient Egyptian objects persists today but it is interesting to note that it was a private collectors' club that made the first attempt to fit this material into an art historical framework. One clear and consistent characteristic of these collectors which emerges from a study of their exhibitionary work is that of broad collecting tastes in terms of region and material and a universalizing concept of objects as 'art'. The expertise of members was similarly wide-ranging in a manner which would be somewhat criticized today, certainly in the institutional art world, where knowledge is more specialized and 'professional'. Yet at the time of the exhibition, Egypt was an interest shared by institutions and individuals in terms of both collecting and the archaeology that made it possible.

Interpretation and Response

Nonetheless, there is a certain bias underpinning the classification of Egyptian objects as 'art'. In writing the catalogue, Henry Wallis demonstrates the application of a Eurocentric model for the study of objects identified as art:

> The eye as readily detects the difference between a *cinque cento* gem or bronze, and a veritable antique, or a picture by Overbeck and one by Perugino, as it does between a work of the time of Psametik and its prototype of the earlier dynasties.[75]

The problem of periodizing Egyptian objects is also compared to that of Italian art which would be the norm for this time in art historical discourse.[76] The desire to summarize and classify a whole culture in terms of discrete periods is a methodology borrowed from the so-called Berlin School of Art History, founded by the Director of the Berlin Gemäldegalerie, Gustav Waagen.[77] As we have seen, Waagen had been a member of both the Fine Arts Club and the BFAC, and his work was a model and inspiration for the members' approach to writing art history in their exhibition catalogues.[78] The Club's art historical framing of the Egyptian objects also reflects contemporary attitudes towards both 'treasures' and decorative arts. A review of the exhibition, published in *The Magazine of Art*, reinforced both of these tropes:

> The art of Ancient Egypt is never likely to be better illustrated in a single exhibition than is at present at a show at the Burlington Fine Arts Club, whose committee, aided by such specialists as Professor Gaston Maspero and Mr Flinders Petrie, has organized such a gathering as the Egyptologist must always remember with interest. Not only private collectors, but important public institutions – the Royal Museum of Berlin for instance – have lent to the Burlington Club what are practically priceless treasures, representing to perfection the smaller and more exquisite of the industrial arts as the Egyptians practised them.[79]

Bearing in mind the role of the South Kensington Museum in the founding of the Club and the interests of its members, the attribution of 'industrial arts' to Egyptian objects is to be expected.

The Magazine of Art also suggested that the subject of the exhibition was not yet one which captured the popular imagination: 'Were the subject of more direct appeal to a large artistic public, we should treat it at greater length.'[80] Nonetheless,

> [T]the whole assemblage … has been brought together with diligence and with rare knowledge … much credit is due … to Mr Henry Wallis, who adds to his gifts as an artist the qualifications of an expert in Egyptian affairs.[81]

While ancient Egypt was a fascinating topic to the Victorian public, it was not, it seems, one popular in museums or indeed in art exhibitions. Framing this archaeological material as art, however, would bring it within the realm of the art museum and the art-viewing public before such time as 'ethnographic' museums became a standard part of the museum community.[82] The attribution of specialist knowledge of Egypt to Wallis further confirms the intellectual context for the exhibition in which artists, archaeologists, military officials, and religious figures came together in the form of the EEF, which became a vehicle for their material appropriation of an 'ancient' and therefore exotic civilization.

Viewing the Club's exhibition would have been a different experience to viewing similar material displayed in Petrie's exhibitions at the Royal Archaeological Institute in the previous decade. The emphasis there was naturally on excavated material and maps and visuals associated with excavations.[83] In contrast, the Club's exhibition was displayed in their purpose-built art gallery space, in their Savile Row townhouse, thus placing the objects within an elegant domestic interior (see Figure I.2, Introduction). Perhaps because visitors to the Club's exhibitions were less interested in archaeology, and by extension the 'art' of ancient Egypt, visitor numbers for this show were not very high by the Club's standards – 2,273, exclusive of members. However, another exhibition in the same year on a seemingly more popular subject only received 2,408 visitors.[84]

1921 Later Approaches to Egypt

The Club would later revisit the subject of Egyptian art with their subsequent exhibition of that topic in 1921: 'Ancient Egyptian Art'. The title was only slightly modified from the earlier exhibition which looked at the art of 'ancient' Egypt but the role of the EEF in the second exhibition was much stronger in that it was a collaborative effort from the outset. The minutes of the Club's General Committee meeting which approved the second Egypt exhibition confirm this collaboration and reveal the Club's unique approach to all the objects it displayed:

> 15.6.1920
> The recommendations of the Exhibition Committee that the forthcoming Winter Exhibition consist of ... and that the subject of the Summer 1921 Exhibition be the Art of Egypt – in conjunction with the Egypt Exploration Fund – subject to the availability of the Rev William MacGregor's collection, failing which an Exhibition of Ivories be held ... was adopted with the following suggestions – for the Winter Exhibition ... – and for the Summer Exhibition that it be an instruction to the Sub Committee, to be elected, that stress be laid on Art as opposed to the archaeological character + qualities of the Exhibits also in view of the financial condition of the Club the Sub-Committee should arrange for the Catalogue to be completed and the Introduction written without entailing expense to the Club.[85]

Clearly there was some concern about the interpretation of the material which would lend itself to an archaeological presentation but, as we have seen with other exhibitions concerned with archaeological subjects, the Club's approach would be firmly to present it as 'art'. The Club was consistent with this interpretation of all objects throughout its history of exhibitions, apart from in a few cases where external experts were invited to curate the objects or write the catalogue essays. In this, the Club was different from institutions which mounted exhibitions as its shows were driven by personal taste and collections, rather than administrative factors such as exhibition schedules, politics, and economics.

At the next General Committee meeting it was noted that 'Sir Hercules Read' had been instructed to approach the EEF with a view to collaboration. Read was co-opted on to the exhibition subcommittee along with:

> 4.1.1921
> The following gentlemen were appointed a Subcommittee for the forthcoming Summer Exhibition of Egyptian Art: – Rev William MacGregor, The Hon Richard Bethell, H R Hall, Dr A Gardiner, Percy Newberry, O C Raphael and Sir Hercules Read. The Rev Wm MacGregor and Mr Newberry were elected temporary Honorary members of the Club for the duration of the Summer Exhibition.[86]

Read, as noted in Chapter 2, had succeeded Franks at the British Museum and was a prominent member of both the Society of Antiquaries and the Royal Anthropological Institute.[87]

The other members of the subcommittee for this exhibition are interesting because two were not Club members – MacGregor and Newberry – but were more than willing to help organize an exhibition for the Club. Throughout its history, the Club was consistently able to call on outside help and expertise for their exhibitions. This indicates both a familiarity with the Club and its activities in the wider art world, a respect for its exhibitions, and of course the richness of the Club members' social networks. The involvement of MacGregor is not surprising as he was on the committee for the previous Egypt exhibition (see above) and had been a member of the Club at that time. He was also an active member of the EEF (which had changed its name to the EES by 1921). In between the two exhibitions, MacGregor had built the museum on the premises of his home at Bolehall Manor that was apparently visited by several prominent persons in the world of Egyptian antiquities, including, as we have seen, Carnarvon and Henry Wallis, the progenitor of the first Egypt exhibition who would publish a catalogue of MacGregor's ceramics collection in 1922.[88] In June of 1922, the MacGregor collection was put up for sale at Sotheby's and by all accounts was a successful sale of Egyptian material. As MacGregor's biographer describes it:

> In 1921, surprisingly, MacGregor decided to sell his collection to the firm Messrs Spink and Son, a highly-regarded London dealer in antiquities. In the summer of the following year the collection was offered in 1800 lots through the auction house Sotheby's. A total of over 8000 pieces were sold over a period of nine days and it was hailed as a '*remarkable collection of Egyptian antiquities ... unparalleled by any other private collection in England, Europe or America*' (Sotheby & Co. 1922).
>
> Museums, dealers and collectors all flocked to purchase items, which as a collection had covered a broad range of subjects, materials and dates. The proceeds reached the staggering total of £34,092 9s. One of the key pieces was an obsidian head of Senwosret III, sold for the highest price of the sale at £10,000 (Araújo 2006: 66–8). This fragmented head, originally believed to be a representation of Amenemhat III, Senwosret III's son, became the property of the Armenian businessman and collector, Calouste Gulbenkian. It can now be found in the Gulbenkian Museum in Lisbon (Inv. No. 138).
>
> The collection as a whole was hailed as being '... *instrumental not only in furthering the progress of Egyptology but also in bringing Egyptian art before the eyes of an educated public*' (Capart 1937). Today, it lies scattered in various museums and private collections around the world. Items such as 'MacGregor Man' in the Ashmolean Museum in Oxford and the ivory plaque of King Den in the British Museum are just two examples of the rare and high quality of items that MacGregor owned. It is unfortunate that whilst many artefacts have retained the MacGregor collection provenance, others through time and distance have lost their link to him. When MacGregor died in 1937, he left behind him the legacy of many beautiful and often unique pieces that have been preserved for future generations to view and study. His life and collection stand testament to how patronage from the middle-classes played an important role in the emerging discipline of Egyptology.[89]

Thus, MacGregor sold off his Egyptian collection after it was featured quite prominently in the Club's exhibition which closed at the end of July 1921. The Club's second Egypt exhibition had therefore appeared at a crucial time for the field of Egyptian art and archaeology and the market for this material.

Percy Newberry (1869–1949), also co-opted as a temporary Club member during the period of the 1921 exhibition, was another significant person in the field. He was director of the EES's Archaeological Survey of Egypt in its second season, which was notable for its excavation of Beni Hasan and the inclusion of 16-year-old Howard Carter (1874–1939) as an artist for the team.[90] Newberry was also Professor of Egyptology at Liverpool and then later Cairo universities.[91] Unfortunately he was also involved in the drama surrounding the MacGregor sale at Sotheby's. It appears that Newberry had been negotiating with Spink and Son for the sale at the same time that Carter and Richard Bethell were also trying to secure the collection for a single client.[92] This apparently led to a great falling-out between Carter and Newberry, and demonstrates that in the early twentieth century, archaeology like art history, intersected with and was connected to the commercial art world.[93]

Richard Bethell (1883–1929), the son of the 3rd Baron Westbury, was involved not only with the MacGregor sale but more importantly, as a member of the committee of the EES, the survey team that found Tutankhamun's tomb and subsequently was on the list of those who allegedly suffered the 'curse of Tutankhamun' after he died in apparently suspicious circumstances.[94] He was a member of the Club, along with Howard Carter, the Earl of Carnarvon, Arthur Evans (1851–1941) and many other lenders to the exhibition. According to the exhibition catalogue, Carnarvon and Carter were also on the exhibition committee, thus confirming the close links between Club members and the EES that underpinned the exhibition. Additionally, the 1921 exhibition demonstrates the development of interpretation in the field since 1895. In his prefatory note, C.H.R. (Read) states the Club's perspective, and possibly that of the wider field, quite clearly:

> The present exhibition of Ancient Egyptian Art has been gathered together and arranged by a joint committee of the Club and of members of the Egyptian Exploration Society.
>
> The interval of five-and-twenty years that has passed since the Club held an exhibition of the kind, has not only seen great changes in the condition of such studies, but is also long enough to produce a new generation of collectors and of others interested in the earlier phases of man's culture.
>
> It is unquestionable that no true idea of the real grandeur of the art of ancient Egypt can be formed except by visiting the country. But, short of that, the present exhibition may claim to be a very comprehensive exposition of what her long-dead artists and craftsmen could do in the minor arts; of a few pieces in the gallery even more might be said.[95]

The exhibition represents ancient Egypt through its things, which were provided by a new generation of collectors, thus providing a benchmark for new interpretations.

The introductory essay to the catalogue, written by committee member P.E.N. (Newberry) is even more explicit, positioning the material in an ethnographic interpretative framework that was current at the time:

> It has been a dogma of writers on art that a 'work which can be proved to serve any utilitarian, non-aesthetic object must not be considered as a genuine work of art.' If this test were applied to the productions of the Ancient Egyptian studios or workshops, then it would have to be confessed at once that no 'genuine' works of art were produced by the dwellers on the banks of the Nile. The Egyptians were an eminently practical people, and their art was the outcome of the practical business of life. Possessing in a high degree the decorative instinct, they delighted to ornament the objects of everyday life—the weapons with which they fought, the vessels from which they drank, the houses in which they dwelt. But they were not idealists like the Greeks, they did not seek to generalize and to idealize the human figure. They endeavoured to copy nature, to transcribe it; they were realists.[96]
>
> The truth is that Egyptian Art, that is to say the art of Dynastic Egypt, suddenly makes its appearance in Upper Egypt thoroughly formed, and no trace has been found of its origins or early development on Upper Egyptian soil. It is the same with the hieroglyphic writing.[97]

For Newberry, from his perspective as an archaeologist and Egyptologist, the ancient Egyptians had no art because they were a practical people. This is very much a primitivist perspective which informed other Club exhibitions of non-western art, as will be discussed in Chapter 4.

In the 1921 catalogue, Newberry concludes that more excavation needs to be carried out to fill in gaps in knowledge, such as those he outlined, and this would subsequently take place, starting with the discovery of the tomb of Tutankhamun a year later. It has been argued that the EES, along with the French archaeological service in Egypt, which directed the key excavations, and its members who collected so much of the material, were exploiting a certain colonial position with respect to Egypt and its material past.[98] Certainly Britain and France's control of the region made this possible and perhaps coloured the interpretation of the excavated material. This is reflected in the contextual interpretation of the Club's two Egypt exhibitions but more significant for our purposes is the Club's insistence on framing the objects as 'art', essentially using art as a benchmark, and applying this approach consistently. Through the Club, 'Ancient Egypt' could at once be a source of fascinating archaeology and seemingly 'the cradle of civilization' but also of aesthetically pleasing decorative art, in spite of Newberry's reductive criticism. At the Club, the same objects were interpreted in two ways at the same time, an approach that would prevail in its exhibitions of primarily non-pictorial material.

1931 The Art of India

The colonial framework noted for the Egypt exhibition of 1921 also informed the exhibition of Indian art mounted by the Club in the next decade and was similarly underpinned by a strong colonial institution but the inclusion of pictorial material saved it from a primitivist-ethnological interpretation. If the Egypt exhibition was dominated by the Egypt Exploration Society, a subsequent and equally ground-breaking exhibition of Asian art at the BFAC was defined by the Indian Civil Service (ICS), the administrative arm of the British Raj.[99] Quite a few lenders to the exhibition had served or were still serving in the ICS, yet unlike previous exhibitions of Indian objects in Britain, there were also a number of lenders from India, including the government and museums. Two former Governors of Bengal, the Earl of Lytton (Victor Bulwer-Lytton, 1876–1947) and the Marquess of Zetland (Lawrence Dundas, 1876–1961) were on the exhibition organizing committee, for example.[100] They were joined by several other influential people in the world of India but also by someone who was a very active member of the Club, Archibald G. B. Russell (1879–1955). At the time of the exhibition, Russell was the Officer of Arms at the College of Arms, holding the post of Lancaster Herald. Apart from heraldry,[101] he was known as a specialist in William Blake,[102] a collector of old master drawings, and latterly a collector of 'Siamese, Indian, Egyptian, Babylonian Antiquities' which were sold in a Sotheby's auction of 30 May 1927.[103]

Russell was joined on the exhibition subcommittee by Laurence Binyon (1869–1943), a Keeper at the British Museum, poet, and dramatist, who was not necessarily known for his expertise on Indian art or India but was a specialist in painting, particularly Asian painting, and he continued the useful institutional affiliation with the British Museum enjoyed by the Club. Binyon contributed one of the two essays to the exhibition catalogue, 'Indian Painting,' which was also the type of material that featured most in the BFAC show. The other catalogue essay was written by Kenneth de Burgh Codrington (1899–1946), aka 'K de B', who after the Club's exhibition was appointed Keeper of the Indian Section at the V&A (from 1935 till 1948). He was also a member of the Club, like Russell, but Binyon was not a member. In the museum field of Indian art, Codrington was seen as unusual because of his direct experience of India. He was born there and several generations of Codrington men had served in the Indian Army.[104]

Russell, Binyon, and Codrington were all lenders to the exhibition, as was the next member of the subcommittee, Sir William Rothenstein (1872–1945), a portrait painter, war artist, and friend of Binyon, as well as of Whistler and numerous other artists and politicians in both Paris and London.[105] He published much art criticism and later became head of the RCA (Royal College of Art). He developed a personal interest in India after visiting in 1910, becoming fascinated with its painting and sculpture.[106] Rothenstein was also a defender of Indian painting and a founder of the India Society, along with Christina Herringham, E. B. Havell, and A.K. Coomaraswamy (1877–1947). Members of the Club and those affiliated with it were also on the committee of the India Society, including Binyon, Roger Fry, and the Marquess of Zetland.[107] Thus the India Society would seem to have played an important role in the BFAC exhibition and it was given special privileges: 'Permission was given to the India Society to meet in the Club gallery on Wednesday, May 13th at 5 o'clock.'[108] Rabindranath Tagore (1861–1931), the Nobel laureate, was also on the India Society Committee, and was closely associated with Rothenstein, who drew a portrait of him on a visit to the Tagore family home in 1912.[109]

The final member of the Club's exhibition subcommittee was the High Commissioner for India at the time, Sir Atul Chandra Chatterjee (1874–1955), whose role was probably both political and expedient. He had been added to the subcommittee after Chester Beatty (1875–1968) declared he was unable to assist in that instance: 'it was reported that ... Mr Chester Beatty regrets that he is unable to join the Committee of the Art of India Exhibition which had co-opted the High Commissioner for India'.[110] Beatty would have been a logical choice as he possessed a collection of Mughal paintings and manuscripts that is still considered one of the finest in the world.[111] A number of these paintings were loaned to the Club's exhibition, however.

The Lenders

The general lenders to the Club's exhibition similarly represent a cross-section of Anglo-Indian relations in the decade before independence. Not all were members of the Club, which demonstrates the continuing influence the Club had in the worlds of politics, society, and government at that time. The lenders who were members of the Club are representative of the membership profile thus established, however. They included collectors such as Chester Beatty and George Eumorfopoulos, who had gained renown for his Chinese art collections (see Chapter 2), the diplomat, Sir Francis Oppenheimer (1870–1961), the collector and champion of Modernists, Sir Michael Sadler (1861–1943), and Rupert Brooke's literary executor and private secretary to Churchill, Edward H. Marsh (1872–1953). The lenders who were not members are somewhat less diverse with the main groups representing current or former members of the Indian Civil Service; museums in England and India, including the Fitzwilliam and the Madras Provincial Museum; curators and experts, such as Louis C. G. Clarke (1881–1960), the academic, Stella Kramrisch (1896–1993) as well as individuals from India, such as the dealer, Imre Schwaiger (1868–1940), Sir Akbar Hydari (1869–1941), the collector and art critic, Ajit Ghose (act. *c.* 1890s–1920s), M. C. Dey (1895–1989) of the Government School of Art and a student of Tagore as well as a couple of Maharajas. Bearing in mind that the BFAC was still a private members' club, this list of lenders is impressive, and indicates that even in 1930 the assumed boundaries between private collectors and public institutions still were not so well defined or even considered an issue, as they are now. The exhibition was also open to the public who would have been able to see who the lenders were, thus defining the collecting field of Indian art through a broad lens.

Other links between members are revealed in a report in the July 1931 issue of *Man*, the journal of the Royal Anthropological Institute (RAI):

> By invitation of the Burlington Fine Arts Club a Special Meeting was held on 9th June to view the exhibition of Indian Art at their house in Savile Row. Our Fellow, Mr. Codrington, who had been entrusted with a large share of the organizing of the exhibition, was present to answer questions and help in the discussion of knotty points, and the meeting proved to be not only very pleasant but also of much value to those interested in the art of India and, especially, its archaeology.
>
> The Indian Government had generously lent a considerable number of objects from the famous excavations of Mohenjo-Daro and Harappa, including examples of all the most significant of them, the privilege of examining which, comfortably and at leisure, was much appreciated.
>
> The amateurs of Indian art had besides a rare opportunity of seeing some fine sculptures, lent also by the Indian Government, of the classical Sanchi and Gupta periods, so little known outside India, and some beautiful products of the medieval period of which, again, few really fine specimens are to be seen in this country; of better known forms of Indian art there was an excellent collection of miniatures of both the Mogul and the Hindu (or 'Rajput') schools.[112]

One of these sculptures is now in the V&A (see Plate 9), having been acquired by bequest from Lord Ampthill (Oliver Russell, 1869–1935), one of the lenders. This was likely acquired when Ampthill was Governor of Madras as this is where the Chola bronze figure of Shiva was made. Chola bronzes are among the most popular sculpture types from India and have been the subject of a number of exhibitions, including 'The Sacred and the Sensuous: Chola Bronzes from South India' at the Asia Society in New York (2002), whose title neatly combined the two standard tropes for interpreting Indian art. The Chola category (Chola dynasty, *c.* 300 BC–1279 AD) was not yet in use at the time of the Club's exhibition[113] but the inclusion of such material in the exhibition represents what was available for collectors at the time, and what was for them representative of 'Indian art'.

From the perspective of the RAI, Codrington could be a guide for visitors interested in both art and archaeology, the two categories of object represented in the display, as they saw it. He was an active member of both the RAI and the BFAC, demonstrating yet again that special interest groups and collectors' clubs were not seen as having exclusive interests. This ability to interpret both categories of object was particularly useful for the members of the Royal Anthropological Institute because they were most interested in the objects representing archaeology, which is somewhat to be expected, but in the review above, there is no dispute with the general presentation of the exhibits as 'art' in the Club's exhibition. Indeed, Indian 'art' is the category used to describe the objects which were nevertheless also 'specimens'. The Club itself was not averse to such language as the catalogue of the Persian and Arab exhibition demonstrated.

The Club's exhibition of Indian art in fact was somewhat dominated by painting, unusually for one of its regionally-defined, non-western shows. The paintings were primarily Mughal (see Figure 3.5) and were accompanied by small archaeological objects such as beads and seals recently excavated from Mohenjo-daro and Harappa.[114] The inclusion of newly excavated material was of interest to members and non-members alike, as the RAI review above noted and these particular finds were significant in defining and identifying the historical origins of what was newly named the 'Indus Valley civilization'.[115] Thus 'ancient India' was being presented here too, contributing to the narrative of Indian art.

The Club's exhibition is not generally seen as innovative, however. For example, the selection of exhibits by the Club has been interpreted as a deliberate decision to exclude monumental sculpture,[116] which would later form the cornerstone of 'Indian art' for art historians. In fact, it was likely due to the limitations of the Club's display space as this problem has been noted before, with other exhibitions, such as 'Milanese and Allied Schools' of 1898 (see Chapter 1). Certainly even if large-scale examples could not be displayed, sculpture was seen as an important category of Indian art by the Club as its two catalogue essays were on sculpture and painting, the former by Codrington and the latter by Binyon.[117] Such essays are also more representative of twentieth-century Club catalogues which were presented as art historical texts that could be consulted independently of the exhibition. This may have been a consistent aim but it was more successfully realized in the later years of the Club's existence when art historical writing became more distant from its connoisseurship origins.

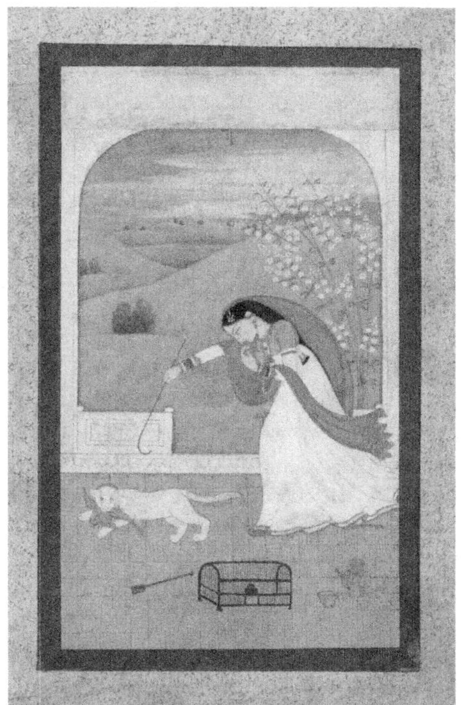

Figure 3.5 Painting, cat thief, Kangra, India, *c.* 1810. Opaque watercolour on paper. Height: 22.3 cm, width: 14.9 cm, IS.140-1955.

Source: © Victoria and Albert Museum, London.

Interpretation

Both of the India catalogue essays attempt to present histories of their respective media and both emphasize an exceptionalism and exoticness grounded in religion, as was common at that time in interpretations of 'Indian art'. Binyon, for example, begins his discussion with 'the great frescoes of the Buddhist period', e.g. those at Ajanta and Bagh.[118] This is followed by a brief discussion of the 'flatness' of Hindu painting and then the rest of the essay focuses on 'the Mogul School', presenting it in traditional painting discourse, e.g. 'schools' of painting. Binyon's perspective is perhaps influenced by the collections of the British Museum where he had organized exhibitions of Indian paintings and drawings in 1922 and 1931. In 1925, wall frescoes from Bagh were exhibited there.[119] He had also published The Court Painters of the Grand Mughals, and he was based in the Department of Prints and Drawings until 1933. His primary interest in West and South Asian painting was actually Persian, and this no doubt influenced his interest in the Mughals. He wrote the essay for the catalogue of the exhibition of Persian art mentioned previously that was held at the Royal Academy in the same year as the Club's India exhibition.

The introductory essay on sculpture by Codrington similarly reflects his own interests, including ethnography and archaeology. The framework is also religious but not as courtly-focussed as Binyon's assessment: 'In summary, it may be said that early Indian sculpture is essentially bas-relief sculpture, and that its inspiration was popular.'[120] We then read about the decline of Buddhism, the rise of Hinduism, and the move towards the dominance of iconographical literature in criticism of sculpture when in fact '[it] represents the dead bones of the working tradition … In the finest work considerable freedom of treatment is won by the sculptor in his acceptance of a convention that is obviously still vital …'.[121] 'Vitality' and 'movement' are two characteristics widely associated with Indian sculpture and are features that, in the mind of the art historian of the time, clearly differentiate it from Classical sculpture (Greek and Roman) – the benchmark.[122] As Codrington notes, 'The broadly conceived planes of such a figure as the *Ilyssos*, especially the powerful, flat treatment of the thighs, is the antithesis of the treatment of mass in Indian sculpture.'[123] The *Ilyssos* he refers to is the sculpture of the river god from the west pediment of the Parthenon which is in the British Museum.[124]

In spite of the bias evident in the introductory essays, and the limitations on the size of objects in the exhibition, it appears, surprisingly, that the Club's show might be the first dedicated survey exhibition of Indian art in London.[125] There are numerous precedents for the display of Indian material, as well as aspects of Indian art such as painting (or paintings of India) but these displays were either part of colonial and empire exhibitions such as the Colonial and Indian Exhibition of 1886, the Indian Museum of the East India Company or in-house gallery displays of institutional collections such as that of the South Kensington Museum in 1874. This latter category would also include themed exhibitions of one aspect of Indian art, such as the paintings in the British Museum (e.g. 1922). But no surveys had yet been attempted in London before 1931 and certainly none with loans from the Indian government.[126] The Club archives do not say why or how the idea of a survey came about but it was very much in keeping with their historical approach to exhibition themes, which ranged from focussed shows of the work of one artist, to a material focus such as ceramics and the art of cultures or nations, such as ancient Egypt, Persia, or 'primitive peoples' (discussed in Chapter 4). If defining all material objects as 'art' is the primary methodology, then themes around which to organize objects had no limitations.

The Club's India exhibition has received very little attention in the literature of the display of Indian art in Britain. It is often dismissed for either not including monumental sculptures,[127] as we have seen, or for being 'small' and not introducing 'an overall portrait of Indian art'.[128] Small could certainly describe the size of many of the exhibits but not the exhibition itself which contained over 330 objects. In spite of differing interpretations of scale, the Club's India exhibition suffers more from comparison with very large-scale institutional exhibitions of Indian art or other arts associated with India. In 1931, for example, as noted above, the Royal Academy staged one of its regular 'national' exhibitions that focussed on the art of a single nation. That year it was Persia and that monumental show (1000 exhibits), *The International Exhibition of Persian Art*, included a room with the arts from other countries that exhibited Persian influence; in the case of India, it was Mughal painting.[129] In the study of the history of Islamic art and its historiography, this exhibition is indeed 'a milestone in Islamic Art History' but it is not the first survey, as we have seen, just a more substantial one in terms of organizer and size. Incidentally, in addition to the major work by Arthur Pope that arose from this exhibition (*A Survey of Persian Art from Prehistoric Times to the Present*, Pope and Ackerman, eds., 1964–1967), Laurence Binyon catalogued the paintings and wrote his own work on them two years later: *Persian Miniature Painting, Including a Critical and Descriptive Catalogue of the Miniatures Exhibited at Burlington House, January–March, 1931*, published in 1933.

Possibly because of the prominence of the Royal Academy exhibition, the Club unusually decided to offer lectures to members about their own exhibition of Indian art around the same time. The lectures were to be given by Binyon and Codrington but it appears that they were not well attended.[130] This is possibly because members were required to request tickets in advance and lectures were not a standard event for the club. In fact, as we have seen, the Club's activities were not event-driven, rather they were focussed on sharing objects both internally among members and externally, with the general public.

Conclusion

As this chapter demonstrates, the Club's approach to the art and objects of nations and cultures beyond Europe, such as Persia, Egypt, and India, was pluralist in that each nation or culture was deemed to be of interest; its objects were collected by Club members and their friends; the objects could be and were treated as 'art'; and there was no limit to what could be borrowed or from whom, apart from the physical space of the galleries. The regionalist approach to classifying the objects was established early on in Club practice, as we have seen, both in the broad cultural sense for non-western material but also on a micro-level for European prints and paintings. For the latter, the Club was following common art historical practice but for the former, it was somewhat pioneering in its choice of nations or cultures to represent. Members owned objects from these areas, they wanted to display them as art, so they found ways to define them that would help to classify them within a familiar art historical framework. Once this was established, as we will see in Chapter 4, no nation, culture, or theme was considered too difficult or too challenging for the Club. Everything could be exhibited in a structured display, in their view, and everything was of interest.

Notes

1 Di Yin Lu, 'On a Shoestring: Small-Time Entrepreneurs and the International Market for Chinese Curios, 1921–1949', *Archives of Asian Art*, vol. 63, no. 1 (2013), pp. 87–102.
2 S. Blair and J. Bloom, eds., *Grove Encyclopedia of Islamic Art and Architecture* (Oxford: Oxford University Press, 2009), p. 58.
3 Minute book vol. 1, pt 2, entry for 31.5.1886. See Appendix A for other visitor numbers.
4 General Committee minutes 4.12.1884, VII.
5 Ben Thomas and Timothy Wilson, eds., *C. D. E. Fortnum and the Collecting and Study of Applied Arts and Sculpture in Victorian England* (Oxford: Oxford University Press, 1999), pp. 129, 147.
6 See Ian Jenkins, *The Lion of Knidos* (London: British Museum Press, 2008), which also details Murdoch Smith's crucial work in removing the sculpture.
7 Isabelle Gadoin, 'British Collectors of Persian Art in the 19th Century: From Personal Culture to Oriental Taste?', *Res Orientales*, vol. XX (2011), pp. 122–123; Stephen Vernoit, ed., *Discovering Islamic Art: Scholars, Collectors and Collections, 1850–1950* (London: I B. Tauris, 2000), pp. 11–12.
8 For example, BFAC, *Catalogue of Specimens Illustrative of Persian and Arab Art Exhibited in 1885* (London, 1885), nos. 258, 574, 597.
9 See www.royalcollection.org.uk/collection/1080368/miscellanea (accessed 9 July 2015).
10 See www.whistler.arts.gla.ac.uk/correspondence/biog/display/?bid=Vaugh_H (accessed 9 July 2015).
11 BFAC (1885), catalogue nos. 261, 262, 265, 145, 250, 268, 305, 313.
12 See exhibition catalogue, BFAC (1885), p. 33; Francesca Vanke Altman, 'William Holman Hunt, Race, and Orientalism', in Thomas J. Tobin, ed., *Worldwide Pre-Raphaelitism: Critical Theory, Popular Culture, Audiovisual Media* (New York: SUNY Press, 2005), p. 47.
13 See www.tate.org.uk/art/artists/william-holman-hunt-287 (accessed 9 July 2015).

14 See, for example, Gadoin (2011), pp. 121–134; see also www.rbkc.gov.uk/leightonarabhall/pdfs/leightons_collection.pdf (accessed 1 Dec. 2015).
15 Vernoit (2000), p. 100. This is now prominently displayed in the Jameel Gallery at the V&A.
16 BFAC (1885), catalogue nos 594, 595, 588, 81, 87, 163, 166, 204, 239, 266, 603.
17 See www.rbkc.gov.uk/subsites/museums/leightonhousemuseum/aboutthehouse/aboutleightonhouse/historyofthehouse.aspx (accessed 9 July 2015).
18 Caroline Dakers, *The Holland Park Circle: Artists and Victorian Society* (New Haven, CT: Yale University Press, 1999).
19 Ibid., pp. 106, 115.
20 Ibid., p. 107.
21 See www.whistler.arts.gla.ac.uk/correspondence/people/biog/?bid=Huth_HR&initial=H (accessed 15 Aug. 2014). The new mansion, Possingworth Park, built from 1866 at a cost of 'more than £60,000' and sited around one kilometre north-east of the old manor, was designed by the celebrated architect Sir Matthew Digby Wyatt in a Tudor-gothic style. See www.parksandgardens.org/places-and-people/site/5082 (accessed 15 Aug 2014).
22 BFAC (1885), catalogue nos 554, 140, 308, 375, 467, 460, 549, 539, 634, 465, 448, 343, 358, 360, 363, 294, 297, 315, 376.
23 Stacey Pierson, *Collectors, Collections and Museums: The Field of Chinese Ceramics in Britain, 1560–1960* (Bern: Peter Lang, 2007), p. 73.
24 Anthony Griffiths, ed., *Landmarks in Print Collecting: Connoisseurs and Donors at the British Museum since 1753* (London: British Museum Press, 1996), p. 190.
25 Franks was one of the first to use this term, in a report on an exhibition at the Society of Antiquaries of Islamic ceramics and a group found at Rhodes. Thomas and Wilson, eds. (1999), p. 220.
26 C.1989–1910. See http://collections.vam.ac.uk/item/O340298/jug-unknown/ (accessed 10 July 2015).
27 This exhibition was noted in the Introduction, BFAC (1885), p. vii. Science and Art Department of the Committee of Council on Education, 1862.
28 Ibid.
29 Gadoin (2011), p. 123.
30 Tate Collection, NO1685.
31 Timothy Wilson, 'A Victorian Artist as Ceramic Collector: The Letters of Henry Wallis', part 1, *Journal of History of Collections*, vol. 14, no. 1 (2002), p. 139.
32 Ibid.
33 Henry Wallis, *Persian Ceramic Art Belonging to Mr F. Du Cane Godman, F.R.S., with Examples from Other Collections: The Thirteenth Century Illustrated Wall-Tiles* (London, 1894).
34 Wilson (2002), part 2, vol. 14, no. 2 (2002), p. 233. At the time of the exhibition. Bode was director of the Sculpture Department at the Berlin Museum. He would later go on to be Director of all the Prussian museums from 1906–1920, and a prominent art historian. See https://dictionaryofarthistorians.org/bodew.htm (accessed 30 Nov. 2015).
35 BFAC (1885), p. v.
36 Ibid., p. vii.
37 Wallis essay in the exhibition catalogue, in ibid., p. viii.
38 Vernoit (2000), p. 11.
39 Gadoin (2011), pp. 122–123.
40 Wallis, in BFAC (1885), p. ix.
41 Ibid, p. x.
42 Ibid.
43 BFAC (1885), p. ix.
44 Vernoit (2000), p. 6.
45 Abraham Thomas, 'Owen Jones and the Islamic World', in G. Maclean, ed., *Britain and the Muslim World: Historical Perspectives* (Newcastle: Cambridge Scholars Publishing, 2011), Chapter 10, p. 144.
46 For a history, see Barry D. Wood, '"A Great Symphony of Pure Form": The 1931 International Exhibition of Persian Art and its Influence', *Ars Orientalis*, vol. 30 (2000), pp. 113–130.
47 General Committee minutes, 26.6.1894.

48 General Committee minutes, 17.7.1894.
49 Jason Thompson, *Wonderful Things: A History of Egyptology 1: from Antiquity to 1881* (Cairo: American University in Cairo Press, 2015), p. 255.
50 Ibid.
51 Amara Thornton, 'Exhibition Season: Annual Archaeological Exhibitions in London, 1880s–1930s', *Bulletin of the History of Archaeology*, 10 March 2015. Available at: http://doi.org/10.5334/bha.252 online journal – no page nos. (accessed 22 July 2015).
52 See www.ees.ac.uk/about-us/history.html (accessed 24 July 2015).
53 *A Catalogue of the Egyptian Antiquities in the Possession of F. G. Hilton Price* (London: Bernard Quaritch, 1897).
54 Thompson (2015), p. 255.
55 See http://heritagearchives.rbs.com/people/list/frederick-george-hilton-price.html (accessed 22 July 2015).
56 Beverley Rogers, 'The Reverend William MacGregor: An Early Industrialist Collector', *Antiquity*, no. 325 (September 2010). Available at: www.antiquity.ac.uk/projall/rogers325/ (accessed 27 July 2015).
57 Ibid.
58 See Burlington Fine Arts Club, *Exhibition of the Art of Ancient Egypt* (London, 1895), pp. 8–39.
59 See Margaret S. Drower, 'Gaston Maspero and the Birth of the Egypt Exploration Fund (1881–3)', *The Journal of Egyptian Archaeology*, vol. 68 (1982), pp. 299–317 and B. U. Schipper, ed., *Ägyptologie als Wissenschaft: Adolf Erman (1854–1937) in seiner Zeit* (Berlin: de Gruyter, 2006).
60 Jason Thompson, *Sir Gardner Wilkinson and His Circle* (Austin, TX: University of Texas Press, 2010), p. 212.
61 BFAC (1895), p. 102.
62 Ibid., p. xviii.
63 See www.ucl.ac.uk/museums-static/digitalegypt/archaeology/edwards.html (accessed 26 July 2015). See also www.brown.edu/Research/Breaking_Ground/ bios/ Edwards_ Amelia%20Blanford.pdf for a professional biography (accessed 26 July 2015).
64 See www.liverpoolmuseums.org.uk/wml/collections/antiquities/egyptology.aspx (accessed 26 July 2015). See also Margaret Gibson and Susan Wright, eds., *Joseph Mayer of Liverpool, 1803–1886* (London: Society of Antiquaries and the National Museums and Galleries on Merseyside, 1988).
65 See www.globalegyptianmuseum.org/detail.aspx?id=4288 (accessed 30 June 2016).
66 Jane E. Buikstra and Charlotte Roberts, eds., *The Global History of Paleopathology: Pioneers and Prospects* (Oxford: Oxford University Press, 2012), p. 211. On the history of mummy unwrapping, see Christina Riggs, *Unwrapping Ancient Egypt* (London: Bloomsbury, 2014), Chapter 2.
67 General Sir Francis Grenfell in the catalogue – not a Club member.
68 This history was described by Charles Ricketts, who was discussed in Chapter 1, in an article for the EEF: 'Head in Serpentine of Amenemmes III in the Possession of Oscar Raphael, Esq.', *Journal of Egyptian Archaeology*, vol. 4, no. 4 (Oct. 1917), pp. 211–212.
69 BFAC (1895), p. ix.
70 See http://data.fitzmuseum.cam.ac.uk/id/object/61606 (accessed 27 July 2015). The museum catalogue entry reveals that the head was a bequest from Oscar Raphael, a Club member.
71 T. A. Heathcote, Grenfell entry in *The British Field Marshals, 1736–1997: A Biographical Dictionary* (Barnsley: Pen & Sword Military) repr. (Casemate, 2012).
72 David Jeffreys, *Views of Ancient Egypt since Napoleon Bonaparte: Imperial Colonialism and Modern Appropriations* (London: Routledge, 2012), p. 90.
73 The correspondence between Hilton Price and Pitt Rivers is preserved at the University of Oxford. The letter in question is available at: http://web.prm.ox.ac.uk/rpr/index.php/primary-documents-index/16-second-collection-1880-1900/527-saswm-pr-papers-l1228/ (accessed 27 July 2015).
74 BFAC (1895), Introduction, p. v.
75 Ibid., p. vi.
76 Ibid., p. xv. The Club had also mounted several Italian exhibitions by this time, see Chapter 1.

77 See https://dictionaryofarthistorians.org/waageng.htm (accessed 27 July 2015).
78 Waagen's popularity among collectors in England was established with his 1854 publication *Treasures of Art in Great Britain*. His role in the development of museum collections in Britain has been studied but less has been said about private collectors. See F. Illies and G. Waterfield, 'Waagen in England: German Influence on 19th Century English Art Museums and Collections', in *Jahrbuch der Berliner Museen* 37 (1995), pp. 47–59; and Elizabeth Pergam, *The Manchester Art Treasures Exhibition of 1857: Entrepreneurs, Connoisseurs and the Public* (Farnham: Ashgate, 2011), p. 33, on his impact on the field. He is noted in the Club's own histories that were written before the 1940s, e.g. *History, Rules, Regulations, and Bye-laws*, 17 Savile Row, London, W.1, 1925, pp. 10–12.
79 'The Art of Ancient Egypt', *The Magazine of Art*, vol. 18 (1895), p. 396.
80 Ibid.
81 Ibid.
82 It was the subject of small archaeological exhibitions, however. See Thornton (2015), fn 318.
83 Ibid.
84 Blue and White Oriental China, see Chapter 2 for discussion.
85 General Committee minute, 15.6.1920. The final exhibition title was 'Ancient Egyptian Art'.
86 General Committee minute, 4.1.1921,
87 David M. Wilson, 'Read, Sir (Charles) Hercules (1857–1929), Museum Curator', in *Oxford Dictionary of National Biography*, available at: http://dx.doi.org/10.1093/ref:odnb/35693 (accessed 1 Dec. 2015).
88 Rogers (2010).
89 Ibid.
90 See www.ees.ac.uk/archive/CarterandtheEES.html (accessed 17 Aug. 2015).
91 See www.ames.cam.ac.uk/library/archive/newberry (accessed 17 Aug. 2015).
92 T. G. H. James, *Howard Carter: The Path to Tutankhamun* (London: Tauris Parke, 1992) (2006 edn), p. 241.
93 Ibid.
94 See www.mirror.co.uk/news/world-news/curse-king-tutankhamun-fatal-fevers-4563888 (accessed 15 Aug. 2015).
95 BFAC, *Catalogue of an Exhibition of Ancient Egyptian Art* (BFAC, 1922), pp. xvii–xviii.
96 Ibid., p. xix.
97 Ibid, p. xxii.
98 Paolo del Vesco, 'Forming and Performing Material Egypt: Archaeological Knowledge Production and Presentation', in S. Quirke, *et al.*, eds., *Forming Material Egypt*, proceedings of the international conference, London, 20–21 May, 2013, EDAL IV 2013/2014, Milan, 2014, pp. 241–260.
99 Chandrahas Singh, *The Civil Service in India, 1858–1947: A Historical Study* (Delhi: Atma Ram and Sons, 1989).
100 BFAC, *Catalogue of an Exhibition of the Art of India*, 1931, p. 3.
101 Russell wrote a review of the Club's heraldry exhibition of 1916 ('A Collection of Objects of British Heraldic Art to the End of the Tudor Period') in *The Burlington Magazine*: 'Heraldry at the Burlington Fine Arts Club', vol. 29, no. 160 (July 1916), pp. 164–168.
102 See Archibald Russell, *The Engravings of William Blake* (London, 1912). The Club mounted has two Blake exhibitions in its history: 1876, 'Works of William Blake', and 1927, 'Blake Centenary Exhibition'.
103 *A Collection of Valuable Ancient Works of Art: The Property of Archibald G. B. Russell...*, Sothebys, London, 30 May, 1927.
104 Saloni Mathur, *India by Design: Colonial History and Cultural Display* (Berkeley, CA: University of California Press, 2007), p. 151.
105 See www.academia.edu/5510654/William_Rothenstein_Short_Biography (accessed 10 Aug. 2015).
106 Partha Mitter, *Art and Nationalism in Colonial India, 1850–1922: Occidental Orientations* (Cambridge: Cambridge University Press, 1994), pp. 309–311; Robert Speaight, *William Rothenstein: The Portrait of an Artist in his Time* (London: Eyre & Spottiswoode, 1962).

107 See www.open.ac.uk/researchprojects/makingbritain/content/india-society (accessed 10 Aug. 2015).
108 General Committee minutes, 5.5.1931.
109 In the British Museum collection today: see www.britishmuseum.org/explore/online_tours/asia/the_art_of_peace/portrait_of_tagore.aspx (accessed 10 Aug. 2015).
110 General Committee minutes, 7.10.1930.
111 See Elaine Wright, *Muraqqa: Mughal Indian Paintings from the Chester Beatty Library* (Dublin: CBL, 2008). Beatty was an Irish-American mining magnate who collected widely and extensively but especially books and manuscripts from around the world. He opened his museum, the Chester Beatty Library in Dublin in 1953. Charles Horton, *Alfred Chester Beatty: From Miner to Bibliophile* (Dublin: Town House, 2003).
112 140. 'Loan Exhibition of Indian Art', *Man*, vol. 31 (July 1931), p. 136. Royal Anthropological Institute of Great Britain and Ireland.
113 The figure was assigned to the Madras Presidency, an administrative subdivision of British India. The Club's exhibition took place before the end of British rule in India.
114 For example, BFAC, *Catalogue of an Exhibition of the Art of India*, 1931, catalogue pages 24–27.
115 The excavations were led by Sir John Marshall and have been noted in the Club's exhibition catalogue's Preface. He is credited with discovering the 'Indus Valley civilisation'. See Douglas Barrett, 'Sir John Marshall', *Journal of the Royal Asiatic Society of Great Britain and Ireland*, no. 1/2 (April 1959), pp. 92–93.
116 Tapati Guha-Thakurta, *Monuments, Objects, Histories. Institutions of Art in Colonial and Postcolonial India* (New York: Columbia University Press, 2004), p. 177.
117 BFAC (1931).
118 Ibid., p. 9. For context, see Partha Mitter, *Much Maligned Monsters: Aa History of European Reactions to Indian Art* (Chicago: University of Chicago Press, 1992).
119 Joanna Bowring, 'Chronology of Temporary Exhibitions at the British Museum', British Museum Research Publication no. 189 (London: British Museum, 2012).
120 BFAC (1931), p. 17.
121 Ibid., p. 18.
122 Mitter (1992).
123 Ibid. p. 17.
124 Item 1816,0610.99. It was also displayed in the recent special exhibition at the British Museum, 'Defining Beauty: The Body in Ancient Greek Art', March–July 2015.
125 The exhibition had somewhat of a rocky start, however. It had first been proposed in 1898 but was postponed and not proposed again until 1930. General Committee minutes 19.7.1898 (viii); 8.11.1898 (iv); 1.7.1930.
126 There was a survey exhibition of 'Arts and crafts, choice examples of Indian art' in Liverpool at the Walker in 1898 but this seems to have been an isolated example. *Spring exhibition comprising arts and crafts, choice examples of Indian art: lent by the Department of Science and Art, London), architectural drawings, photographs, &c.*, D. Marples & Co. Printers, 50A Lord Street, Liverpool, 1898.
127 For example, Guha-Thakurta (2004), p. 177.
128 Devika Singh, 'Indian Nationalist Art History and the Writing and Exhibiting of Mughal Art, 1910–1948', *Art History*, vol. 36, no. 5 (Nov. 2013), p. 1049.
129 Ibid. and B. W. Robinson, 'The Burlington House Exhibition of 1931: A Milestone in Islamic Art History', in Vernoit, ed. (2000), pp. 147–149.
130 General Committee minutes, 28.5.1931.

4 Indigenous and Primitive Art

Chapter Contents

Introduction

As demonstrated in Chapter 3, Club members and associates of the Club had very wide interests in collecting, from traditional art objects to archaeological things, but even with that in mind, there are some subject areas that would seem to be far outside the Club members' interests. Among these were areas of art production that were geographically far from England, such as the Americas, and areas that were conceptually quite new, such as what was called 'primitive art' for much of the twentieth century. Both of these subject areas, however, were related to Club members' other professional interests, indicating that Club members wished to exhibit not only collected items that reflected the Club's traditional areas of interest but also those that related to professional activities beyond the Club that were also associated with acquiring things. Two Club exhibitions mounted in the first part of the twentieth century clearly demonstrate this inclination and provide another perspective on the exhibitionary and collecting work of the Club.

1920 Objects of Indigenous American Art

Early in 1920, it was agreed by the Club's General Committee that the forthcoming Summer exhibition would be on 'Aboriginal American Art'.[1] The title was eventually changed to 'Objects of Indigenous American Art', which neatly combined the ethnographic and art historical categories of things that were first combined by the Club in the Egypt exhibition of 1895 (see Chapter 3). As usual, a subcommittee for the exhibition was appointed:

> The following Gentlemen were appointed a Sub Committee for the forthcoming Summer Exhibition of Aboriginal American Art: -

Sir Hercules Read
T. A. Joyce
O. C. Raphael
Louis C. G. Clarke.

Professor Henry Balfour and Mr T A Joyce BT were elected Honorary Members of the Club for the period of the Summer Exhibition.

Mr A P Maudslay was elected a temporary Honorary member of the Club for the period of the Summer Exhibition.[2]

As noted in the General Committee minutes above, several non-members were temporarily elected so that they could serve on the committee: Professor Henry Balfour, T. A. Joyce and A. P. Maudslay.[3] The catalogue of the exhibition confirms that both Balfour and Maudslay were on the final subcommittee for the show.[4]

The justification for this exhibition theme may not be noted in Club minutes but there is a comment in the exhibition catalogue which confirms that this was the first exhibition in Britain to concentrate solely on 'American' art, and by this the Club meant North (Canada and the USA), Central, and South America.[5] This was not a widely exhibited category of art or object in Britain at that time even though there were collections on display in the British Museum and the Museum of Archaeology and Anthropology (MAA) at Cambridge University. Neither institution had presented its own temporary exhibitions of 'American' art but both were lenders to the Club's exhibition, either officially or through their staff, who participated individually. The subcommittee, for example, included Read from the British Museum and Louis Clarke (1881–1960) from the MAA, Cambridge University, where he later became Director of the Fitzwilliam Museum (1937). T. A. Joyce (Thomas Athol, 1878–1942) was also at the British Museum, as assistant to Read, and was a specialist in American archaeology. He later became a president of the Royal Anthropological Institute (RAI, discussed in Chapter 3), thus demonstrating yet another link between the Club and members of other special interest groups not necessarily concerned with objects as 'art'. Joyce is known for some unfortunate views as a scholar but was clearly respected by the members of the Club regardless.[6] In a review of several of Joyce's publications on aspects of 'ancient American art', Roger Fry (a fellow Club member), for example, states that: 'we owe Mr Joyce a debt of gratitude for the careful and thorough accumulation of all the material which the archaeological remains afford'.[7]

Henry Balfour (1863–1939), also a president of the RAI, was curator of the Pitt Rivers Museum at the time of the exhibition. Subsequently, he was also appointed Professor of Ethnology at Oxford University and he continued as curator until his death.[8] The next member of the exhibition subcommittee is a little more mysterious because no detailed biography or biographical information exists for him, yet he was an active member of the Club and a collector of some repute: Oscar C. Raphael whose bequest to the British Museum included Egyptian, 'Oriental', and American antiquities.[9] He also left a range of Chinese and other material to the Fitzwilliam Museum, Cambridge, such as the Grenfell head discussed in Chapter 3.[10] Raphael was yet another link to the RAI, having been a fellow for some years until his death[11] and to the Egypt Exploration Fund (EEF, later EES), of which he was a member.[12] Not surprisingly, he was a lender to the Club's later Egypt exhibition in 1921 (see Chapter 3).

The final member of the exhibition subcommittee, A. P. Maudslay (Alfred Percival, 1850–1931) was a British diplomat who had worked in Trinidad, Fiji, Tonga, and Samoa.[13] Upon leaving the colonial service, he went to Guatemala to work as an archaeologist at various Maya ruins. He had completed this work by the time of the Club's exhibition and would clearly have been a logical and useful member of the subcommittee. In his obituary of Maudslay in *Man*, T. A. Joyce noted that he was a meticulous independent archaeologist who photographed everything he found and made plaster casts of many of the monuments. He was also a president of the RAI,[14] thus confirming that all the members of the Club's exhibition subcommittee were also members of the RAI. This suggests a rather formal link that would have been intentional on behalf of the Club but it was not a joint exhibition, as the following year's Egypt exhibition with the EES was (see Chapter 3).

Interpretation

Nonetheless, the link with the RAI and its interests and perspective would clearly colour the Club's approach to the material and its subject. T. A. Joyce wrote the introductory essay to the exhibition catalogue, after all, and the selection of objects to include was made by the subcommittee. Joyce's own perspective would seem to be strongly anthropological, somewhat in contrast to those reflected in some of the other exhibitions of non-Western objects, but he still framed the objects as art in the BFAC manner:

> The Committee of the Burlington Club may lay claim, I think, to the distinction of being first in the field with an exhibition of an American art which owes nothing to any other continent. The archaeology or ethnology of the indigenous race, or races, of America have had their students and their literature for a couple of generations or more. But their autochthonous art, viewed as art, is here seen grouped together for the first time, at any rate, in this country.
>
> … What will be noticed at once is that though the art is at times naturalistic, the dominant note is one of symbolism, expressed in terms that are not perhaps easy for us to understand, but nearly always productive of fine decorative motives of original type … For this exhibition, it surely may be claimed that it avoids the commonplace as successfully as the merely pretty, and, of a certainty, it has a near relation to the primitive.[15]

The interpretation of these objects as both art and artefact is not unusual for its time or place, when ethno-archaeology was developing as a scholarly specialism. As Joyce suggested, American 'art' was primitive, natural, and ritualistic, providing evidence that the peoples who created these objects were possessed of the same qualities. It is also finely decorated and therefore possessed of two contradictory, yet to the anthropologist, complementary qualities. Joyce also suggests that the Club is unusual in even considering American art as a category for display. In that time period this indeed would have been unusual in Britain, as is noted in some of the reviews of the show. In *The Burlington Magazine*, for example, one reviewer stated:

> That such an exhibition should be arranged by so distinguished a body (the BFAC) must be source of much gratification to all Americanists. For it would seem to suggest that the British art-world has at length awakened to the importance of

American autochthonous art. We may now perhaps look forward to the time when it will be given the consideration that it merits by students on this side of the Atlantic as it already is on the other side.[16]

The same reviewer gives credit to Joyce for the high quality of the exhibits and also describes the objects as an antidote to the insincerity of the art of the day.[17] In this view, American art is naturally sincere because it is actually 'primitive' rather than theoretically so. Joyce compares it with 'the primitive' in the catalogue and as Stallabrass (1990) noted, the period 1918–1930 was an important one for the establishment of primitivism as a theme in writing on art and anthropology in Britain, including the Club, as we will see. The American art in the Club's show was seen to possess this primitive quality because it was truly 'savage', unlike the theoretical primitivism of the avant-garde.[18] As Joyce stated in the catalogue, the indigenous art of America possessed the 'naturalism' which was considered a key characteristic of primitive objects and people.[19]

However, the Club's presentation of the subject in one of its exhibitions also incorporates it into its own universalist view of 'art' which, as we have seen, is not constrained by medium, location of production, or authorship. The very few other exhibitions of American objects at the time took a very different approach. One of the earliest was an 'Exhibition of Maya Sculptures' in the British Museum in 1923 (until 1939) that was a display of the Maudslay collection which had arrived in 1922 due to the efforts of Joyce[20] (Figure 4.1). The Rymill Collection arrived at the Museum of Anthropology and Archaeology at Cambridge after 1929 but it too was displayed as ethnography, and not in special exhibitions until the Club's 'Primitive Peoples' exhibition in 1935 (discussed below).[21] Public collections of American objects were rare in Britain in 1920 but the subject was not unfamiliar to the general public as Joyce noted. As early as 1840, the American artist and collector George Catlin had opened the Gallery of the North American Indian at the Egyptian Hall in London.[22] In fact, Native American[23] artifacts, that is from North and South America, had been privately collected in Britain since at least the late sixteenth century.[24] They were on display in various venues, including the British Museum, which was founded in 1753 with the collection of Sir Hans Sloane (1660–1753) that included such artifacts.[25] As Brown noted:

British museums, art, and literature have a long history of representing the indigenous peoples of North America (S. Pratt 2005). Moreover, throughout the nineteenth century, with increased travel and emigration, and the resulting global circulation of Native-made arts, the British public was not unfamiliar with First Nations artifacts or with the images and descriptions of them that appeared in journals, newspapers, and letters from friends and relatives.[26]

The British collections that continued to be formed up to the time of the Club's exhibition in 1920 were clearly linked with British colonial and military activities in that region, in a similar way to the collecting of Egyptian and Chinese material, as we have seen in Chapters 2 and 3. The British Museum possessed some of the earliest Native American material collected in England, acquired by Sloane.[27] These were of the type typically found in the natural history collections formed in the eighteenth century, such as tobacco pipes or ivory combs.[28] Some of these objects might be referred to (and are usually today) as 'African-American' because they were remnants of the slave trade

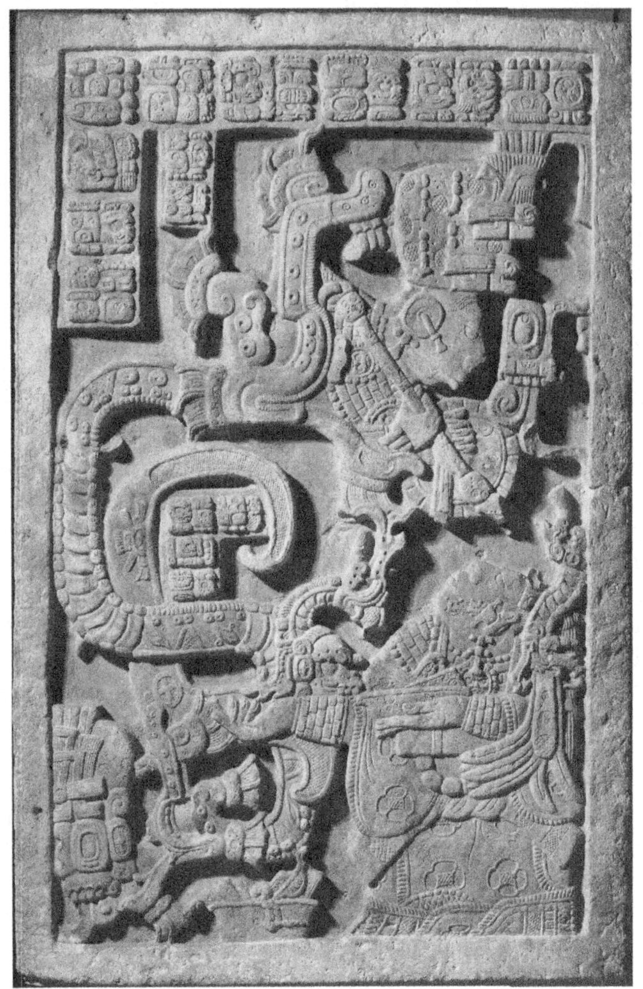

Figure 4.1 Lintel 25, the Yaxchilan Lintels, Chiapas, Mexico, *c.* 725–760. Limestone. Height: 121 cm, width: 85.5 cm, Am1923, Maud.5.

Source: © Trustees of the British Museum, London.

and brought to America from Africa.[29] Pacific objects (also known as Polynesian), that are often included in the category of 'American art', formed part of a collection created by Sir Ashton Lever (1729–1788), including material from Cook's voyages. Lever's collection had been on display to the public in several locations in London and Manchester and therefore it was quite well known.[30] Later in the nineteenth century, a large collection formed by Captain Savage came to the Liverpool Museum in 1857 to be joined by Joseph Mayer's (of Egyptian Museum fame – see Chapter 3) collection in 1867.[31]

Unlike the British Museum, which was not a lender to the Club's exhibition (but of course its curator Joyce was, and he was on the exhibition subcommittee), Liverpool Museum was one of four institutional lenders to the Club's exhibition:

Cambridge – the MAA, Oxford – the Pitt Rivers Museum, Liverpool – primarily from the Savage and Mayer collections, and the Warrington Museum. One of the items singled out in the Introduction to the Club's exhibition catalogue and in reviews of the exhibition (e.g. *The Connoisseur*)[32] was an Aztec manuscript known today as the *Codex Fejérváry-Mayer* and it is today considered one of the most important Aztec texts in existence[33] (Figure 4.2 a and b). It is one of the few to survive the Spanish Conquest and is a calendar codex of some significance.

The Pitt Rivers Museum was formed when Pitt Rivers donated half of his collection to the University of Oxford in 1884.[34] The items loaned by this Museum to the Club's exhibition came from various donors, including Pitt Rivers himself. The curator of the Pitt Rivers Museum at the time of the exhibition was Henry Balfour, who, as we have seen, was on the organizing committee. He was not, in addition, an independent lender like some others on the committee, however. The Pitt Rivers loan also would not have included the Rymill Collection, discussed above, as this was formed after 1929. But it did include some material that had been in the founding collection, such as the buckskin coat (Pitt Rivers 1884.88.8), which was displayed in 'Case B. North-West America in the exhibition.'[35]

The General List of Lenders

In spite of the fact that there were few institutional collections of American material in Britain at that time, due to colonial service, there were quite a few private collectors of 'American' objects, that is both North and South American. Not surprisingly, several of the lenders to the Club's exhibition had colonial service or military connections, such as Captain A. W. F. Fuller (1882–1961), Lt-Col. F. K. McClean, Major Charles F. Meek (a Club member), and Major Royall Tyler (also a Club member). Fuller's collection is now mainly in the Field Museum in Chicago which purchased it in 1958. It is considered one of the finest collections of Polynesian artifacts in the world but he also collected material from part of what is today Canada, including a large number of objects loaned to the Club's exhibition. Among collectors of Pacific material, there does seem to have been a parallel interest in 'American' objects, and the connection is related to a wider interest in anthropology and objects of that type at that time. This is demonstrated by Fuller's fellowship of the RAI, what is clearly a defining feature of the Club's exhibition.[36] Statistically, Fuller was one of the most prolific lenders to the Club's exhibition, so clearly his assumed collecting focus on the Pacific region needs to be reconsidered as his collection contained quite a lot of American objects.

Another collector whose collection is not well studied is F. K. McClean, who may possibly be the aviation pioneer Frank McClean (1876–1955) but none of the existing biographies of him mention any collecting interests, beyond airplanes.[37] McClean loaned 11 objects to the Club's exhibition, and all were identified as being from Peru.[38] Major Royall Tyler (1884–1953) was an American historian, based in Paris, who most famously helped form the art collections of the Blisses (Robert Woods and Mildred), who founded Dumbarton Oaks Library and Collection in Washington, DC.[39] Tyler was educated in England but served as a Major in the US Army during the First World War.[40] In studies of the Bliss collection, which is famous for its Byzantine and Pre-Columbian material, it is noted that Tyler was entirely responsible for introducing the Blisses to Pre-Columbian and Byzantine art. In 1913, the Blisses were encouraged by Tyler to buy some newly arrived Peruvian objects from the Paris dealer Brummer,

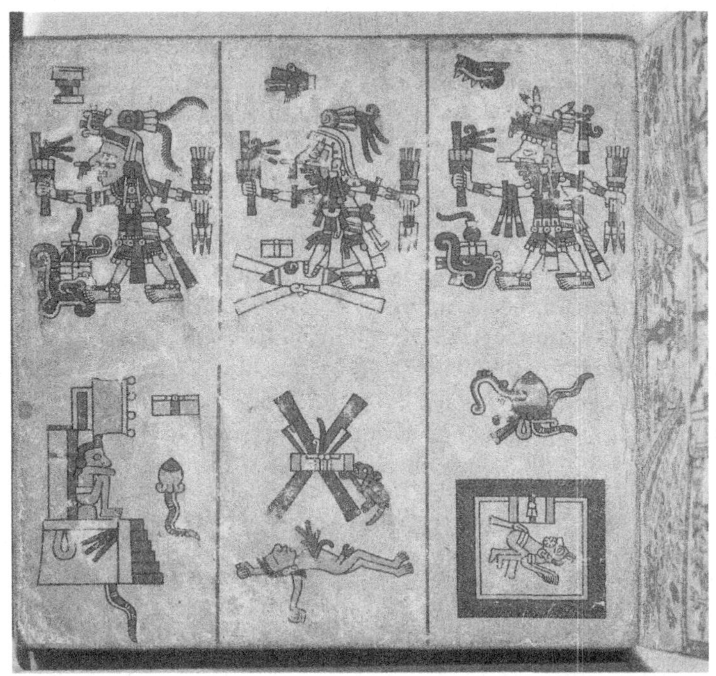

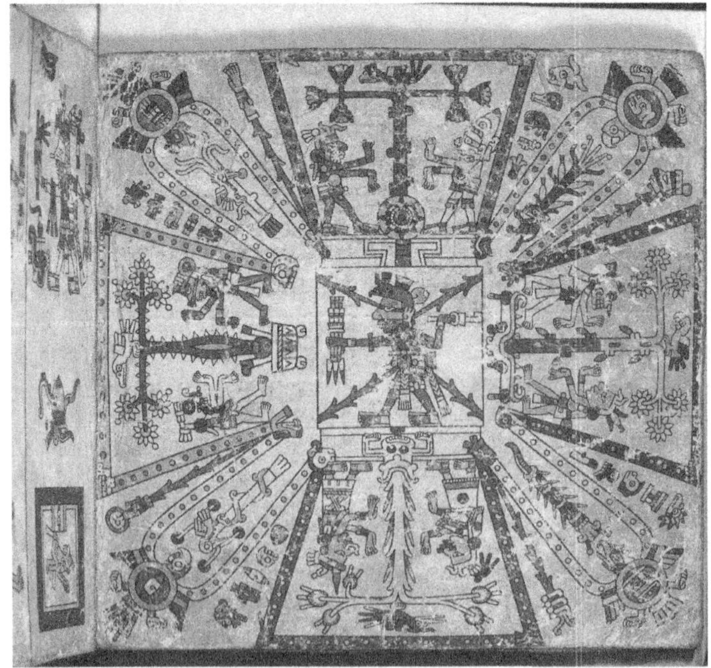

Figure 4.2 (a) and (b) *Codex Fejérváry-Mayer*, Mixteca/Aztec, Central Mexico, before 1521. Deer hide, gesso and paint, 175 × 175 × 4040 mm. Gift of Joseph Mayer, 1867. M12014.

Source: © National Museums Liverpool, World Museum.

who had acquired the collection of a German doctor who had lived in Peru for many years.[41] Pre-Colombian art was popular in Paris long before any other type of non-Western art and was displayed at the Louvre as early as 1850.[42] Thus, Tyler's interest was influenced by his Paris location. As an independent lender, Tyler contributed only one object to the Club's exhibition (a stone carving said to be from Oaxaca, 'mantelpiece above Case E, no. 1') but Tyler was also a member of the Club, which is mentioned elsewhere in connection with his collecting activities.[43]

Most of the private lenders to the Club's exhibition were not military, however, but several did have experience of travel and study in South America, including 'Miss A. Breton' who was the Victorian artist Adela Breton (1849–1923). At one stage she was hired by Maudslay to verify and further study what he had recorded and seen at Chichén Itza in the Yucatan, one of the most famous archaeological sites of the Maya in Mexico, with its stepped pyramid and jade throne in the shape of a jaguar.[44] Not surprisingly, Breton was an active fellow of the RAI, particularly under the presidency of Maudslay, and she took part in the International Congress of Americanists, which took place in London in 1912.[45] To accompany the Congress, there was an exhibition, to which Breton loaned several items, including some of her own drawings[46] (see Plate 10). Maudslay made a comment about the state of the field at the time of the congress, which also confirms the existence of that exhibition:

> [W]e have probably more pre-Columbian objects of interest here than any other European country. Most of these are, of course, preserved in Museums, but there are many in private hands, and we should be most grateful for any information which may enable us to trace them, as we hope to exhibit a loan collection during the session of the [Americanist] Congress at the Imperial Institute [later that year] ... [47]

What actually transpired was that an exhibition was arranged for the week of the Congress.[48] It comprised mostly paintings, pictures and photographs, but also some archaeological objects such as 'Ancient Peruvian pottery' lent by one of the organizers, the geographer and explorer Sir Clements Markham (1830–1916: active there in 1852–1853 especially), and finds from British Guiana lent by the naturalist and colonial officer Sir Everard im Thurn (1852–1932: active there 1870s–1890s).[49] The International Congress of Americanists was founded in 1875 and a meeting has taken place every two or three years until the present day.[50]

Another lender with direct experience of Mexico was 'Lord Cowdray' who was the first Viscount Cowdray (Weetman Pearson, 1856–1927), scion of the Pearson Group and founder of an oil company in Mexico. He was a Liberal MP and a good friend of the dictator Porfiro Diaz (1830–1915), having completed a number of major construction projects there, including a railroad. Cowdray most likely acquired the items loaned to the Club's exhibition before the oil company was sold in 1919.[51] He loaned six pottery objects from Mexico which were displayed in 'Case D. Mexico'.[52] Cowdray was a prolific collector of mainly European art and much of this, as well as the family collection, was sold by Christie's in 2010.[53] Connected to Cowdray was Lord Murray of Elibank, who loaned one object. He was a partner in Pearson and Son.

Cowdray was not a member of the Club but nor was another lender who loaned more objects than anyone else: C. L. Fenton (Charles Ludwig, née Fleischmann, 1867–1932), who is best known today for the 'Fenton vase', which is now in the British

Museum and was loaned to the Club's exhibition in 1920 (Figure 4.3).[54] This piece was illustrated in *The Burlington Magazine*'s review of the exhibition, on p. 44, fig. H, and is considered significant because of its inscriptions and imagery which illustrate aspects of elite life. Fenton loaned over 70 objects to the exhibition, all of which were either from Mexico or Guatemala, where he lived and where his brother was, apparently, British Consul in Coban for many years. Charles Fenton was, not surprisingly, a fellow of the RAI from 1911.[55] At the time of the Congress of Americanists, however, Fenton was apparently still known as 'Fleischmann', as is noted in the 1913 publication: 'the delegates would have seen the "Museum of Central American antiquities collected by Mr Fleischmann from Guatemala",[56] when the latter hosted them at his home in Hampstead (this material came to the British Museum in 1930).'[57]

A less prolific lender but perhaps more famous contributor than Fenton was Thomas Gann (1867–1938), Principal Medical Officer in British Honduras (later Belize) from 1894 till 1923, and amateur archaeologist.[58] By the time of the exhibition, Gann had published several texts on the archaeology of British Honduras, including the recent *The Maya Indians of Southern Yucatan and Northern British Honduras* (Washington, DC: Bureau of American Ethnology, Smithsonian Institution, 1918). He was not a member of the Club at that time. Another interesting non-member who loaned but

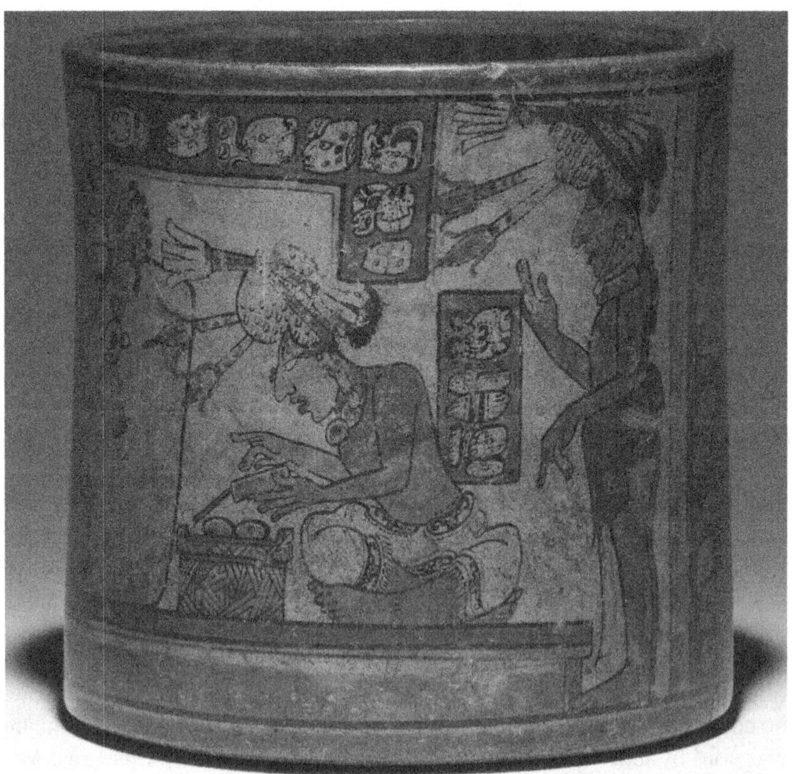

Figure 4.3 The Fenton vase, Nebaj, Guatemala, Late Maya, 600–800. Slip-painted earthenware. Height: 17.2 cm, diameter: 17 cm. Am1930.F.1.

Source: © Trustees of the British Museum, London.

one object was 'Mrs Murray Guthrie', who was Olive Leslie (1872–1945), the daughter of Sir John Leslie, Bt, who married Walter Murray Guthrie (1869–1911), MP and merchant banker.[59] Later she remarried, then divorced and seems to have reverted to her first married name at the time of the Club's exhibition.

Confirming the diversity of lenders to the Club's exhibition, and collectors of 'American' art, the next lender on the list is E. F. Gye, who was Ernest Frederick Gye (1879–1955), grandson of the famous Frederick Gye (1810–1878), the Covent Garden theatre impresario and manager of the Royal Opera House, and son of the Victorian soprano, Emma Albani (1847–1930).[60] Ernest Gye seems later to have become a diplomat, serving in Venezuela from 1936 till 1939.[61] Gye is followed on the list of lenders by Edward Huth (1847–1935), who was a member of the Club along with his uncle Louis, the famous art collector who was discussed in Chapter 2, and his father Henry (1815–1878). All were prominent bankers, with Edward inheriting from Louis on his death in 1905.

More in keeping with the anthropologically-inclined collector lenders was St. George Littledale (1851–1931), who loaned eight objects, all seemingly from an expedition to North America. Most are identified as being from 'North America, Haida people', which is an indigenous group still resident in the former Queen Charlotte Islands territory of British Columbia (Haida Gwaii) and in Alaska (Kaigani Haida).[62] Quite a few objects in the exhibition are identified as being from this culture and represent the North American aspect of the selection. Today, such material would not be included in a general 'Americas' exhibition but rather 'indigenous America' which is now identified specifically with Native North American cultures. Littledale is probably best described today as an explorer, as he was independently wealthy and spent much time pursuing adventurous travel in the late nineteenth century, including to Japan, Tibet, Mongolia, Siberia, the Caucasus, and North America.[63] He was generous in collecting natural history specimens for museums but clearly also collected objects for himself. He visited Alaska twice, in 1884 and 1904,[64] and it is likely therefore that it was that branch of the Haida with which his loaned objects can be associated.

George A. Lockett (1855–1923) had even more interesting connections with his loaned objects, which were mainly from Peru. Lockett was a partner in the merchant firm of W. and J. Lockett, originally of Liverpool, which also had substantial business interests in Peru, including in nitrates and sugar.[65] He was a member of the Club and seems, like others, to have had wide interests in works of art. For the America exhibition, he loaned six objects from Peru, mainly gold and silver but also two pottery items, including a figure captioned: 'from a child's grave, Ancon, Peru' (cat. 'Case P Peru, no. 4'). Like the Egyptian funerary objects discussed in Chapter 3, this gives a further indication of how provenance was conceptualized at that time and for that place, the present-day restrictions against and aversion towards grave goods not yet in force. Lockett, incidentally, also came from a prominent polo-playing family. He founded the Lima Polo Club and his brother Vivian won the Olympic gold medal for polo in 1920.[66] A similar business was run in Lima by another exhibition lender, J. Guthrie Reid (James, 1855–1920) who loaned 34 objects. His company was Duncan, Fox and Co, and while in Peru, he and his wife Clarissa (made a Dame in 1918) amassed collections of Peruvian antiquities and furniture. The antiquities were given to the British Museum by bequest on the death of his wife in 1933 and her descendants gave the furniture to Temple Newsom House in Leeds.[67]

A Peruvian object of a different type was loaned by 'A. E. Macandrew' (dates unknown), which seems to be one that was donated by the Colchester Museum to the

MAA Cambridge in 1947: 'Feather-work head-dress, Truxillo region, Peru' (On cases N, O and P; now MAA 1947.302 A & B).[68]

Jewellery was also loaned to the exhibition. Mrs Percy Macquoid (Theresa, 1858–1939), who along with Miss Lillian Elliott, Mrs Murray Guthrie, Lady Kennedy, and Mrs Van den Bergh, was one of several lady lenders of single, jewellery-like objects, in her case, a gold frog (Case L Central and South America, no. 27). Percy Macquoid (1852–1925) was the artist, designer, and furniture collector, who wrote extensively about English furniture, including the collection of Henry Hirsch, discussed in Chapter 2.

Drawings collectors, a major area of collecting for the Club, as we have seen, made a contribution to the exhibition as well. Philip Norman (1842–1931) was an active Club member, artist, Fellow of the Society of Antiquaries, and historian of London buildings, both collecting and making drawings of many of them.[69] He loaned a substantial number of his drawings to the other Club exhibition of 1920: 'A Collection of Early Drawings and Pictures of London', to which he also contributed the introductory essay.[70] The fact that he participated in both exhibitions of 1920, with such widely different subjects, again illustrates the diverse nature of the Club members' collections and exhibitionary activities. A.P. Oppé was (Adolph) Paul Oppé (1878–1957), also a drawings scholar and collector, and a member of the Club, who became Deputy Director of the V&A in 1910.[71] He was an expert on the Cozens and wrote the biography *Alexander and John Robert Cozens* (1952). Much of his collection, considered to be of national importance, is in the Tate Gallery today.[72] He was a major lender to the Club's John Robert Cozens exhibition in 1923 and was on its organizing committee.[73] He was also a lender to the Indian Art exhibition in 1931 (see Chapter 3). Another lender of but one object was Henry Yates Thompson (1838–1929; not Sir Henry mentioned previously), a Club member and collector of illuminated manuscripts. He was a benefactor to the British Museum, the Fitzwilliam Museum and Newnham College, Cambridge, giving the college its original library in 1897.[74] He was on the committee of and a lender to the Club's 1908 Exhibition of Illuminated Manuscripts.[75]

As we have seen, this diverse lender profile is not unusual for the Club, yet it is also representative of this subject area which was populated by geographically and disciplinarily disparate specialists. In true Club fashion, in spite of an unfamiliarity with the exhibition subject, they embraced the challenge and gathered together the most significant collectors, lenders, and specialists in that very narrow field. Their broad and far-reaching network was used to great effect here, leading to a truly innovative exhibition. The Club's reputation in the art world was also sufficient to attract such contributors and was seen as a boon to the field of indigenous American art, bringing archaeological specimens to the attention of the art world.

Yet since their exhibition in 1920, while the field has developed to some extent, there have not been many displays of American art in Britain, apart from the Horniman Museum's 'American Indian Arts and Crafts' in 1966, and its 'The First Americans' of 1975. Fairly recently, however, there have been several exhibitions of 'Native American' material including one at the British Museum: 'Warriors of the Plain: 200 Years of Native American Honour and Ritual' (2012–2013), which continued to frame the objects and their associated cultural origins in terms of ritual. Also in 2013, 'George Catlin's Portraits of Native American Indians' went back on display for the first time in Britain since the 1850s (Birmingham Museum and Art Gallery). These exhibitions collectively have had the effect of reinforcing the 'lost civilization' trope associated with Native American cultures which is even promulgated in America today. Only recently (in 2015), the Seattle Art Museum, echoing the Club's interpretation from nearly 100 years earlier, presented the exhibition 'Indigenous Beauty: Masterworks of American Indian Art from the Diker Collection' which, according to the publicity materials:

> reflects the diversity of Native cultures. This superb exhibition offers more than great works of art and cultural artifacts—it is an invitation to explore other worlds.
>
> Deeply engaged with cultural traditions and the land, indigenous artists over the centuries have used art to represent and preserve their ways of life. Even during the 19th and 20th centuries, when drastic changes were brought by colonization, artists brilliantly adapted their talents and used the new materials available to them to marvellous effect.[76]

Thus, indigenous 'art' is still closer to nature, imbued with tradition, and the tension between art and ethnography still has currency with this category of object as does the framing of its cultural origins in terms of threatened peoples who nonetheless 'adapt'. Such tension is perhaps even more notable in the next exhibition considered in this chapter: 'The Art of Primitive Peoples' of 1935. In fact, some of the same objects and object origins would be featured, thus conflating the two categories of object, and suggesting that the categorization of these objects was still in flux. The Club's efforts to do so were not entirely successful, as we will see.

1935 The Art of Primitive Peoples

Some of the objects exhibited in the American exhibition of 1920 were exhibited in a later exhibition at the Club: The Art of Primitive Peoples of 1935, which included objects from Alaska and North-west America. But in another categorical innovation presented by the Club, the 'primitive' category also included objects from Africa, New Zealand, the Polynesian Islands, and Japan. The organizing committee was similar as well, including Louis Clarke once again, as well as Henry Balfour and Archibald Russell from the India exhibition. Captain Fuller, the Pitt Rivers Museum, and the MAA at Cambridge were also lenders again. In the two exhibitions, there is seemingly a lot of overlap in both object origins and participants but this is both a consequence of the displays being Club exhibitions and of the way in which such objects continued to be interpreted in Britain, albeit through the art lens imposed by the Club. If the Club's definition of 'America' was broad, then its conception of 'Primitive art' was even broader. According to the Introduction in the catalogue, written by 'AD', Adrian Digby, from the subcommittee:

> For the purposes of the exhibition ... the term primitive people is intended to describe a tribe or group living in a cultural phase in which metal working is either non-existent or in its infancy, and in which economic, religious, or political contact with the industrialized civilizations such as our own is almost negligible. In short, the primitive man is one who is frequently, but with little justification, called a savage.[77]

This definition is both materialist and isolationist, but very much in keeping with the contemporary interpretations used in anthropological and archaeological studies of the day, as we have seen with the interpretation of the American material as 'primitive'.[78] In archaeology and anthropology texts, metal- and stone-working technology was the standard method for periodizing cultures, giving rise to such divisions as 'Bronze Age' or 'Iron Age', 'neolithic', 'paleolithic'. The so-called 'three age system', developed in the early nineteenth century,[79] was complemented by evolutionary notions of progress so that technological ability became the benchmark for defining a people or culture as 'civilized'.[80] This in turn is supported by comparative theories of ethnography which exceptionalized groups of people who were 'untouched' by European culture or colonization and therefore technology or progress.[81] In the discipline of anthropology, such ideas were falling out of fashion in the first quarter of the twentieth century but in archaeology, there were still some theorists who practised an early form of ethnoarchaeology, in which objects defined people and provided documentary evidence for human society and activities.[82]

The Club's definition of primitive, therefore, was not mainstream in the academic disciplines of the day but is representative of a kind of old-fashioned notion of material culture and human society that is grounded in the activity of object collecting. The Club was a collectors' club, after all, and their universalizing approach to what constituted 'art' meant that all objects could be collected in the same way and by extension, exhibited in the same way. Interestingly, the subcommittee of the Primitive exhibition was dominated by museum curators, who were grounded in the older ethnography approach to 'primitive' things: Clarke, Adrian Digby (1909–2001), and Balfour. Clarke, as we have seen, was curator of the MAA, Cambridge; Digby had recently joined the Department of Ceramics and Ethnography at the British Museum,[83] and Balfour was curator of the Pitt Rivers Museum. Interestingly, Tancred Borenius was also on the committee but, in contrast to the other members, he was a traditional art historian specializing in Italian and British painting, and a Professor of Art History at the time of the exhibition (see Chapter 1). His interest in 'primitive' art is not documented nor is his influence noticeable anywhere in the exhibition catalogue. This catalogue, apart from the prefatory note by Russell, is almost thoroughly anthropological in its tone and taxonomy. None of the objects is dated, in contrast to those in the American exhibition, and the introductory essay provides no art historical framework or analysis of the objects, just mentioning art almost apologetically: 'the material exhibited may not appear to be art'.[84] In fact, the essay goes on to refer to 'aesthetic activities' in order, almost, to avoid the word 'art'. The themes explored in the essay are ethnographic as well: religion, environment, and technology, similarly to the America exhibition. Man is said to have 'religious needs' and the objects are evidence of this. Ornament and design, where present, are a substitute for language, and, as such, evidence of a cultural history.[85] Technology, however, is a limited skill: 'primitive peoples seem very often to develop one industry and to specialize in one technique alone'.[86] Ultimately, the objects look the way they do because primitive man is closer to nature, a trope which had maintained its currency from the time of the America exhibition.

Exhibits and their Lenders

The nearly 300 objects included in the exhibition were for the most part recently 'discovered', which adds to the non-historical nature of the exhibition and its interpretation. Among these were objects collected in the Rymill expedition of 1929, discussed in relation to the American exhibition above. These were loaned by the MAA, which had sponsored the expedition. Brown noted that:

> [T]he MMA loaned eighty-two specimens from the ethnology collection for the show. The two items from the Rymill Collection were a horn spoon whose handle was carved in the image of a duck's head and a shallow wooden food bowl with a carved head of a bear protruding from the rim. The Art of Primitive People's catalogue did not refer to the bowl, but the listing for the spoon (exhibition number 141) repeated the information that Robert Rymill had transferred to the catalogue card when he processed the objects in 1930: 'Sheep horn spoon, with carved head in form of a duck. Length 9". Dakota (Wahpeton), Canada. Collected by R. Rymill 1929' (Burlington Fine Arts Club 1935, 37). In the Burlington show, Native American pieces were outnumbered by artifacts from other world cultures ... [87]

This newly discovered material is praised in the exhibition catalogue for its untainted purity:

> The only material in use ... in the exhibition comes from places that have been fairly recently explored, such as the Sepik River in New Guinea, which although well known to anthropologists and colonial administrators still remains undefiled by the contact of the trader selling cheap Birmingham ware, and hardly influenced as yet by the activities of the missionaries.[88]

For the author of the catalogue, Digby, there was evidently some anxiety about acculturation and its impact on objects. With respect to the numerous objects from the Congo ('Belgian Congo', 'Upper Congo') lent by Captain Fuller (see above), this type of anxiety has been explained by Mirzoeff (1999) as a desire to define the area as primitive even in the face of contrary evidence. It needs to be less advanced to keep it exotic.[89] Fuller was, in fact, one of the two main lenders to this exhibition, which was much more in keeping with his taste as a collector than the American one. Much of the material in this exhibition was 'Polynesian', an area of collecting that had a long history in Britain but at the time Fuller was collecting, it was popular because it had somewhat fallen out of favour, and therefore was cheap. As Hooper (2006) noted:

> The relatively low commercial value of Polynesian 'curios' circulating in Britain in the early twentieth century allowed several dedicated collectors to form large private collections of Polynesian material. William Oldman (who began his career as a dealer), Harry Beasley, Alfred Fuller and James Hooper drew on material which was being sold or discarded from private collections and museums, and on the large quantities of souvenirs which had accumulated in the attics of the families of missionaries, travellers and colonial officers, and which was finding its way into street markets and 'junk shops' all over Britain. These men, together with Franks, Balfour and von Hugel, were all acting in the context of what might be called a 'salvage paradigm'. Although they were to a large extent following their own interests, they were also aware of the finite nature of the material they collected, and conjectured that the cultures which had made these things would soon 'die out'.[90]

Another collector cited by Hooper was William Oldman, listed as 'W. O. Oldman' in the Club's exhibition catalogue. Oldman (1879–1949) was a collector and dealer of ethnographic objects, building up major collections of Polynesian and Maori material.[91] Oldman was the second major lender to the Club's Primitive exhibition, despite, like Fuller, not being a member.[92] In his time, he was described as 'the greatest ethnographic dealer in the world'[93] and in 1948, he sold his Polynesian collection to the New Zealand government where it is now distributed among several museums.[94] A *Moai Kavakava* (human figure) (item OL000342) is now in the Museum of New Zealand and was acquired from the Oldman Collection in 1948 (Figure 4.4). It is very similar to, if not the same as no. 207 in the exhibition. Another of the items probably loaned to the Club's exhibition was part of this sale to New Zealand and was featured in the recent exhibition 'Pacific Encounters: Art and Divinity in Polynesia, 1760–1860' (Hooper 2006) where it was catalogued as: 'No. 172, whisk handle, Austral Islands, late 18th–early 19th century'. It appears to be no. 193 in the Club's catalogue where it is described as: 'Wooden handle for a fly whisk, Society Islands.'[95] Oldman's participation in this exhibition as a dealer highlights a common feature noted in other more conventional exhibitions mounted by the Club: the role of the art market in both members' and the Club's activities. With a subject area somewhat unclaimed by scholarship at the time, like 'primitive art', this involvement would necessarily be stronger.

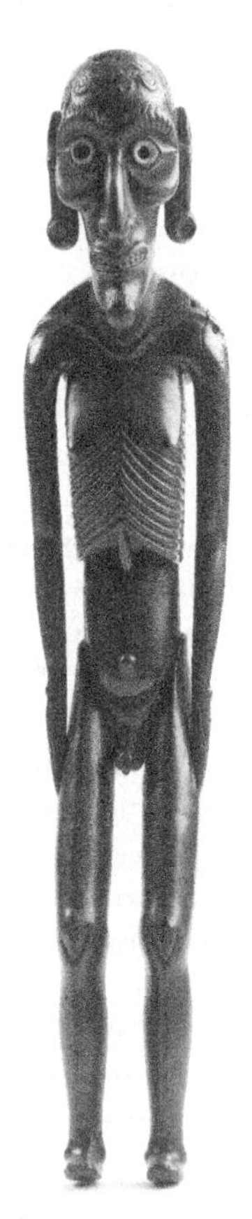

Figure 4.4 *Moai Kavakava* (human figure), Easter Island, 1800s. Wood, bone, shell, obsidia. Height: 40.5 cm, width: 80 cm. Oldman Collection, gift of the New Zealand Government, 1992. Museum of New Zealand Te Papa OL000342.

Interpretation

The Pacific objects loaned by Oldman at that time had yet to be described or classified in more specific forms, such as 'Polynesian' or 'Maori' but much of the same language is in use today for such objects. What is more indicative of its time are the colonial names for places used in the exhibition ('Belgian Congo') and the collective classification of all the objects into the category of 'primitive art'. Clifford (1988) assigns the origins of this category of art to Paris in the early twentieth century but it was also embraced by anthropologists in the USA, for example, in Franz Boas's classic book, *Primitive Art*, which had been published in 1927.[96] It was less current in art historical classifications so in some ways the Club's treatment of it as an exhibition topic situates the category in art history at a relatively early date in Britain. The tone (and author) of the catalogue essay are not art historical, as we have seen, but the prefatory note states clearly that, 'The scientific aspect has on this occasion been ignored, and the selection of the exhibits has been made from the point of view of artistic effort alone.'[97] While this is contradicted by the introductory essay, one can assume that this is how the committee – consisting of three anthropologists and two art historians – made their selection.

Thus, as essentially an art exhibition, as determined by the Club's presentation of it, the Primitive display appears to be the earliest presentation of the subject in a temporary exhibition in Britain. For art collectors at that time, and the Club by extension, 'primitive art' was familiar through artists' encounters with ethnographic things and critical responses to this[98] but because of the nature of the material and its acquisition, anthropologists were also associated with the subject and were needed in this case to both supply museum loans and interpret the material in the essay and object entries for the Club's catalogue. There were quite different forms of appropriation of these types of objects operating at the time of the exhibition therefore. The Club's exhibition also took place before more specific category names were commonly used in Britain for the regional art represented, e.g. 'Pacific art', 'African art', Polynesian art', etc., and therefore before such objects were clearly distinguished regionally. As the Club exhibition demonstrates, the 'primitive' category was still a broad one. While this combination of disparate regional arts seems strange today, it makes some kind of sense here especially when viewed from the perspective of artists' interest in 'the primitive'. Plenty of artists were members of the Club, as we have seen, and the exhibition lenders included three artists: Walter P. Belk (1872–1963), the silversmith and designer, Sir William Reynolds-Stephens (1862–1943, a Club member), the sculptor[99] as well as the designer and photographer Curtis Moffat (1887–1949).[100] For artists at that time, 'primitive' could also refer to an attitude or style,[101] and this informed the Club's attempt to present 'primitive' as an art historical category for displayed objects (somewhat defeated by the exhibition's ahistorical approach), and this was reinforced by the exhibition's title, 'The Art of Primitive Peoples'.

Within this framework, if we further consider the sub-categories of 'art' represented on a large scale in the exhibition, then Polynesian art and African art are also being displayed as 'art' for the first time. Coombes ([1994] 2007) has examined the display and collecting of African art in Britain during the late Victorian and Edwardian periods but not from an art historical perspective. In spite of the ethnographic nature of the exhibits and the absence of dates for the objects, the Club's standard approach and philosophy of display demand that their exhibition be examined as an 'art' display, and therefore from an art historical perspective. Reviews of the show from the time it was opened similarly treat the material in this way, even when the review is in a more scientific publication such as *Nature* or *Man*. The review in *Nature*, for example, in fact complains that the exhibition is too aesthetically pleasing and the quality of the craftsmanship on display is too high:

> [W]hile it is true that this collection contains some of the finest known examples of so-called primitive art – it is indeed a possible criticism of the exhibition that it includes so little that is crude, but at the same time scientifically instructive – the general level of execution is higher than might reasonably be expected.[102]

Clearly the expectation for this kind of material is that it should look like the popular perception of 'ethnographic' objects, that is, not high quality or artistic, and the reviewer is nonetheless surprised that it can be of such quality. This is possibly because it is presented in an 'art' exhibition, within an 'art' category, in an elegant interior, making the contrast to the usual presentation more stark. Indeed, the review describes the objects as 'treasure' and 'a demonstration of the artistic capacity of those backward peoples'.[103]

A similar perspective is demonstrated in the report in *Man* which noted that 'the exhibits were chosen for their artistic excellence, which was very high'.[104] The report also noted that members of the RAI were given a tour of the show by Tancred Borenius, one of the organizers.[105] The art press responded similarly but in contrast praising the aestheticization of 'primitive art' and attributing the 'discovery' of the artistic merits of 'primitive art' to modern artists. In *The Burlington Magazine*, the reviewer stated:

> The Burlington Fine Arts Club is to be congratulated on giving its aesthetic patronage to this exhibition of objects which, twenty years ago, would have been regarded as of merely ethnological interest. That revolution in taste, or rather that miracle of making the blind see, which has made such an exhibition possible, here or anywhere else where connoisseurs of the fine arts foregather, has been due largely to the active interest of modern artists, who first recognised the analogies between their mode of sensibility and that of the so-called savages.
>
> ... Connoisseurs took a hint from the artists, and the best of these objects are now prized almost as much as the masterpieces of antiquity or the Renaissance. Such a revolution in taste or sensibility no doubt has its explanation in more fundamental sociological changes; we turn to the art of primitive peoples as a reaction from the excessive intellectuality of our civilization, or even from its excessive snobbery.[106]

The collectors made this 'discovery' possible but yet here they are said to be taking their cue from artists. The constant refrain repeated here is the anxiety surrounding avant-garde contemporary art of the time, of which 'primitive' objects are seen to be the antithesis.[107] The *Burlington* review further repeats the notion of child-like simplicity supposedly embodied in the objects but also states that some of the objects in the Club's exhibition are completely the opposite. The 'art' on display is difficult to understand, and ethnographic knowledge is required to do so.

> It is impossible in a short notice to differentiate between the very diverse aesthetic qualities revealed by the objects gathered together in this exhibition. Coming from regions as far apart as Greenland and the South Seas, they represent many different varieties of so-called primitive culture. That the aesthetic qualities are parallel in some way to the type of culture is evident enough, but it would need a wide

> knowledge of ethnography to establish an exact correspondence. The general distinction between animistic and magical forms of primitive religion seems to be related to the equally general distinction between naturalistic and geometric types of art, and to a certain extent this is an obvious development; in one case efficacy depends on resemblance, in the other case on disguise or escape from reality. But the aesthetician is faced by more awkward questions.[108]

The exhibition is therefore challenging to view and understand because the objects themselves, apparently, are not well studied – in fact, not conforming to traditional art historical classifications – and perhaps the Club's exhibition made the lack of conformity more apparent. However, there does seem to be more knowledge and therefore appreciation of some of the African objects in the show as the *Burlington* reviewer recommends two recently published books about African art to the potential viewer of the exhibition. African art makes up a significant proportion of the objects in the show (about 25 per cent) and most were loaned by two individuals: Captain Fuller and William Oldman. Both are perhaps better known for their 'Polynesian' or Pacific object collections, yet both Fuller and Oldman clearly appreciated objects from Africa, particularly Benin, as they loaned a number of bronze pieces from this location (see Figure 4.5).[109]

Benin bronze objects came onto the market after the British punitive expedition in 1897.[110] The material that went into museum collections is well studied but private collections, formed before 1935, are less known. The interest of Fuller and Oldman in Benin objects is not widely published but their participation in the Club's exhibition provides good evidence for private collectors' activities in this area. One private collection that was well known, and that came up for sale in 1930, was that of Captain G. W. Neville (1852–1930), who was a local agent for the Liverpool shipping company, Elder Dempster, and manager of the new British Bank of West Africa.[111] Neville appears to have

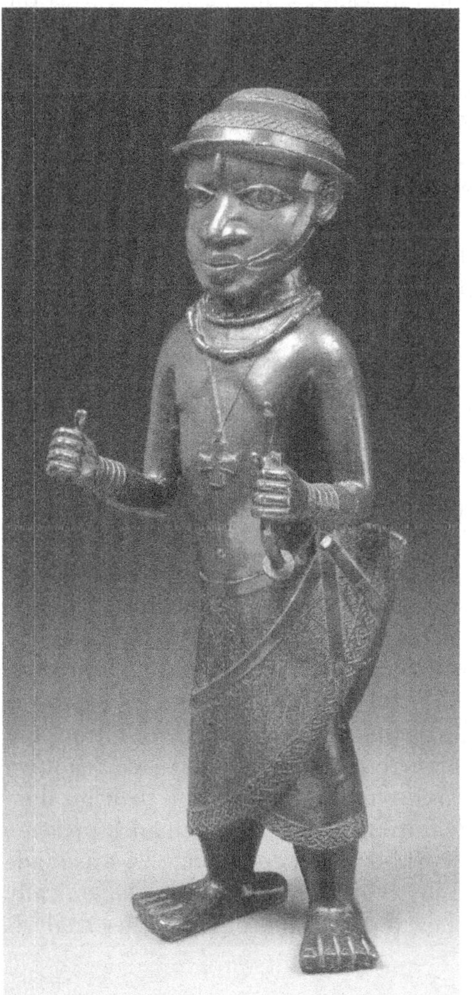

Figure 4.5 Figure of a man, Benin City, Edo State, Nigeria. Cast bronze. Height: 64 cm, width: 22 cm. Af1949, 46.157.

Source: © Trustees of the British Museum, London.

accompanied the expedition and massacre at Benin and subsequently acquired a collection of bronzes from there. These were exhibited quite early in London, partly at the Royal Anthropological Institute and another group at the British Museum.[112]

Many of the Benin 'bronzes' ended up in the British Museum, and C. H. Read would describe them in 1898 as 'works of art'.[113] This was an early categorization of African art as 'art' but not a consistent one, however. Interestingly, African art was regionally categorized separately quite early on, compared to much of the 'Polynesian' material in the Club's exhibition. It was not always called 'African', however. For example, one of the earliest exhibitions in London of what we would call 'African Art' was the Chelsea Book Club's exhibition of 'Negro Sculpture' in 1920, which was reviewed very favourably by Roger Fry (a Club member) and included in his *Vision and Design* of 1920.[114] Another exhibition of the same name was held at the Lefevre Galleries in London in 1933,[115] and an article by Dora Clarke in the *Journal of the Royal African Society* (April 1935) even goes so far as to say that there is now a 'field of negro sculpture' and notes that the appreciation of 'negro art' has developed considerably since Neville brought back a collection from the expedition in 1897.[116] In the same year as the Club's exhibition of Primitive Art, the MOMA in New York opened its groundbreaking exhibition of 'African Negro Art'[117] so it leads us to question whether the Club was a little old-fashioned in its elision of African art in the general category of Primitive art. Certainly, this was one of the earlier exhibitions in England of Primitive art and that general category would continue to be used for decades after the Club's exhibition in 1935 but other groups were already distinguishing African art as a separate category. At the same time, a parallel category to 'primitive' that also usually included African objects emerged: 'tribal art', a term which is still current in the commercial art world. The terminology and classification of African art thus remain fluid.

Seligman and 'the Primitive'

As we have seen, the role of anthropology and anthropologists in this exhibition is significant. While papers concerned with the internal Club discussions about the Primitive exhibition do not survive, much can be gleaned from the participants in the exhibition who were primarily anthropologists or collectors of anthropological material, and this would have coloured the interpretation of the objects, their classification, and the exhibition theme. Unlike art history, in anthropology, 'primitive' was a relevant and established category of object in 1935. In fact, this subject was taught at the London School of Economics from the 1920s, for example, in the academic year 1921–1922, 'The Useful Arts of Primitive Peoples' was taught by Charles Seligman (1873–1940), a lender to the Club's exhibition and a Club member. In the year 1936–37, the course title was changed to 'Primitive Crafts', more specifically placing the emphasis on 'useful' objects and their production, as opposed to the connoisseurship definition of art.[118] Seligman represents the infusion of this perspective into the art world through collecting. He was made Emeritus Professor of Ethnology at the LSE in 1934, but he was not academically trained in social anthropology.[119] As Nicky Levell (2001) has noted, in her analysis of Seligman as a collector:

> [H]is research focused on tropical pathology while harbouring a growing interest in physical anthropology. In 1898 he joined the ground-breaking Cambridge Anthropological Expedition to the Torres Strait. Only during the expedition, which revolutionised anthropological methodology, did Seligman receive his first anthropological training in ethnology, physical anthropology and experimental psychology under Alfred Cort Haddon (1855–1940) and William Halse Rivers. This was followed, six years later, by a second period of fieldwork, under his [Seligman's] scientific leadership, in Papua New Guinea (the Cooke-Daniels expedition of 1904). On returning to London he was appointed on a three-year contract as pathologist to the Zoological Society of London ... The publication of his research undertaken during the Cooke-Daniels expedition, *The Melanesians of British New Guinea* (1910), definitely established his reputation as an anthropologist, and in 1910 he joined the LSE, University of London, as Lecturer in Ethnology.[120]

The objects Seligman loaned to the Club's exhibition were accordingly, mostly from this area: Sarawak, Borneo, and New Guinea, with one object from the Sudan.[121] The exhibition objects in general are thus a strange combination of very finely decorated, such as the Benin material, and much cruder, as has been noted in the contemporary reviews. But it is perhaps this juxtaposition which emphasizes the 'primitiveness' of the peoples represented as there is inconsistency rather than a clear sophistication in the visual aspects of the objects in spite of the observations of some critics. The selection thus validates the anthropological perspective presented in the main catalogue essay, along with the undated objects and the title of the exhibition which was not 'Primitive Art' but 'The Art of Primitive Peoples'. Studies of other geographical regions represented in this exhibition, such as 'First Nations' objects, confirm this while suggesting that the mere fact of such objects being displayed by an art collecting club demonstrates a different approach and attitude.[122] As we have seen, the First Nations objects were those acquired during the MAA's Ford Motor Expedition discussed above. They were first loaned to a public exhibition in the Club's Primitive show. Yet Brown (2014) notes that their display by the Club was in marked contrast to how their home museum approached it – emphasizing 'social context rather than form'.[123] The Club space, both physical and conceptual, thus transformed the objects, giving them a new identity as objects displayed and interpreted through an art historical prism. This in turn provided them with an exhibited history which gave them a history *as* art, whatever kind of object they may be. Once identified as art, especially collected art, these objects can then enter the connoisseurship system of the art market which drives collecting: their exhibited history, identification, and association with an owner confer legitimacy, authenticity, and provenance.

Conclusion

The exhibitions examined here suggest therefore that for certain objects without traditional art historical classifications, their identification was still in flux in the 1920s and 1930s, and able to be shaped by the Club. This is partly due to the fact that many of the objects were newly excavated or collected from distant regions so encounters with them were also new. Standards for identification and canonized classifications did not yet exist, so objects such as these could be identified specifically both geographically or nationally (American –North and South at that time) or more generally by representativeness (primitive products). It was later in the twentieth century that specific categories for these objects became more commonly used, but even then not until the second half of the twentieth century. The broad primitive category in particular would be surprisingly long-lasting. For example, the Club's exhibition title was borrowed for a similar show at the Berkeley Galleries in London, 1945: 'Primitive Art: the Art of Primitive Peoples', suggesting that such a designation was still meaningful and descriptive enough for the commercial art world at that time.[124] It would take the rise of post-colonial studies for this terminology and approach to classification to be questioned and to disappear but studies of 'primitive' notions in the arts need also to include not just artists and their 'discovery' of such objects, and literary/textual reception, but also private collectors and their role in initiating and sustaining such categorization.

Through all its exhibitions, but especially the two considered here, the Club both engineered and reflected a confluence of interests in objects and their collecting. A further desire to display such objects as aesthetic items for viewing and interpret them art historically unified both the objects and members' interests through the frame of an art historical presentation, albeit in a new type of space, neither museum nor home. For 'primitive' objects, it was this space that enabled the worlds of ethnography and art to intersect, demonstrating that the two worlds were in fact complementary. The space thus functioned in a similar way to that of Clifford's (1988) art-culture system (his 'machine for making authenticity') wherein the relative value and identity of objects change in response to different contexts. In the Club's exhibitions rooms, a tomb object collected by an archaeologist becomes, by virtue of display by the Club, an 'art' object associated with fine art collecting. This setting and approach were unique, and their examination has provided a window into a hitherto unexplored aspect of exhibitionary practice and art historical agency in nineteenth- and twentieth-century London.

Notes

1 General Committee minutes, 3.2.1920.
2 General Committee minutes, 3.2.1920; 2.3.1920; 13.4.1920.
3 General Committee minutes, 2.3.1920; 13.4.1920.
4 Burlington Fine Arts Club, *Catalogue of an Exhibition of Objects of Indigenous American Art* (London, 1920).
5 BFAC 1920, prefatory note, C H R [Read].
6 For example, his notorious chapter on the 'Negro' in the *Encyclopaedia Britannica*, 1911, where he declares their inferiority. Thomas Athol Joyce, 'Negro', in *Encyclopædia Britannica*. Volume XIX, 11th edn. (New York: Encyclopædia Britannica, 1911), p. 344. (accessed 20 Aug. 2015).
7 Roger Fry, 'Ancient American Art', first printed in *The Burlington Magazine* in 1918, reprinted in Roger Fry, *Vision and Design* (London: Chatto and Windus, 1920), pp. 69–75, p. 69. Incidentally, this review is also interesting for what it reveals about Fry's own perspective on aspects of 'American art', particularly sculpture, which, in his view, reveals 'Eastern Asiatic influence' and can be compared favourably with Chinese sculpture: ibid., pp. 73–74.
8 See http://history.prm.ox.ac.uk/collector_balfour.html (accessed 20 Aug. 2015).
9 C. J. Gadd, The Raphael Bequest: I. Egyptian and West Asiatic Antiquities', *The British Museum Quarterly*, vol. 15 (1941–1950), pp. 57–60; William Watson, Soame Jenyns, Basil

Gray, and D. E. Barrett, 'The Raphael Bequest: II. Oriental Antiquities', *The British Museum Quarterly*, vol. 15 (1941–1950), pp. 82–95; H. J. Braunholtz, 'The Raphael Bequest: III. Ancient Stone Mask from Mexico', *The British Museum Quarterly*, vol. 15 (1941–1950), pp. 106–107.

10 Basil Gray, 'The Oscar Raphael Collection for the Nation', *The Burlington Magazine for Connoisseurs*, vol. 87, no. 512 (Nov. 1945), pp. 276, 278–283.

11 Report of the Council for the Session July 1941 to June 1942, *The Journal of the Royal Anthropological Institute of Great Britain and Ireland*, vol. 72, no. 1/2 (1942), pp. 71–72.

12 Raphael is mentioned as being on the council in the 1929 report of the EES AGM. Egypt Exploration Society, *Report of the Forty-third Ordinary General Meeting (Forty-seventh Annual General Meeting)* (Bristol: Arrowsmith, 1929), p. 3.

13 Robert J. Sharer, 'Alfred P. Maudslay: Pioneer Maya Archaeologist', *Expedition Magazine* vol. 26, no. 1 (Oct. 1983): n.p., *Expedition Magazine*. Penn Museum, October 1983, web. 1 Jan 2016, available at: www.penn.museum/sites/expedition/?p=4949 (accessed 31 Dec. 2015); Ian Graham, *Alfred Maudslay and the Maya: A Biography* (Norman, OK: University of Oklahoma Press, 2002).

14 T. A. Joyce, 'Alfred Percival Maudslay', *Man*, vol. 32 (May 1932), pp. 123–125.

15 BFAC (1920), introductory essay.

16 Cyril G. E. Bunt, 'American Art at the Burlington Fine Arts Club', *The Burlington Magazine*, vol. 37, no. 208 (July 1920), p. 40.

17 Ibid.

18 Julian Stallabrass, 'The Idea of the Primitive: British Art and Anthropology 1918–1930', *New Left Review*, vol. 183 (1990), p. 96; Bunt (1920), p. 40.

19 Stallabrass (1990), p. 99.

20 Graham (2002), p. 260.

21 Alison K. Brown, *First Nations, Museums, Narrations: Stories of the 1929 Franklin Motor Expedition to the Canadian Prairies* (Vancouver, BC: University of British Columbia, 2014).

22 Robert M. Lewis, 'Wild American Savages and the Civilized English: Catlin's Indian Gallery and the Shows of London', *European Journal of American Studies*, vol. 3, no. 1 (2008). Available at: https://ejas.revues.org/2263 (accessed 25 Sept. 2016); Benita Eisler, *The Red Man's Bones: George Catlin, Artist and Showman* (New York. W. W. Norton, 2013); David M. Wrobel, *Global West, American Frontier: Travel, Empire and Exceptionalism from Manifest Destiny to the Great Depression* (Albuquerque, NM: University of New Mexico Press, 2013).

23 The terminology used to classify these objects is still somewhat fluid, and often relates to geography. 'First Nations', for example, refers to Canada and parts of Alaska, whereas 'Native American' tends to be associated with the United States. 'American Indian' is also used, along with specific tribe names such as Cree. For simplicity, 'Native American' will be used here.

24 For a history of early collecting, see Christian F. Feest, 'The Collecting of American Indian Artifacts in Europe, 1493–1750', in Karen Ordahl Kupperman, ed., *America in European Consciousness, 1493–1750* (Chapel Hill, NC: University of North Carolina, 1995), pp. 324–360.

25 David Wilson, *The British Museum: A History* (London: British Museum Press, 2002).

26 Brown (2014), p. 78.

27 See www.britishmuseum.org/explore/highlights/article_index/s/sir_hans_sloane_and_ethnograph.aspx (accessed 26 Aug. 2015).

28 Christian F. Feest, 'European Collecting of American Indian Artefacts and Art', *Journal of the History of Collections*, 5, no. 1 (1993), p. 6.

29 One of these pieces from Sloane's collection was even selected as one of the 'History of the World in 100 Objects' in the British Museum exhibition of that name. See www.britishmuseum.org/explore/highlights/highlight_objects/aoa/a/akan_drum.aspx (accessed 26 Aug. 2015).

30 H. Waterfield and J. C. H. King, *Provenance: Twelve Collectors of Ethnographic Art in England, 1760–1990* (London: Paul Holborton Publishing, 2009), pp. 27–36.

31 See www.liverpoolmuseums.org.uk/wml/collections/ethnology/americas-collections.pdf (accessed 26 Aug. 2015).

32 'Indigenous American Art at the Burlington Fine Arts Club', *The Connoisseur*, vol. LVII (May–August 1920), p. 241.
33 *Codex Fejervary-Mayer*, in *Codices Selecti*, vol. 26, commentary by C.A. Burland (Graz: Akademische Druck-und Verlagsanstalt, 1971). For a recent scholarly reference citing the Codex, see Anne S. Dowd and Susan Milbrath, eds., *Cosmology, Calendars, and Horizon-Based Astronomy in Ancient Mesoamerica* (Boulder, CO: University Press of Colorado, 2015), e.g. pp. 88–90.
34 Waterfield and King (2009), pp. 37–54.
35 See http://web.prm.ox.ac.uk/rpr/index.php/article-index/12-articles/604-pitt-rivers-south-american-collections.html (accessed 26 Aug. 2015).
36 For brief biographical details about Fuller and a discussion of his Pacific collections, see Waterfield and King (2009), pp. 93–104; For his collections in Chicago, see www.field museum.org/node/5061 (accessed 26 Aug. 2015).
37 Philip Jarrett, *Frank McClean: Godfather of British Naval Aviation* (Barnsley: Seaforth Publishing, 2011).
38 See exhibition catalogue, BFAC 1920, Case nos. M–P.
39 James Nelson Carder, ed., *A Home of the Humanities: The Collecting and Patronage of Mildred and Robert Woods Bliss* (Cambridge, MA: Harvard University Press, 2010). Robert Woods and Mildred Bliss were Americans who served in various diplomatic posts, including Argentina and Paris in the period of the 1890s–1919. They began collecting art in earnest in Paris and later returned to America for further government service and founded the Dumbarton Oaks Research Library and Collection at their former estate, to be administered by Harvard. For a biography of the Blisses and a history of the library, see 'Mildred and Robert Woods Bliss, a Brief Biography', in Carder (2010), pp. 1–25.
40 Royall Tyler, *Dictionary of American Biography* (New York: Charles Scribner's Sons, 1977). *Biography in Context*. Web. 28 June 2016, available at: http://ic.galegroup.com/ic/bic1/ReferenceDetailsPage/ReferenceDetailsWindow?displayGroupName=Reference&disableHighlighting=false&prodId=BIC2&action=e&windowstate=normal&catId=&documentId=GALE%7CBT2310001718&mode=view&userGroupName=fairfax_main&jsid=28d94d5cb3fad467191be7f50b1b1def (accessed 26.8 2015); https://dictionaryofarthistorians.org/tylerr.htm (accessed 26.8 2015); Julie Jones, 'Mildred and Robert Woods Bliss and the Pre-Colombian Collection at Dumbarton Oaks', in Carder (2010), pp. 53–72.
41 Jones, in Carder (2010), p. 55.
42 Ibid., p. 53.
43 Ibid., pp. 58–59.
44 Mary F. McVicker, *Adela Breton: A Victorian Artist Amid Mexico's Ruins* (Albuquerque, NM: University of New Mexico Press, 2005), pp. 55–57. On Chichén Itza, see, for example, Clemency Chase Coggins and Orrin C. Shane, III, *Cenote of Sacrifice: Maya Treasures from the Sacred Well at Chichen Itza* (Austin, TX: University of Texas Press, 2014).
45 McVicker (2005), p. 162.
46 Ibid.
47 A. Maudslay, 'Some American Problems', *Journal of the Royal Anthropological Institute*, vol. 42 (1912), p. 22.
48 A. C. Breton, E. N. Fallaize, A. C. Haddon, T. A. Joyce and A. P. Maudslay, eds., *Proceedings of the XVIII. Session, London, 1912 International Congress of Americanists* (London: Harrison & Sons, 1913), pp. lxxi–lxxvi.
49 Breton, *et al.* (1913), p. lxxv; Colin Wallace, 'Reconnecting Thomas Gann with British Interest in the Archaeology of Mesoamerica: An Aspect of the Development of Archaeology as a University Subject,' *Bulletin of the History of Archaeology*, 2011, UCL, Institute of Archaeology. Available at: www.archaeologybulletin.org/articles/10.5334/bha.2113/#r39 (accessed 31 Dec. 2015).
50 See www.ica55.ufg.edu.sv/historia (accessed 29 Aug. 2015).
51 Paul Garner, *British Lions and Mexican Eagles: Business, Politics, and Empire in the Career of Weetman Pearson in Mexico, 1889–1919* (Stanford, CA: Stanford University Press, 2011).
52 BFAC (1920), Case D. Mexico.

53 See www.christies.com/about/press-center/releases/ press release.aspx?press releaseid=4957 (accessed 29 Aug. 2015); see www.antiquestradegazette.com/news/2011/oct/01/a-winning-formula-on-the-fields-of-cowdray/ (accessed 29 Aug. 2015).
54 See www.britishmuseum.org/explore/highlights/highlight_objects/aoa/t/the_fenton_vase.aspx (accessed 29 Aug. 2015). BFAC (1920), 'Case K: Central America'; Pottery beaker (with figurative scene), 'a line drawing of the design is exhibited above Case L', 'Nebaj Guatemala, early Maya, Fenton', p. 43.
55 Graham (2002), p. 305; Report of the Council, June, 1932, to June, 1933, *The Journal of the Royal Anthropological Institute of Great Britain and Ireland*, vol. 63 (Jan.–Jun. 1933), p. iii.
56 Breton, *et al.* (1913), p. lxx.
57 Wallace (2011).
58 Ibid.
59 See http://lafayette.org.uk/gut1324a.html (accessed 29 Aug. 2015).
60 Michelle Labreche-Laroushe, *Emma Albani: International Star* (Montreal: Dundum, 1994), p. 106.
61 A brief biography of Gye can be found in the catalogue of the archives of Reginald Farrer at the Royal Botanic Garden Edinburgh, p. 11. Available at: www.rbge.org.uk/assets/files/science/Library%20-Archives/GB235RJF_ReginaldJFarrer.pdf (accessed 16 Feb. 2016).
62 Kathleen Kuiper, ed., *Indigenous Peoples of the Arctic, Subarctic, and Northwest Coast* (New York: Rosen Education Service, 2012), pp. 106–107.
63 E. Clinch and N. Clinch, *Through a Land of Extremes: The Littledales of Central Asia* (Seattle, WA: Mountaineers Books, 2008).
64 Ibid., p. 11.
65 Jones (2000), pp. 64–65.
66 Horace Laffaye, *Polo in Britain: A History* (Jefferson, NC: Macfarland, 2012).
67 Nigel Glendinning and Hilary Macartney, *Spanish Art in Britain and Ireland, 1750–1920: Studies in Reception in Memory of Enriquetta Harris Frankfort* (Rochester, NY: Tamesis Books, 2010), p. 7; Geoffrey Jones, *Merchants to Multinationals: Trading Companies in the Nineteenth and Twentieth Centuries* (Oxford: Oxford University Press, 2000), p. 305; T. A. J. (Joyce), 'Bequest of the Late Dame Clarissa Reid', *British Museum Quarterly*, vol. VIII, no. 2 (1933), pp. 75–76.
68 http://maa.cam.ac.uk/maa-highlights/central_south_america/peru/372/ (accessed 1 Sept. 2015). It has not been possible to trace Macandrew's biography but he was active in 1927–1931, when he submitted building plans for Mount Hall, Great Horkesley, Essex. See https://secureweb1.essexcc.gov.uk/SeaxPAM/result_details.aspx?DocID=880583 (accessed 1 Sept. 2015).
69 'Obituary: Philip Norman', *Notes and Queries* (1931), CLX (May 30): 396. doi: 10.1093/nq/CLX.may30.396-b (accessed 5 Dec. 2015).
70 BFAC, *Catalogue of a Collection of Early Drawings and Pictures of London* (London, 1920).
71 Brinsley Ford, 'Obituary. Paul Oppé', *The Burlington Magazine*, vol. 99, no. 651 (June 1957), pp. 207–208.
72 www.tate.org.uk/research/prints-and-drawings-rooms/oppe-collection (accessed 5 Dec. 2015).
73 He also contributed a short essay to the catalogue. BFAC, *Catalogue of a Collection of Drawings by John Robert Cozens*, 1923.
74 See www.newn.cam.ac.uk/about-newnham/college-history/biographies/content/henry-elizabeth-yates-thompson (accessed 5 Dec. 2015).
75 BFAC, *Catalogue of an Exhibition of Illuminated Manuscripts* (London, 1908), p. viii.
76 See www.seattleartmuseum.org/exhibitions/indigenous (accessed 5 Dec. 2015).
77 BFAC, *Catalogue of an Exhibition of the Art of Primitive Peoples* (London, 1935), p. 9.
78 Stallabrass (1990).
79 Ian Shaw and Robert Jameson, eds., *A Dictionary of Archaeology* (Chichester: Wiley-Blackwell, 2002); Bruce Trigger, *A History of Archaeological Thought*, 2nd edn (Cambridge: Cambridge University Press, 2006).

80 R. Bentley, H. Maschner and C. Chippendale, eds., *A Handbook of Archaeological Theories* (Walnut Creek, CA: Alta Mira Press, 2009).
81 Ibid.
82 James Urry, *Before Social Anthropology: Essays on the History of British Anthropology* (London: Routledge, 1993), p. 7.
83 See www.britishmuseum.org/about_us/departments/africa,_oceania,_americas/history_of_the_collection.aspx (accessed 6 Dec. 2015).
84 BFAC (1935), p. 9.
85 Ibid., pp. 10, 11, 13.
86 BFAC (1935), p. 13.
87 Brown (2014), p. 230. The spoon is now acc. No. MMA 1930.854.
88 BFAC (1935), p. 9.
89 Nicholas Mirzoeff, 'Transculture: From Kongo to Congo', in Nicholas Mirzoeff, *An Introduction to Visual Culture* (London: Routledge 1999), Chapter 4.
90 Steven Hooper, *Pacific Encounters: Art and Divinity in Polynesia, 1760–1860* (Honolulu: University of Hawaii Press, 2006), p. 72.
91 Ibid., pp. 72; 273; Paul van der Grijp, *Passion and Profit: Towards an Anthropology of Collecting* (Berlin: Lit Verlag, 2006), pp. 101–103.
92 This is likely because he was a dealer and would not have been allowed to become a Club member.
93 Van der Grijp (2006), p. 102.
94 Hooper (2006), p. 273; see http://collections.tepapa.govt.nz /Topic/1337 (accessed 3 Sept. 2015).
95 Museum of New Zealand, no. OL000390, today.
96 Franz Boas, *Primitive Art* (Oslo: H. Aschehoug and Company, 1927). Incidentally, this is still in print.
97 BFAC (1935), p. 7.
98 Julia Kelly, *Art, Ethnography and the Life of Objects in Paris, c. 1920–1930* (Manchester: Manchester University Press, 2012).
99 See www.tate.org.uk/art/artists/sir-william-reynolds-stephens-1833 (accessed 3 Sept. 2015).
100 See www.vam.ac.uk/content/articles/c/curtis-moffat-biography/ (accessed 3 Sept. 2015).
101 Stallabrass (1990), p. 97.
102 News, 'The Art of Primitive Peoples', *Nature*, vol. 135 (1 June 1935), p. 927.
103 Ibid.
104 Royal Anthropological Institute Proceedings. 146. Exhibition of the Art of Primitive Peoples. *Man*, vol. 35 (September 1935), p. 137.
105 Ibid.
106 H. R., 'The Art of Primitive Peoples', *The Burlington Magazine for Connoisseurs*, vol. 67, no. 388 (July 1935), p. 42.
107 Sally Price, *Primitive Art in Civilized Places*, second edn (Chicago: University of Chicago Press, 1989).
108 Ibid.
109 Fuller's collection of Benin bronzes was donated to the Chicago Natural History Museum (now the Field Museum) in 1963 by his wife. See Chicago Natural History Museum, 'Report of the Director to the Board of Trustees for the Year 1963', 'Collections. Anthropology', p. 38.
110 Laszlo Mathe-Shires, 'Benin Kingdom: British Conquest, 1897', in K. Shillington, ed., *Encyclopaedia of African History*, vol. 1, A–G (New York: Routledge, 2005), pp. 136–137.
111 F. S., 'Obituary for George W. Neville', *Journal of the Royal Africa Society*, vol. 29, no. 114 (Jan. 1930), p. 201; Eddy Chicka Ndekwu, *First Bank of Nigeria: A Century of Banking* (London: Spectrum Books, 1994), p. 17; Coombes (2007, [1994]), p. 46.
112 See www.britishmuseum.org/research/collection_online/collection_object_details.aspx?objectId=8849&partId=1 (accessed 9 Sept. 2015); C. H. Read and O. M. Dalton, 'Works of Art from Benin City', *Journal of the Anthropological Institute*, vol. XXVII (1898), pp. 362–382.
113 Read and Dalton (1898).

114 Fry (1920), pp. 65–68.
115 Raymond Firth, 'Art and Anthropology', in J. Cooke and A Shelton, eds., *Anthropology, Art, and Aesthetics* (Oxford: Clarendon Press, 1992), p. 21.
116 Dora Clarke, 'Negro Art: Sculpture from West Africa', *Journal of the Royal African Society* 34 (April 1935), pp. 129, 130.
117 Christopher B. Steiner, 'The Tradition of African Art: Reflections on the Social Life of a Subject', in M. Phillips and G. Schochet, eds., *Questions of Tradition* (Toronto: University of Toronto Press, 2004), p. 100.
118 Michael O'Hanlon and Robert Welsch, *Hunting the Gatherers: Ethnographic Collectors, Agents and Agency in Melanesia, 1870s–1930s* (Oxford: Berghahn, 2000), pp. 197–199.
119 Nicky Levell, 'Scholars and Connoisseurs: Knowledge and Taste. The Seligman Collection of Chinese Art', in A. Shelton, ed., *Collectors: Expressions of Self and Other* (London: Horniman Museum and Gardens, 2001), p. 75. Seligman was also therefore representative of many Club members with pluralistic tastes in object collecting.
120 Ibid., pp. 75–76.
121 BFAC (1935), nos. 110, 138, 140, 147–149, 155, 157, 176.
122 Brown (2014), pp. 230–231.
123 Ibid., p. 231.
124 Berkeley Galleries, *Primitive Art: Exhibition of the Art of Primitive Peoples at the Berkeley Galleries, June–July 1945* (London: Berkeley Galleries, 1945). This exhibition has an interestingly ambiguous title, combining both 'art' and the 'art of peoples', suggesting a strong anthropological association attaching to these kinds of objects.

Part 3

Epilogue

5 The Club, its Legacy, and the Historiography of Collecting and Display

In spite of its forays into the worlds of ethnographic objects, the Club's exhibition programme still maintained its traditional focus in its later years. The last exhibition mounted by the Club was British Medieval Art, which was presented from May to July of 1939.[1] While it took place just a few months before the beginning of the Second World War, it was timed to be on display during the meeting of the International Congress of the History of Art, a semi-annual conference that was founded in Vienna in 1873.[2] As reported in *The Burlington Magazine*, that year's congress was held at the University of London and its theme was 'British art and its relationship with other countries'.[3] For the Club, this was an opportunity to participate in and support a major event in the academic art history calendar and it was commended by Pevsner for showing 'medieval British art at its best'.[4] This exhibition was to be followed by one on 'Flower paintings and gardens in art' but it had to be abandoned because the Club's premises were bombed during the war. After the war ended, the Club was unable to continue and on 5 June 1950, the Club's General Committee voted to close the Club for good. The Chairman, the Earl of Ilchester, had noted that in order to reopen the Club, after leaving its premises in Savile Row during the War, it would be necessary to secure the support of 250 members. Unfortunately, considerably fewer than that responded to a circular previously sent round. New premises had been found in Great Cumberland Place, but an annual income of £2500 would have been required to support this.[5] At the next and final meeting of the committee, on 7 February 1951, it was decided to place the Club into voluntary liquidation, but also that:

> [T]he liquidation be authorised on the conclusion of the winding up to offer the net proceeds of sale of the asset of the Club to the National Art Collections Fund as the only disinterested Institution which covers the whole field of art, the gift to be recorded as in memory of the Burlington Fine Arts Club.[6]

The National Art Collections Fund (NACF), which several Club members had helped to set up and had complementary aims, was thus the beneficiary of the Club's financial legacy, in total about £13,000.

The issue with the premises does not seem substantial enough to warrant the dissolution of the Club. It is worth considering, therefore, what other reasons might have underlain this decision. In an obituary, of sorts, the author of an editorial in *The Burlington Magazine* explained it thus:

> It is generally felt that, sad as the occasion was, it was wisest to bring the Club to an end in this abrupt manner rather than to allow it to drag on for a few more years and eventually fade out. It is hard to see how it could have continued to fulfil its original function even if funds had been found to keep it going. In its early days it proved an outstanding feature of the cultural life of London, the only institution in the country which held regular Old Master Exhibitions of real distinction. Its role is now more effectively carried on by the Royal Academy, the Arts Council, and other official bodies. Its constitution was moulded to suit a leisurely, gentlemanly way of life; it was essentially a private enterprise. It could never have adapted itself to modern conditions without radically altering its character.[7]

From the perspective of the 1950s, the Club's old-fashioned character and the demise of the social life of its heyday were to blame, in the author's view. This is to some extent true. The demise of the Club was partly financial but it was also temporal. The Club was a victim of the changing landscape for the presentation of art collections, the London art market, and gentlemen's clubs beginning with the First World War.

From that time, art and objects were increasingly moving out of the country house and into public museums, sometimes permanently because of financial hardship, with the demise and breaking up of the great landed estates[8] but also because of the increasing popularity of museum exhibitions, and greater museum attendance, so that museums became the natural home for showing privately (and publicly) collected objects. It was no longer about showing and discussing works with your peers but rather moving these works away from the cloistered elites towards the general public, who had much more access to art works than ever before.

Perhaps a more significant factor in the decline of the Club was the demise of Victorian clubland and the concept of the club as an insular, protected world of privilege.[9] Throughout its history, the Club's situation was somewhat precarious because of its premises, which were acquired on fixed-term leases. The first lease was renewed but by the time the second lease came up for renewal in the 1920s, the world around the Club, both immediately in the West End and more generally in Britain, was changing. As we have seen, new members had to pay more for the club privileges available but also those wealthy enough to join and maintain their memberships had to do so in a time when, during the 1930s and 1940s, there were major changes in Britain's economy, politics, society, social class distinctions, and ways of living, even in social life such as going out in the West End, where the Club had been located.[10]

While the membership profile did not change significantly in its later years, it was wealth and art collecting that had brought the Club members together. The former was disappearing in many areas, or at least becoming harder to acquire and maintain, but the latter was also changing, at least in the way practised by the members of the Club. Their reason for being members was to bring together their objects, present them to their peers (becoming peers in the process), study and practise connoisseurship, and present their learning and collecting interests in the form of themed exhibitions. The desire to do this collectively did not survive the Second World War because of both the post-war economic and social situation in England but more importantly, the loss of their premises in 1940 which meant the loss of the anchor which grounded the members and brought them together. Unlike museums, the Club was an exclusive space and did not rely on external visitors or even paying visitors to survive, nor did it require the presence of external visitors to continue its exhibition programme, which was designed by and for its members. Visitors were welcome but they are not mentioned as a criterion for justifying or maintaining the exhibition programme anywhere in the Club archives. A significant post-war change was therefore the members' own attitudes towards appropriate spaces for sharing collections and practising art historiography.

The continuation of the Club after the War may also have seemed less essential because if members wanted to share and interpret their collections, they could do so in the increasing number of collecting clubs that arose from the 1920s onwards and have yet to be the subject of a dedicated study, in spite of becoming a significant element of the art world in the twentieth century. These collecting clubs were quite different in character to the BFAC, not being gentlemen's clubs essentially, but they were the same in intention, that is sharing, learning from and developing collections – traditional connoisseurship activities. The Burlington Fine Arts Club can therefore be seen as one of the first (with its predecessor) such clubs. Yet later collectors clubs were somewhat different in that they tended to be more specialized than the Burlington which embraced almost all types of art and media, as long as it was not contemporary. One of the first specialist collector's clubs to emerge was one that had considerable overlap in membership to the BFAC: the Oriental Ceramic Society, which was founded in 1921.[11] This club is perhaps closer to a learned society than the BFAC in that it produces its own scholarly journal (TOCS), but it is nonetheless a club for collectors with a museum presence on its council. Similar organizations include the English Ceramic Circle, also formed in the 1920s (in 1927), the Silver Society formed in 1958, and the Furniture History Society in 1964. Notably, these are concentrated on the decorative arts and their main activity is lectures, not exhibitions, though some groups do the occasional show of members' objects. Sharing collections and interest in art are also undertaken in another new way by museum friends groups. The oldest was founded at the Fitzwilliam (1909) but these are designed to support the museums and share *their* collections, not necessarily those of members.

Thus, the BFAC had no real successor but that is not surprising because it was unique - an unusual confluence of gentlemen's club for art collectors, exhibition space in London, and site for curatorial practice and the writing of art history. It provided an alternative space for display and curating by private collectors as well as those involved in the public management of art in museums. These seemingly different groups came together through and at the Club which became an unregulated and therefore unrestricted space in which to appreciate, interpret, and promote non-contemporary art. Its unique approach and circumstances enabled the Club to have an impact that deserves to be recognized more widely. For private collecting, the Club also brought both collectors and collections to wider public attention and in doing so, promoted collecting in its many forms.

As we have seen, these collected objects were combined and often interpreted in new ways through displays at the Club, bringing objects from private and sometimes distant public spaces to audiences in London. Through their unique mode of presentation, which applied the museum approach to display and interpretation to a grand domestic-style gallery space, they also brought two forms of curatorial and art historical practice together in one unusual place. As this was an unprecedented and therefore unclassified space, it enabled an unrestricted form of art historical practice where new categories of art were defined and old ones expanded. Objects of all types were identified as and presented as art and situated in the literature of art history through the

Club's regular production of catalogues with historiographical essays. As we have seen, many of these combined such writing with traditional catalogue lists of objects that were essential for Club readers and viewers for whom connoisseurship was a priority. Significantly, it should also be noted that the Club's universalizing approach to all objects, regardless of type or geographical origins, much prefigures an approach which is standard practice today, when art history, anthropology, and archaeology are part of an interdisciplinary analysis of the world of things.

This study has brought to light many such innovative interventions and has positioned the Club in the map of the London art world as defined by Helmreich and Fletcher, demonstrating that the Club is a hitherto unrecognized agent in this world. It was through the Club that the many parts of the art world, including the market, can be seen to have intersected and were interrelated. That the Club did not survive and was not imitated in the same form is not only indicative of circumstances but also suggests that such a confluence of art world agents was untenable. The boundaries that exist today (often unacknowledged) between the private and the public, the market and academia have developed with the increasing institutionalization of art historical practice in its widest sense and funding of such activity. The world before regulation in the form of loan agreements, national insurance, research assessment, and ethical restrictions has disappeared. The public and private do still intersect but not in the untethered way that the Club enabled.

It might be asked therefore whether the Club could have survived in another form, for example, as a special interest group without the gentlemen's club element, but this is unlikely because the lectures and journals that sustain such groups were never a regular part of the Club's programme. In this way, collectors' clubs tend to emulate learned societies and generally have at least a veneer of educational motives. For the Club, the few lectures that were scheduled were notably poorly attended and its literary output was in the service of the objects. Exhibitions were its key activity and the medium through which the Club's aims and objectives were achieved but these required the unique conceptual space of the club environment and the physical framework of premises.

In spite of its uniqueness, the BFAC did leave a legacy, however, beyond the financial one gifted to the NACF on its closure. This can be seen in scholarship, where its exhibitions have become both a historiographic record of art history, collecting, and curatorial practice, as well as the art market, where the provenance that developed for the many objects displayed by the Club is noted. In the twenty-first century, such a provenance is still relevant and desirable commercially. A lot in a recent sale at Sotheby's in London, 'A Roman marble head of a Dionysiac Child' (Lot 40), had a Club exhibition (and member) listed in its provenance and history:

> **PROVENANCE**
>
> The wine-merchant and art collector Henry J. Pfungst, Esq. (1844–1917), London, acquired in or prior to 1904.
>
> **EXHIBITED**
>
> Burlington Fine Arts Club, London, 1904.[12]

The Club has become part of the life history of this object, which was changed forever by its presence at 17 Savile Row.

The final word should perhaps go to the Club itself and the journal linked with its later history. As summed up in a *Burlington Magazine* editorial in 1952:

> The exhibitions at the Burlington Fine Arts Club did more to stimulate appreciation in London of the art of the past than any similar enterprises, at least until the first war.
>
> The Club has left its permanent mark on the history of exhibitions, and indirectly on the history of criticism.[13]

Notes

1 Burlington Fine Arts Club, *Catalogue of an Exhibition of British Medieval Art* (London, 1939).
2 Ibid., Introduction.
3 'The History of Art Congress', *The Burlington Magazine for Connoisseurs*, vol. 75, no. 436 (July 1939), p. 3.
4 Nikolaus Pevsner, 'An Exhibition of British Medieval Art', *The Burlington Magazine for Connoisseurs*, vol. 75, no. 436 (July 1939), p. 13.
5 Special General Meeting minutes, 5.6.1950.
6 General Committee minutes for the meeting, 7.2.1951.
7 'The Burlington Fine Arts Club', *The Burlington Magazine*, vol. 94, no. 589 (Apr. 1952), pp. 97–99.
8 David Cannadine, *The Decline and Fall of the British Aristocracy* (Harmondsworth: Penguin, 2005).
9 Amy Milne-Smith, *London Clubland: A Cultural History of Gender and Class in Late Victorian Britain* (Basingstoke: Palgrave, 2011), epilogue.
10 Judith Walkowitz, *Nights Out: Life in Cosmopolitan London* (New Haven, CT: Yale University Press, 2012); Fiona MacCarthy, *Last Curtsey: The End of the Debutantes* (London: Faber & Faber, 2006).
11 For a comprehensive history of the OCS, see Stacey Pierson, 'The History of the London Oriental Ceramic Society, 1921–1947', *Diancang* 典蔵 (Taipei), part 1, vol. 220 (January 2011), pp. 152–159; part II, vol. 221 (February 2011), pp. 132–139; part III, vol. 222 (March 2011), pp. 186–195.
12 Sotheby's London, 13 June 2016, 'Ancient Marbles: Classical Sculpture and Work of Art', Lot 40.
13 Editorial, *The Burlington Magazine* (Apr. 1952), pp. 98, 99.

Appendix A

List of Special Exhibitions Mounted by the Club with Visitor Numbers (where Available) from 1869[1]

Number	*Title*	*Date*	*Visitor numbers*
1	Rembrandt etchings	1867	
2	Marc Antonio Raimondi	1868	
3	Oriental porcelain	1869	
4	Albert Dürer and Lucas van Leyden	1869	477
5	Oriental art and manufactures	1870	1524
6	Raphael Sanzio and Michelangelo Buonarroti	1870	851
7	The works of Old Masters	1871	940
8	Drawings in watercolours by artists born anterior to 1800, and now deceased	1871	1884
9	Exhibition illustrative of Turner's *Liber Studiorum*	1872	2192
10	Drawings and etchings by Claude le Lorrain	1872	
11	Watercolour drawings by William Muller	1872–1873	507
12	Collected works of the late George Mason, ARA	1873	2968
13	English and Continental porcelain	1873	1745
14	Watercolour drawings by the late Peter de Wint and the late David Cox	1873–1874	2436
15	Illuminated manuscripts	1874	1518
16	The work of Wenceslas Hollar	1875	1869
17	Drawings of Thomas Girtin	1875	1863
18	Japanese lacquerware	1875–1876	1113
19	Artistic painted glass	1876	180
20	Paintings, drawings and engravings by William Blake	1876	6143
21	Etched work of Rembrandt	1877	3379
22	Engravings and woodcuts by Hans Sebald Beham and Barthel Beham	1877–1878	196
23	Pictures by the late Samuel Raven	1878	1673
24	Drawings by Dutch Masters	1878	1590
25	Chinese and Japanese art	1878–1879	2835
26	Bronzes and ivories of European origin	1879	1519
27	Etched work of Charles Meryon	1879–1880	1634
28	Collection of drawings in watercolours by deceased English artists born in or subsequent to 1800 and now deceased	1880	1500
29	Collection of engravings and mezzotints	1881	1751

Number	*Title*	*Date*	*Visitor numbers*
30	Collection of woodcuts of the German School, 15th–16th century	1882	560
31	Pictures and drawings by the late D. G. Rossetti	1883	12,133
32	Collection of etchings by Renier Zeeman and Karel du Jardin	1884	414
33	Collection of drawings by the late Robert Hills	1884	214
34	Collection of drawings of architectural subjects by deceased British artists	1885	1055
35	Persian and Arab art	1885	4198
36	Collection of engravings in mezzotints by James McArdell	1886–1887	590
37	Hispano-Moresque and maiolica wares	1887	1056
38	Prints and books to illustrate the history of engravings in Japan	1888	1406
39	Greek ceramic art	1888	1370
40	Drawings of John Sell Cotman	1888–1889	2011
41	Portrait miniatures	1889–1890	12,031
42	Collection of drawings in watercolour and in black and white by the late Spencer Vincent	1890	1939
43	Collection of bookbindings	1891	2999
44	Pictures by masters of the Netherlandish and allied schools	1892	3181
45	Luca Signorelli	1893	1965
46	Specimens of Japanese lacquer and metalwork	1894	3905
47	Pictures of the School of Ferrara-Bologna	1894	2459
48	Blue and White Oriental porcelain	1895	2408
49	Art of Ancient Egypt	1895	2273
50	Coloured Chinese porcelain	1896	1338
51	Drawings in watercolour by Alfred William Hunt	1897	4565
52	A collection of European enamels from the earliest date to the end of the seventeenth century	1897	3086
53	Pictures by masters of the Milanese and allied schools of Lombardy	1898	4512
54	Chased and embossed steel and iron work of European origin	1900[2]	2611
55	Pictures by Dutch masters of the seventeenth century	1900	2456
56	A collection of silversmiths' work of European origin	1901	11,501
57	English mezzotint portraits from circa 1750 to circa 1830	1902	2366
58	Ancient Greek art	1903	11,346
59	Pictures of the School of Siena and examples of the minor arts of that city	1904	4253

(Continued)

(Continued)

Number	*Title*	*Date*	*Visitor numbers*
60	A collection of English embroidery executed prior to the middle of the XVI century	1905	4110
61	Pictures and sketches by Charles Wellington Furse, ARA	1906	5237
62	Early German art	1906	4624
63	Pictures and sketches by Robert Brough, ARSA	1907	3304
64	Faience of Persia and the Nearer East	1907	3976
65	Exhibition of illuminated manuscripts	1908	5053
66	Early English portraiture	1909	7184
67	Early Chinese pottery and porcelain	1910	3548
68	A collection of pictures and other works of art including examples of the works of the brothers Le Nain and other works of art	1911	2117
69	Venetian painting of the eighteenth century	1911	1716
70	Pictures of the early Venetian School and other works of art	1912	5356
71	A collection of Italian sculpture and other plastic art of the Renaissance	1912	3450
72	Pictures, decorative furniture and other works of art[3]	1913	3019
73	A collection of pictures, drawings etc., of the French School of the eighteenth century	1913	2915
74	A collection of Early English earthenware and other works of art	1913–1914	3225
75	Pictures of the Venetian School, including works by Titian and his contemporaries	1914	2858
76	A collection of old embroideries of the Greek islands and Turkey	1915	1858
77	A collection of objects of Chinese art	1915	2674
78	Objects of British heraldic art to the end of the Tudor period	1916	1943
79	The Herbert Horne collection of drawings with special reference to the works of Alexander Cozens	1917	2352
80	A collection of drawings by deceased masters	1918	3411
81	A collection of early drawings and pictures of London with some contemporary furniture	1919	illegible
82	Exhibition of Florentine painting before 1500	1920	4876
83	Exhibition of objects of Indigenous American art	1920	1360
84	A collection of pictures and English furniture of the Chippendale period	1920	4286

Number	*Title*	*Date*	*Visitor numbers*
85	An exhibition of Ancient Egyptian art	1921	4863
86	Exhibition of pictures and other works of art selected from the collection of Mr Robert Holford [1808–1892] mainly from Westonbirt in Gloucestershire	1921–1922	3655
87	Pictures, drawings and sculpture of the French School of the last 100 years	1922	3683
88	A collection of drawings by John Robert Cozens, with some decorative furniture and other works of art	1922–1923	2946
89	An exhibition of carvings in ivory	1923	1764
90	A collection of counterfeits, imitations and copies of works of art	1924	3068
91	An exhibition of Italian art of the seventeenth century	1925	1282
92	An exhibition of Late Elizabethan art in conjunction with the tercentennial of Bacon	1926	2020
93	An exhibition to celebrate the 150th anniversary of the birth of William Blake	1927	2893
94	An exhibition of Spanish art, including pictures, drawings and engravings by Goya	1928	3596
95	An exhibition of marine art	1929	n.a.
96	A collection of pictures, drawings and furniture from the Empire and Regency periods: select examples of Romano-British art; watercolour drawings by Francis Towne	1929–1930	806
97	Exhibition of art in the Dark Ages in Europe (c.400–1000 A.D.)	1930	2423
98	An exhibition of the art of India	1931	1462
99	A collection of English caricature	1931–1932	1284
100	An exhibition of the works of some neglected English masters, c.1759–c.1830	1932	1028
101	A collection of Japanese prints and drawings	1933	868
102	An exhibition of English paintings and drawings c. 1780–1830 and Holbein's portrait of Henry VIII from Althorp	1933–1934	2415
103	An exhibition of sport in British Art	1934	704
104	An exhibition of pictures, furniture, Italian maiolica and other works of art	1934–1935	1354
105	An exhibition of the art of primitive peoples	1935	978
106	An exhibition of Chinoiserie	1935–1936	1705
107	An exhibition of Gothic art in Europe, c.1200–c.1500	1936	1395

(Continued)

(Continued)

Number	*Title*	*Date*	*Visitor numbers*
108	An exhibition of pictures and drawings by Richard Parkes Bonington and his circle	1937	1338
109	An exhibition of the works of British-born artists of the seventeenth century	1938	812
110	An exhibition of British Medieval art	1939	124
111	Flower paintings and gardens in art	abandoned	

Notes

1 The exhibition titles recorded in meeting minutes are often slightly different from those published in the catalogues. The latter have been used here. In addition, exhibition titles can vary with the edition of the catalogue published. The illustrated catalogues often have shorter titles.
2 There was no special exhibition in 1899 but an ordinary exhibition was mounted.
3 This was an ordinary exhibition but it is included here to demonstrate visitor numbers.

Appendix B

Biographical Index of Active Members and Contributors[1]

NB *denotes non-members.

Samuel Addington (*c.* 1807–86) was a wool merchant and original member of both the Fine Arts Club and the Burlington Fine Arts Club.[2] He collected porcelain, coins, and prints.

William Agnew*(1825–1910), was founder of Agnews art dealership in Mayfair and is best known for paintings. He was created a baronet in 1895.

Baron Aldenham (see Henry Hucks Gibbs).

William Cleverly Alexander (1840–1916) was a wealthy banker, art patron, and collector, whose daughters were painted by Whistler, and was therefore a great patron of the artist, who decorated Alexander's house in Holland Park.[3] He also collected Japanese woodblock prints and Chinese ceramics.

Lord Ampthill* (see Sir Arthur Oliver Villiers Russell).

William Arkwright Esq. (1857–1925) was possibly the 'descendant of the famous Sir Richard Arkwright of Spinning Jenny fame. He was a very keen dog breeder and published 'The Pointer and His Predecessors'.[4]

Walter Armstrong (1850–1914) was an art critic, author, and Director of the National Gallery of Ireland.

Sir Hickman Bacon (1855–1945) was the 11th/12th Baronet Redgrave/Mildenhall, High Sheriff of Lincolnshire and a JP.[5] He is best known today for his collection of prints and English watercolours.

Henry Balfour*(1863–1939), a president of the RAI, was curator of the Pitt Rivers Museum and Professor of Ethnology at Oxford.

Thomas Baring MP, Earl of Northbrook (1799–1873) was the first Earl of Northbrook and a distinguished politician who was Viceroy of India under Gladstone.

Lord Battersea (see Cyril Flower).

Chester Beatty (1875–1968) was an Irish-American mining magnate who collected widely and extensively but especially books and manuscripts from around the world. He opened his museum, the Chester Beatty Library in Dublin, in 1953.

Walter Behrens (1861–1913) worked as a merchant for the firm of S. L. Behrens and Co in Manchester, where he lived and collected mainly Japanese art.[6]

Walter P. Belk (1872–1963)* was a silversmith and designer.

Sir William H. Bennett KCVO (1852–1931) was a prominent surgeon.[7] The bulk of his Chinese collection was sold in 1906.[8]

Robert Henry Benson (1850–1929) was a banker, connoisseur and collector. In 1887, he married Evelyn Holford, the daughter of the collector, Robert Stayner Holford. Earning his fortune as senior partner in the merchant bank, Robert Benson and Co., London, he became a trustee of the National Gallery in 1912 and was also a member of the Council of the Royal College of Music.[9]

Bernard Berenson* (1865–1959) was an art critic, connoisseur, and scholar of Italian Renaissance art, who was particularly influential in the USA.[10]

Richard Bethell (1883–1929) was the son of the 3rd Baron Westbury and a member of the committee of the Egypt Exploration Society, the survey team that found Tutankhamun's tomb.

Laurence Binyon* (1869–1943) was a Keeper at the British Museum, poet, and dramatist.

Charles Blanc (1813–1882) was a French art critic and scholar of French and Italian art.[11]

Mrs Edward Bloxam* was probably Anne Jane Bloxam who was married to Edward Bloxam (d. 1891), who had been Chief Clerk in the Chancery. One of their children was J. F. Bloxam (d. 1928).[12]

William (Wilhelm) von (fr. 1914) Bode (1845–1929) was a German art historian who was Director of the Prussian museums from 1906–1920.

Tancred Borenius (1885–1948) was a Professor of Art History, writer, and specialist in Italian and British painting, who helped found the magazine *Apollo*.[13]

George H. Boughton (1833–1905), A.R.A, was the painter/writer/illustrator who lived in the USA, and was a friend of Whistler and Henry James.

Sir William Boxall (1800–1879), RA, was a portrait painter and Director of the National Gallery in London.

Adela Breton*(1849–1923) was an artist and fellow of the RAI, who recorded a number of archaeological sites in Mexico.

Dr Justus Brinckmann*(1843–1915) was Director of the Museum für Kunst und Gewerbe in Hamburg and a specialist in Modern art.

Henry Broadhurst* (1840–1911) was a Member of Parliament for Stoke-on-Trent (and other constituencies) and a prominent trade unionist.[14]

Victor Bruce (1849–1917) was the 9th Earl, and son of James Bruce who had been Governor-General of Canada. He was Viceroy of India from 1894 to 1899.[15]

J. Annan Bryce (1841–1923) was a Scottish businessman and MP who worked in India, Burma and 'Siam' (Thailand) and was Director of the Burma railway.

Victor Bulwer-Lytton (the 2nd Earl of Lytton, 1876–1947)* was a politician who held various prominent colonial positions including Governor of Bengal and acting Viceroy of India. His home was Knebworth House.[16]

Edward Burne Jones (later Burne-Jones, 1833–1898) was the painter, illustrator, and designer, who was associated with William Morris and the Pre-Raphaelite Movement.[17]

Stephen Bushell* (1844–1908) was a medical doctor with the British legation in Peking and a buying agent for the V&A.[18] He was married to Florence Matthews. While in Peking, he collected the key Chinese texts on ceramics that he translated and were used as foundation texts for the study of Chinese ceramics in Britain.[19]

Charles Butler (1821–1910) was High Sheriff of Hertfordshire and JP for the same county. He was also a committee member for the New Gallery.[20]

The Earl of Carnarvon (George Herbert, the 5th Earl, 1866–1923) was famous for the co-discovery of the tomb of Tutankhamun with Howard Carter, an excavation he also financed. His home was Highclere Castle.[21]

Howard Carter (1874–1939) was an Egyptologist and archaeologist who worked for the Egyptian Antiquities Service and then Lord Carnarvon, with whom he discovered the tomb of Tutankhamun.

Boddam Castle (1819–1891) of Bristol (not the place Boddam Castle of the same name), was a barrister descended from a long line of East India Company employees.

Spencer Cavendish, 8th Duke of Devonshire* (1833–1908) was a prominent statesman whose home was Chatsworth.

Victor Christian William Cavendish* (1868–1938), the 9th Duke of Devonshire was Governor of Canada from 1916–1921.[22] Before this, he held numerous parliamentary positions in Britain.[23]

Sir Atul Chandra Chatterjee* (1874–1955) was High Commissioner for India in London from 1924–1931.[24]

Edward Cheney (1803–1884) was a collector of Renaissance art, especially the Tiepolo family and was based at Badger Hall in Shropshire. He seems to have known Ruskin (Club member) and his wife.[25]

Joseph H. P. Chitty (1861-1942) was a solicitor from a prominent legal family and Chief Master of the Chancery Division at Lincoln's Inn.[26]

Sir Arthur Church (1834–1915) was a painter and Professor of Chemistry at the Royal Academy.

Louis C. G. Clarke (1881–1960)* was a curator at the Museum of Anthropology and Archaeology, Cambridge, and then later Director of the Fitzwilliam Museum at the same institution.

Alfred Cock (1848–98), QC, was a barrister who was known for his book and manuscript collection.[27]

Kenneth de Burgh Codrington (1899–1946) was Keeper of the Indian section at the V&A from 1935–1948.

Arthur Colefax (1866–1936) was a patent lawyer and Conservative MP, and also the son of the woollen merchant Colefax, whose firm would later become Colefax and Fowler.

Sidney Colvin (1845–1927) was Keeper of Prints and Drawings at the British Museum from 1883–1912, and the first Director of the Fitzwilliam Museum. He was also an art critic and friend of Ruskin as well as of Robert Louis Stevenson.[28]

Sir Martin Conway (1856–1937) was Baron Conway of Allington, an art historian, politician and author who specialized in Dutch art. He was also known as an accomplished mountaineer.

Sir Francis Cook (1817–1901) was the 1st Baronet and head of the family firm Cook, Son and Co. Aided by J. C. Robinson, he built up an impressive art collection at Doughty House, which was inherited by his son Frederick (and his brother) on his death.

Sir Frederick Cook (1844–1920) was the 2nd Baronet and MP for Kennington.

Herbert Cook (1868–1939, later Sir, the 3rd Baronet) was the son of Frederick Cook, a barrister and an active member of the art world as co-founder of the National Art Collections Fund, *The Burlington Magazine* and the Arundel Club. He took possession of Doughty House and the collection upon his father's death and built up his own collection in addition.

James B. Coughtrie* (active 1863–1914) is listed as 'Secretary, China Fire Insurance Company, Ltd', Hong Kong, in the Jardine Matheson archive[29] and was an artist who specialized in Hong Kong topographical scenes. His daughter Phyllis married Lionel Giles.

Viscount Cowdray (Weetman Pearson, 1856–1927) was the first Viscount and scion of the Pearson Group. He was also a Liberal MP and founder of an oil company in Mexico. He was a prolific collector of mainly European art but also some South American objects.

Wilson Crewdson (1856–1918) was a Fellow of the RGS and the Society of Antiquaries. He was an investor and collector, especially of Japanese art and was on the council of the Japan Society.[30]

Lt Col. G. B. Croft Lyons (1855–1926) was a Fellow of the Society of Antiquaries and a collector who left his collection to the V&A by bequest.

Dr A. E. Cumberbatch* (d. 1929) was an aural surgeon who taught surgery to the cricketer W. G. Grace.[31]

S. A. R. Le Duc d'Aumale (1822–1897) was Henri Eugène Philippe Louis d'Orléans, a French aristocrat (Duke of Orleans), general and owner of the Château de Chantilly, as well as a house in Twickenham.

George R. Davies (1844–1918) of Agden Hall, Cheshire, was a cotton merchant. His collection was purchased by Edgar Gorer.

Marchese d'Azeglio (see Vittorio Emanuelle Taparelli).

St John Dent* (d. *c.* 1884) His collection of engravings was sold by Sotheby's in 1884. Further biographical information has not been sourced.

Alfred A. De Pass (1861–1952)* was from a prominent Jewish mercantile family based in South Africa, where Alfred also worked for a time before moving to Falmouth.

M. C. Dey (Mukul Chandra, 1895–1989)* was Principal of the Government College of Art and Craft in Calcutta.[32]

W. W. Fitzwilliam Dick (William Wentworth, 1805– 1892) was MP for Wicklow.

Edward Dillon (d.1914) was an assayer to the Japanese mint and after living in Japan developed an expertise in Japanese art, which he wrote about in *The Arts of Japan* (1906). He was an active member of the London art world and was involved in the National Art Collections Fund, *The Burlington Magazine*, the Society of Antiquaries (a Fellow), and the BFAC.[33]

Bonamy Dobree (1819–1907) was the son of a Governor of the Bank of England, of the same name.

Campbell Dodgson (1868–1948) succeeded Sidney Colvin as Keeper of Prints and Drawings at the British Museum and was an expert on German art, particularly Dürer.[34]

Sir William Drake (1817–1890) was a prominent lawyer and Fellow of the Society of Antiquaries.[35]

Lawrence Dundas (2nd Marquess of Zetland, 1876–1961)* was an MP, Governor of Bengal, Secretary of State for India, President of the RGS and Chairman of the National Trust.[36]

Eugene Dutuit (1807–1886) was a prominent French art collector and connoisseur whose collection was displayed in Paris.[37]

Charles Eastlake (1836–1906) was the nephew of Sir Charles Locke Eastlake (1793–1865) and a prominent architect and furniture designer.

Lady Eastlake* (see Elizabeth Rigby).

Robert W. Edis (later Sir, 1839–1927) was a prominent architect, Fellow of the RIBA, and the Society of Antiquaries, and is associated with the Aesthetic Movement.[38]

Wynne Ellis (1790–1875) was a silk merchant, MP, Club member, and collector of paintings, whose collection was sold by Christie's in 1876.[39]

Professor Dr Adolf Erman (1854–1937)* was a German Egyptologist, attributed with being one of the founders of the field.[40]

George Eumorfopoulos (1863–1939) worked for the shipping firm Ralli Brothers and became a prominent collector of Asian art which he displayed at his home in London. He was actively involved in the London art world and was a founder of the Oriental Ceramic Society.[41]

Arthur Evans (1851–1941) was an archaeologist and Keeper of the Ashmolean Museum, who is best known today for his work at Knossos.[42]

C. L. Fenton* (Charles Ludwig, née Fleischmann, 1867–1932) was the British Consul in Guatemala and a Fellow of the RAI, and on the committee of the International Congress of Americanists.[43]

Heneage Finch (1786–1859) was the 5th Earl of Aylesford and an MP.[44]

Richard Fisher (1809–1890) was a solicitor and print collector who lived at Hill Top farm near Midhurst, Sussex.

Cyril Flower (1843–1907) (see Lord Battersea), was a Whistler patron and Liberal MP.

Wickham Flower (b. *c.* 1836) was a solicitor and Whistler patron. His residence, Swan House, was built for him in Chelsea by Norman Shaw and decorated by William Morris.[45]

C. D. E. Fortnum (aka Charles Drury, 1820–99) was the last Fortnum of Fortnum and Mason, Piccadilly, an art collector and connoisseur.

A. W. Franks (Sir Augustus Wollaston, 1826–1897) was a Keeper at the British Museum from 1851–1896.

Gustavo Frizzoni*(1840–1919) was an Italian art historian, connoisseur and collector.[46]

Francis Fry (1803–1886) was another grandson of the founder of Fry's chocolate who worked in railways and collected books and ceramics.[47]

Lewis Fry (1832–1921) was a member of the chocolate manufacturing family (son of Joseph, grandson of the founder), a Liberal MP for Bristol, and an art collector.

Roger Fry (1866–1934) was the influential art critic, painter and Bloomsbury Group member who helped found *The Burlington Magazine*.

Captain A. W. F. Fuller*(1882–1961) was a solicitor who upon retirement collected mainly ethnographic objects from the Pacific region but also African art.

Thomas Gann* (1867–1938) was Principal Medical Officer.in British Honduras (later Belize) from 1894–1923, and an amateur archaeologist.

Ajit Ghose* (act. 1890s–1920s) was an art critic and collector in India.

Henry Hucks Gibbs (later Baron Aldenham, 1819–1907) was a Director and Governor of the Bank of England, then an MP for the City of London.

Lionel Giles* (1875–1958) was a Keeper at the British Museum and a renowned translator of Chinese texts.

Frederick du Cane Godman (1834–1910) was a scientist and fellow of the Royal Society, who collected mainly Islamic art.

Robert Charles Goff (Col. Goff) (1837–1922) was a printmaker and painter.

Elizabeth Hamilton Gray* (*c.* 1801–1887) was married to John Hamilton Gray and became a specialist in the Etruscans and a collector of Etruscan antiquities.

Field Marshal Francis Wallace (Lord) Grenfell* (1821–1945) had a distinguished military career, having served in Africa and Egypt. He later went on to become Governor of Malta and Commander-in-Chief of Ireland. He was made a peer in 1902 (1st Baron Grenfell).

Rev. J. Griffiths* (1806–1885) was Warden of Wadham College, Oxford.

James Walter Grimston* (1809–1895), the 2nd Earl of Verulam, was a Conservative politician who was based at Gorehambury House near St Albans.

Mrs Murray Guthrie* (Olive Lesley, 1872–1945) was married to Walter Murray Guthrie (1869–1911), MP and merchant banker.

Ernest Frederick Gye (1879–1955) was the grandson of the famous Frederick Gye (1810–1878), Covent Garden theatre impresario and manager of the Royal Opera House and son of the Victorian soprano Emma Albani (1847–1930). He seems later to have become a diplomat, serving in Venezuela from 1936–1939.

Seymour Haden (1818–1910) was a prominent surgeon who was also an etcher and print collector. He was married to Whistler's step-daughter and was founder and first president of the Royal Society of Painter-etchers and Engravers.

Edward Hamilton MD (?1815–1903?) may have been the prominent physician who helped found the London Homeopathic Hospital.

W. S. Halsey* was Commissioner of Customs at Cawnpore, India.[48]

Henry Harris (*c.* 1870–1950) was a collector who lived in Florence and was friends with both Bernard Berenson and Roger Fry.

George Herbert* (1850–1895) was the 13th Earl of Pembroke and a politician. His family seat was Wilton House, near Salisbury,

J. P. Heseltine (John Postle, 1843–1929) was a stockbroker, etcher, and collector, primarily of Old Master pictures. He was also a trustee of the National Gallery and a good friend of Whistler.

Rev. J. J. Heywood (John James, 1827–1887) was an MP from a prominent banking family who knew Whistler.

Henry Hirsh (d. *c.* 1934) was an art collector who specialized in furniture but also acquired ceramics and paintings. He resided at 23 Park Lane and his collection was sold by Christie's in 1934.[49]

R. L. Hobson* (1872–1941) was a Keeper at the British Museum from 1897–1938. He was an authority on ceramics and other works of art.

J. Stewart Hodgson (James, 1827–1899) was a banker and close friend and patron of Lord Leighton (a Club member) who painted a portrait of Hodgson's daughters.

Sir George Lindsay Holford (1860–1926) was the son of Robert Holford and equerry to Prince Albert and Edward VII.

Robert Stayner Holford (1808–1892) was an MP, art collector, and founder of the Westonbirt Arboretum at his home, Westonbirt.

J. A. Holms (John Augustus, 1866–1938) was a paintings collector and stockbroker from a wealthy family, whose collection 'was on a par with William Burrell'.[50] He owned a famous Safavid carpet, later purchased by Burrell, which can be seen in his museum today: 'the Wagner Garden Carpet'.[51]

Marcus B. Huish (Marcus Bourne, 1843–1921), was the founder of the Fine Art Society and its first managing director. He was also a barrister, art dealer, and editor of the *Art Journal*.

William Holman Hunt* (1827–1910) was the painter and founder of the Pre-Raphaelite Brotherhood.

Edward Huth (1847–1935) was the nephew of Louis Huth and inherited his collection in 1905.

Louis Huth (1821–1905), with his brothers Charles and Henry, was the son of the merchant banker, Frederick Huth. He was based at Possingworth Park and was a patron of Whistler and G. F. Watts.

Sir Akbar Hydari* (Muhammad Akbar Nazar Ali, 1869–1941) was Prime Minister of Hyderabad from 1937–1941.

Constantine Ionides (1833–1900) was a stockbroker from a wealthy Greek family, who built up a substantial art collection that was left to the V&A by bequest.[52]

Lady Jekyll, Dame Agnes* (1861–1937) was an artist and the daughter of William Graham (1817–1885), patron of the Pre Raphaelites, whose collection was sold in 1886. She was also the sister-in-law of the garden designer, Gertrude Jekyll.

Owen Jones (1809–1874) was an architect and designer who was closely involved with the founding of the South Kensington Museum (now the V&A). He is most famous for his *Grammar of Ornament* (1856).

T. A. Joyce* (Thomas Athol, 1878–1942) was a Keeper at the British Museum and a specialist in American archaeology. He later became President of the Royal Anthropological Institute.

Sydney Kennedy (Sydney Ernest, 1855–1933) was a trustee of the London Stock Exchange and a partner in the family firm of Sydney Kennedy and Co.

Sir John Kirk (1832–1922) was a surgeon and naturalist who went on Livingstone's second Zambezi expedition.[53]

Stella Kramrisch (1896–1993)* was an American art historian and curator who specialized in Indian art. She was professor at the University of Pennsylvania.[54]

Sir Trevor Lawrence (1831–1913) was a surgeon, as well as an MP and orchid collector, who had served as President of the RHS.[55]

Alfred Lawson* (?–1921) was Director of the Ottoman Bank in Smyrna.

Sir Henry Layard (Austen Henry, 1817–1894) was an archaeologist, trustee of the National Gallery, and commissioner of works under Gladstone, who is famous for his discovery of Nineveh.[56]

Sir Frederick Leighton, PRA (1st Baron Leighton, 1830–1896) was the prominent Victorian painter and sculptor.

James Lindsay, 26th Earl of Crawford and 9th Earl of Balcarres* (1847–1913) was an astronomer and politician.

St George Littledale (1851–1931) was a traveller and explorer who collected natural history specimens for museums.

Richard R. Duppa Lloyd (d. *c.* 1913) was a well-travelled English engineer and art connoisseur who had also lived in Sydney between 1868 and 1873.

George A. Lockett (1855–1923) was a partner in the merchant firm of W. and J. Lockett, originally of Liverpool which also had substantial business interests in Peru, including in nitrates and sugar.

Willoughby Loudon (b. 1820) seems to have been a barrister but also was a porcelain collector as his objects are noted in a number of publications, including Franks' catalogue of 1876.

Charles Luard (Maj.-Gen. Charles Edward Luard, 1839–1908) was a professional soldier who possibly murdered his wife.

Lord Lyveden (see Robert Vernon).

Rev. William MacGregor* (1842–1937) was a minister, industrialist, and collector who had his own museum at his home, Bolehall Manor, in Staffordshire. He left his Liverpool parish to go to Egypt in 1885 and joined the EEF, becoming a benefactor.

Mrs Percy Macquoid* (Theresa, 1858–1939) was married to the artist, designer, and furniture collector, Percy Macquoid (1852–1925).

John Malcolm of Poltalloch (1803–93) was from a prominent landowning family and inherited the title of laird in 1857 upon the death of his older brother. The family seat was located near Argyll but the landholdings included plantations in the West Indies and a cattle station in Australia.

Murray Marks* (1840–1918) was an art and antiques dealer based in Bond Street, who helped many collectors build up collections, especially of ceramics. He was a donor to and buyer for the V&A and was active in the London literary and artist circles, befriending Whistler and Rossetti.

C. Brinsley Marlay (Charles, 1831–1912) was a wealthy landowner with estates in Ireland and a London house. He also built up a substantial art collection which was left to the Fitzwilliam.

Baron Marochetti (Carlo, 1805–67) was an Italian sculptor with a studio and foundry in Kensington who created a number of public commissions in France and Britain.

Edward H. Marsh (1872–1953) was Rupert Brooke's literary executor and Churchill's private secretary. He edited volumes of poetry and was a patron of many of the artists associated with the Bloomsbury Group.[57]

Gaston Maspero* (Professor, 1846–1916) was an Egyptologist and philologist in Paris who became Director General of Excavations and Antiquities in Egypt.

Florence Matthews* (n.d., see Stephen Bushell).

A. P. Maudslay* (Alfred Percival, 1850–1931) was a British diplomat who worked in Trinidad, Fiji, Tonga, and Samoa. Upon leaving the colonial service, he went to Guatemala to work as an archaeologist at various Maya ruins, recording them and bringing back a number of fragments and objects which are now in the British Museum.

Joseph Mayer* (1803–86) was a Liverpool jeweller and antiquary who had his own Egyptian museum and then donated his collection to Liverpool Museum in 1867.

Lt-Col. F. K. McClean* (Sir Francis Kennedy McClean 1876–1955) was an aviation pioneer and civil engineer who travelled widely, flying a number of early planes.

L. (Leander) Hamilton McCormick (1859–1934) was an American author, inventor, and sculptor who lived in the UK with his English wife for 17 years.

L. C. R. Messel (1872–1953) was the son of a prominent German Jewish businessman who was married to Maud, the daughter of Linley Sambourne. They lived at Nymans, in East Sussex, which he inherited in 1915 and rebuilt.[58]

Richard Mills (d. 1901) was a solicitor and collector of the work of several Pre-Raphaelite painters as well as Chinese porcelain.

William Mitchell (1820–1908) was a wealthy collector based in London's West End, who was good friends with Malcolm of Poltalloch.

Curtis Moffat (1887–1949) was a designer and society photographer who was involved in the avant-garde art worlds in both Paris and London. He lived in Fitzroy Square and had a collection of African and Chinese art.

Sir Alfred Mond, 1st Baron Melchett was a Liberal politician and Cabinet minister under Lloyd George (although he switched to the Conservative Party after a falling out). He became a passionate Zionist after visiting Palestine in 1921.

Ludwig Mond (1839–1909) was a distinguished chemist and father of Alfred Mond.

Cosmo Monkhouse (William Cosmo, 1840–1901) was a Victorian art critic who worked at the Board of Trade and was a prolific writer about painting and ceramics.

J. P. Morgan (J. Pierpont Morgan, 1837–1913) was the scion of the American banking family, a financier, and prolific collector of a wide range of art objects.

William Morris* (1834–1896) was the Victorian designer, writer and social activist who founded the Kelmscott Press.

Alfred Morrison (1821–1897) was the son of the very wealthy businessman and MP James Morrison (1790–1857) and a prominent collector with homes at Fonthill and Carlton House Terrace in London.

Mrs Alfred Morrison* (Mabel Chermside, 1847–1933).

Lady Dorothy Nevill*(1826–1913) was a plant collector, writer, and friend of Whistler and Disraeli. She wrote memoirs and corresponded with Darwin, to whom she supplied rare plants.

Captain G. W. Neville* (1852–1930) was a local agent for the Liverpool shipping company Elder Dempster and manager of the new British Bank of West Africa.[59] Neville appears to have accompanied the expedition and massacre at Benin.

Percy Newberry* (1869–1949) was Professor of Egyptology at Liverpool and then later Cairo University and Director of the EES's Archaeological Survey of Egypt in its second season, which was notable for its excavation of Beni Hasan.

J. E. Nightingale (James Edward, 1838–1908) was a ceramics collector and specialist in Worcester porcelain.

Philip Norman (1842–1931) was an artist, Fellow of the Society of Antiquaries, and historian of London buildings.

Northampton – Admiral William Compton* **(1818–1897)** was the 4th Earl of Northampton, a navy commander, and MP in the House of Lords.

William Oldman* **(1879–1949)** was a collector and dealer of ethnographic objects, building up major collections of Polynesian and Maori material.

A. P. Oppé (Adolph Paul, 1878–1957) was a drawings scholar and collector who became deputy director of the V&A in 1910.[60] He was an expert on the Cozens and wrote the biography *Alexander and John Robert Cozens* (1952). Much of his collection, considered to be of national importance, is in the Tate Gallery today.

Sir Francis Oppenheimer (1870–1961) was a career diplomat who also spent time in India.

Henry Oppenheimer (1859–1932) was a partner in the bank Speyer Brothers and was instrumental in securing storage for the National Gallery collections during WWI.

J. F. Payne, MD appears to have been the dermatologist, who when published in the *British Journal of Dermatology*, was described as 'Physician to St. Thomas's Hospital, and to the Hospital for Diseases of the Skin'.

Weetman Pearson* (see Viscount Cowdray).

Flinders Petrie* **(Sir William Matthew, 1853–1942)** was Edwards Professor of Egyptian Archaeology at UCL who worked as an excavator for the Egypt Exploration Fund. He was a pioneer of archaeological methodologies.

Sir Claude Phillips* **(1846–1924)** was the first Keeper of the Wallace Collection and an art critic.

General Pitt Rivers (Augustus Henry Lane-Fox, 1827–1900) was a land owner, army officer, and archaeologist with a prodigious collection of ethnographic objects, who pioneered excavation methodologies and donated his collections to Cambridge.[61]

Gerald Ponsonby (Gerald Henry Brabazon, 1829–1908) was one of eleven children of the 4th Earl of Bessborough and private secretary to the Lord-lieutenant of Ireland.

Sir Edward Poynter* **(1836–1919)** was a painter, a Director of the National Gallery and a President of the Royal Academy.

Colonel Poyser (Richard, 1842–1919) served in India and South Africa and was a veterinary officer.

Frederick Hilton Price (1842–1909) was a banker, amateur archaeologist, head of the EEF, friend of Pitt Rivers, and a collector of Egyptological material.

Val Princep (Valentine Cameron, 1838–1904), RA, was a painter and a member of the Pre-Raphaelite Brotherhood.

William Proby (1836–1909) was the 5th Earl of Carysfort, based at Elton Hall, Peterborough.[62] He was High Sheriff and Lord-Lieutenant of Wicklow before entering the House of Lords.

Richard Popplewell Pullan* **(1825–1888)** was a prominent architect and the brother-in-law of the Victorian architect-designer William Burges (1827–1881). He worked in Knidos and is famous for the discovery of the 'lion of Knidos', now in the British Museum.

General Sir Julius Raines* **(1827–1909)** served in the Crimean War and the Indian Mutiny campaign.

Oscar Raphael (1874–1941), very little is known about Raphael who was a collector of a wide range of objects from Egyptian to Chinese and Mexican. He was member of the RAI, the EEF and the OCS and left bequests to the British Museum and the Fitzwilliam.

W. G. Rawlinson (1840–1928) was a partner in a firm of silk merchants, a Turner scholar, and collector.

C. H. Read (Charles Hercules, 1857–1929) after being knighted in 1912, he was commonly known Sir Hercules Read and succeeded Franks at the British Museum. He was a member of the RAI.

J. Guthrie Reid (James, 1855–1955) was a partner in Duncan, Fox and Co and spent time in Peru. He was a collector whose objects are in the British Museum and at Temple Newsom in Leeds.

Sir Richard Temple Rennie* **(1839–1905)** was a barrister and judge, and had served in China and Japan.

Charles Ricketts (1866–1931) was an artist, collector, and co-founder with Charles Shannon of the Vale Press.

Sir William Ridgeway (1858–1926) was a classical scholar and Disney Professor of Archaeology at Cambridge.

Elizabeth Rigby (1809–93)* (see Lady Eastlake) was the wife of Sir Charles Eastlake (1793–1865), who was the painter, writer, and Director of the National Gallery (not his nephew of the same name, who was a Club member).

J. C. Robinson (John Charles, 1824–1913) was curator of the Museum of Ornamental Art and then Superintendent of Art Collections at the South Kensington Museum. An influential figure in the art world of the late nineteenth century, Robinson also co-founded the Royal Society of Painter-Etchers, collected art himself and guided others in building up their collections.

Max Rosenheim (1849–1911) was a wine merchant and a trustee of the British Museum, who co-founded its Friends Society and collected mainly Renaissance engravings and medals.[63]

D. G. Rossetti (Dante Gabriel, 1828–1882) was the artist, poet and illustrator, who co-founded the Pre-Raphaelite Brotherhood.

W. M. Rossetti (William Michael, 1829–1919) was an art critic and author, who worked as a civil servant and co-founded the Pre-Raphaelite Brotherhood with his brother Dante.

Sir William Rothenstein (1872–1945) was a portrait painter, war artist, art critic, founder of the India Society, and head of the RCA.

John Ruskin (1819–1900) was the influential critic, author, historian, patron, and philanthropist.

Archibald Russell (G. B., 1879–1955) was the Officer of Arms at the College of Arms, holding the post of Lancaster Herald. A specialist in William Blake, he also collected Old Master drawings, and various antiquities.

Sir Arthur Oliver Villiers Russell* (1869–1935) (see Lord Ampthill) was the second Baron Ampthill with a distinguished military, colonial service and sporting history. He was Governor of Madras from 1899–1906 and briefly served as Viceroy of India in 1904.[64]

Sir Michael E. Sadler (1861–1943) was the historian and university administrator who was President of the Leeds Art Club and a pioneer collector of Expressionist art. He served on the Sadler Commission, which investigated education in India.[65]

George Salting (1835–1909) devoted his life to collecting, building up substantial collections of paintings, ceramics and Renaissance bronzes that are now in the National Gallery, the British Museum, and the V&A.

W. S. Salting (William Severin, 1837–1905) was the brother of George Salting. His daughter married Lord Binning, George Baillie-Hamilton.

William Bell Scott (1811–1890) was a poet, artist, and engraver, who was friends with the Rossettis.

Charles Schreiber (1826–1884) was an academic, MP, and art collector with his wife Lady Charlotte (1812–1895).

Imre Schwaiger* (1868–1940) was a Hungarian art dealer based in India and London who looked after the interests of Jacques Cartier.[66]

Charles Seligman (1873–1940) was medical doctor turned anthropologist who was made Emeritus Professor of Ethnology at the LSE in 1934.

H. Danby Seymour (Henry, 1820–77) was an MP for Poole, Committee member of the Nineveh Fund, and patron of G. F. Watts.

Charles Shannon (1863–1937) was an artist, collector, and co-founder with Charles Ricketts of the Vale Press.

George Bernard Shaw (1856–1950) was the influential Irish playwright, critic, and activist.

Osbert Sitwell (Sir Francis Osbert Sacheverell, 1892–1969) was the author, art critic, collector and journalist. who became the 5th Baronet in 1843. His sister was Edith Sitwell.

Harold Clifford Smith (1876–1960) was a Keeper at the V&A and a furniture specialist.

W. H. Smith (William Henry, 1825–1891), of the bookseller and newsagent family, was an MP who held several prominent government offices, including Leader of the House of Commons.

John Poyntz Spencer* (1835–1910) was the 5th Earl Spencer and an MP.

E. G. Spencer-Churchill (Captain, 1876–1964) served in the First World War and was based at Northwick Park, the family estate. He was a cousin of Winston Churchill.

R. Phene Spiers* (Richard, 1838–1916) was an architect who worked for Digby Wyatt.

Lady Stern (Sybil Alice, fl. 1919–1967) was possibly the wife of Sir Frederick Stern (1884–1967), merchant banker and horticulturalist, who lived at Highdown, Sussex, where he also created the famous garden.[67]

S. Arthur Strong (Sanford, 1863–1904) was a linguist and an Orientalist scholar who was Professor of Arabic at UCL. He also became librarian/curator for the Duke of Devonshire, the Earl of Pembroke, and the House of Lords. He catalogued the paintings collection at Chatsworth.

Vittorio Emanuelle Taparelli (1816–1890) (see Marchese d'Azeglio) was a career diplomat and the Sardinian Ambassador in London, who also collected art and co-founded the St. James' Club.

Henry Virtue Tebbs (1833–1899) was a solicitor, friend of Holman Hunt and Rossetti, and a collector of books and other objects.

H. S. Theobald (Henry Studdy, 1847–1934) was a barrister and a collector of etchings and mezzotints, including those of Whistler.[68]

Sir Henry Thompson (1820–1904) was a prominent surgeon and friend of Whistler, who built up a collection of Chinese ceramics with the help of Murray Marks.

Walter E. Tower (see E. J. Wythes).

Alfred Trapnell* (1838–1917) worked in the metal smelting business and collected Chinese ceramics and other objects.

Lady Trevelyan was possibly **Caroline Phillips (1849–1928)**, mother of Sir Charles Philips Trevelyan, the 3rd baronet.[69]

Royall Tyler (1884–1953) was an American historian and major in the US Army who was based in Paris and is associated with the Blisses of Dumbarton Oaks.

Alphonse van Branteghem (d. 1911) was a Belgian lawyer who collected Greek antiquities.

Henry Vaughan (1809–1899) was a collector and philanthropist who developed a substantial collection of Turner drawings that were given by bequest to the Scottish National Galleries and owned Constable's *The Haywain* which was given to the National Gallery in London.[70]

G. T. Veitch (n. d.) appears to have worked for Jardine Matheson in Asia for five years in the 1880s. This would explain how his collection was mainly acquired in China, according to reviews of an exhibition of his collection at the Birmingham Art Gallery.

Adolfo Venturi (1856–1941) was an Italian art historian who was General Inspector of the *Belle Arti* at the Ministry of Public Instruction in Rome and then Professor of Art at the University of Rome.

Robert Vernon (d. 1873) or his son Fitzpatrick Henry Vernon (d. 1900) (see Lord Lyveden). The first Lord was a prominent MP who held a range of important political offices. He was also a member of several gentlemen's clubs, including the BFAC.[71]

Gustav Waagen (d. 1868) was the Director of the Berlin Gemäldegalerie, who founded the Berlin School of Art History.

Henry Wallis (1830–1916) was a painter and associate of the Pre-Raphaelite Brotherhood. He later became a collector and connoisseur of ceramics.

O. C. Waterfield (Ottiwell Charles, 1831–1898) was headmaster of Temple Grove School from 1863–1880.

G. F. Watts (George Frederic, 1817 –1904) was the painter and sculptor based in Holland Park who was friends with many in that circle, including the Princeps, teaching Val, and Tennyson.[72]

John Webster was possibly the MP for Aberdeen from 1880–1885,[73] whose collection of etchings by Cruikshank and Rembrandt was sold by Sotheby's in May 1889.

Henry Willett (1823–1903/05) gave his collection to Brighton and was a friend of Ruskin, who was a long-term member of the Club.[74]

W. H. Willshire (1816–1899), MD, was President of the Medical Society of London,[75] and a collector and writer on prints. He published a book for the British Museum, entitled: *Catalogue of Early Prints in the British Museum*, II, German and Flemish Schools, London, 1883.

J. M. Whistler (James Abbott McNeill, 1834–1903) was the American painter, etcher, and designer who worked mainly in London and was associated with the Aesthetic Movement.

R. C. Witt (Sir Robert Cleremont, 1872–1952) was a solicitor, art historian and collector of prints and drawings who co-founded the Courtauld Institute and the National Art Collections Fund.

Ralph Wornum (1812–1877) was a Keeper at the National Gallery, a print collector, and proponent of design education.

Sir M. Digby Wyatt (Matthew, 1820–1877) was an architect and historian. As a collector, his main expertise was in paintings and architecture but he also seems to have collected some porcelain, both English and European.

E. J. Wythes (d. 1949) was the grandson of the railway magnate George Wythes (1811–1883) and resided at Copped Hall in Epping. He hired C. E. Kempe (1837–1907) to extend it in 1887 and Kempe, a Victorian stained glass designer and manufacturer, was a partner of another exhibition lender, Walter E. Tower, an architect (1873 – 1955) who appears to have been Kempe's cousin.[76]

Notes

1 Some of this biographical information is also provided in the main text, where relevant. Where not provided in the main text, sources are provided here.
2 See www.whistler.arts.gla.ac.uk/correspondence/biog/display/?bid=Addi_S (accessed 2 Nov. 2015).
3 See http://etchings.arts.gla.ac.uk/catalogue/biog/?nid=AlexWC (accessed 8 Oct. 2015).
4 See www.the-saleroom.com/en-gb/auction-catalogues/woolley-and-wallis/catalogue-id-srwo10018/lot-cd8937dd-05bf-44ba-946d-a401007831bd (accessed 19 Oct. 2015).

5 See www.thepeerage.com/p12774.htm#i127740 (accessed 10 Dec. 2015).
6 See http://rusholmearchive.org/fallowfield-brow-and-oak-drive (accessed 27 Oct. 2015).
7 See http://livesonline.rcseng.ac.uk/biogs/E003829b.htm 10.12.15. His KCVO medals were recently sold.
8 See www.liverpoolmuseums.org.uk/ladylever/collections/chinese/dealersessay/ (accessed 27 Oct. 2015).
9 See www.oxfordartonline.com/subscriber/article/grove/art/T007959 (accessed 26 Nov. 2015).
10 See https://dictionaryofarthistorians.org/berensonb.html (accessed 25 June 2016).
11 See https://dictionaryofarthistorians.org/blancc.htm (accessed 25 June 2016).
12 Wills and Bequests, *Flintshire Observer*, Thursday August 17, 1893.
13 See https://dictionaryofarthistorians.org/boreniust.htm (accessed 26 June 2016).
14 John Simkin, 'Henry Broadhurst', *Spartacus International*, September 1997 (updated August 2014). Available at: http://spartacus-educational.com/TUbroadhurst.htm (accessed 25 June 2016).
15 R. Hyam, 'Bruce, Victor Alexander, Ninth Earl of Elgin and Thirteenth Earl of Kincardine (1849–1917)', in *Oxford Dictionary of National Biography*, first published 2004; online edn, Jan 2008. Available at: http://dx.doi.org/10.1093/ref:odnb/32136 (accessed 25 June 2016).
16 Jason Tomes, 'Lytton, Victor Alexander George Robert Bulwer-, Second Earl of Lytton (1876–1947)', in *Oxford Dictionary of National Biography*, first published 2004; online edn, Jan 2008. Available at: http://dx.doi.org/10.1093/ref:odnb/32169 (accessed 25 June 2016).
17 See Fiona MacCarthy, *The Last Pre-Raphaelite: Edward Burne-Jones and the Victorian Imagination* (Cambridge, MA: Harvard University Press, 2012).
18 Pierson (2007), pp. 74, 79.
19 Such as the *Tao shuo* of 1774 which he translated as *Chinese Porcelain Before the Present Dynasty* (Peking, 1886) as noted above. See Pierson (2007), p. 74.
20 See www.thepeerage.com/p52640.htm#i526394 (accessed 25 May 2016).
21 Fiona Carnarvon, *Carnarvon & Carter: The Story of the Two Englishman who discovered the Tomb of Tutankhamun* (Highclere Enterprises LPP, 2007).
22 Irma Coucill, *Canada's Prime Ministers, Governors General and Fathers of Confederation* (Ontario, 2005), p. 74.
23 R. Whiddington, 'Victor Christian William Cavendish, the Duke of Devonshire. 1868-1938'. *Obituary Notices of Fellows of the Royal Society*, vol.2, no. 7 (1939), pp. 557–526. doi:10.1098/rsbm.1939.0016 (accessed 29 Nov. 2015).
24 See www.open.ac.uk/researchprojects/makingbritain/content/atul-chandra-chatterjee (accessed 25 June 2016).
25 Tim Knox, 'Edward Cheney of Badger Hall: Forgotten Collector of Italian Sculpture', *Sculpture Journal*, vol. 16, no. 1 (2007), pp. 5–20. See www.historywebsite.co.uk/articles/Albrighton/Ruskin/Ruskin.htm (accessed 2 Nov. 2015).
26 See www.lincolnsinn.org.uk/images/word/Newsletter/LI_Annual_Review_2013.pdf (accessed 27 Oct. 2015).
27 *Country Life Illustrated*, vol. 3 (May 24 1898), p. 650.
28 See https://dictionaryofarthistorians.org/colvins.htm (accessed 25 June 2016).
29 Letters re: Hong Kong Fire Insurance Co., Ltd, Oct. 1876– Jun. 1878, Manuscripts/MS JM/C37, Jardine Matheson Archive, Cambridge University: http://janus.lib.cam.ac.uk/db/node.xsp?id=EAD%2FGBR%2F0012%2FMS%20JM%2FC37 (accessed 29 Jan. 2016).
30 Mark Rawitsch, *The House on Lemon Street: Japanese Pioneers and the American Dream* (Boulder, CO: University of Colorado Press, 2012), pp. 55–58.
31 Simon Rae, *W. G. Grace: A Life* (London: Faber & Faber, 1999).
32 See http://gcac.edu.in/our-college/history/ (accessed 25 June 2016).
33 M. A. 'Mr. Edward Dillon', *The Burlington Magazine for Connoisseurs*, vol. 25, no. 136 (1914),p. 260. See www.jstor.org/stable/859740 (accessed 25 June 2016).
34 Edmund. Schilling, 'Campbell Dodgson', *The Burlington Magazine*, vol. 90, no. 547 (1948), pp. 293–294. See www.jstor.org/stable/869842 (accessed 25 June 2016).
35 Hopkinson (1999), pp. 13–14.

36 Philip Woods, 'Dundas, Lawrence John Lumley, Second Marquess of Zetland (1876–1961)', in *Oxford Dictionary of National Biography*, first published 2004; online edn, Jan 2011. Available at: http://dx.doi.org/10.1093/ref:odnb/32932 (accessed 25 June 2016).
37 Kingsley, Rose, and Gronkowski Camille, 'The Dutuit Collection. Article I. Its Makers and Its History', *The Burlington Magazine for Connoisseurs*, vol. 1, no. 3 (1903), pp. 381–386. See www.jstor.org/stable/855682 (accessed 25 June 2016).
38 See www.scottisharchitects.org.uk/architect_full.php?id=200377 (accessed 25 June 2016).
39 G. C. Boase, 'Ellis, Wynne 1800–1881', in *Dictionary of National Biography, 1885–1900*, vol. 17 (1885), pp. 298–299.
40 Kateryna Gamaliia, 'International School of Egyptology of Adolf Erman', *Sociology Study*, vol. 4, no. 1 (January 2014), pp. 52–60.
41 See www.asia.si.edu/collections/downloads/Eumorfopoulos-George-Aristedes.pdf (accessed 25 June 2016),
42 See http://sirarthurevans.ashmus.ox.ac.uk/biography/ (accessed 25 June 2016).
43 Graham (2002), p. 305.
44 See http://hansard.millbanksystems.com/people/mr-heneage-finch-1/ (accessed 26 June 2016).
45 E. Jones and C. Woodward, *A Guide to the Architecture of London* (revised and updated ed.) (London: W&N, 2013), p. 364.
46 Jaynie Anderson, 'Frizzoni, Gustavo', *Grove Art Online. Oxford Art Online*. Oxford University Press. Available at: www.oxfordartonline.com/subscriber/article/grove/art/T030018 (accessed 26 June 2016).
47 For the Frys, see Paul Chrystal, *Chocolate: The British Chocolate Industry* (London: Bloomsbury, 2013).
48 Yalland, 1994, p. 165.
49 P. Macquoid, 'Mr Henry Hirsch's Furniture – I', *Country Life*, 25 October 1924, pp. 630–631.
50 Frances Fowle, 'Alexander Reid in Context: Collecting and Dealing in Scotland in the late 19th and early 20th Centuries', vol. 1, unpublished PhD thesis, University of Edinburgh, 1993, p. 365.
51 Burrell Collection 9.2. See http://collections.glasgowmuseums.com/starobject.html?oid=33061 (accessed 2 Nov. 2015).
52 See www.vam.ac.uk/content/articles/t/the-constantine-ionides-collection/ (accessed 26 June 2016).
53 Obituary: Sir John Kirk, G. C. M. G., K. C. B., F. R. S., M. D., LL. D., D. Sc., D. C.L., H. H. Johnston, *The Geographical Journal*, vol. 59, no. 3 (Mar. 1922), pp. 225–228.
54 See www.nytimes.com/1993/09/02/obituaries/stella-kramrisch-indian-art-expert-and-professor-97.html (accessed 26 May 2016).
55 See www.liverpoolmuseums.org.uk/ladylever/collections/chinese/dealersessay/Dealers%20and%20collectors.pdf [2.11 2015); 'The Trevor Lawrence Orchid Collection at the Royal Gardens, Kew', *Nature*, 93 (7 May 1914), pp. 244–245.
56 Shawn Malley, *From Archaeology to Spectacle in Victorian Britain: The Case of Assyria, 1845–1854* (Farnham: Ashgate, 2012).
57 Christopher Hassall, *Edward Marsh, Patron of the Arts: A Biography* (Harlow: Longmans, 1959).
58 Now National Trust. See: See www.nationaltrust.org.uk/nymans (accessed 1 Nov. 2015).
59 F. S., 'Obituary for George W. Neville', *Journal of the Royal Africa Society*, vol. 29, no. 114 (Jan. 1930), p. 201; Eddy Chicka Ndekwu, *First Bank of Nigeria: A Century of Banking* (London: Spectrum Books, 1994, p. 17; Coombes (2007 [1994]), p. 46.
60 Brinsley Ford, 'Obituary. Paul Oppé', *The Burlington Magazine*, 99, no. 651 (Jun, 1957), pp. 207–208.
61 Mark Bowden, *Pitt Rivers: The life and archaeological work of Lieutenant-General Augustus Henry Lane Fox Pitt Rivers* (Cambridge; Cambridge University Press, 1991).
62 See www.historicengland.org.uk/listing/the-list/list-entry/1164802 (accessed 28 June 2016).
63 Mary Lago, *Christiana Herringham and the Edwardian Art Scene* (Columbia, MO: University of Missouri Press, 1995), p. 82. See www.britishmuseum.org/research/search_the_collection_database/term_details.aspx?bioId=109390 (accessed 1 Nov. 2015).

64 Katherine Prior, 'Russell, (Arthur) Oliver Villiers, second Baron Ampthill (1869–1935)', in *Oxford Dictionary of National Biography*, Oxford University Press, 2004; online edn, Jan 2008. See www.oxforddnb.com/view/article/35874 (accessed 25 June 2016).
65 J. H. Higginson, 'Michael Ernest Sadler (1861–1943)', *PROSPECTS*, vol. 24, no. 3/4 (1994), pp. 455–469.
66 Hans Nadelhoffer, *Cartier* (London: Chronicle Books, 2007), p. 159.
67 Rubinstein (2011), p. 958.
68 See http://etchings.arts.gla.ac.uk/catalogue/biog/?nid=TheoHS (accessed 10 Oct. 2015). He published a text, *Treatise on the Construction of Wills*, in 1876 and he contributed to several Club exhibitions relating to printed works, such as 1891, Exhibition Illustrative of the French Revival of Etching; 1902, Exhibition of English Mezzotints from circa 1750 to circa 1830.
69 See www.bbc.co.uk/arts/yourpaintings/paintings/caroline-philips-18491928-lady-trevelyan-with-her-son-cha167931 (accessed 26 Oct. 2015).
70 See www.nationalgalleries.org/collection/jmw-turner/the-vaughan-bequest (accessed 28 June 2016).
71 See www.historyofparliamentonline.org/volume/1820-1832/member/smith-robert-1800-1873 (accessed 10 Dec. 2015).
72 V. Gould, *G. F. Watts: The Last Great Victorian* (New Haven, CT: Yale University Press, 2004).
73 Hamish Fraser and Howard Lee, *Aberdeen, 1800–2000: A New History* (Montreal: Dundurn, 2000), p. 187.
74 See http://myweb.tiscali.co.uk/speel/otherart/willett.htm (accessed 26 Oct. 2015). And see the Introduction for Ruskin.
75 See notice in the *British Medical Journal*, Reports of Societies, volume for 1859, p. 235.
76 Margaret Stavridi, *Master of Glass: Charles Eamer Kempe 1837-1907 and the Work of his firm in Stained Glass and Church Decoration*, Kempe Society, 1988. For Wythes and Copped Hall: See www.coppedhalltrust.org.uk/index.php?option=com_content&view=article&id=9&Itemid=7 (accessed 29 Nov. 2015).

Bibliography

Primary Sources

BFAC papers and correspondence, National Art Library (NAL), V&A

BFAC Rules and Regulations, I, 1866, NAL archives, 200.b.110.

Burlington Fine Arts Club, *History, Rules, Regulations, and Bye-laws*, 17 Savile Row, London, W.1, 1925.

Candidates books, 1867–1940, 11 vols, 86.KK.25–36.

Draft History, 1895, NAL 200.B.110.

General Committee minute books, 1866–1951, 6 vols., 86.KK.11–16.

General Meeting minute books (AGMs), 1866-1951, 2 vols, 86.KK.37–38.

Secondary sources

Fred Aftalion, *A History of the International Chemical Industry*, second edn, Philadelphia: Chemical Heritage Foundation, 2001.

Malcolm Allbrook, *Henry Prinsep's Empire: Framing a Distant Colony*, Canberra: ANU Press, 2014.

Francesca Vanke Altman, 'William Holman Hunt, Race, and Orientalism', in Thomas J. Tobin, ed., *Worldwide Pre-Raphaelitism: Critical Theory, Popular Culture, Audiovisual Media*, New York: SUNY Press, 2005.

Bruce Altschuler, *Salon to Biennial: Exhibitions that Made Art History, vol. 1, 1863–1959*, London: Phaidon, 2008.

Jaynie Anderson, 'Frizzoni, Gustavo.' *Grove Art Online. Oxford Art Online.* Oxford University Press. See www.oxfordartonline.com/subscriber/article/grove/art/T030018 (accessed 26 June 2016).

Antiques Trade Gazette, 'A Winning Formula on the Fields of Cowdray'. Available at: www.antiquestradegazette.com/news/2011/oct/01/a-winning-formula-on-the-fields-of-cowdray/ (accessed 29 Aug. 2015).

Archives. Faculty of Asian and Middle Eastern Studies, Cambridge University, 'Newberry'. Available at: www.ames.cam.ac.uk/library/archive/newberry (accessed 17 Aug. 2015).

Arts Council, *English Watercolours from the Hickman Bacon Collection*, London: Arts Council, 1946.'The Arundel Club', *The Burlington Magazine for Connoisseurs*, vol. 4, no. 12 (Mar. 1904), p. 203.

ASCE (Association de Sauvegarde de Chantilly et de son Environnement), 'Le duc d'Aumale'. Available at: www.asce-chantilly.com/portraits/aumale.html (accessed 25.6 2016).

Ashmolean Museum. Available at: www.ashmolean.org/ash/objects/makedetail.php?pmu=730&mu=732>y=qsea&sec=&dtn=15&sfn=Artist%20Sort,Title&cpa=1&rpos=0&key=WA1850.31 (accessed 15.11 2015).

Louise Auchincloss, *J. P. Morgan: The Financier as Collector*, New York: Harry N. Abrams, 1990.

Australian Dictionary of Biography, 'Severin Kanute Salting'. Available at: www.adb.anu.edu.au/biography/salting-severin-kanute-2626 (accessed 10 Dec. 2015).

C. T. Bailey, 'Colonel Croft Lyons', *The Burlington Magazine for Connoisseurs*, vol. 49, no. 284 (Nov. 1926), p. 240.

Joseph Banks, 'Collections on the subject of Old China and Japan wares with Some Remarks on these Interesting Manufactures Made in Lady Banks's Dairy at Spring Grove', manuscript, 1807. Published by Rose Kerr, "Chinese Porcelain at Spring Grove Dairy: Sir Joseph Banks's Manuscript"', *Apollo* (January 1989), pp. 30–34.

Paul Barlow and Colin Trodd, *Governing Cultures: Art Institutions in Victorian London*, Farnham: Ashgate, 2000.

Douglas Barrett, 'Sir John Marshall', *Journal of the Royal Asiatic Society of Great Britain and Ireland*, no. 1/2 (April 1959), pp. 92–93.

T. J. Barringer, *Reading the Pre-Raphaelites*, New Haven, CT: Yale University Press, 1998.

John Batchelor, 'Scott, William Bell (1811–1890)', in *Oxford Dictionary of National Biography*, first published 2004; online edition, October 2007. Available at: http://dx.doi.org/10.1093/ref:odnb/24938 (accessed 22 Dec. 2015).

Andrea Bayer and Mina Gregori, *Painters of Reality: The Legacy of Leonardo and Caravaggio in Lombardy*, New York: Metropolitan Museum of Art, 2004.

BBC. 'Lewis Fry'. Available at: www.bbc.co.uk/arts/yourpaintings/paintings/the-right-honourable-lewis-fry-pc-mp-185181 (accessed 24 Nov. 2015).

Rhona Beare, *A Guide to Our Stained Glass Windows*, Clifton: Christ Church, 2015.

R. Bentley, H. Maschner and C. Chippendale, eds., *A Handbook of Archaeological Theories*, Walnut Creek, CA: Alta Mira Press, 2009.

'Bequest to the Nation'. *The Straits Times*, 17 June 1909.

Bernard Berenson, 'Burlington Fine Arts Club, Exhibition of Pictures, Drawings and Photographs of Works of the School of Ferrara-Bologna', *Revue Critique d'Histoire et de Littérature* 29, no. 18 (May 6 1895), pp. 348–352.

Berkeley Galleries, *Primitive Art: Exhibition of the Art of Primitive Peoples at the Berkeley Galleries, June–July 1945*, London: Berkeley Galleries, 1945.

The Earl of Bessborough, ed., *Lady Charlotte Schreiber, Extracts from her Journal, 1853-1891*, London, 1952.

Bidamount, 'Chinese Qing Porcelains: The George Davies Collection'. Available at: www.bidamount.com/chinese-qing-porcelains-the-george-davies-collection/ (accessed 28 Nov. 2015).

Laurence Binyon, *Persian Miniature Painting, Including a Critical and Descriptive Catalogue of the Miniatures Exhibited at Burlington House, January–March, 1931*, London, 1933.

S. Blair and J. Bloom, eds., *Grove Encyclopedia of Islamic Art and Architecture*, Oxford: Oxford University Press, 2009.

Franz Boas, *Primitive Art*, Oslo: H. Aschehoug and Company, 1927.

Hector Bolitho, *Alfred Mond: First Lord Melchett*, London: Martin Secker, 1933.

Mark Bowden, *Pitt Rivers: The Life and Archaeological Work of Lieutenant-General Augustus Henry Lane Fox Pitt Rivers*, Cambridge: Cambridge University Press, 1991.

Joanna Bowring, 'Chronology of Temporary Exhibitions at the British Museum', British Museum Research Publication no. 189, London: British Museum, 2012.

H. J. Braunholtz, 'The Raphael Bequest: III. Ancient Stone Mask from Mexico', *The British Museum Quarterly*, vol. 15 (1941–1950), pp. 106–107.

A. C. Breton, E. N. Fallaize, A. C. Haddon, T. A. Joyce and A. P. Maudslay (eds) *Proceedings of the XVIII. Session, London, 1912 International Congress of Americanists*, London: Harrison & Sons, 1913.

Bristol Law Society, 'Lewis Fry'. Available at: www.bristollawsociety.com/lewis-fry/ (accessed 24 Nov. 2015).

British History. Available at: www.british-history.ac.uk/ report. aspx? compid=40571 (accessed 19.9.14).

British Museum, 'History of the collection: Department of Africa, Oceania and the Americas'. Available at: www.britishmuseum.org/about_us/departments/africa,_oceania,_americas/history_of_the_collection.aspx (accessed 2 Sept. 2015).

British Museum, 'Online Tour: Asia'. Available at: www.britishmuseum.org/explore/online_tours/asia/the_art_of_peace/portrait_of_tagore.aspx (accessed 10.8 2015).

British Museum, 'The Akan Drum'. Available at: www.britishmuseum.org/explore/highlights/highlight_objects/aoa/a/akan_drum.aspx (accessed 26 Aug. 2015).

British Museum, 'Sir Hans Sloane and Ethnography'. Available at: www.britishmuseum.org/explore/highlights/article_index/s/sir_hans_sloane_and_ethnograph.aspx (accessed 26 Aug. 2015).

British Museum, 'The Fenton Vase'. Available at: www.britishmuseum.org/explore/highlights/highlight_objects/aoa/t/the_fenton_vase.aspx (accessed 29 Aug. 2015).

British Museum, 'Henry Oppenheimer (Biographical Details)'. Available at: www.britishmuseum.org/research/search_the_collection_database/term_details.aspx?bioId=93105 (accessed 14 Nov. 2015).

British Museum, 'Sir Hickman Bacon (Biographical Details)'. Available at:www.britishmuseum.org/research/search_the_collection_database/term_details.aspx?bioId=133681 (accessed 10 Dec. 2015).

British Museum, 'Rev J F Bloxam (Biographical Details)'. Available at: www.britishmuseum.org/research/search_the_collection_database/term_details.aspx?bioId=142038 (accessed 19 Oct. 2015).

P. O. Bronsted, *A Brief Description Of Thirty-Two Ancient Greek Painted Vases, Lately Found In Excavations Made at Vulci, in the Roman Territory, by Mr. Campanari and Now Exhibited by him in London, no. 15, Leicester Place*, London, 1832.

Alison K. Brown, *First Nations, Museums, Narrations: Stories of the 1929 Franklin Motor Expedition to the Canadian Prairies*, Vancouver, BC: University of British Columbia, 2014.

Bill Brown, 'Objects, Others, and Us (the Refabrication of Things)', *Critical Inquiry* vol. 36, no. 2 (Winter 2010), pp. 183–217. Available at: www.brown.edu/Research/Breaking_Ground/bios/Edwards_Amelia%20Blanford.pdf (accessed 26 July 2015).

Barbara Bryant, *G. F. Watts Portraits: Fame and Beauty in Victorian Society*, London: National Portrait Gallery, 2004.

Alessandra Buccheri, *The Spectacle of Clouds, 1439–1650: Italian Art and Theatre*, Farnham: Ashgate, 2014.

Jane E. Buikstra and Charlotte Roberts, eds., *The Global History of Paleopathology: Pioneers and Prospects*, Oxford: Oxford University Press, 2012.

Cyril G. E. Bunt, 'American Art at the Burlington Fine Arts Club', *The Burlington Magazine* vol. 37, no. 208 (July 1920), p. 40.

Burlington Fine Arts Club, *Marc Antonio Raimondi*, London, 1868.

Burlington Fine Arts Club, *A Short Description of the English and Continental Porcelain, Exhibited June 1873*, London, 1873.

Burlington Fine Arts Club, *Catalogue of the Etched Work of Rembrandt, Selected for Exhibition at the Burlington Fine Arts Club*, London, 1877.

Burlington Fine Arts Club, *Catalogue of Specimens Illustrative of Persian and Arab Art Exhibited in 1885*, London, 1885.

Burlington Fine Arts Club, *Catalogue of Objects of Greek Ceramic Art, Exhibited in 1888*, London, 1888.

Burlington Fine Arts Club, *Pictures by Masters of the Netherlandish and Allied Schools of the XV and Early XVI Centuries*, London, 1892.

Burlington Fine Arts Club, *The Work of Luca Signorelli and His School*, London, 1893.

Burlington Fine Arts Club, *Exhibition of Pictures, Drawings and Photographs of Works of the School of Ferrara-Bologna, 1450–1540*, London, 1894.

Burlington Fine Arts Club, *Catalogue of Blue and White Oriental Porcelain, Exhibited in 1895*, London, 1895a.

Burlington Fine Arts Club, *Exhibition of the Art of Ancient Egypt*, London, 1895b.

Burlington Fine Arts Club, *Catalogue of Coloured Chinese Porcelain, Exhibited in 1896*, London, 1896.

Burlington Fine Arts Club, *Catalogue of an Exhibition of Ancient Egyptian Art*, London, 1897.

Burlington Fine Arts Club, *Exhibition of Pictures by Masters of the Milanese and Allied Schools of Lombardy*, London, 1898.

Burlington Fine Arts Club, *Exhibition of Early Chinese Pottery and Porcelain*, London, 1910.

Burlington Fine Arts Club, *Exhibition of Florentine Painting before 1500*, London, 1919.

Burlington Fine Arts Club, *Catalogue of an Exhibition of Objects of Indigenous American Art*, London, 1920.

Burlington Fine Arts Club, *Catalogue of an Exhibition of Ancient Egyptian Art*, London, 1922.

Burlington Fine Arts Club, *Catalogue of the Loan Exhibition of Flemish and Belgian Art: A Memorial Volume*, London, 1927.

Burlington Fine Arts Club, *Catalogue of an Exhibition of the Art of India*, London, 1931.

Burlington Fine Arts Club, *Exhibition of the Art of Primitive Peoples*, London, 1935.

Burlington Fine Arts Club, *Catalogue of an Exhibition of British Medieval Art*, London, 1939.

'The Burlington Fine Arts Club', *The Burlington Magazine* 589, vol. XCIV, April 1952, pp. 97–99.

S. W. Bushell, *Chinese Pottery and Porcelain Before the Present Dynasty*, Peking, 1886.

David Cannadine, *The Decline and Fall of the British Aristocracy*, Harmondsworth: Penguin, 2005.

James Nelson Carder, ed., *A Home of the Humanities: The Collecting and Patronage of Mildred and Robert Woods Bliss*, Cambridge, MA: Harvard University Press, 2010.

Fiona Carnarvon, *Carnarvon & Carter: The Story of the Two Englishman who Discovered the Tomb of Tutankhamun*, Highclere Enterprises LPP, 2007.

CARP, 'Trapnell, Alfred Esq.'. Available at: http://carp.arts.gla.ac.uk/image.php?id=pe_193&t=1&urltp=search.php%3Fstart%3D0%26end%3D6%26what%3D%26who%3D1089020817%26where%3D%26when%3D%26period%3D%26search%3D99 (accessed 1 Nov. 2015).

Cartelen. Available at: http://cartelen.louvre.fr/cartelen/visite?srv=car_not_frame&idNotice=13898 (accessed 13 Nov. 2015).

Bill Cash, *John Bright: Statesman, Orator, Agitator*, London: Tauris, 2011.

Marjorie Caygill and John F. Cherry, eds. *A. W. Franks: Nineteenth Century Collecting and the British Museum*, London: British Museum Press, 1997.

William Chaffers, *Marks and Monograms on Pottery and Porcelain of the Renaissance and Modern Periods, with Historical Notices of Each Manufactory; Preceded by an Introductory Essay of the Vasa Fictilia of England, of the Romano-British and Mediaeval Eras*, J. Davy, London, first edition 1863; fourth edition 1874.

Deborah Cherry, 'The Hogarth Club: 1858–1861', *The Burlington Magazine*, vol. 122, no. 925 (Apr. 1980), pp. 236–244.

Chicago Natural History Museum, 'Report of the Director to the Board of Trustees for the year 1963', 'Collections. Anthropology', Chicago: Chicago Natural History Museum, p. 38.

'Chinese Porcelain in the Davies Collection', *The Burlington Magazine for Connoisseurs*, vol. 23, no. 123 (June 1913), pp. 162–167.

'Chinese Porcelain. Purchase of a Well-Known Collection', *The Times*, 20 February 1913, p. 9.

Christie's, Lot Finder. Available at: www.christies.com/lotfinder/LotDetailsPrintable.aspx?intObjectID=3041641 (accessed 13 Nov. 2015).

Christie's, Press Release. Available at: www.christies.com/about/press-center/releases/ press release.aspx? pressreleaseid =4957 (accessed 29 Aug. 2015).

Paul Chrystal, *Chocolate: The British Chocolate Industry*, London: Bloomsbury, 2013.

A. H. Church, *Cantor Lectures on Some Points of Contact Between the Scientific and Artistic Aspects of Pottery*, London: Trounce, 1881.

Clark Art. Available at: www.clarkart.edu/exhibitions/mystery/index.cfm (accessed 4.11 2015).

Dora Clarke, 'Negro Art: Sculpture from West Africa', *Journal of the Royal African Society* vol. 34 (April 1935), pp. 129–137.

James Clifford, *The Predicament of Culture: Twentieth-Century Ethnography, Literature and Art*, Cambridge, MA: Harvard University Press, 1988.

E. Clinch and N. Clinch, *Through a Land of Extremes: The Littledales of Central Asia*, Seattle, WA: Mountaineer Books, 2008.

Codex Fejervary-Mayer, *Codices Selecti*, Vol. 26, commentary by C.A. Burland, Graz: Akademische Druck-und Verlagsanstalt, 1971.

Clemency Chase Coggins, and Orrin C. Shane, III, *Cenote of Sacrifice: Maya Treasures from the Sacred Well at Chichen Itza*. Austin, TX: University of Texas Press, 2014.

Rachel Cohen, *Bernard Berenson: A Life in the Picture Trade*, New Haven, CT: Yale University Press, 2013.

Collection of Old Chinese Porcelains Formed by George R. Davies, Esq., ... London: Gorer and Son, 1913.

G. Contenau, 'Les nouvelles salles d'art musulman au Musée du Louvre' (Deuxième article), *Syria*, T. 3, Fasc. 3 (1922), pp. 251–260.

Martin Conway, *The Sport of Collecting*, London: F.A. Stokes, 1914.

Annie E. Coombes, *Reinventing Africa: Museum, Material Culture and Popular Imagination in Late Victorian and Edwardian England*, New Haven, CT: Yale University Press, 2007.

J. Coote and A. Shelton, eds., *Anthropology, Art, and Aesthetics*, Oxford: Clarendon Press, 1994.

Stephen Coppel, 'Malcolm, John, of Poltalloch (1805–1893)', in *Oxford Dictionary of National Biography*, online edn, May 2005. Available at: www.oxforddnb.com/view/article/62981 (accessed 18 Dec. 2015).

Corsair. 'CORSAIR. The Online Catalog of the Pierpont Morgan Library'. Available at: http://corsair.themorgan.org/cgi-bin/Pwebrecon.cgi?BBID=161984 (accessed 11 March 2016).

Corsair. 'CORSAIR. The Online Catalog of the Pierpont Morgan Library'. Available at: http://corsair.themorgan.org/cgi-bin/Pwebrecon.cgi?BBID=179962 (accessed 11 March 2016).

Irma Coucill, *Canada's Prime Ministers, Governors General and Fathers of Confederation*, Ontario: Pembroke Publishers, 2005.

F. R. Cowell, *The Athenaeum: Club and Social Life in London 1824–1974*, London: Heinemann, 1975.

Robert Cumming, ed., *'My Dear BB...' The Letters of Bernard Berenson and Kenneth Clark, 1925–1959*, New Haven, CT: Yale University Press, 2015.

Caroline Dakers, *The Holland Park Circle: Artists and Victorian Society*, New Haven, CT: Yale University Press, 1999.

Caroline Dakers, *A Genius for Money: Business, Art and the Morrisons*, New Haven, CT: Yale University Press, 2011.

Elon Danziger, 'The Cook Collection, Its Founder and Its Inheritors', *The Burlington Magazine*, vol. 146, no. 1216, Collectors and Patrons (July, 2004), pp. 444–458.

Martin J. Daunton, *State and Market in Victorian Britain: War, Welfare and Capitalism*, Woodbridge: Boydell, 2008.

Helen Davies, 'John Charles Robinson's Work at the South Kensington Museum, Part I: The Creation of the Collection of Italian Renaissance Objects at the Museum of Ornamental Art and the South Kensington Museum, 1853–62', *Journal of the History of Collections*, vol. 10, no. 2 (1998), pp. 169–188.

Helen Davies, 'John Charles Robinson's Work at the South Kensington Museum, Part II. From 1863 to 1867: Consolidation and Conflict', *Journal of the History of Collections*, vol. 11, no. 1 (1999), pp. 95–115.

Aileen Dawson, *The Art of Worcester Porcelain, 1751–1788: Masterpieces from the British Museum Collection*, Lebanon, NH: University Press of New England, 2007.

Charles Dawson, 'In Search of the Marksman – William Chaffers', *English Ceramic Circle Transactions*, vol. 24 (2013), pp. 195–222.

Colleen Denney, *At the Temple of Art: The Grosvenor Gallery, 1877–1890*, Madison, NJ: Fairleigh Dickinson University Press, 2000.

Patrizia Di Bello, *Women's Albums and Photography in Victorian England: Ladies, Mothers and Flirts*, London: Routledge, 2007.

Charles Dickens (Jr.), *Dickens's Dictionary of London*, London, 1879.

Dictionary of Art Historians, 'Bernard Berenson'. Available at: https://dictionaryofarthistorians.org/berensonb.htm (accessed 11 Nov. 2015).

Dictionary of Art Historians, 'Wilhelm Bode'. Available at: https://dictionaryofarthistorians.org/bodew.htm (accessed 30 Nov. 2015).

Dictionary of Art Historians, 'William Boxall'. Available at: www.dictionaryofarthistorians.org/boxallw.htm (accessed 13 Aug.2014).

Dictionary of Art Historians, 'Justus Brinckmann'. Available at: https://dictionaryofarthistorians.org/brinckmannj.htm (accessed 27 Oct. 2015).

Dictionary of Art Historians, 'Giovanni Morelli'. Available at: https://dictionaryofarthistorians.org/morellig.htm (accessed 11 Nov. 2015).

Dictionary of Art Historians, 'Adolphus Paul Oppé'. Available at: https://dictionaryofarthistorians.org/oppea.htm (accessed 1 Sept. 2015).

Dictionary of Art Historians, 'Claude Phillips. Available at: https://dictionaryofarthistorians.org/phillipsc.htm (accessed 24 Nov. 2015).

Dictionary of Art Historians, 'William George Rawlinson'. Available at: https://dictionaryofarthistorians.org/rawlinsonw.htm (accessed 7 Oct. 2015).

Dictionary of Art Historians, 'Elizabeth Rigby'. Available at: https://dictionaryofarthistorians.org/rigbye.htm (accessed 11 Feb. 2015).

Dictionary of Art Historians, 'Arthur Sandford Strong'. Available at: https://dictionaryofarthistorians.org/strongs.htm (accessed 11 Dec. 2015).

Dictionary of Art Historians, 'Royall Tyler'. Available at: https://dictionaryofarthistorians.org/tylerr.htm (accessed 26 Aug. 2015).

Dictionary of Art Historians, 'Adolfo Venturi'. Available at: https://dictionaryofarthistorians.org/venturia.htm (accessed 11 Nov. 2015).

Dictionary of Art Historians, 'Gustav Friedrich Waagen'. Available at: https://dictionaryofarthistorians.org/waageng.htm (accessed 27 July 2015).

Dictionary of Art Historians, 'Ralph Nicholson Wornum'. Available at: www.dictionaryofarthistorians.org/wornumr.htm (accessed 13 Aug. 2014).

Dictionary of Art Historians, 'Matthew Digby Wyatt'. Available at: https://dictionaryofarthistorians.org/wyattm.htm (accessed 6 Oct. 2015).

Campbell Dodgson, 'Una Vilana Windisch', *The Burlington Magazine*, 1930. Reprinted in M. Levey, ed., *The Burlington Magazine: A Centenary Anthology*, New Haven, CT: Yale University Press, 2003, p. 40.

Anne S. Dowd and Susan Milbrath, eds., *Cosmology, Calendars, and Horizon-Based Astronomy in Ancient Mesoamerica*, Boulder, CO: University Press of Colorado, 2015.

William Richard Drake, *A Descriptive Catalogue of the Etched Work of F. S. Haden*, London, 1880 and *Notes on Venetian Ceramics*, London, 1868.

Margaret S. Drower, 'Gaston Maspero and the Birth of the Egypt Exploration Fund (1881–3)', *The Journal of Egyptian Archaeology*, vol. 68 (1982), pp. 299–317.

Dumbarton Oaks, 'Bliss-Tyler Correspondence'. Available at: www.doaks.org/resources/bliss-tyler-correspondence/1909-1919 (accessed 26 Aug. 2015).

Ann Eatwell, 'The Collector's or Fine Arts Club 1857–74. The First Society for Collectors of the 'Decorative Arts', *DAS: The Decorative Arts Society 1850 to the Present, Journal Number Eighteen, Omnium Gatherum*, Suffolk, 1994, pp. 25–30.

Ann Eatwell, 'Private Pleasure, Public Beneficence: Lady Charlotte Schreiber and Ceramic Collecting', in Clarissa Campbell Orr, ed., *Women in the Victorian Art World*, Manchester: Manchester University Press, 1995, pp. 125–145.

Ann Eatwell, 'Borrowing from Collectors: The Role of the Loan in the Formation of the Victoria and Albert Museum and its Collection (1852–1932)', *DAS: The Decorative Arts Society 1850 to the Present, Journal Number Twenty-four, Omnium Gatherum*, Suffolk, 2000, pp. 21–29.

Editorial, *The Burlington Magazine for Connoisseurs*, Vol. 1, No. 1 (Mar. 1903), pp. 3–5.

Egypt Exploration Society, *Report of the Forty-Third Ordinary General Meeting (Forty-Seventh Annual General Meeting)*, Bristol: Arrowsmith, 1929.

Egypt Exploration Society, 'History'. Available at: www.ees.ac.uk/about-us/history.html (accessed 24 July 2015).

Egypt Exploration Society, 'Carter and the EES'. Available at: www.ees.ac.uk/archive/CarterandtheEES.html (accessed 17 Aug. 2015).

Benita Eisler, *The Red Man's Bones: George Catlin, Artist and Showman*, New York: W.W. Norton & Co., 2013.

Caroline Elam, '"A more and more important work": Roger Fry and *The Burlington Magazine*', *The Burlington Magazine*, vol. 145, no. 1200, Centenary Issue (Mar. 2003), pp. 142–152.

Jas Elsner and Roger Cardinal, eds., *The Cultures of Collecting*, London: Reaktion, 1994.

Essex Record Office, 'Building Plan of Gardener's Cottage, Mount Hall, Great Horkesley. Reference: D/RLwPB1/1607'. Available at: https://secureweb1.essexcc.gov.uk/SeaxPAM/result_details.aspx?DocID=880583 (accessed 1 Sept. 2015).

George Eumorfopoulos, 'Preface', in R. L. Hobson, *The Eumorfopoulos Collection*, vol. I, London: Ernest Benn Ltd, 1925.

J. K. Fairbank, K. F. Bruner and E.M. Matheson, eds., *The I.G. in Peking: Letters of Robert Hart, Chinese Maritime Customs, 1868–1907*, vol. 1, New Haven, CT: Harvard University Press, 1975.

Christian F. Feest, 'European Collecting of American Indian Artefacts and Art', *Journal of the History of Collections*, vol. 5, no. 1 (1993), pp. 1–11.

Christian F. Feest, 'The Collecting of American Indian Artefacts in Europe, 1493–1750', in Karen Ordahl Kupperman, ed., *America in European Consciousness, 1493–1750*, Chapel Hill, NC: University of North Carolina Press, 1995, pp. 324–360.

James Fenton, *School of Genius: A History of the Royal Academy of Art*, London: Royal Academy, 2006.

W. N. Fergusson, *Adventure, Sport and Travel on the Tibetan Steppes*, London, 1911.

Ophelia Field, *The Kit-Kat Club*, London: HarperCollins, 2009.

Field Museum, 'A.W.F. Fuller Collection'. Available at: www.fieldmuseum.org/node/5061 (accessed 26 Aug. 2015).

Fine Art Society, *125 Years of Exhibitions at the Fine Art Society PLC, 1876–2001*, London: Fine Art Society, 2001.

Raymond Firth, 'Art and Anthropology', in J. Coote and A Shelton, eds., *Anthropology, Art, and Aesthetics*, Oxford: Clarendon Press, 1992, pp. 15–39.

David R. Fisher, 'MARRYAT, Joseph II (1790–1876), of Wimbledon House, Surr. and 6 Richmond Terrace, Whitehall, Mdx.', in D. Fisher, ed., *The History of Parliament: The House of Commons 1820–1832*, 2009. Available at: www.historyofparliamentonline.org/volume/1820-1832/member/marryat-joseph-1790-1876 (accessed 19 June 2016).

Fitzwilliam Museum, 'Hidden Histories: Charles de Sousy Ricketts and Charles Haslewood Shannon'. Available at: www.fitzmuseum.cam.ac.uk/gallery/hiddenhistories/biographies/bio/friendship/rickettsshannon_biography.html (accessed 29 June 2016).

Fitzwilliam Museum, 'From Pigsty to Palace'. Available at: www.fitzmuseum.cam.ac.uk/gallery/cockerell/pigstytopalace/marlay.html (accessed 7 Oct. 2015).

Fitzwilliam Museum, 'Collections Explorer: Shelly Limestone Statue of Amenenhat III'. Available at: http://data.fitzmuseum.cam.ac.uk/id/object/61606 (accessed 27 July 2015).

J. D. Flam and M. Deutch, eds., *Primitivism and Twentieth-century Art: A Documentary History*, Berkeley, CA: University of California Press, 2003.

Carol Flores, *Owen Jones: Design, Ornament, Architecture and Theory in an Age in Transition*, New York: Rizzoli, 2006.

Brinsley Ford, 'Obituary: Paul Oppé', *The Burlington Magazine*, vol. 99, no. 651 (June 1957), pp. 207–208.

Frances Fowle, 'Alexander Reid in Context: Collecting and Dealing in Scotland in the Late 19th and Early 20th Centuries', vol. 1, unpublished PhD thesis, University of Edinburgh, 1993.

Isabelle Frank, ed., *The Theory of Decorative Art: An Anthology of European and American Writings, 1750–1940*, New Haven, CT: Yale University Press, 2001.

A. W. Franks, *Catalogue of a Collection of Oriental Pottery and Porcelain*, 2nd edn., London: Bethnal Green Branch Museum, 1878 (1st edition, 1876).

Hamish Fraser and Howard Lee, *Aberdeen, 1800–2000: A New History*, Montreal: Dundurn, 2000.

M. Friedländer, *Early Netherlandish Painting*, New York: Springer, 1969.

M. J. Friedländer, *Zeitschrift für bildende Kunst*, vol. L, Leipzig, 1915.

Roger Fry, 'An Essay in Aesthetics', *New Quarterly*, 1909, reprinted in Roger Fry, *Vision and Design*, London: Chatto and Windus, 1920, pp. 11–25.

Roger Fry, 'The Chinese Exhibition', *The Nation*, vol. VII, no. 17 (23 July 1910), pp. 593–594.

Roger Fry, 'Ancient American Art', first printed in *The Burlington Magazine* in 1918, reprinted in Roger Fry, *Vision and Design*, London: Chatto and Windus, 1920, pp. 69–75.

Roger Fry, 'Negro Sculpture', reprinted in Roger Fry, *Vision and Design*, London: Chatto and Windus, 1920, pp. 65–68.

C. J. Gadd, 'The Raphael Bequest: I. Egyptian and West Asiatic Antiquities', *The British Museum Quarterly*, vol. 15 (1941–1950), pp. 57–60.

Isabelle Gadoin, 'British Collectors of Persian Art in the 19th Century: From Personal Culture to Oriental Taste?', *Res Orientales*, vol. XX (2011), pp. 121–134.

Kateryna Gamaliia, 'International School of Egyptology of Adolf Erman', *Sociology Study*, vol. 4, no. 1 (January 2014), pp. 52–60.

Paul Garner, *British Lions and Mexican Eagles: Business, Politics, and Empire in the Career of Weetman Pearson in Mexico, 1889–1919*, Stanford, CA: Stanford University Press, 2011.

Dana Garvey, 'Cosmo Monkhouse: A Conservative Reconsidered', *Nineteenth-Century Art Worldwide*, vol. 14, no. 2 (Summer 2015). Available at: www.19thc-artworldwide.org/summer 15/garvey-on-cosmo-monkhouse-a-conservative-reconsidered (accessed 7 Oct. 2015).

Luca Giacomelli, 'The Marquis Vittorio Emanuele d'Azeglio and his Activity as a Collector, Connoisseur and Socialite in London, 1848–1880', Seminars in the History of Collecting, June 2012. Available at: www.academia.edu/2936431/The_Marquis_Vittorio_Emanuele_dAzeglio_and_his_activity_as_a_collector_connoisseur_and_socialite_in_London_1848-1880_ (accessed 27 Nov. 2015).

Margaret T. Gibson and Susan M. Wright, eds., *Joseph Mayer of Liverpool, 1803–1886*, London: Society of Antiquaries and the National Museums and Galleries on Merseyside, 1988.

Nigel Glendinning and Hilary Macartney, *Spanish Art in Britain and Ireland, 1750–1920: Studies in Reception in Memory of Enriquetta Harris Frankfort*, Rochester, NY: Tamesis Books, 2010.

Global Egyptian Museum, 'Mummy Hand'. Available at: www.globalegyptianmuseum.org/detail.aspx?id=4288 (accessed 30 June 2016).

Denise M. Glover, Stevan Harrell, Charles F. McKhann, and Margaret Byrne Swain, *Explorers and Scientists in China's Borderlands, 1880–1950*, Seattle, WA: University of Washington Press, 2012.

Edgar Gorer and J. F. Blacker, *Chinese Porcelain and Hard Stones*, vol. 1, London: Gorer and Son, 1911.

S. Gorer and Son, *The Trapnell Collection of Old Chinese Porcelain*, London: Gorer and Son, 1906.

Christopher Gosden, *Anthropology and Archaeology: A Changing Relationship*, London: Routledge, 1999.

V. Gould, *G. F. Watts: The Last Great Victorian*, New Haven, CT: Yale University Press, 2004.

Government of New Zealand, 'Tepapa'. Available at: http://collections.tepapa.govt.nz / Topic/1337 (accessed 3 Sept. 2015).

Ian Graham, *Alfred Maudslay and the Maya: A Biography*, Norman, OK: University of Oklahoma Press, 2002.

Basil Gray, 'The Oscar Raphael Collection for the Nation', *The Burlington Magazine for Connoisseurs*, vol. 87, no. 512 (Nov. 1945), pp. 276, 278–283.

Frank Greenaway, 'Church, Sir Arthur Herbert (1834–1915), chemist', *Oxford Dictionary of National Biography* online. Available at: http://dx.doi.org/10.1093/ref:odnb/51472 (accessed 29 Nov. 2015).

Anthony Griffiths, ed., *Landmarks in Print Collecting: Connoisseurs and Donors at the British Museum since 1753*, London: British Museum Press, 1996.

Grove Art Online, 'Benson, R. H.'. Oxford Art Online, Oxford University Press. Available at: www.oxfordartonline.com/subscriber/article/grove/art/T007959 (accessed 26 Nov. 2015).

Grove Art Online, 'Tura, Cosimo [Cosmè]'. Oxford Art Online, Oxford University Press, Available at: www.oxfordartonline.com/subscriber/article/grove/art/T086559?q=cosme+tura&search=quick&pos=1&_start=1#firsthit (accessed 9 Nov. 2015).

Tapati Guha-Thakurta, *Monuments, Objects, Histories. Institutions of Art in Colonial and Postcolonial India*, New York: Columbia University Press, 2004.

H. R., 'The Art of Primitive Peoples', *The Burlington Magazine for Connoisseurs*, vol. 67, no. 388 (July 1935), p. 42.

Anne Håbu and Dawn Rooney, eds., *Royal Porcelain from Siam: Unpacking the Ring Collection*, Oslo: Hermes Publishing, 2013.

David J. Hall, 'Fry, Francis (1803–1886)', in *Oxford Dictionary of National Biography* online, 2004 http://dx.doi.org/10.1093/ref:odnb/10209 (accessed 30 Dec. 2015).

Hansard, 'Royal Academy of Arts (Sale of Works of Art)'. Available at: http://hansard.millbanksystems.com/commons/1962/mar/28/royal-academy-of-arts-sale-of-works-of (accessed 15 Nov. 2015).

John Harris, *Moving Rooms: The Trade in Architectural Salvages*, New Haven, CT: Yale University Press, 2007.

Jessica Harrison-Hall, *Ming Ceramics in the British Museum*, London: British Museum Press, 2001.

Paul Hartwig, *Die Griechische Meisterschalen der Blüthezeit des strengen rothfigurigen Stiles*, Stuttgart, 1893.

Francis Haskell, *The Ephemeral Museum: Old Master Paintings and the Rise of the Art Exhibition*, New Haven, CT: Yale University Press, 2000.

Christopher Hassall, *Edward Marsh, Patron of the Arts: A Biography*, Harlow: Longmans, 1959.

T. A. Heathcote, *The British Field Marshals, 1736–1997: A Biographical Dictionary*, Barnsley: Pen & Sword Military (Casemate, 2012 reprint).

Anne Helmreich, 'The Socio-Geography of Art Dealers and Commercial Galleries in Early Twentieth-Century London', in Helena Bonett, Ysanne Holt, and Jennifer Mundy, eds., *The Camden Town Group in Context*, London: Tate Research Publication, May 2012. Available at: www.tate.org.uk/art/research-publications/camden-town-group-/anne-helmreich-the-socio-geography-of-art-dealers-and-commercial-galleries-in-early-r1105658 (accessed 9 May 2016).

Anne Helmreich and Pamela Fletcher, eds., *The Rise of the Modern Art Market in London, 1850–1939*, Manchester: Manchester University Press, 2013.

James Hevia, 'Loot's Fate: The Economy of Plunder and the Moral Life of Objects "From the Summer Palace of the Emperor of China"', *History and Anthropology*, vol. 6, no. 4 (1994), pp. 319–345.

Robert Hewison, *John Ruskin*, Oxford: Oxford University Press, 2007.

Carola Hicks, *Girl in a Green Gown: The History and Mystery of the Arnolfini Portrait*, London: Vintage, 2011.

Histoire et fabrication de la porcelaine chinoise, ouvrage tr. du chin. par S. Julien, accompagné de notes et d'additions par A. Salvétat, et augmenté d'un mémoire sur la porcelaine du Japon, tr. du jap. par J. Hoffmann, Paris, 1856.

History website, 'The Sage at Badger'. Available at: www.historywebsite.co.uk/articles/Albrighton/Ruskin/Ruskin.htm (accessed 2 Nov. 2015).

'The History of Art Congress', *The Burlington Magazine for Connoisseurs*, vol. 75, no. 436 (July, 1939), p. 3.

History of Parliament online, 'Robert Vernon Smith'. Available at: www.historyofparliamentonline.org/volume/1820-1832/member/smith-robert-1800-1873 (accessed 10 Dec. 2015).

R. L. Hobson, 'Some Old Chinese Pottery', *The Burlington Magazine*, vol. xix (1911), p. xxx.

R. L. Hobson, *Chinese Pottery and Porcelain*, London, 1915.

Holfords of Westonbirt Trust. Available at: www.holfordtrust.com/textonly.asp (accessed 11 Dec. 2015).

Steven Hooper, *Pacific Encounters: Art and Divinity in Polynesia, 1760–1860*, Honolulu: University of Hawaii Press, 2006.

Martin J. Hopkinson, *No Day Without a Line: The History of the Royal Society of Painter-Printmakers 1880–1999*, Oxford: Ashmolean Museum, 1999.Charles Horton, *Alfred Chester Beatty: From Miner to Bibliophile*, Dublin: Town House, 2003.

Virginia Hoselitz, *Imagining Roman Britain: Victorian Responses to a Roman Past*, Woodbridge: Boydell and Brewer, 2007.

Edmond Hoyle. Available at: http://edmondhoyle.blogspot.co.uk/2011/12/from-pen-and-library-of-henry-hucks.html (accessed 6 Oct. 2015).

Ellen Huang, '*China's China: Jingdezhen Porcelain and the Production of Art in the Nineteenth Century*', PhD dissertation, University of California, San Diego, 2008.

Gervase Huxley, *Victorian Duke: The Life of Hugh Lupus Grosvenor, First Duke of Westminster*, Oxford: Oxford University Press, 1967.

Laura Iamurri, 'Art History in Italy: Connoisseurship, Academic Scholarship and the Protection of Cultural Heritage', in M. Rampley, *et al.*, eds., *Art History and Visual Studies in Europe: Transnational Discourses and National Frameworks*, Leiden: Brill, 2012, pp. 393–406.

F. Illies and G. Waterfield, 'Waagen in England: German Influence on 19th Century English Art Museums and Collections', in *Jahrbuch der Berliner Museen*, 37 (1995), pp. 47–59.

'Indigenous American Art at the Burlington Fine Arts Club', *The Connoisseur*, vol. LVII (May–August 1920), p. 241.

Institute of Historical Research, 'The Jobbing System of the London Stock Exchange'. Available at: www.history.ac.uk/projects/research/jobbing (accessed 1 Nov. 2015).

International Congress of Americanists, 'Historia: El Congreso Internacional de Americanistas, 1875–2006'. Available at: www.ica55.ufg.edu.sv/historia (accessed 29 Aug. 2015).

Invaluable auctioneers, 'Auction Lot 17: Sir Edward Coley Burne-Jones'. Available at: www.invaluable.com/auction-lot/sir-edward-coley-burne-jones-bt.,-a.r.a.,-r.w.s.-17-c-lmjd4wzz4y (accessed 27 Nov. 2015).

Irish Arts Review. 'Island Paradise'. Available at: www.irishartsreview.com/island-paradise/ (accessed 10 Dec. 2015).

I Tatti. Available at: http://itatti.harvard.edu/ (accessed 11 Nov. 2015).

Albert Jacquemart, *Histoire de la céramique: étude descriptive et raisonné des poteries de tous le temps et de tous les peoples*, Paris, 1873.

Elizabeth James, *The Victoria and Albert Museum: A Bibliography and Exhibition Chronology, 1852–1996*, London: Routledge, 1998.

T. G. H. James, *Howard Carter: The Path to Tutankhamun*, London: Tauris Parke, 1992 (2006 edn.).

Janus, 'Jardine Matheson Archive. Contract of Jardine Matheson and George Veitch', MS JM/F11/176'. Available at: http://janus.lib.cam.ac.uk/db/node.xsp?id=EAD%2FGBR%2F0012%2FMS%20JM%2FF11%2F176;sib0=180 (accessed 29 Nov. 2015).

Philip Jarrett, *Frank McClean: Godfather of British Naval Aviation*, Barnsley: Seaforth Publishing, 2011.

David Jeffreys, *Views of Ancient Egypt since Napoleon Bonaparte: Imperial Colonialism and Modern Appropriations*, London: Routledge, 2012.

Ian Jenkins, *The Lion of Knidos*, London: British Museum Press, 2008.

H. H. Johnston,' Obituary: Sir John Kirk, G. C. M. G., K. C. B., F. R. S., M. D., LL. D., D. Sc., D. C.L.', *The Geographical Journal*, vol. 59, no. 3 (Mar. 1922), pp. 225–228.

E. Jones and C. Woodward, *A Guide to the Architecture of London* (revised and updated ed.), (London: W&N, 2013), p. 364.

Geoffrey Jones, *Merchants to Multinationals: Trading Companies in the Nineteenth and Twentieth Centuries*, Oxford: Oxford University Press, 2000.

Julie Jones, 'Mildred and Robert Woods Bliss and the Pre-Colombian Collection at Dumbarton Oaks', in James Nelson Carder, ed., *A Home of the Humanities: The Collecting and Patronage of Mildred and Robert Woods Bliss*, Cambridge, MA: Harvard University Press, 2010, pp. 53–72.

Margaret Jourdain, 'Lace in the Collection of Mrs. Alfred Morrison at Fonthill', *The Burlington Magazine for Connoisseurs*, vol. 2, no. 4 (Jun. 1903), pp. 95–97, 99, 101, 103.

Thomas Athol Joyce, 'Negro', in *Encyclopædia Britannica.* Volume XIX (11th ed.). New York: Encyclopædia Britannica, 1911, p. 344 (accessed 20 Aug. 2015).

T. A. Joyce, 'Alfred Percival Maudslay', *Man*, vol. 32 (May 1932), pp. 123–125.

T. A. J. (Joyce), 'Bequest of the Late Dame Clarissa Reid', *British Museum Quarterly*, vol. VIII, no. 2 (1933), pp. 75–76.

Laurence Kanter and Pia Palladino, *Fra Angelico*, New York: Metropolitan Museum of Art, 2005.

Gaynor Kavanaugh, *Museums and the First World War: A Social History*, London: Bloomsbury, 1998 reprint.

Julia Kelly, *Art, Ethnography and the Life of Objects in Paris, c. 1920–1930*, Manchester: Manchester University Press, 2012.

Wilhelm Klein, *Die griechischen Vasen mit Meistersignaturen*, C. Gerolds Sohn, 1887.

Tim Knox, 'Edward Cheney of Badger Hall: Forgotten Collector of Italian Sculpture', *Sculpture Journal*, vol. 16, no. 1 (2007), pp. 5–20.

Kathleen Kuiper, ed., *Indigenous Peoples of the Arctic, Subarctic, and Northwest Coast*, New York: Rosen Education Service, 2012.

Udo Kultermann, *The History of Art History*, revised edition, New York: Abaris Books, 1993.

Michelle Labreche-Laroushe, *Emma Albani: International Star*, Montreal: Dundum, 1994.

Mary Lago, *Christiana Herringham and the Edwardian Art Scene*, Columbia, MO: University of Missouri Press, 1995.

Lady Lever Art Gallery, 'William Lever's Collecting of Famille Noire Porcelain'. Available at: www.liverpoolmuseums.org.uk/ladylever/collections/chinese/noiressay/page3.aspx#_ftn15 (accessed 19 Oct. 2015).

Lady Lever Art Gallery, 'Chinese Dealers and Collectors: C.S. Holberton'. Available at: www.liverpoolmuseums.org.uk/ladylever/collections/chinese/dealersessay/page2.aspx (accessed 19 Oct. 2015).

Lady Lever Art Gallery, 'Chinese Dealers and Collectors': S. E. Kennedy. Available at: www.liverpoolmuseums.org.uk/ladylever/collections/chinese/dealersessay/ (accessed 27 Oct. 2015).

Lady Lever Art Gallery, 'Chinese Dealers and Collectors: Gore v Lever: Edgar Gorer and William Hesketh Lever'. Available at: www.liverpoolmuseums.org.uk/ladylever/collections/chinese/goreressay/page4.aspx#_ftn84 (accessed 2 Nov. 2015).

Lady Lever Art Gallery, 'Chinese Dealers and Collectors: Huish'. Available at: www.liverpoolmuseums.org.uk/ladylever/collections/chinese/dealersessay/Dealers%20and%20collectors.pdf (accessed 1 Nov. 2015).

Horace A. Laffaye, *Polo in Britain: A History*, Jefferson, NC: Macfarland, 2012.

Lafayette Negative Archive, 'Walter Murray Guthrie'. Available at: http://lafayette.org.uk/gut1324a.html (accessed 29 Aug. 2015).

Mary Lago, *Christiana Herringham and the Edwardian Art Scene*, Columbia, MO: University of Missouri Press, 1995.

Mogens Trolle Larsen, *The Conquest of Assyria: Excavations in an Antique Land*, London: Routledge, 2014.

Legacies of British Slave Ownership database, 'Joseph Marryat: Profile and Legacies Summary'. Available at: www.ucl.ac.uk/lbs/person/view/11416 (accessed 19 June 2016).

Leighton House Museum, 'Leighton and the Middle East Website: Leighton and Collecting Art'. Available at: www.rbkc.gov.uk/leightonarabhall/pdfs/leightons_collection.pdf (accessed 1 Dec. 2015).

Leighton House Museum, 'About the House'. Available at: www.rbkc.gov.uk/subsites/museums/leightonhousemuseum/aboutthehouse/aboutleightonhouse/historyofthehouse.aspx (accessed 9 July 2015).

Anthony Lejeune, *The Gentlemen's Clubs of London*, London: Stacey International, 1979.

Julie L'Enfant, *William Rossetti's Art Criticism: The Search for Truth in Victorian Art*, Lanham, MD: University Press of America, 1998.

Nicky Levell, 'Scholars and Connoisseurs: Knowledge and Taste. The Seligman Collection of Chinese Art', in A. Shelton, ed., *Collectors: Expressions of Self and Other*, London: Horniman Museum and Gardens, 2001, pp. 73–90.

Robert M. Lewis, 'Wild American Savages and the Civilized English: Catlin's Indian Gallery and the Shows of London', *European Journal of American Studies*, vol. 3, no. 1 (2008). Available at: https://ejas.revues.org/2263 (accessed 29 Nov. 2015).

Lincoln's Inn Society, 'Newsletter'. Available at: www.lincolnsinn.org.uk/images/word/Newsletter/LI_Annual_Review_2013.pdf (accessed 27 Oct. 2015).

Richard Lines, *A History of the Swedenborg Society, 1810–2010*, London: The Swedenborg Society, 2012.

Nigel Llewellyn, 'The History of Western Art History', in Michael Bentley, ed., *The Routledge Companion to Historiography*, London: Routledge, 1997, pp. 828–848.

Adrian Locke, 'Exhibitions and Collectors of Pre-Hispanic Mexican Artefacts in Britain', in E. Matos Moctezuma and F. Solis Olguin, eds., *Aztecs*, London: Royal Academy of Arts, 2002, pp. 80–87, 90–91.

Di Yin Lu, 'On a Shoestring: Small-Time Entrepreneurs and the International Market for Chinese Curios, 1921–1949', *Archives of Asian Art*, vol. 63, no. 1 (2013), pp. 87–102.

Fiona MacCarthy, *Last Curtsey: The End of the Debutantes*, London: Faber & Faber, 2006.

Fiona MacCarthy, *The Last Pre-Raphaelite: Edward Burne-Jones and the Victorian Imagination*, Cambridge, MA: Harvard University Press, 2012.

Percy Macquoid, 'Mr Henry Hirsch's Furniture – I', *Country Life*, 25 October 1924, pp. 630–631.

Shawn Malley, *From Archaeology to Spectacle in Victorian Britain: The Case of Assyria, 1845–1854*, Farnham: Ashgate, 2012.

Murray Marks, *A Catalogue of Blue and White Nankin Porcelain Forming the Collection of Sir Henry Thompson*, London, 1878.

Joseph Marryat, *Collections Towards a History of Pottery and Porcelain in the 15th–18th Centuries*, London, 1850.

Herbert B. Mason, *Encyclopedia of Ships and Shipping*, London: The Shipping Encyclopedia, 1923.

Laszlo Mathe-Shires, 'Benin Kingdom: British Conquest, 1897', in K. Shillington, ed., *Encyclopaedia of African History*, vol. 1, A–G, New York: Routledge, 2005, pp. 136–137.

Saloni Mathur, *India by Design: Colonial History and Cultural Display*, Berkeley, CA: University of California Press, 2007.

Alfred Maudslay, 'Some American Problems', *Journal of the Royal Anthropological Institute vol.* 42 (1912), pp. 9–22.

Sir Herbert Maxwell, Bart., M.P. (1894). Life of the Right Honourable William Henry Smith M.P. (New ed.). London: William Blackwood and Sons, repr. Cambridge: Cambridge University Press, 2010.

Alison McQueen, *The Rise of the Cult of Rembrandt: Reinventing an Old Master in Nineteenth-Century France*, Amsterdam: Amsterdam University Press, 2003.

Mary F. McVicker, *Adela Breton: A Victorian Artist Amid Mexico's Ruins*, Albuquerque, NM: University of New Mexico Press, 2005, pp. 55–57.

MeasuringWorth, 'Five Ways to Compute the Relative Value of a UK Pound Amount, 1270 to Present'. Available at: www.measuringworth.com/ukcompare/relativevalue.php (accessed 17 Dec. 2015).

Merriam-Webster dictionary, 'Gadarene'. Available at: www.merriam-webster.com/word-of-the day/2011/12/15/#i0SYHelD3eUOpZQv.99 (accessed 11 Aug. 2014).

Metropolitan Museum of Art, 'Cosmè Tura, "The Flight into Egypt"'. Available at: www.metmuseum.org/collection/the-collection-online/search/437849?=&imgno=0&tabname=object-information (accessed 9 Nov. 2015).

Metropolitan Museum of Art, 'Pesellino, "Madonna and Child with Six Saints"'. Available at: www.metmuseum.org/collection/the-collection-online/search/437276?=&imgno=0&tabname=object-information (accessed 15 Nov. 2015).

Metropolitan Museum of Art, 'Bernardo Daddi, "The Crucifixion"'. Available at: www.metmuseum.org/collection/the-collection-online/search/438423 (accessed 15 Nov. 2015).

Amy Milne-Smith, *London Clubland: A Cultural History of Gender and Class in Late Victorian Britain*, Basingstoke: Palgrave, 2011.

John Minford, 'Sinology, Old and New', *China Heritage Quarterly*, no. 13 (March 2008). Available at: www.chinaheritagequarterly.org/articles.php?searchterm=013_giles.inc&issue=013 (accessed 29 Nov. 2015).

The Mirror, 'The Curse of King Tutankhamun'. Available at: www.mirror.co.uk/news/world-news/curse-king-tutankhamun-fatal-fevers-4563888 (accessed 15.8 2015).

Nicholas Mirzoeff, 'Transculture: From Kongo to Congo', in *An Introduction to Visual Culture*, London: Routledge, 1999.

Partha Mitter, *Much Maligned Monsters: A History of European Reactions to Indian Art*, Chicago: University of Chicago Press, 1992.

Partha Mitter, *Art and Nationalism in Colonial India, 1850–1922: Occidental Orientations*, Cambridge: Cambridge University Press, 1994.

Elizabeth Moignard, *Greek Vases: An Introduction*, Bristol: Bristol Classical Press, 2006.

Museo Thyssen-Bornemisza, 'The Virgin and Child Enthroned'. Available at: www.museothyssen.org/en/thyssen/ficha_obra/55 (accessed 5 Nov. 2015).

Museum of Archaeology and Anthropology, 'Feather Poncho and Headdress'. Available at: http://maa.cam.ac.uk/maa-highlights/central_south_america/peru/372/ (accessed 1 Sept. 2015).

Museum of Fine Arts, Boston, 'Oil Flask, Lekythos'. Available at: www.mfa.org/collections/object/oil-flask-lekythos-153982 (accessed 7 Oct. 2015).

Museum of Fine Arts, Boston, 'Drinking Cup, Kylix'. Available at: www.mfa.org/collections/object/drinking-cup-kylix-153673 (accessed 7 Oct. 2015).

Hans Nadelhoffer, *Cartier* (London: Chronicle Books), 2007.

National Gallery, 'Giovanni Antonio Boltraffio: "Portrait of a Man in Profile"'. Available at: www.nationalgallery.org.uk/paintings/giovanni-antonio-boltraffio-portrait-of-a-man-in-profile/*/key-facts (accessed 13 Nov. 2015).

National Gallery, 'Correggio: "Christ Taking Leave of his Mother"'. Available at: www.nationalgallery.org.uk/paintings/correggio-christ-taking-leave-of-his-mother (accessed 9 Nov. 2015).

National Gallery, 'Piero di Cosimo, "The Fight between the Lapiths and the Centaurs"'. Available at: www.nationalgallery.org.uk/paintings/piero-di-cosimo-the-fight-between-the-lapiths-and-the-centaurs (accessed 15 Nov. 2015).

National Gallery, 'Exhibition Guide: Leonardo da Vinci'. Available at: www.nationalgallery.org.uk/media/15705/exhibition-guide_leonardo-da-vinci.pdf (accessed 29 June 2016).

National Gallery, 'Image NG3627, God the Father'. Available at: www.nationalgalleryimages.co.uk/Imagedetails.aspx?q=NG3627&ng=NG3627&frm=1 (accessed 15 Nov. 2015).

National Gallery, 'Lodovico Mazzolino: "Christ Disputing with the Doctors"'. Available at: www.nationalgallery.org.uk/paintings/lodovico-mazzolino-christ-disputing-with-the-doctors (accessed 9 Nov. 2015).

National Gallery, 'Sir Edward Poynter'. Available at: www.nationalgallery.org.uk/paintings/history/directors/sir-edward-poynter (accessed 9 Nov. 2015).

National Gallery, 'George Salting'. Available at: www.nationalgallery.org.uk/paintings/history/collectors-and-benefactors/george-salting (accessed 25 Sept. 2016).

National Gallery of Art, Washington, DC, 'Tura, Cosmè, "The Virgin Annunciate [middle right panel]"'. Available at: www.nga.gov/content/ngaweb/Collection/art-object-page.41587.html (accessed 24 Nov. 2015).

National Gallery of Art, Washington, DC, 'The Adoration of the Magi'. Available at: www.nga.gov/collection/gallery/gg4/gg4-41581.html (accessed 15 Nov. 2015).

National Gallery of Ireland, 'Sir Walter Armstrong'. Available at: www.nationalgallery.ie/en/aboutus/History/NGI_Directors/Walter_Armstrong.aspx (accessed 4 Nov. 2015).

National Museums Liverpool, 'Egyptology'. Available at: www.liverpoolmuseums.org.uk/wml/collections/antiquities/egyptology.aspx (accessed 26 July 2015).

National Museums Liverpool. 'Early History of the Americas'. Available at www.liverpoolmuseums.org.uk/wml/collections/ethnology/americas-collections.pdf (accessed 26 Aug. 2015).

National Trust, 'Nymans'. Available at: www.nationaltrust.org.uk/nymans (accessed 1 Nov. 2015).

Eddy Chicka Ndekwu, *First Bank of Nigeria: A Century of Banking*, London: Spectrum Books, 1994.

The New Gallery, Regent Street, 'Exhibition of Early Italian Art, from 1300–1550', 1893–1894.

Newnham College, 'Henry and Elizabeth Yates Thompson'. Available at: www.newn.cam.ac.uk/about-newnham/college-history/biographies/content/henry-elizabeth-yates-thompson (accessed 5 Dec. 2015).

News, 'The Art of Primitive Peoples', *Nature*, vol. 135 (1 June 1935), p. 927.

A D. Nicholl, 'Agnew, Sir William Gladstone (1898–1960)', rev. Marc Brodie, in *Oxford Dictionary of National Biography*, first published 2004; online edn, Jan 2011. Available at: http://dx.doi.org/10.1093/ref:odnb/30349 (accessed 10 Dec. 2015).

Notes of the Quarter, January, February, March, 'J. Arthur Strong', *Journal of the Royal Asiatic Society of Great Britain and Ireland for 1904* (1904), pp. 387–394.

Vinnie Norskov, *Greek Vases in New Contexts*, Aarhus: Aarhus University Press, 2002.

'Obituary: Philip Norman', *Notes and Queries*, vol. CLX (May 30, 1931), p. 396. doi: 10.1093/nq/CLX.may30.396-b (accessed 5 Dec. 2015).

Official Catalogue of the Great Exhibition of the Works of Industry of All Nations, 1851, London: Spicer Brothers, 1851.

M. B. Ogilvie and J. D. Harvey, eds., *The Biographical Dictionary of Women in Science*, vol. 2, L–Z, London: Routledge, 2000, pp. 936–937.

Michael O'Hanlon and Robert L. Welsch, *Hunting the Gatherers: Ethnographic Collectors, Agents and Agency in Melanesia, 1870s–1930s*, Oxford: Berghahn, 2000.

Open University, 'India Society'. Available at: www.open.ac.uk/researchprojects/makingbritain/content/india-society (accessed 10 Aug. 2015).

Clarissa Campbell Orr, ed., *Women in the Victorian Art World*, Manchester: Manchester University Press, 1995.

Hugh Owen, *Two Centuries of Ceramic Art in Bristol. Being a History of the Manufacture of "The True Porcelain" by Richard Champion...*', London, 1873.

Jonathan Parry, 'Cavendish, Spencer Compton, Marquess of Hartington and Eighth Duke of Devonshire (1833–1908)', first published 2004; online edn, Jan 2008. Available at: http://dx.doi.org/10.1093/ref:odnb/32331 (accessed 11. Dec. 2015).

Reginald Herbert Pembroke (15th Earl of), *The History and Treasures of Wilton House: Home of the Earls of Pembroke and Montgomery for over 400 Years*, Andover: Pitkin Pictorials, 1957.

Elizabeth Pergam, *The Manchester Art Treasures Exhibition of 1857: Entrepreneurs, Connoisseurs and the Public*, Farnham: Ashgate, 2011.

Nikolaus Pevsner, 'An Exhibition of British Medieval Art', *The Burlington Magazine for Connoisseurs*, vol. 75, no. 436 (July 1939), p. 13.

Philadelphia Museum of Art, 'Vincenzo Foppa: "Virgin and Child before a Landscape"'. Available at: www.philamuseum.org/collections/permanent/102013.html (accessed 12 Nov. 2015).

Claude Phillips, 'Florentine Painting Before 1500', *The Burlington Magazine for Connoisseurs*, vol. 34, no. 195 (Jun. 1919), pp. 208–211, 214–217, 219.

Stacey Pierson, 'The Sung Standard: Chinese Ceramics and British Studio Pottery in the 20th Century', in S. Pierson, ed., *Song Ceramics: Art History, Archaeology and Technology*, Colloquies on Art and Archaeology in Asia, no. 20. London: School of Oriental and African Studies, 2004a, pp. 81–102.

Stacey Pierson, 'Private Collecting, Teaching and Institutionalisation: the Percival David Foundation and the Field of Chinese Art in Britain, 1920–1964', unpublished DPhil dissertation, University of Sussex, 2004b.

Stacey Pierson, *Collectors, Collections and Museums: The Field of Chinese Ceramics in Britain, 1560–1960*, Bern: Peter Lang, 2007.

Stacey Pierson, 'The History of the London Oriental Ceramic Society, 1921–1947', *Diancang* 典藏 (Taipei), part 1, vol. 220 (January 2011), pp. 152–159; part II, vol. 221 (February 2011), pp. 132–139; part III, vol. 222 (March 2011), pp. 186–195.

Stacey Pierson, *From Object to Concept: Global Consumption and the Transformation of Ming Porcelain*, Hong Kong: Hong Kong University Press, 2013.

Pitt Rivers Museum. 'Henry Balfour' Available at: http://history.prm.ox.ac.uk/collector_balfour.html (accessed 20 Aug. 2015).

Marcia Pointon, 'W. E. Gladstone as an Art Patron and Collector', *Victorian Studies*, vol. 19, no. 1 (Sept. 1975), pp. 73–98.

Andrea Geddes Poole, *Stewards of the Nation's Art: Contested Cultural Authority, 1890–1939*, Toronto: University of Toronto Press, 2010.

Possingworth Park. Available at: www.parksandgardens.org/places-and-people/site/5082 (accessed 15 Aug. 2014).

Scott Pratt, 'Wounded Knee and the Prospect of Pluralism', *Journal of Speculative Philosophy*, New Series, vol. 19, no. 2 (2005), pp. 150–166.

Elizabeth Prettejohn, ed. *Cambridge Companion to the Pre-Raphaelites*, Cambridge: Cambridge University Press, 2012.

Sally Price, *Primitive Art in Civilized Places*, second edn, Chicago: University of Chicago Press, 1989.

Katherine Prior, 'Russell, (Arthur) Oliver Villiers, Second Baron Ampthill (1869–1935)', *Oxford Dictionary of National Biography*, Oxford University Press, 2004; online edn, Jan. 2008. Available at: www.oxforddnb.com/view/article/35874 (accessed 25 June 2016).

H. R., 'The Art of Primitive Peoples', *The Burlington Magazine for Connoisseurs*, vol. 67, no. 388 (July 1935), p. 42.

Simon Rae, *W. G. Grace: A Life*, London: Faber & Faber, 1999.

Mark Rawitsch, *The House on Lemon Street: Japanese Pioneers and the American Dream*, Boulder, CO: University of Colorado Press, 2012.

RBS Heritage Hub. 'Frederick George Hilton Price'. Available at: http://heritagearchives.rbs.com/people/list/frederick-george-hilton-price.html (accessed 22 July 2015).

C. H. Read and O. M. Dalton, 'Works of Art from Benin', *The Journal of the Anthropological Institute of Great Britain and Ireland*, vol. 27, London: Trübner & Co., 1898, pp. 362–382.

Herbert Read, *Art and Industry: The Principles of Industrial Design*, London, 1934.

Hercules Read (C. H.) 'Lieut.-Colonel George Babington Croft Lyons', *The Antiquaries Journal*, vol. 6 (1926), pp. 451–452. doi:10.1017/S0003581500057024 (accessed 8 Oct. 2015).

'Report of the Council', June, 1932, to June, 1933, *The Journal of the Royal Anthropological Institute of Great Britain and Ireland*, vol. 63 (Jan.–Jun. 1933), p. iii.

'Report of the Council for the Session July 1941 to June 1942', *The Journal of the Royal Anthropological Institute of Great Britain and Ireland*, vol. 72, no. 1/2 (1942), pp. 71–72.

Rethinking Pitt Rivers, 'Primary Documents, Letter of Jan. 22, 1897'. Available at: http://web.prm.ox.ac.uk/rpr/index.php/primary-documents-index/16-second-collection-1880-1900/527-saswm-pr-papers-l1228/ (accessed 27 July 2015).

Rethinking Pitt Rivers, 'Pitt Rivers' South American Collections'. Available at: http://web.prm.ox.ac.uk/rpr/index.php/article-index/12-articles/604-pitt-rivers-south-american-collections.html accessed (accessed 26 Aug. 2015).

Jean Paul Richter, 'Italian Pictures at the New Gallery and at Burlington House', *The Art Journal*, new series (1894), p. 62.

Charles Ricketts, 'Head in Serpentine of Amenemmes III in the Possession of Oscar Raphael, Esq.', *Journal of Egyptian Archaeology*, vol. 4, no. 4 (Oct. 1917), pp. 211–212.

Bernhard Ridderbos *et al*., eds., *Early Netherlandish Paintings: Rediscovery, Reception and Research*, Amsterdam: Amsterdam University Press, 2005.

Christina Riggs, *Unwrapping Ancient Egypt*, London: Bloomsbury, 2014.

B. W. Robinson, 'The Burlington House Exhibition of 1931: A Milestone in Islamic Art History', in Stephen Vernoit, ed., *Discovering Islamic Art: Scholars, Collectors and Collections, 1850–1950*, London: I B. Tauris, 200, pp. 147–149.

J. C. Robinson, *A Descriptive Catalogue of a Collection of Oriental and Old Sèvres Porcelain, the Property of Her Majesty the Queen: Deposited for Exhibition in the Museum of the Department*, London: HMSO, 1853.

Dinah Roe, *The Rossettis in Wonderland. A Victorian Family History*, London: Haus Publishing, 2011.

Beverley Rogers, 'The Reverend William MacGregor: An Early Industrialist Collector', *Antiquity*, no. 325 (September 2010). Available at: antiquity.ac.uk/projall/rogers325/ (accessed 27 July 2015).

'Romney', *Masters in Art: A Series of Illustrated Monographs, Issued Monthly*, vol. 4, part 37, Boston: Bates and Guild Company, 1903.

William Michael Rossetti, *Some Reminiscences*, vol. I, Cambridge: Cambridge University Press, 2013 (1906).

Eliot Woodridge Rowlands, *Masaccio: Saint Andrew and the Pisa Altarpiece*, New York: J Paul Getty Museum, 2003.

Royal Academy, 'About the RA: Our Story'. Available at: www.royalacademy.org.uk/about-the-ra#our-story (accessed 22 Jan. 2016).

Royal Anthropological Institute of Great Britain and Ireland, 'Miscellaneous Business of the Meeting on November 9th, 1897', *The Journal of the Anthropological Institute of Great Britain and Ireland*, vol. 27 (1897), p. 361. Available at: www.jstor.org/stable/2842835 (accessed 9 Sept. 2015).

Royal Anthropological Institute of Great Britain and Ireland, 'Loan Exhibition of Indian Art', *Man*, vol. 31 (July 1931), p. 136.

Royal Anthropological Institute Proceedings. 146. Exhibition of the Art of Primitive Peoples. *Man* vol. 35 (September 1935), p. 137.

Royal Botanic Gardens of Edinburgh, 'The Reginald Farrar Collection'. Available at: www.rbge.org.uk/assets/files/science/Library%20-Archives/GB235RJF_ReginaldJFarrer.pdf (accessed 16 Feb. 2016).

Royal Collection, 'Benozzo Gozzoli: "The Fall of Simon Magus"'. Available at: www.royalcollection.org.uk/collection/403372/the-fall-of-simon-magus (accessed 15 Nov. 2015).

Royal Collection, 'Angelo Poliziano: "Miscellanea"'. Available at: www.royalcollection.org.uk/collection/1080368/miscellanea (accessed 9 July 2015).

Royal College of Physicians, 'Sir Hermann Weber'. Available at: http://munksroll.rcplondon.ac.uk/Biography/Details/4672 (accessed 7 Oct. 2015).

Royal College of Surgeons, 'Sir William Henry Bennett'. Available at: http://livesonline.rcseng.ac.uk/biogs/E003829b.htm (accessed 10 Dec. 2015).

Royall Tyler. *Dictionary of American Biography*. New York: Charles Scribner's Sons, 1977. *Biography in Context*. Web. 28 June 2016. Available at: http://ic.galegroup.com/ic/bic1/ReferenceDetailsPage/ReferenceDetailsWindow?displayGroupName=Reference&disableHighlighting=false&prodId=BIC2&action=e&windowstate=normal&catId=&documentId=GALE%7CBT2310001718&mode=view&userGroupName=fairfax_main&jsid=28d94d5cb3fad467191be7f50b1b1def (accessed 26.8 2015).

Patricia Rubin, '"The Outcry": Despoilers, Donors and the National Gallery in London, 1909', *Journal of the History of Collections* vol. 25, no. 2 (2012), pp. 253–275.

William D. Rubinstein, *et al.*, eds., *Palgrave Dictionary of Anglo-Jewish History*, Basingstoke: Palgrave Macmillan, 2011.

Rusholme and Victoria Park Archive, 'Fallowfield Brow and Oak Drive'. Available at: http://rusholmearchive.org/fallowfield-brow-and-oak-drive (accessed 27 Oct. 2015).

Archibald Russell, *The Engravings of William Blake*, London, 1912.

Archibald Russell, 'Heraldry at the Burlington Fine Arts Club', *The Burlington Magazine*, vol. 29, no. 160 (July 1916), pp. 164–168.

S. R., 'A van Branteghem', *Revue Archéologique*, Quatrième Série, T. 18 (JUILLET– DÉCEMBRE 1911), pp. 362–363.

St James Hotel and Club, 'History'. Available at: www.stjameshotelandclub.com/history (accessed 18 Dec. 2015).

Ernest Samuels, *Bernard Berenson: The Making of a Connoisseur*, Cambridge, MA: Harvard University Press, 1979.

'Sanford Arthur Strong', Notes from the Quarter, *Journal of the Royal Asiatic Society of Great Britain and Ireland* (1904), pp. 387–394.

B. U. Schipper, ed., *Ägyptologie als Wissenschaft: Adolf Erman (1854–1937) in Seiner Zeit*, Berlin: De Gruyter, 2006.

Science and Art Department of the Committee of Council on Education. *Catalogue of the Special Exhibition of Works of Art of the Mediaeval, Renaissance and More Recent Periods on Loan at the South Kensington Museum*, June, 1862.

Seattle Art Museum, 'Indigenous Beauty'. Available at: www.seattleartmuseum.org/exhibitions/indigenous (accessed 5 Dec. 2015).

Charles Sebag-Montefiore, 'Holford, Robert Stayner (1808–1892)', in *Oxford Dictionary of National Biography*, online edition, rev. first published 2004. Available at: http://dx.doi.org/10.1093/ref:odnb/37559 (accessed 18 Dec. 2015).

Simon Sebag-Montefiore, 'R. H. Benson as a Collector', Appendix 3, in Jehanne Wake, *Kleinwort Benson: The History of Two Families in Banking*, Oxford: Oxford University Press, 1997, pp. 480–487.

Thomas Seccombe, 'Wornum, Ralph Nicholson (1812–1877)', rev. David Carter, first published 2004, in *Oxford Dictionary of National Biography*. Available at: http://dx.doi.org/10.1093/ref:odnb/29978 (accessed 18 Dec. 2015).

Meryl Secrest, *Duveen: A Life in Art*, Chicago: University of Chicago Press, 2004.

Eric Shanes, *The Golden Age of Watercolours: The Hickman Bacon Collection*, London: Dulwich Picture Gallery, 2001.

Robert J. Sharer, 'Alfred P. Maudslay: Pioneer Maya Archaeologist', *Expedition Magazine* 26.1 (October 1983): n.p..*Expedition Magazine*. Penn Museum, October 1983, Web. 1 Jan 2016. Available at: www.penn.museum/sites/expedition/?p=4949 (accessed 31 Dec. 2015).

Ian Shaw and Robert Jameson, eds., *A Dictionary of Archaeology*, Chichester: Wiley-Blackwell, 2002.

Samuel Shaw, 'William Rothenstein (1872–1945)'. Available at: www.academia.edu/5510654/William_Rothenstein_Short_Biography (accessed 10 Aug. 2015).

Chandrahas Singh, *The Civil Service in India, 1858–1947: A Historical Study*, Delhi: Atma Ram and Sons, 1989.

Devika Singh, 'Indian Nationalist Art History and the Writing and Exhibiting of Mughal Art, 1910-1948', *Art History*, vol. 36, no. 5 (November 2013), pp. 1042–1069.

H. Clifford Smith, *The Danny Unicorn Jewel*, London, 1914.

H. Clifford Smith, *Victoria and Albert Museum: Catalogue of English Furniture & Woodwork*, London: Board of Education, 1931.

H. Clifford Smith, *Some Mid-Georgian Furniture from the Royal Collections*, London, 1935.

Nicholas Smith, 'A Stitch in Time: The V&A and the Bayeux Tapestry, I', V&A blog, May 14, 2013. Available at: www.vam.ac.uk/blog/tales-archives/stitch-time-va-and-bayeux-tapestry-1 (accessed 13 June 2016).

C. Hugh Smyth and P. M. Lukehart, eds., *The Early Years of Art History in the United States: Notes and Essays on Departments, Teaching, and Scholars*, Princeton, NJ: Princeton University Press, 1993.

Nahum Sokolow (1919) *History of Zionism: 1600–1918*, London: Longmans, Green & Co.; republished by Forgotten Books, London, 2013.

Sotheby, Wilkinson and Hodge, *Catalogue of the MacGregor Collection of Egyptian Antiquities*, London, June 26–July 6 1922.

David Sox, *Bachelors of Art: Edward Perry Warren and the Lewes House Brotherhood*, London: Fourth Estate, 1991.

Penny Sparke, Brenda Martin, and Trevor Keeble, eds.,*The Modern Period Room: The Construction of the Exhibited Interior, 1870–1950*, London: Routledge, 2006.

Robert Speaight, *William Rothenstein: The Portrait of an Artist in His Time*, London: Eyre & Spottiswoode, 1962.

Spring Exhibition Comprising Arts and Crafts, Choice Examples of Indian Art: Lent by the Department of Science and Art, London, architectural drawings, photographs, &c., D. Marples & Co. Printers, 50A Lord Street, Liverpool, 1898.

Julian Stallabrass, 'The Idea of the Primitive: British Art and Anthropology, 1918–1930', *New Left Review*, no. 183 (1990), pp. 95–116.

Margaret Stavridi, *Master of Glass: Charles Eamer Kempe 1837–1907 and the Work of his Firm in Stained Glass and Church Decoration*, Kempe Society, 1988.

Christopher B. Steiner, 'The Tradition of African Art: Reflections on the Social Life of a Subject', in M. Phillips and G. Schochet, eds., *Questions of Tradition*, eds., Toronto: University of Toronto Press, 2004, pp. 88–109.

Stock Exchange Gazette, 'Directory of Directors…, Thomas Skinner and Co, East Grinstead', 1914.

George W. Stocking, *Victorian Anthropology*, New York: Free Press, 1987.

Jean Strouse, *Morgan: American Financier*, New York: HarperCollins, 2000.

Christine Sylvester, *Art/Museums: International Relations Where We Least Expect It*, London: Routledge, 2009.

Tate, 'History of Tate'. Available at: www.tate.org.uk/about/who-we-are/history-of-tate (accessed 24 Nov. 2015).

Tate, 'William Holman Hunt'. Available at: www.tate.org.uk/art/artists/william-holman-hunt-287 (accessed 9 July 2015).

Tate, 'The Oppé Collection'. Available at: www.tate.org.uk/research/prints-and-drawings-rooms/oppe-collection (accessed 5 Dec. 2015).

Tate, 'Sir William Reynolds Stephens', Available at: www.tate.org.uk/art/artists/sir-william-reynolds-stephens-1833 (accessed 3 Sept. 2015).

Brandon Taylor, *Art for the Nation: Exhibitions and the London Public, 1747–2001*, Manchester: Manchester University Press, 1999.

'The Art of Ancient Egypt', *The Magazine of Art*, vol. 18 (1895), p. 396.

The Esoteric Curiosa, 'Shaking the Family Tree of Lord Romsey'. Available at: http://theesotericcuriosa.blogspot.co.uk/2013/03/shaking-family-tree-of-lord-romsey-art.html (accessed 7 Oct. 2015).

The London Gazette, Friday, Nov. 1, 1901. Available at: www.thegazette.co.uk/London/issue/27370/page/7098/data.pdf (accessed 27 Nov. 2015).

The Peerage, 'Clare Reynold Rolston'. Available at: www.thepeerage.com/p3027.htm#i30267 (accessed 10 Dec. 2015).

The Peerage, 'Lady Margaret McCarty'. Available at: www.thepeerage.com/p12774.htm#i127740 (accessed 10 Dec. 2015).

This is Money, 'Historic Inflation Calculator: How the Value of Money Has Changed Since 1900'. Available at: www.thisismoney.co.uk/money/bills/article-1633409/Historic-inflation-calculator-value-money-changed-1900.html (accessed 17 Dec. 2015).

Abraham Thomas, 'Owen Jones and the Islamic World', in G. Maclean, ed., *Britain and the Muslim World: Historical Perspectives*, Newcastle: Cambridge Scholars Publishing, 2011, pp. 143–163.

Ben Thomas and Timothy Wilson, eds., *C. D. E. Fortnum and the Collecting and Study of Applied Arts and Sculpture in Victorian England*, Oxford: Oxford University Press, 1999.

Jason Thompson, *Sir Gardner Wilkinson and His Circle*, Austin, TX: University of Texas Press, 2010.

Jason Thompson, *Wonderful Things: A History of Egyptology 1: from Antiquity to 1881*, Cairo: American University in Cairo Press, 2015.

Amara Thornton, 'Exhibition Season: Annual Archaeological Exhibitions in London, 1880s–1930s', *Bulletin of the History of Archaeology*, 10 March 2015. Available at: http://doi.org/10.5334/bha.252 (accessed 22 July 2015).

Timken Museum of Art, 'Giovanni Antonio Boltraffi, "Portrait of a Youth Holding an Arrow"'. Available at: www.timkenmuseum.org/collection/italian/portrait-youth-holding-arrow (accessed 11 Nov. 2015).

Toledo Museum, 'Classes'. Available at: http://classes.toledomuseum.org:8080/emuseum/view/objects/asitem/People$00402996/0?t:state:flow=7c1703b3-d942-4708-b76b-d3b2727b661c (accessed 11 March 2016).

'The Trevor Lawrence Orchid Collection at the Royal Gardens, Kew', *Nature*, vol. 93 (7 May 1914), pp. 244–245.

Bruce Trigger, *A History of Archaeological Thought*, 2nd ed., Cambridge: Cambridge University Press, 2006.

Athena Tsingarida, 'The Search for the Artist. The van Branteghem and Bourquignon Collections and the Connoisseurship of Greek Vases', in S. Schmidt and M. Steinhardt, eds., *Sammeln und Erforschen: Griechische Vasen in Neuzeitlichen Sammlungen*, Munich: C.H. Beck, 2014. pp. 115–122.

University College London, 'Pre-history of the Petrie Museum'. Available at: www.ucl.ac.uk/museums-static/digitalegypt/archaeology/edwards.html. (accessed 26 July 2015).

University of Glasgow History of Art and HATII, 'William Chaffers' in *Mapping the Practice and Profession of Sculpture in Britain and Ireland 1851–1951*, online database 2011. Available at: http://sculpture.gla.ac.uk/view/organization.php?id=msib1_1234176170 (accessed 14 June 2016).

University of Glasgow Research Project on Exhibition Culture in London, 1878–1908. Available at: www.exhibitionculture.arts.gla.ac.uk/ (accessed 22 Dec. 2015).

James Urry, *Before Social Anthropology: Essays on the History of British Anthropology*, London: Routledge, 1993.

W. R. Valentiner, 'Simon van Herlam, the Master of the Morrison Triptych', *Gazette des Beauxs-Arts*, vol. XLV (Jan. 1955), pp. 7, 10.

Paul van der Grijp, *Passion and Profit: Towards an Anthropology of Collecting*, Berlin: Lit Verlag, 2006.

Stephen Vernoit, ed., *Discovering Islamic Art: Scholars, Collectors and Collections, 1850–1950*, London: I B. Tauris, 2000.

Michael Vickers, 'Value and Simplicity: Eighteenth-Century Taste and the Study of Greek vases', *Past and Present*, no. 116 (1987), pp. 98–137.

Victoria and Albert Museum, 'A Grand Design'. Available at:www.vam.ac.uk/vastatic/microsites/1159_grand_design/essay-an-encyclopedia-of-treasures_new.html (accessed 11 Aug. 2014). No longer available.

Victoria and Albert Museum, 'Lieutenant-Colonel George Babington Croft Lyons'. Available at: www.vam.ac.uk/content/articles/l/lt-col-george-babington-croft-lyons/ (accessed 27 Oct. 2015).

Victoria and Albert Museum, 'Jug'. Available at: http://collections.vam.ac.uk/item/O340298/jug-unknown/ (accessed 10 July 2015).

Victoria and Albert Museum, 'Curtis Moffat'. Available at: www.vam.ac.uk/content/articles/c/curtis-moffat-biography/(accessed 3 Sept. 2015).

Victoria and Albert Museum, ' George Salting'. Available at: www.vam.ac.uk/content/articles/g/george-salting/ (accessed 13 Aug. 2014).

Victoria and Albert Museum, 'Charlotte Schreiber'. Available at: www.vam.ac.uk/content/articles/c/charlotte-schreiber/ (accessed 13 Sept. 2015).

Victoria and Albert Museum, 'Richard Phene Spiers'. Available at: http://collections.vam.ac.uk/item/O179344/richard-phene-spiers-plaquette-lanteri-edouard/ (accessed 8.10 2015).

Victoria and Albert Museum, 'Sword Guard by Michitoshi'. Available at: http://collections.vam.ac.uk/item/O77413/sword-guard-michitoshi/ (accessed 28 Nov. 2015).

Victorian web, 'Carlo Marochetti'. Available at: www.victorianweb.org/sculpture/marochetti/biography.html (accessed 18 Dec. 2015).

Tasha Vorderstrasse and Tanya Treptow, eds., *A Cosmopolitan City: Muslims, Christians, and Jews in Old Cairo*, Oriental Institute Publications 38, Chicago: The Oriental Institute of the University of Chicago, 2015.

W, 'Notes on the Veitch Collection of Chinese Porcelains in the Birmingham Art Gallery', *The Burlington Magazine*, vol. iv. (1904), p. 232.

Gustav Waagen, *Treasures of Art in Great Britain*, 4 vols., 1854. Rep. Cambridge: Cambridge University Press, 2015.

Rebecca Wade, 'Pedagogic Objects: The Formation, Circulation and Exhibition of Teaching Collections for Art and Design Education in Leeds, 1837–1857', unpublished PhD thesis, University of Leeds, 2012.

Clive Wainwright, "'A gatherer and disposer of other men's stuffe": Murray Marks, Connoisseur and Curiosity Dealer', *Journal of the History of Collections*, vol. 14, no. 2 (2002), pp. 161–176.

Walker Art Gallery, 'Watermark: Works on Paper'. Available at: http://www.liverpoolmuseums.org.uk/walker/collections/works-on-paper/watermark/explore.aspx?coll=4&per=69017&rdir=/walker/collections/works-on-paper/watermark/&page=1 (accessed 10 Oct. 2015).

Judith Walkowitz, *Nights Out: Life in Cosmopolitan London*, New Haven, CT: Yale University Press, 2012.

Colin Wallace, Research Papers: 'Reconnecting Thomas Gann with British Interest in the Archaeology of Mesoamerica: An Aspect of the Development of Archaeology as a University Subject', *Bulletin of the History of Archaeology*, UCL, Institute of Archaeology, 12 May 2011. Available at: www.archaeologybulletin.org/articles/10.5334/bha.2113/ (accessed 31 Aug. 2015).

Henry Wallis, *Persian Ceramic Art Belonging to Mr F. Ducane Godman, F.R.S., With Examples From Other Collections: The Thirteenth Century Illustrated Wall-Tiles*, London, 1894.

Minette Walters, *A Dreadful Murder: The Mysterious Death of Caroline Luard*, London: Pan, 2013.

H. Waterfield and J. C. H. King, *Provenance: Twelve Collectors of Ethnographic Art in England 1760–1990*, London: Paul Holborton Publishing, 2009.

Mark Westgarth, *A Biographical Dictionary of Nineteenth Century Antique and Curiosity Dealers*, Regional Furniture, vol. XXIII, Glasgow: Regional Furniture Society, 2009a.

Mark Westgarth, 'The Art Market and its Histories'. *Perspectives: The Art Book*, vol. 16, issue 2 (May 2009b), pp. 32–33.

Mark Westgarth, *The Emergence of the Antique and Curiosity Dealer 1815-c.1850: the Commodification of Historical Objects*, Farnham: Ashgate, 2012.

R. Whiddington, 'Victor Christian William Cavendish, the Duke of Devonshire. 1868-1938', *Obituary Notices of Fellows of the Royal Society*, vol. 2, no. 7 (1939), pp. 557–526. doi:10.1098/rsbm.1939.0016 (accessed 29 Nov. 2015).

The Correspondence of James McNeill Whistler, University of Glasgow, 'Samuel Addington'. Available at: www.whistler.arts.gla.ac.uk/correspondence/biog/display/?bid=Addi_S (accessed 2 Nov. 2015).

The Correspondence of James McNeill Whistler, University of Glasgow, 'George Henry Boughton'. Available at: www.whistler.arts.gla.ac.uk/correspondence/people/biog/?bid=Boug_GH&firstname=george&surname=boughton (accessed 10 Dec. 2015).

The Correspondence of James McNeill Whistler, University of Glasgow, 'Robert William Edis'. Available at: www.whistler.arts.gla.ac.uk/correspondence/biog/display/?bid=Edis_RW (accessed 21 Sept. 2015).

The Correspondence of James McNeill Whistler, University of Glasgow, 'Cyril Flower'. Available at: www.whistler.arts.gla.ac.uk/correspondence/people/biog/?bid=Flow_C&firstname=cyril&surname=flower (accessed 10 Dec. 2015).

The Correspondence of James McNeill Whistler, University of Glasgow, 'Wickham Flower'. Available at: www.whistler.arts.gla.ac.uk/correspondence/biog/display/?bid=Flow_W (accessed 8 Oct. 2015).

The Correspondence of James McNeill Whistler, University of Glasgow, 'Robert Charles Goff'. Available at: http://www.whistler.arts.gla.ac.uk/correspondence/people/biog/?bid=Goff_RC&firstname=robert&surname=goff (accessed 10 Dec. 2015).

The Correspondence of James McNeill Whistler, University of Glasgow, 'James John Heywood'. Available at: www.whistler.arts.gla.ac.uk/correspondence/people/biog/?bid=Heyw_JJ&firstname=J&surname=Heywood (accessed 2 Nov. 2015).

The Correspondence of James McNeill Whistler, University of Glasgow, 'Marcus Bourne Huish'. Available at: www.whistler.arts.gla.ac.uk/correspondence/biog/display/?bid=Huis_MB (accessed 10 Dec. 2015).

The Correspondence of James McNeill Whistler, University of Glasgow, 'Helen Rose Huth'. Available at: www.whistler.arts.gla.ac.uk/correspondence/people/biog/?bid=Huth_HR&initial=H (accessed 15 Aug. 2014).

The Correspondence of James McNeill Whistler, University of Glasgow, 'Vittorio Emanuelle Taparelli'. Available at: www.whistler.arts.gla.ac.uk/correspondence/biog/display/?bid=D_Az_Mq (accessed 11 Aug. 2014).

The Correspondence of James McNeill Whistler, University of Glasgow, 'Henry Vaughan'. Available at: www.whistler.arts.gla.ac.uk/correspondence/biog/display/?bid=Vaugh_H (accessed 9 July 2015).

Whistler Etchings Project. 'William Cleverly Alexander'. Available at: http://etchings.arts.gla.ac.uk/catalogue/biog/?nid=AlexWC (accessed 8 Oct. 2015).

Whistler Etchings Project. 'Francis Seymour Hadens'. Available at: http://etchings.arts.gla.ac.uk/catalogue/biog/?nid=HadeFS (accessed 12 Aug. 2014).

Whistler Etchings Project. 'Henry Studdy Theobald. Available at: http://etchings.arts.gla.ac.uk/catalogue/biog/?nid=TheoHS (accessed 10 Oct. 2015).

Whistler Etchings Project. 'Frederick Wedmore'. Available at: http://etchings.arts.gla.ac.uk/catalogue/biog/?nid=WedmF (accessed 10 Oct. 2015).

Lisa White, 'A Collector of Distinction: Sir William Holburne (1793–1874)', *Apollo Magazine*, (September 2003), pp. 46–54.

Christopher Whitehead, *The Public Art Museum in Nineteenth Century Britain: The Development of the National Gallery*, London: Routledge, 2005.

Christopher Whitehead, *Museums and the Construction of Disciplines: Art and Archaeology in Nineteenth-Century Britain*, London: Bloomsbury Academic, 2009.

Dyfri Williams, 'Etruscan Production and Interpretation: The Hamilton Gray Vase', in J. Swaddling and P. Perkins, eds., *Etruscan by Definition: The Cultural, Regional and Personal Identity of the Etruscans; Papers in Honour of Sybille Haynes*, London: British Museum Press, 2009, pp. 10–20.

Dyfri Williams and Jack Ogden, *Greek Gold: Jewelry of the Classical World*, London: British Museum Press, 1994.

David Wilson, *The British Museum: A History*, London: British Museum Press, 2002.

David M. Wilson, 'Read, Sir (Charles) Hercules (1857–1929), Museum Curator', in *Oxford Dictionary of National Biography*. Available at: http://dx.doi.org/10.1093/ref:odnb/35693 (accessed 1 Dec. 2015).

Timothy Wilson, 'A Victorian Artist as Ceramic-Collector: The Letters of Henry Wallis', Parts 1 and 2, *Journal of the History of Collections*, vol. 14, no. 1 and vol. 14, no. 2 (2002), pp. 139–159. 231–269.

Barry D. Wood, '"A Great Symphony of Pure Form": The 1931 International Exhibition of Persian Art and its Influence', *Ars Orientalis*, vol. 30 (2000), pp. 113–130.

Elaine Wright, *Muraqqa: Mughal Indian Paintings from the Chester Beatty Library*, Dublin: CBL, 2008.

David M. Wrobel, *Global West, American Frontier: Travel, Empire and Exceptionalism from Manifest Destiny to the Great Depression*, Albuquerque, NM: University of New Mexico Press, 2013.

Zoe Yalland, *Boxwallahs: The British at Cawnpore, 1857–1901*, Norwich: Michael Russell Wilson, 1994.

Jacqueline Yallop, *Magpies, Squirrels and Thieves: How the Victorians Collected the World*, London: Atlantic Books, 2011.

Catalogues

A Catalogue of the Egyptian Antiquities in the Possession of F. G. Hilton Price, London: Bernard Quaritch, 1897.

A Catalogue of the Collection of Old Nankin Porcelain Whole Coloured & Old Chinese Enamelled Porcelain Formed by Richard Mills,... Many of the Pieces Were Exhibited at the Burlington Fine Arts Club in 1895 and 1896, Christie, Manson and Woods, 10 April 1908.

A Collection of Valuable Ancient Works of Art: the Property of Archibald G. B. Russell... , London: Sotheby's, 30 May 1927.

A Catalogue of the Highly Important Collection of Benin Bronzes Formed By The Late G. W. Neville: Which Will Be Sold by Auction on May 1st, 1930, London: Foster, 1930.

Index

Made in the USA
Middletown, DE
17 June 2024

55924761R00137